Recovery from schizophrenia

Does social class or the state of the economy influence whether people with schizophrenia recover from their illness? Has industrial development affected the number of people with this illness who become severely disabled? Does the level of economic development determine which citizens become insane? These questions are at the heart of *Recovery from Schizophrenia*. Acclaimed as a major work on its first publication, this fully revised and updated second edition draws on new research and experience to consider whether recent changes in approach to treatment are really an advance.

The author argues that we have been too pessimistic about the course of untreated schizophrenia and overconfident about the benefits of modern treatment. Despite the increased use of new antipsychotic drugs and massive annual investment in the treatment of schizophrenia, the outcome from the illness in modern industrial society is no better than in the Third World. Much of what is called community treatment is, in fact, the antithesis of treatment, resulting in people with psychosis living a life in which even basic needs, such as food and shelter, are not met.

To explain how society has come to respond in this way to the person with schizophrenia, Richard Warner, a psychiatrist, anthropologist and medical director of a public mental health system, steps outside the usual confines of the mental health field and draws on information from sociology, history and economics as well as medicine to make his case.

Dr. Richard Warner is the Medical Director of the Mental Health Center of Boulder County, Colorado, and Associate Professor-Adjunct at the University of Colorado, U.S.A.

"Warner's 2nd edition [of *Recovery from Schizophrenia*] remains a refreshingly different view of psychiatry's favorite conundrum – schizophrenia; a problem psychiatry wants to own, to legitimise itself, but does not want to deal with its socio-contextual origins. Warner, in this updated and rewritten text continues to prick the mythological balloons that have come to be associated with this so-called 'disease'".

Loren Mosher MD
Associate Director
Department of Addiction, Victim and Mental Health Services
Maryland, U.S.A.

Recovery from schizophrenia

Psychiatry and political economy

Second edition

Richard Warner

London and New York

First published 1994
by Routledge
11 New Fetter Lane, London EC4P 4EE

Simultaneously published in the U.S.A. and Canada
by Routledge
29 West 35th Street, New York, NY 10001

Typeset in Times by J&L Composition Ltd, Filey, North Yorkshire
Printed and bound in Great Britain by
T.J. Press (Padstow) Ltd, Padstow, Cornwall

British Library Cataloguing in Publication Data
A catalogue record for this book is available from the British Library

Library of Congress Cataloging in Publication Data
Warner, Richard, 1943–
    Recovery from schizophrenia/Richard Warner.—2nd ed.
        p.   cm.
    Includes bibliographical references and index.
    1. Schizophrenia—Treatment—Political aspects.   2. Schizophrenia—
Treatment—Economic aspects.   3. Schizophrenia—Treatment.
I. Title
    [DNLM: 1. Deinstitutionalization—history.   2. Psychotropic Drugs—
therapeutic use.   3. Schizophrenia—drug therapy.
4. Schizophrenia—history.   5. Socioeconomic Factors.   WM 11.1
W283r 1994]
RC514.W24 1994
362.2'6—dc20
DNLM/DLC
for Library of Congress   93–38556
                                                                            CIP

ISBN 0–415–09260–4 (hbk)
ISBN 0–415–09261–2 (pbk)

To those who suffer from schizophrenia

Contents

Acknowledgments

Several people were kind enough to give me criticism and encouragement when some of the ideas in this book were first drafted in the form of a long article. Among these reviewers were John Strauss, John Wing, Loren Mosher, Solomon Goldberg, Lewis Wolberg, Bernard Bloom and Maxwell Jones. I am most grateful for their advice.

I am also indebted to those who have discussed this research with me and reviewed sections of the book. I have received valuable critiques from the following colleagues in various departments of the University of Colorado: Robert Freedman, Thomas Mayer, Edward Greenberg, Gary Kiger and Paul Shankman. At the Mental Health Center of Boulder County, my associates Phoebe Norton and Ruth Arnold have made useful comments on sections of the manuscript. Julian Leff and Andrew Scull carefully reviewed large sections of the work and made many helpful suggestions.

I gained a great deal from discussions with Loren Mosher, Julian Leff, Paul Polak and Robert Freedman. Robert Freedman contributed to the development of the theory about the occurrence of schizophrenia in Chapter 9 of this, the second, edition. Much of the discussion in Chapter 10 about the economic advancement of the mentally ill in the community is a result of my collaboration with Paul Polak.

A great deal of credit is due to Marilyn Rothman, the librarian, who, with great energy and skill, helped me assemble the many sources cited here. I am especially grateful to my wife, Lucy Warner, for her unflagging support, astute criticism and skillful editing. I also appreciate the fine job of manuscript preparation by Betty Grebe and Irene Marconnet.

The following figures are reprinted from other sources by permission of the publisher or author. Figure 1.3 is taken from Gottesman, I. I., *Schizophrenia Genesis: The Origins of Madness*, New York: W. H. Freeman, 1991, p. 96, ©1991 Irving I. Gottesman. Figure 2.1 is taken from Brenner, M. H., "Fetal, infant and maternal mortality during periods of economic instability," *International Journal of Health Services*, 3: 145–59, 1973, p. 153, ©1973 Baywood Publishing, Farmingdale, New York. Figure

5.1 is taken from Bockoven, J. S., *Moral Treatment in Community Mental Health*, New York: Springer, 1972, p. 56, ©1972 J. Sanbourne Bockoven. Figure 9.1 is reprinted from Barker, D. J. P., "Rise and fall of Western diseases", *Nature*, 338: 371–2, 1989, p. 371, © 1989 Macmillan Magazines Limited, London.

Material in Chapters 3 and 6 has previously been published in Warner, R., "The influence of economic factors on outcome in schizophrenia,' *Psychiatry and Social Science*, 1: 79–106, 1981, ©1981 Universitetsforlaget, Oslo. The research at the end of Chapter 4 has previously been published in Warner, R., "The effect of the labor market on mental hospital and prison use: an international comparison," *Administration in Mental Health*, 10: 239–58, 1983, ©1983 Human Sciences Press, New York. Chapter 7 has previously appeared in essentially similar form as Warner, R., "Recovery from schizophrenia in the Third World," *Psychiatry*, 46: 197–212, 1983, ©1983 William Alanson White Psychiatric Foundation, Washington, D.C.

Introduction

Does the way we make our living or the level of economic development of our country affect whether or not we become insane? Do social class or the state of the economy influence whether schizophrenics recover from their illness? Has industrial development affected the number of schizophrenics who become permanently and severely disabled – lost to their families, costly to the community and leading lives of emptiness and degradation? These questions are at the heart of this book.

My original intent was to uncover what the natural course of schizophrenia had been before the antipsychotic drugs were introduced, but this simple goal led to the realization that some current beliefs about the illness, widely accepted in psychiatry, are not accurate. We may well have been too pessimistic about the course of untreated schizophrenia and over-confident about the benefits of modern treatment. The antipsychotic drugs, it emerges, have not appreciably improved the long-term outcome from the illness; these drugs alone did not unlock the doors of our mental institutions and make possible the community treatment of psychotics. Despite a massive annual investment in the treatment of schizophrenia, the outcome from the illness in modern industrial society is no better than in the Third World.

Each change in our treatment approach to schizophrenia, moreover, is not necessarily an advance. A treatment method of demonstrated effectiveness – moral management – was laid to rest in the mid-nineteenth century only to be resurrected in a similar form nearly a hundred years later. Much of what today is called community treatment is, in fact, the antithesis of treatment: people suffering from psychosis are consigned to a sordid, impoverished existence in which even basic needs, such as food and shelter, are not met. To understand how such aberrations and misconceptions have come about, to appreciate what has shaped the course and occurrence of schizophrenia, and to see what has molded psychiatric ideology and the social response to the schizophrenic, we need to step outside psychiatry. We have to venture into the territory of the sociologist, the anthropologist and the historian; we must enter the province of epidemiologists, social psychologists, economists and political scientists.

A NOTE ON THEORY

The materialist theoretical approach I have used throughout this book is not commonly applied to questions in psychiatry. The central premise of the approach is that in order to understand human thought and behavior it is essential to begin with the material conditions of mankind's existence and productive processes. The origins of philosophical and social change, the materialist argues, are likely to be found in changes in technology. Values, attitudes and ideology are likely to be shaped by political and domestic economy (for example, family patterns, social stratification and political organization); and these aspects of society, in turn, tend to be molded by the forces of production and reproduction, by the technology of subsistence and population control and by labor requirements.[1]

A materialist research strategy, for example, allows us to generate the hypothesis that social attitudes towards the insane partly reflect the usefulness of the psychotic person in the productive process; that psychiatric ideology is influenced by economic conditions; that the course of schizophrenia is influenced by class status, sex roles and labor dynamics; or that variations in the occurrence of the illness may reflect differences in the circumstances of different classes and castes under different modes of subsistence and production. Such hypotheses, of course, must be tested against alternative explanations, and that is what this book sets out to do.

I do not wish to suggest that material conditions *create* schizophrenia in any simple, deterministic way, but rather that they *mold* the course and outcome of the illness and *influence*, along with other factors, its incidence. Psychiatric ideology is obviously not wholly determined by the economy, but it could be significantly affected by such factors. The materialist perspective allows for the operation of any number of causes besides technological, environmental and production-related forces. People in similar environmental settings will not all develop schizophrenia; biology is crucial in determining who becomes psychotic. Inbreeding could produce isolated populations with an increased genetic predisposition to schizophrenia. Individual psychology is also relevant; the psychotic or pre-psychotic person's behavior or response to circumstances may sometimes create the stresses that precipitate or worsen his or her illness. The materialist researcher would expect, however, that if we look at a large number of instances we will often find material forces to be important. It is not only biological, genetic or psychological factors which determine the distribution and course of schizophrenia. We should be prepared to expand our concern with social factors beyond family dynamics and socioeconomic status. It is in the relationship between all of these potential causes and the economic, technological and environmental facts of our existence that we may gain the broadest understanding of why some people become schizophrenic and why some of them never recover.

CHAPTER TOPICS

The opening chapters of the book establish the background for the subsequent analysis. The first chapter outlines what is known about the factors that promote the appearance of schizophrenia and that shape the course of the illness. The material is presented in such a way that readers who are not already familiar with the facts and features of the illness will learn enough to understand the rest of the book. The next chapter provides details of the ways in which mental and physical health are influenced by the economy, by social class and by the conditions of labor.

The middle section of the book looks at the impact of political economy on schizophrenia. Chapter 3 is an analysis of outcome studies of schizophrenia since the turn of the century and tries to establish whether changes in the long-term course of the illness are linked to large-scale fluctuations in the economy. The extent to which political, economic and labor market forces shaped the postwar policy of deinstitutionalization is examined in Chapter 4; and the role of similar forces in the development of institutions for the insane in the eighteenth and nineteenth centuries and in molding the treatment philosophy of the period is discussed in the following chapter.

Chapter 6 looks at possible reasons for the link between the economy and outcome from schizophrenia, and Chapter 7 attempts to explain why schizophrenia is a less malignant condition in the Third World. The plight of the Western schizophrenic person and the way in which the social role and alienation of the psychotic person shape the course of the illness are examined in Chapter 8. Moving from the course of schizophrenia to its incidence, Chapter 9 analyzes how economic development, social stratification and birth complications influence the appearance of the illness.

The final section deals with treatment issues. Chapter 10 evaluates the limitations of the antipsychotic drugs and the place of low-dose and drug-free treatment. The importance of work, economic opportunities, consumer involvement and community support in the management of psychosis is covered in the final two chapters.

Part I

Background

Chapter 1

What is schizophrenia?

Schizophrenia is an illness which is shaped, to a large extent, by political economy. The thrust of the following chapters will be to document this claim. First, though, we must be clear what it means. What is political economy? What is schizophrenia, and how can it be "shaped"?

WHAT IS POLITICAL ECONOMY?

All social groups survive by exploiting their environment and by limiting their population size to whatever their technology and the environment can sustain. The !Kung Bushmen subsist in the arid Kalahari Desert by camping in small bands near the few waterholes that exist and foraging over wide areas for nuts, berries, roots and melons.[1] Industrial societies sustain dense populations through increasingly intensive exploitation of land and sea for food, fuel and raw materials by means of elaborate forms of technology. Whatever the level of complexity of a society, however, it must possess a social structure which regulates the basic mechanisms of production and reproduction – a structure which governs the relationships among the productive and non-productive members of the society; which controls population size; and which regulates the distribution of labor power and energy in the society. All these functions may be subsumed under the term *economy*. Where the social structure is primarily seen as influencing domestic roles and relationships we speak of *domestic economy*. When we are considering larger political groupings (clans, bands, classes, castes and nations) we refer to *political economy*.[2]

We shall be looking, then, for influences on the occurrence and course of schizophrenia which lie in differences in the modes of production of various societies – hunting and gathering, subsistence farming and industrial capitalism, for example. What was the impact of the Industrial Revolution upon insanity and the insane? How is schizophrenia affected by styles of labor use, by Third World nutrition and childbearing, by unemployment, by the social stratification of class and caste, by the fluctuations of the business cycle, by poverty, by welfare support and by variations in family organization which are consequences of political-economic forces?

WHAT IS SCHIZOPHRENIA?

Schizophrenia is an illness (or, equally, a group of illnesses). Psychiatrist Thomas Szasz would disagree, arguing that the whole concept of mental illness is a fabrication – scientifically worthless and socially harmful.[3] Indeed there are many conditions treated as illnesses by psychiatrists which might more logically be considered as non-medical forms of deviance – for instance, nicotine dependence, transvestism and conduct disorder of childhood (to name just a few), all mental disorders listed in the third edition (revised) of the American Psychiatric Association *Diagnostic and Statistical Manual* (DSM-III-R).[4] Schizophrenia, nevertheless, fulfills any criteria we might wish to establish to define an illness. It is a non-volitional and generally maladaptive condition which decreases the person's functional capacity and which may be identified by a reasonably circumscribed set of characteristic features. Within rather broad limits, the age of onset and the expected course of the condition may be specified. Researchers are beginning to identify anatomical, physiological and biochemical abnormalities in the brains of people exhibiting features of schizophrenia. The predisposition to develop the condition appears to be, to a certain extent, inherited, and in essentially similar forms the disorder is universally identifiable in all societies around the globe with (as we shall see, in Chapter 9) a surprisingly similar incidence rate. We may regard schizophrenia as an illness, but it will be apparent that it is an illness which is strongly affected by the patient's environment.

Schizophrenia is a *psychosis*. That is to say, it is a severe mental disorder in which the person's ability to recognize reality and his or her emotional responses, thinking processes, judgment and ability to communicate are so affected that his or her functioning is seriously impaired. Hallucinations and delusions are common features of psychosis.

Schizophrenia is one of the *functional* psychoses. These are the disorders in which the changes in functioning cannot definitely be attributed to any specific organic abnormality in the brain. As more is learned of brain pathology in mental illness this distinction has become less relevant. It allows us, however, to distinguish certain mental illnesses from such organic mental disorders as the pre-senile dementias (like Huntington's chorea), drug-induced psychoses (such as those the amphetamines may cause) or delirium tremens (secondary to alcohol withdrawal).

The two most common functional psychoses are schizophrenia and manic-depressive illness (also known as bipolar affective disorder). The distinction between the two is often not easy to make and, as we shall see, psychiatrists in different parts of the world at different times have not drawn the boundaries in the same way. In essence, however, manic-depressive illness is an episodic and recurrent disorder in which the [psychotic symptoms are associated with severe alterations in mood]- at times elated, agitated episodes of *mania*, at other times *depression*, with physical and mental slowing, despair, guilt feelings and low self-esteem.

Schizophrenia, on the other hand, while it may be episodic, will tend to relapse at irregular intervals, unlike the regular, cyclical pattern of manic-depressive psychosis; or it will demonstrate a continuous but fluctuating course. Furthermore, although schizophrenia may be associated with depression, elation or agitation at times, it is often free of these features and the mood is likely, instead, to be blunted, lacking in spontaneity or incongruous. Markedly illogical thinking is common in schizophrenia. Auditory hallucinations may occur in either manic-depressive illness or schizophrenia, but in the latter they are more likely to be commenting on the patient's thoughts and actions or to be conversing one with another. Delusions, also, can occur in both conditions; in schizophrenia they may give the individual the sense that he or she is being controlled by outside forces or that his or her thoughts are being broadcast or interfered with. Both manic-depressive illness and schizophrenia are most likely to begin in late adolescence or in early adult life.

Despite common features, different forms of schizophrenia can appear quite dissimilar. One patient, for example, may be paranoid and hostile in certain circumstances but show good judgment and high functioning in many areas of life. Another may be bizarre in manner and appearance, preoccupied with delusions of bodily disorder, passive and withdrawn. So marked are these differences, in fact, that many psychiatrists believe that, when the underlying neurophysiological and biochemical mechanisms of schizophrenia are worked out, the illness will prove to be a set of different but related conditions which lead, *via* a final common pathway of bio-chemical interactions, to a similar series of consequences. This view of schizophrenia as a federation of states has been present from the time of its earliest conception. To understand why these conditions were united in the first instance we must look at the history of the development of the idea.

EMIL KRAEPELIN

The concept of schizophrenia was formulated by the German psychiatrist Emil Kraepelin. Studying, over the course of years, patients admitted to the insane asylums of the late nineteenth century, he observed that certain types of insanity with an onset in early adult life and initially rather varied features seemed to progress ultimately to a similar deteriorated condition. To accentuate the progressive destruction of mental abilities, emotional responses and the integrity of the personality which he saw as central to

Table 1.1 Features of dementia praecox identified by Emil Kraepelin

Feature	Description
Hallucinations:	
Auditory	At the beginning these are usually simple noises, rustling, buzzing, ringing in the ears (p. 7). Then there develops . . . the *hearing* of voices. Sometimes it is only whispering (p. 7). What the voices say is, as a rule, *unpleasant* and *disturbing* (p. 9). Many of the voices make remarks about the thoughts and doings of the patient (p. 10). It is quite specially peculiar to dementia praecox that the patients'' own *thoughts appear to them to be spoken aloud* (p. 12).
Visual	Everything looks awry and wrong (p. 14). People appear who are not there (p. 14).
Delusions:	
Paranoia	The patient notices that he is looked at in a peculiar way, laughed at, scoffed at . . . . People spy on him . . . persecute him, poison the atmosphere (p. 27).
Guilt	The patient has by a sinful life he believes destroyed his health of body and mind (p. 27).
Grandiosity	The patient is "something better," born to a higher place, . . . an inventor, a great singer, can do what he will (p. 29).
Ideas of influence	Characteristic of the disease . . . is the feeling of one's thoughts being influenced (p. 12).
Thought transference	The patient sometimes *knows the thoughts of other people* (p. 13).
Ideas of reference	Indifferent remarks and chance looks, the whispering of other people, appear suspicious to the patient (p. 31).
Thought disorder:	
Poverty of thought	There is invariably at first a *loss of mental activity* and therewith a certain poverty of thought (p. 19).
Loose associations	The patients lose in a most striking way the faculty of *logical ordering* of their trains of thought . . . .The most self-evident and familiar associations with the given ideas are absent (p. 19).
Incoherence	By these disorders, which . . . remind one of thinking in a dream, the patients'' mental associations often have that peculiarly bewildering incomprehensibility . . . .It constitutes the essential foundation of *incoherence of thought* (p. 20).
Thought block	There can be a sudden "blocking" of their thought, producing a painful interruption in a series of ideas (p. 22).
Affect (emotional expression):	
Blunting	Singular indifference . . . towards their former emotional relations, the extinction of affection for relatives and friends. . . . "No grief and no joy" (p. 33).

Inappropriateness	✳	One of the most characteristic features of the disease is a frequent, causeless, sudden outburst of laughter (p. 33).
Lability		*Sudden oscillations of emotional equilibrium* of extraordinary violence may be developed (p. 35).
Speech: Abnormal flow	✳	The patients become monosyllabic, sparing of their words, speak hesitatingly, suddenly become mute ... let all answers be laboriously pressed out of them (p. 56). In states of excitement ... a prodigious *flow of talk* may appear (p. 56).
Neologisms		There may be produced ... quite senseless collections of syllables, here and there still having a sound reminiscent of real words (p. 68).
Autism:		Patients with dementia praecox are more or less inaccessible, ... they shut themselves off from the outside world (p. 49).
Stupor:		The rigid, impenetrable shutting up of themselves from all outer influences (p. 50).
Negativism:	✳	Stubborn opposition to interference of all sorts (p. 47). *Self*
Lack of drive:	✳	The patients have lost every independent inclination for work or action (p. 37).
Automatic obedience: Waxy flexibility		The preservation of whatever positions the patient may be put in, even though they may be very uncomfortable (p. 38).
Echolalia		✳ The involuntary repetition of words said to them (p. 39).
Echopraxia		The imitation of movements made in front of them (p. 39).
Mannerisms:		They add flourishes by which the movements become unnatural, affected and manneristic (p. 45).
Stereotypy:		Continuance in the *same positions* as well as ... the reception of the *same movements* or *actions* (p. 43).
Intellectual deterioration:	✳	The patients are distracted, inattentive, tired, dull, ... their mind wanders, they have no perseverance (p. 23).
Deterioration of judgment:		The faculty of judgment in the patient suffers without exception severe injury (p. 25).
Personality deterioration:	✳	Their thinking, feeling, and acting have lost the unity ... of the psychic personality, which provides the healthy human being with the feeling of inner freedom (p. 53).

Source: Kraepelin, E., *Dementia Praecox and Paraphrenia*, Edinburgh: Livingstone, 1919.

this condition, Professor Kraepelin termed it dementia praecox – dementia of early life. Against considerable professional opposition, he took the position in 1887 that three conditions, previously considered separate, were in fact subtypes of this single disease entity. These conditions were hebephrenia, marked by aimless, disorganized and incongruous behavior; catatonia, in which the individual might be negativistic, motionless or even stuporose or, at other times, extremely agitated and incoherent; and finally, dementia paranoides, in which delusions of persecution and grandeur were predominant.

In defining dementia praecox, Kraepelin was particularly concerned to show how it differed from other forms of insanity and from idiocy. Unlike cerebral syphilis, no specific cause of the condition could be identified; in contrast to the psychogenic psychoses, dementia praecox did not appear to be an acute response to stress; and it was to be distinguished from manic-depressive insanity by its progressive deteriorating course and by the absence of clear-cut mood swings from elation to melancholia.

Emil Kraepelin's description of dementia praecox continues to serve us well, with some exceptions, as a picture of modern-day schizophrenia. Some of the characteristic features which he identified are listed in Table 1.1. Where his observations no longer appear relevant is in his description of the symptoms associated with catatonic schizophrenia – automatic obedience, stereotypic movements, waxy flexibility, echolalia and echopraxia (see Table 1.1). Kraepelin's treatise on dementia praecox is illustrated with photographs of catatonic patients sitting and standing rigidly in bizarre and contorted postures, preserving poses into which they were set by the photographer. It was not unusual for Kraepelin's patients to repeat involuntarily the words and movements of those around them or to stand or kneel for days or longer in the same spot.[5] Patients with such features could still be seen on the wards of old-style institutions after the Second World War, but they are now very rarely seen in the industrial world. Catatonic schizophrenia, however, is still one of the commonest forms of the disorder in the Third World.

It is possible, as social psychiatrist Julian Leff argues, that these catatonic symptoms are a somatic expression of delusions of influence, symbolic thinking and pathological fear, much as the bodily symptoms of hysteria are a somatic conversion of anxiety. Both hysteria and catatonic symptoms have receded in the West, Dr. Leff suggests, as the population has developed a capacity for expressing emotions in verbal and psychological terms rather than as somatic symptoms.[6] It may also be true that the harsh and regressive conditions of asylums around the turn of the century tended to provoke and worsen catatonic symptoms which persisted as a physical expression of the patient's dependent status and barren existence.

Even more probable, these same asylum conditions may have brought about the deteriorating course which Kraepelin saw as central to his concept of the illness. Therapeutic nihilism, extended hospital stays and coercive management within the asylum walls, and poverty and unemployment beyond them, during these years of the late nineteenth-century Great

Depression combined to limit the chances of recovery from dementia praecox. Few psychiatrists since Kraepelin, as we shall see in Chapter 3, have found the course of schizophrenia to be as malignant as originally portrayed. As Kraepelin's classification was adopted around the world, nevertheless, so was the impression that the illness was inevitably progressive and incurable. To varying degrees the same view holds sway today – that without treatment the outlook is hopeless – despite considerable evidence to the contrary.

EUGEN BLEULER

Twelve per cent of Emil Kraepelin's patients with dementia praecox recovered more or less completely – few enough, but a sufficient number to cause concern about the central diagnostic criterion being poor outcome. In the more prosperous years of the early twentieth century in Switzerland and in the therapeutically progressive atmosphere of the renowned Burgholzi Hospital, psychiatrist Eugen Bleuler presented a more optimistic view of the outcome from the illness. Stimulated by the psychoanalytic theories of his assistant, Carl Jung, Dr. Bleuler formulated a new unifying concept for the condition and gave it a new name. To Dr. Bleuler the identifying characteristic of the illness was not poor outcome but a specific psychological picture – a lack of continuity in the associations between the patient's thoughts and a restricted or incongruous expression of emotion. Other symptoms which he regarded as fundamental were ambivalence and autism (a preoccupation with the inner world leading to detachment from reality). From the fragmentation of thinking and feeling, Eugen Bleuler derived the term *schizophrenia* – split mind. The hallucinations and delusions which were commonly part of the psychotic picture, Dr. Bleuler considered to be merely secondary to the more fundamental defects.[7]

Dr. Bleuler's 1911 monograph, *Dementia Praecox or the Group of Schizophrenias*, contains many examples of patients who fail to show Kraepelin's progressive deterioration and who often recover a high level of functioning.

A young farm girl, age seventeen, has been catatonic for a period of two years. Then she became a nursing attendant. Two years later she was released. She then became a midwife. She married, her husband had a difficult time with her. For example, she would not permit him to sing while he worked. She formed strong unfounded sympathies and antipathies. At the age of thirty-eight, she was again mildly catatonic for some six months. Since then she has been working for eight years outside the hospital, but not as a midwife.[8]

Another of Bleuler's examples:

Physician: Neurasthenia at twenty-nine. Then at thirty-one after typhoid fever, catatonic. At forty-seven, apparently "cured". He then resumes his practice, marries. Has been well for the past two years.[9]

Bleuler's impression was that few, if any, of his schizophrenic patients completely recovered without some vestige of their illness remaining. Far-reaching improvement, however, was common. Fully 60 per cent of his patients recovered sufficiently from their first schizophrenic episode to return to work and support themselves.[10] Such "social recoveries" cannot be directly compared with Kraepelin's 12 per cent of patients, who may well have shown signs of more complete symptomatic recovery. There can be no doubt, though, that the course of the illness in Bleuler's patients was much more benign than in Kraepelin's hospital in Munich. So much so, that Bleuler was able to assert that

> the therapy of schizophrenia is one of the most rewarding for the physician who does not ascribe the results of the natural healing processes of psychosis to his own intervention.[11]

It would be hard to find in modern psychiatry such an optimistic view of the natural course of schizophrenia.

Bleuler's treatment methods

Why should the outcome for Bleuler's patients have been so superior? He may well have broadened the diagnosis of schizophrenia to include some less severely disturbed patients. But it is also likely that Bleuler was too modest about the value of treatment, and that his methods of management maximized the chances of his patients" recovery. The description of his treatment methods from the first decade of the twentieth century reads like a model of the approaches introduced a half-century later in the social-psychiatry revolution of postwar northern Europe (to be described in Chapter 4) or like the principles of humane care abandoned half a century earlier at the end of the moral-treatment era (described in Chapter 5).

Institutional care, for instance, was to be minimized. "It is preferable to treat these patients under their usual conditions and within their habitual surroundings," Dr. Bleuler insisted. "The patient should not be admitted to hospital just because he suffers from schizophrenia, but only when there is a definite indication for hospitalization." Furthermore, "one can consider it an established rule that earlier release produces better results."[12] If the patient cannot return to his own family, "the care he may receive from a strange family often serves as an adequate substitute."[13] In pursuing this policy of active community rehabilitation Bleuler may have been aided by the low levels of poverty and unemployment in Switzerland at that time.

It is certain, at any rate, that his discharge policies were much more liberal than those of Kraepelin.

The return to an appropriate occupation, Bleuler believed, was vital to the patient's health. "Idleness facilitates the predomination by the complexes over the personality," he argued, "whereas regulated work maintains the activity of normal thinking."[14] But he emphasized that "faultless performance can hardly be expected and the unavoidable rebukes can greatly endanger the entire pleasure that the patients take in their work."[15] Dr. Bleuler recognized that a number of other stresses might threaten the patient's recovery ⊢ too much responsibility at work, for example, family troubles or a sense of failure.

Within the institution close attention was to be given to the quality of the patient's environment. "Good surroundings have a very different influence on the patient than unpleasant and noisy ones."[16] The use of mechanical restraints was limited. Patient self-reliance was encouraged and occupational therapy was considered essential. "Every mental institution should have the kind of set-up that will make it possible to offer every patient some kind of work at all times."[17] On Sundays, "generally a bad day" for the patients as there was no work, "special care should be taken to provide sufficient opportunity for entertainment."[18]

Although Bleuler demonstrated that the outcome of schizophrenia was often benign, Kraepelin's more pessimistic view has proven more popular. Why should this have been so? Partly, perhaps, because patient management, economic conditions and community acceptance of the mentally ill in most places through many of the subsequent years have been sufficiently poor that outcome from the illness has seemed closer to Kraepelin's experience than to Bleuler's. (This possibility will be examined in some detail in subsequent chapters.) In part, the modern pessimistic view of the untreated course of schizophrenia may have developed because the introduction of the antipsychotic drugs in the mid-1950s and their subsequent, virtually universal, employment in the treatment of psychosis has masked what was previously known of the natural history of the illness. Finally, some diagnostic reforms have tended to follow Kraepelin's lead in attempting to limit the use of the term schizophrenia to only those cases that do not recover.

DIAGNOSIS

It is by no means universally clear what is schizophrenia and what is not, and before we can study the course of the illness in more detail it will be necessary to examine the different approaches to defining its boundaries.

Scandinavian psychiatrists have tended to use a rather narrow definition of schizophrenia in an attempt to adhere to Kraepelin's emphasis on poor outcome. In this they have followed the course set by psychiatrist

G. Langfeldt in 1937. He distinguished between a core group of *process* or *nuclear* schizophrenics, on the one hand, who demonstrated an insidious onset of illness and a deteriorating course and, on the other, a *reactive* group, who tended to show signs of better social functioning before becoming psychotic, to have a more acute onset and to display a better prognosis. The reactive psychotics, for whom the outlook is brighter, have been separated from "true" schizophrenics in Scandinavian psychiatric terminology and labeled as suffering from *schizophreniform psychoses*.[19] In Britain this approach has not been generally adopted, nor was it much used in the United States until recently.

Russian psychiatrists, particularly in Moscow, also emphasized the course of the illness in developing their classification of schizophrenia. In this instance, however, the result is a broad definition. The Moscow-school psychiatrists speak of *periodic* schizophrenia, consisting of acute episodes with normal remission; *stepwise* schizophrenia, in which each acute episode leads to a period of lowered social functioning; and *sluggish* schizophrenia, with a course of progressive deterioration. Among the periodic schizophrenics are to be found patients who would probably be diagnosed in Western Europe as suffering from manic-depressive psychosis. The Soviet emphasis on social adjustment in diagnosing schizophrenia, in a society where dissidence and non-conformity were seen as pathological, led to the use of the label schizophrenia for individuals who might elsewhere have been considered merely eccentric or iconoclastic.[20]

In the United States, until the mid-1970s, the diagnostic approach to schizophrenia was also extremely broad, leading to the labeling of many patients as schizophrenic who in Europe would have been considered manic-depressive or non-psychotic. This diagnostic practice came about not through an emphasis on the course of the illness but as a result of giving weight to certain intrapsychic mechanisms (under the influence of psychoanalytic theory) which were thought to be basic to schizophrenia. Thus, American psychiatry, like the Russian system, expanded the concept of schizophrenia to include patients with no clear psychotic features. In the United States these patients were labeled *latent* and *pseudoneurotic* schizophrenics.

In the 1960s a research project used a standardized method of diagnosis (built around British criteria) to compare the diagnostic approaches of psychiatrists in New York and London. Comparing the hospital diagnoses given to hundreds of patients admitted in these two cities on opposite sides of the Atlantic, it was found that American psychiatrists were roughly twice as likely to diagnose schizophrenia, compared with the research team's standardized approach, four times as likely to diagnose psychotic depression and ten times less likely to label a psychotic patient as suffering from mania. The diagnoses given by the psychiatrists working in London hospitals, as might be expected, were very close to those of the project psychiatrists (who were using a British diagnostic approach).[21] Plainly, at this time, American psychiatrists were labeling patients as schizophrenic who would have been considered manic-depressive in Britain.

The underlying problem was that schizophrenia and manic-depressive illness share many common symptoms. During an acute episode it may not be possible to tell them apart. The distinguishing feature is often likely to be the prior history of the illness. The records of patients with manic-depressive illness (unless they are too early in the course of the illness) should reveal prior episodes of depression and mania with interludes of normal functioning. From 1950 until the mid-1970s, however, American psychiatrists paid little attention to the course of the psychosis in diagnosing schizophrenia and emphasized instead the presence of supposedly "schizophrenic" symptoms and defects. The result was an overinclusive pattern of diagnosis in comparison with European approaches.

We may view the problem of the diagnosis of schizophrenia in even broader cross-cultural perspective through the findings of the International Pilot Study of Schizophrenia. This large-scale project of the World Health Organization looked at two issues – the diagnosis of schizophrenia around the world (which is what concerns us here) and the course and outcome of the illness. Their findings on the latter question will be discussed later in the book. Using a standardized, British diagnostic approach (incorporated in a computer program), the project evaluated the symptoms of psychotic patients admitted to treatment in nine centers in the developed and developing world – in cities in Colombia, Czechoslovakia, Denmark, India, Nigeria, Taiwan, the U.K., the U.S.A. and the U.S.S.R.

Comparing the diagnoses made by the local hospital psychiatrists and the uniform research method, the project revealed that the diagnosis of psychosis, in general, and schizophrenia, in particular, was reasonably similar in the European and Third World centers. The serious discrepancies lay in the Russian and American diagnostic approaches. A large proportion of the patients who were labeled schizophrenic by psychiatrists in Moscow and Washington, D.C. did not meet the research definition and would have been diagnosed as suffering from manic-depressive psychosis or a neurosis elsewhere in the world.[22]

The diagnostic approaches of American psychiatrists changed suddenly and radically in the late 1970s. Much greater attention was paid to discriminating manic-depressive illness from schizophrenia. The stimulus to this movement was clearly the introduction of lithium carbonate to U.S. psychiatry. This drug, a simple salt, is highly effective in the control of manic-depressive illness in many patients and it is more pleasant and probably less potentially harmful to use than the most common alternative category of drugs, the antipsychotics. Lithium carbonate, however, is generally not beneficial for schizophrenic patients.

Research published as early as 1949 in Australia[23] and in 1954 by researchers in Scandinavia[24] demonstrated the effectiveness of lithium salts in manic-depressive illness, and the use of the drug was widespread in Europe and other countries throughout the 1960s. Despite these facts, lithium carbonate was not commonly used in the United States until the mid-1970s. This delay of ten years or more is usually attributed to the concern over accidental poisonings resulting from the use of lithium chloride as a salt substitute for cardiac patients in the United States during the 1940s. Lithium was taken off the market until the U.S. Food and Drug Administration gave permission for its use in the treatment of mania in 1970.[25]

Some observers, however, have suggested that the delay in the marketing of lithium in the United States was due to a lack of enthusiasm on the part of the major pharmaceutical companies. Lithium carbonate is such a simple substance that it cannot be patented. Nor can patentable alternatives be developed from it (as is common with psychiatric medications). Lithium carbonate, consequently, sells for only slightly more than the cost of aspirin. The profit margin for manufacturers is therefore a good deal lower than with other products. (As an illustration of this point, most psychiatrists in the United States receive several visits a month from representatives of pharmaceutical companies marketing patented antipsychotic or antidepressant drugs, but salesmen for lithium carbonate are not seen from one year to the next.)

Whatever the reasons for the delay in the introduction of lithium to the United States, the advent of the drug was followed within a few years by a major revision of the U.S. classification system for mental disorders. These changes meant more for the diagnosis of schizophrenia, however, than a tightening of the criteria to exclude manic-depressive illness. The concept of schizophrenia was narrowed down to include only those patients with the worst prognostic outlook. With the publication in 1980 of the third edition of the American Psychiatric Association *Diagnostic and Statistical Manual* (DSM-III), American psychiatry switched from one of the broadest concepts of schizophrenia in the world to one of the narrowest – a diagnostic approach similar to the Scandinavian system. No psychotic patient, for example, could any longer be labeled as suffering from schizophrenia if he or she had been continuously disturbed for less than six months. Thus, a patient who had experienced several schizophrenia-like episodes, each briefer than six months, was not to be considered schizophrenic. Nor was a patient who did not show a clear deterioration in functioning. Patients who failed to meet these criteria but appeared schizophrenic in other ways were to be diagnosed as suffering from brief reactive psychosis, schizophreniform disorder or atypical psychosis. Those patients who could not be definitely diagnosed as either manic-depressive or schizophrenic, having features of both conditions, were previously labeled schizoaffective and included within the schizophrenia category; now they were to be excluded.[26]

A number of practical implications flow from these geographic and temporal variations in the diagnosis of schizophrenia. In particular, whatever we have to say about the prevalence and course of the illness has meaning only if we define which diagnostic approach is being used. For every narrowly defined case of schizophrenia in the population there are about four more people who meet broadly defined criteria for the illness.[27] Where the diagnostic concept is deliberately shaped to exclude patients who recover, we must expect the outcome to be worse. In this book, the term schizophrenia, unless otherwise qualified, refers to a middle-of-the-road definition – not as exclusive as the Scandinavian or modern American approach, nor as broad as the Russian or earlier American systems. The definition used here will essentially be the one in use in British psychiatry and the one which, as the WHO Pilot Study shows, is most commonly used around the world. This definition, while clearly differentiating cases of manic-depressive illness, does not exclude psychoses of short duration or those with features of good prognosis. It does, however, exclude patients who fail to show clear-cut psychotic symptoms.

COURSE AND OUTCOME OF SCHIZOPHRENIA

A thorough analysis of the outcome of schizophrenic illness will be attempted in Chapter 3. At this point it is necessary to give an idea of the wide variation which occurs in the course of the condition. A Swiss psychiatrist, Professor Luc Ciompi, provides a useful analysis of the course of schizophrenia followed into old age. In the late 1960s Dr. Ciompi traced 289 patients, all more than 65 years of age, who had been admitted for treatment of schizophrenia to the University Psychiatric Clinic of Lausanne at various times throughout the century. For most of these patients the history of the illness extended back for more than thirty-five years, in many cases for more than fifty years. This is one of the longest follow-up studies in the literature. Dr. Ciompi describes in detail his diagnostic criteria, which are those of Emil Kraepelin and Eugen Bleuler – neither particularly narrow nor broad.

Figure 1.1 is a diagrammatic representation (adapted from Dr. Ciompi's paper) of the onset, course and outcome of the illness in the 228 patients for whom the information could be determined with certainty. Dr. Ciompi found that the onset of the illness had been either acute (with less than six months from first symptoms to full-blown psychosis) or, conversely, insidious, in roughly equal numbers of cases. Similarly, the course of the condition was episodic or continuous in approximately equal numbers of patients; and the outcome was moderate to severe disability in half the cases and mild disability or full recovery in the other half. Full recovery was noted in more than a quarter of the patients.[28] The outcome from schizophrenia varies from one period to another and from place to place.

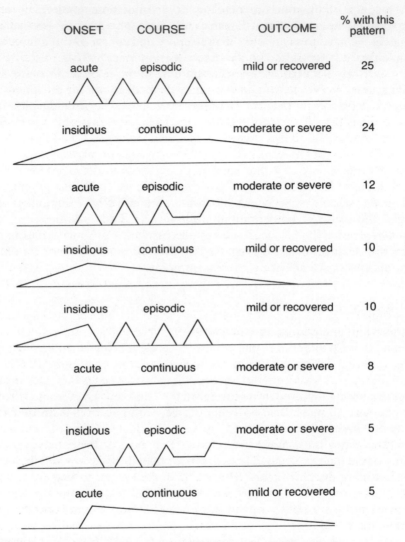

ONSET	COURSE	OUTCOME	% with this pattern
acute	episodic	mild or recovered	25
insidious	continuous	moderate or severe	24
acute	episodic	moderate or severe	12
insidious	continuous	mild or recovered	10
insidious	episodic	mild or recovered	10
acute	continuous	moderate or severe	8
insidious	episodic	moderate or severe	5
acute	continuous	mild or recovered	5

Figure 1.1 The long-term course of schizophrenia in 228 patients
Source: Ciompi, L., "Catamnestic long-term study on the course of life and aging of schizophrenics," *Schizophrenia Bulletin*, 6: 606–18, 1980.

These results, like Eugen Bleuler's, are somewhat better than average and, as we shall see (in Chapter 6), this may be a consequence of the superior economic conditions in Switzerland throughout the century. We can see from these results, nevertheless, that the course of schizophrenia varies a good deal between patients and that the outcome is often favorable – regardless of treatment.

Many attempts have been made to predict which patients will have a benign course and a good outcome – good-prognosis schizophrenia – and to identify the features that will distinguish them from patients with poor-prognosis schizophrenia. (This distinction is similar to Dr. Langfeldt's differentiation of process and reactive schizophrenia mentioned earlier.) The results of this work will be discussed in some detail in Chapter 10. Here we may briefly state that it is the patients with the higher levels of functioning (social, sexual and vocational) before becoming psychotic who tend to do better. A sudden onset to the illness and an onset late in life are also good prognostic features.

HOW WIDESPREAD IS SCHIZOPHRENIA?

Results of prevalence studies range from as few as one schizophrenic for every 1,000 adults in one community to one for each 60 adults in others. This wide variation is in part due, as we have seen, to differences in diagnostic practices and, in part, to differences in recovery and death rates for people with schizophrenia in different parts of the world. It is possible that there are also variations in the true frequency of occurrence of the illness, but a recent World Health Organization multi-national study makes this seem unlikely. The WHO research demonstrates that the rate of occurrence of *new* cases (the incidence) of narrowly defined schizo-phrenia is extraordinarily similar in ten widely dispersed countries.[29] Chapter 9 will examine differences in the incidence and prevalence of schizophrenia in detail and the possibility of environmental effects on the frequency of the illness. The studies analyzed in that chapter indicate that in many industrial world settings the prevalence of schizophrenia is close to one in every 200 adults.

Schizophrenia is found in every culture. The content of the patient's hallucinations and delusions varies from one social group to another – the delusions of villagers living in the north of Ghana are associated with the local fetish system, for example, but among the city dwellers of Accra in the south of that country ideas of influence and control by electricity and radio are more common.[30] The form and basic features of schizophrenia, nevertheless, are similar around the world, as the WHO Pilot Study shows.

WHAT CAUSES SCHIZOPHRENIA?

Tuberculosis is the result of an infection by a bacillus. In the early decades of the century, however, when the disease was widespread, although a huge proportion of the population became infected with the organism, only a relatively small number went on to develop clinically recognizable evidence of the disease. What caused the manifest symptoms of the illness to appear in those few, in some cases years after the initial infection? Poor social conditions were known to increase the susceptibility to the illness, and improvements in diet and housing were linked to a decline in the death rate from tuberculosis long before effective drug treatment was introduced. The irritant effects of coal dust on miners, pregnancy in women and the debilitating influence of secondary illnesses all could reduce an individual's resistance to the disease. What, then, is the cause of tuberculosis? The tubercle bacillus? Overcrowding? Poor diet? The stresses of lower-class living? Or any of the other environmental, occupational or constitutional factors that increase the individual's susceptibility? Clearly any and all of these factors may be considered contributory, and the reduction in the prevalence of the illness had as much to do with elimination of some of the social causes and with the increase in the resistance of the population by vaccination as with the direct attack on the infective organism by chemotherapy.

The same principles apply to schizophrenia. We do not know with certainty of a specific organic defect or infective agent which is critical in the development of schizophrenia (although there are a number of theories and there has been an expansion of knowledge in this area). We do know, however, of several factors which increase the susceptibility to this illness and which may provoke its appearance. To grasp how these factors may influence the development and the course of schizophrenia we need to use an interactive conceptual model such as the one proposed by American psychiatrists John Strauss and William Carpenter.

An adaptation of the conceptual scheme offered by these authors[31] is given in Figure 1.2. An interactional model allows for various types of explanation to assume importance at different stages in the individual's development. The genetic contribution, damaging intrauterine effects and birth trauma might each play a part in forming the newborn infant's predisposition to developing schizophrenia. The vulnerability to the illness might theoretically be heightened during childhood development by brain damage, for example, or by unusual family communication patterns.

Whether or not the illness becomes manifest in later life will depend upon the extent of the vulnerability and the subsequent exposure to a variety of stresses. Precipitating stresses may be biological in nature (such as hallucinogenic drug abuse), or psychosocial. In the latter category are life events (such as starting work, leaving home or bereavement), environmental influences (criticism or intrusiveness at home, for example) or existential concerns (loss of a sense of purpose or belonging).

Once an episode of psychosis has begun, these same stressors and new ones, together with the degree of vulnerability, will determine the subsequent course and outcome of the illness. Labeling and social stigma may affect the individual's sense of self-worth, as may his or her success in reintegrating with the social group and in returning to a valued social role. Criticism, rejection, restriction, confinement or idleness might well limit the individual's capacity for recovery from schizophrenia.

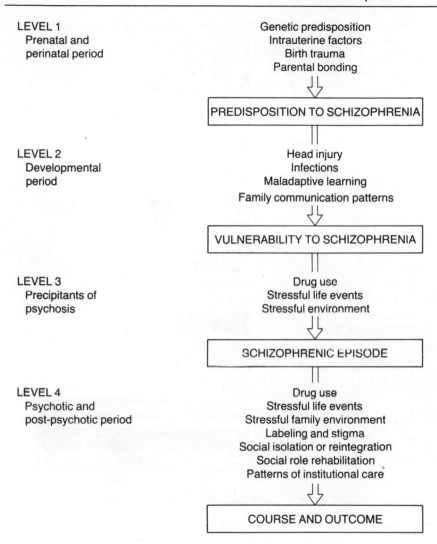

LEVEL 1
Prenatal and
perinatal period

Genetic predisposition
Intrauterine factors
Birth trauma
Parental bonding

PREDISPOSITION TO SCHIZOPHRENIA

LEVEL 2
Developmental
period

Head injury
Infections
Maladaptive learning
Family communication patterns

VULNERABILITY TO SCHIZOPHRENIA

LEVEL 3
Precipitants of
psychosis

Drug use
Stressful life events
Stressful environment

SCHIZOPHRENIC EPISODE

LEVEL 4
Psychotic and
post-psychotic period

Drug use
Stressful life events
Stressful family environment
Labeling and stigma
Social isolation or reintegration
Social role rehabilitation
Patterns of institutional care

COURSE AND OUTCOME

Figure 1.2 Interactional model for factors possibly affecting the onset, course and outcome of schizophrenia

The strength of some of these potential causes of vulnerability and precipitants of psychosis has been better demonstrated than others. On the following pages a few of the more important will be briefly outlined.

Inheritance

If inheritance is important in the development of schizophrenia, relatives of schizophrenic people will have a greater risk of developing the illness than

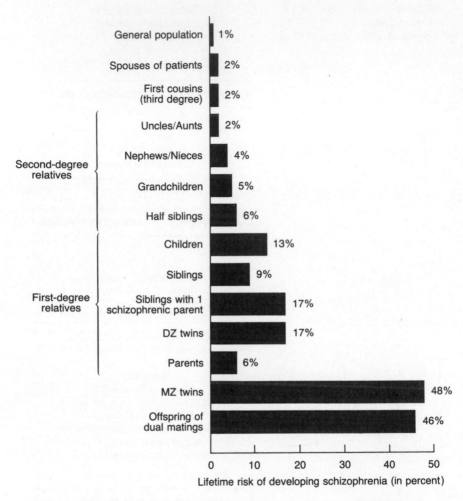

Figure 1.3 The average risk of developing schizophrenia for relatives of a person with the illness; compiled from family and twin studies conducted in Europe between 1920 and 1987
Source: Reprinted by permission of the author. From Gottesman, I. I., *Schizophrenia Genesis: The Origins of Madness*, New York: W. H. Freeman, 1991, p. 96, © 1991 Irving I. Gottesman.

others – and they do. One would also expect the risk to be progressively greater in relatives who are more genetically similar to the schizophrenic person. Epidemiologist Irving Gottesman, drawing data from about 40 European studies conducted between 1920 and 1987, has compiled a comparison of the average lifetime risk of developing schizophrenia for people with different degrees of relationship to someone with schizophrenia. His findings, shown in Figure 1.3, indicate that the closer the similarity in genetic make-up the greater the risk. The identical twins of schizophrenic people, who have precisely the same genetic constitution, run the greatest risk of developing the illness – nearly 50 per cent. The offspring of two schizophrenic parents have a similar risk. The rate is less for first-degree relatives such as non-identical siblings and progressively declines through second-degree and third-degree relatives to the general population risk of around 1 per cent.[32]

Studies of people adopted in infancy suggest that the increased risk of schizophrenia in the relatives of identified cases is related to inheritance rather than environment. The children of schizophrenic people have a similar increased prevalence of the illness whether they are raised by their biological parents or by adoptive parents. Likewise, the family history of schizophrenic people brought up by adoptive parents reveals an increased prevalence of the illness among their biological relatives but not among their relatives by adoption.[33]

Genetic factors appear to be important in the development of schizophrenia but are not sufficient to explain the entire pattern of occurrence. As we have seen, although identical twins have exactly the same genetic make-up, the risk of the second twin developing schizophrenia is only 50 per cent. One may conclude that genetic factors play a major part in establishing the vulnerability to the illness but that environmental factors (including the intrauterine experience) must also play important roles before schizophrenia becomes manifest. Nearly two-thirds of schizophrenic people, moreover, have no relative at all with the illness;[34] so it is questionable whether everyone with schizophrenia carries a genetic vulnerability.

Studies of twins reveal additional information about the inheritance of schizophrenic vulnerability.[35] When one of a pair of identical twins has a severe and deteriorating form of schizophrenia, it is virtually certain that the other twin will show signs of the illness; but if one identical twin has a mild form of the psychosis, the chances of the other twin developing schizophrenia are very much lower – around 25 per cent.[36] This observation suggests that the genetic vulnerability influences both the onset and the course of the illness. The identical twins of schizophrenic people, furthermore, if they do not develop schizophrenia, run an increased risk of developing other psychiatric disorders – alcoholism, neurosis or personality problems.[37] What is inherited is, perhaps, not specifically a vulnerability to schizophrenia but, instead, an underlying biochemical and functional disturbance which may express itself in somewhat different ways under the influence of environmental stresses.

Just what is the deficit that might be inherited?

Brain chemistry

Emotions and thought processes are regulated by the complex interaction of systems of nerve cells throughout the brain. Each nerve cell (or neuron) exerts its effect by the release of a chemical mediator at the synapse – the point of contact with another neuron. Biochemical theories attempting to explain the appearance of schizophrenic symptoms have focused on abnormalities in the action of some of these chemical neurotransmitters.

The predominant biochemical theory of schizophrenia – the dopamine hypothesis – suggests that the underlying abnormality may be a relative overactivity of tracts of neurons in which dopamine is the chemical mediator. Acute stress, leading to sudden increases in dopamine turnover, could thus precipitate an episode of psychosis in a vulnerable individual.[38] It is likely, however, that the disturbance of dopamine function is a consequence of other abnormalities elsewhere in the brain which have not yet been clearly identified. Recently, for example, attention has been focused on whether an abnormality in the functioning of neurons which release gamma-amino butyric acid (GABA) is responsible for producing changes in the dopamine-releasing neurons.[39] The dopamine hypothesis is dealt with in some detail in Chapter 10.

Research on other neurochemical substances – indoleamines, neuropeptides and amino acids – has not produced clear-cut findings.[40] This may be because our research techniques are too crude to elucidate the complex interactions between neuronal systems in the brain. Our eventual understanding of the neurochemical malfunction in schizophrenia, however, will probably involve different neurotransmitters in various parts of the brain.

Brain structure

That there *are* biochemical differences in schizophrenia is certain – just as certain as that there are biochemical correlates in the brain to rage, anxiety and learning Spanish. That there are *anatomical* differences in the brains of schizophrenic people (as in some organic brain disorders) is not a foregone conclusion, however, and in fact the evidence for such abnormalities in the structure of the brain has been slow in accumulating. Decades of post-mortem study of the brains of schizophrenic people failed to produce agreement on any neuroanatomical changes specific to the illness. In recent years, however, the application of more advanced research techniques has shown indications of injury in an area of the brain known as the limbic system. Several researchers have identified such degenerative changes in schizophrenic patients which were not evident in non-schizophrenic people.[41] These findings are of interest as they point to abnormalities in the same area of the brain (the limbic system) that neurochemical research has incriminated as functioning abnormally in schizophrenia. This interconnecting network of terminals and tracts is believed to be central to the regulation of emotion and to the individual's response to stress.

Important evidence for anatomical changes in the brain in schizophrenia has been provided by computed tomographic (CT) scans. Over 50 studies using brain scans have found evidence of mild cerebral atrophy in a proportion of schizophrenic patients.[42] The changes, which include enlargement of the fluid-containing ventricles of the brain and widening of the fissures between folds of brain tissue, can also occur in degenerative brain conditions and in some other psychiatric patients.[43]

The cause of such cerebral atrophy in schizophrenia is not known. Since the abnormalities are found equally in first-break, acute schizophrenic people and in chronic patients, it is unlikely that the changes are due to treatment.[44] The atrophy does not indicate that schizophrenia is a degenerative brain disease: it is not progressive, it is not specific to schizophrenia, nor is it present in all cases.[45] The changes occur in only about a quarter of schizophrenic patients, but there is not a well-defined group with enlarged cerebral ventricles and another with normal-size ventricles: the CT-scan changes are distributed along a smooth gradient from normal to large.[46] The most probable explanation is that the cerebral atrophy found in some schizophrenic people is an indicator of some earlier non-specific brain injury which increases the vulnerability to developing the illness. Such brain damage might result, for example, from intrauterine drug effects or infection, birth trauma or one of a list of similar assaults.

It is likely that inheritance and early brain damage are both risk factors for schizophrenia and that the two together create double jeopardy. Studies of identical twins show that if one twin has schizophrenia and the other does not, the one with the illness is more likely to have a history of obstetric complications at birth[47] and, with brain-imaging techniques such as CT-scans, to show evidence of brain damage.[48]

CT-scan changes are not restricted to one clinical subtype of the illness, but schizophrenic patients with these signs of brain damage have some characteristic clinical features. Patients with evidence of cerebral atrophy have more severe "negative" symptoms of schizophrenia, such as apathy, withdrawal and poverty of ideas: "positive" symptoms such as hallucinations and delusions are less prominent. They also are more likely to have functioned poorly through childhood and adolescence before the onset of illness, and more likely to show signs of neurological impairment, to respond poorly to treatment with medication and to have an unfavorable outcome.[49]

Viral infection

Evidence of early brain damage in some schizophrenic patients raises the possibility of harm to the foetus in the uterus. The risk of intrauterine brain damage is increased if the mother contracts a viral illness in pregnancy. Interest in the possibility of such damage in schizophrenia has been generated by the discovery that more schizophrenic people are born in the late winter or spring than at other times of year:[50] the proportion born at this time is approximately 10 per cent higher than in other seasons of the year.[51] Many possible reasons have been suggested for this finding,[52] maternal infection during pregnancy being one. Foetal brain damage might be caused by a virus or, equally, by medicines taken by the mother to combat symptoms of the illness.[53] Studies from countries as widely dispersed as Denmark, the United States, Finland and England have shown that the proportion of schizophrenic people born in winter and spring increases after epidemics of such viral illnesses as influenza, measles and chickenpox.[54] A smaller number of studies have failed to find a connection with viral epidemics.[55] A recently published report, from the United Kingdom, found that maternal influenza between the third and seventh month of pregnancy is associated with an increased risk of schizophrenia to the child in adult life.[56]

Another recent study from Milan, Italy, indicates that schizophrenic people born between December and April are more likely to show signs of ventricular enlargement. These brain abnormalities, moreover, were more common in winter-born schizophrenic people with no family history for the disorder than in those with a positive family history.[57] Again the evidence suggests that either inheritance or early brain damage (in this case, an intrauterine effect) may put someone at risk of developing schizophrenia.

Brain functioning

Vulnerability to schizophrenia, then, may have a number of biological sources. How it is expressed as abnormal brain *functioning* has also been studied. Researchers in Colorado have detected a functional abnormality in the limbic system. They have measured differences between people from the general population, people with schizophrenia and their relatives in their response to such stimuli as audible clicks and flashing lights. Computerized averaging of multiple electroencephalograph tracings of subjects' responses to these stimuli (evoked potentials) has been used in this work. The research has shown that most schizophrenic people, as well as half of their close relatives, have an abnormal pattern of response to environmental stimuli. They appear to be overly responsive to pieces of sensory information – sights, sounds, smells and touch – and more limited in their ability to blot out irrelevant material.[58]

It is essential to our capacity to concentrate on what is happening to us that we be able to attend to one aspect of our environment at a time and screen out the multiplicity of other bits of sensory data with which we are constantly bombarded. This capacity to discriminate stimuli and to focus attention may be disrupted in those who are vulnerable to schizophrenia. Such a "sensory gating" deficit would be a possible result of abnormal functioning in the limbic system. Given sufficient stress the affected individual will become overwhelmed and highly aroused. Withdrawal into an isolated, inner world may thus be a useful maneuver against the effects of the person's excessive vigilance towards irrelevant stimuli.[59]

The knowledge that half of the first-degree relatives of schizophrenic people share a neurophysiological abnormality with schizophrenic people themselves suggests that the defect is transmitted by a single dominant gene. It raises another question, however: why do only some of those with the defect develop schizophrenia? Recent research by the Colorado team using a brain imaging technique known as magnetic resonance imaging (MRI) reveals that schizophrenic people have a smaller area in the hippocampus (part of the limbic system) than their healthy siblings who have the same sensory gating abnormality. It is possible that early damage to this brain area, combined with an inherited sensory gating defect, is sufficient to produce schizophrenia.[60]

A new and interesting wrinkle to this research is the discovery that abnormal sensory gating in schizophrenia is linked to the function of brain nicotine receptors and to the gene that controls them. The sensory gating defect is transiently improved by high doses of nicotine. This finding raises the possibility that some schizophrenic people may use tobacco as self-medication, and helps to explain why cigarette smoking is heavier and twice as common among schizophrenic patients as in the general population.[61]

Some research workers, using radioactive tracer substances, have demonstrated that blood flow through the frontal lobes of the brain does not increase in schizophrenic patients, as it does in other people, when they undertake tasks requiring attention and effort. People with schizophrenia may not be able to turn on a specific region of their frontal lobes, the prefrontal cortex, when needed – a problem which could explain the withdrawal, apathy and thinking difficulties in schizophrenia.[62] The prefrontal cortex and the limbic system are linked: an abnormality in one could affect the other, though it is not certain which area is primarily disturbed.[63]

Step by step, links are being forged between inheritance patterns, biochemical and anatomical abnormalities and the symptoms of schizophrenia. We can begin to understand how early biological factors, development and environmental stresses may interact with an individual's physiological response pattern to precipitate an episode of schizophrenia.

The family

"In my own very self," wrote D. H. Lawrence in his last work, "I am part of my family."[64] Psychiatrists since Sigmund Freud have regarded the family as crucial to the development of human personality and mental disorder. Anti-psychiatrist David Cooper sees Western family life as a form of imperialism crushing individual autonomy.[65] It is to be expected, therefore, that many will have looked to the family for dynamic forces capable of creating schizophrenia.

In 1948 psychoanalyst Frieda Fromm-Reichmann proposed that some mothers fostered schizophrenia in their offspring through cold and distant parenting.[66] Others have pointed to parental schisms and power imbalances within the family as important in the genesis of the illness.[67] The double-bind theory, put forward by anthropologist Gregory Bateson and his colleagues, postulates that schizophrenia is promoted by contradictory parental injunctions from which the child is unable to escape.[68] Existential psychoanalysts R. D. Laing and Aaron Esterton offer a similar formula for the production of schizophrenia through the mystification of the child with confusing patterns of communication.[69]

While enjoying broad public recognition, such theories have seldom been adequately tested. Recent research has claimed to find abnormalities in the patterns of communication within the families of schizophrenic people that are not evident in the families of non-schizophrenic people.[70] These findings, not confirmed by later research,[71] have been the subject of controversy.[72] None of the work in this area, furthermore, satisfactorily resolves the question of whether the patterns of deviance alluded to in the families of schizophrenic people are the *cause* or the *effect* of psychological abnormalities in the psychotic family member.

A Finnish study of the offspring of schizophrenic mothers who were given up for adoption, for example, found that the children who became schizophrenic themselves were more likely to have been raised in adoptive families which were rated as being disturbed than in normal families. Although the findings suggest that schizophrenia may be the result of an interaction between genetic factors and the family environment, it is also likely that the higher levels of disturbance in the adoptive families were, at least in part, a consequence of rearing a disturbed schizophrenic or pre-schizophrenic child.[73]

While there may be stresses in the rearing of children which could increase vulnerability to schizophrenia, their nature and existence have not yet been verified. One thing only is certain in this field: thousands, if not millions, of family members of Western schizophrenic people have suffered shame, guilt and stigma as a consequence of the widespread acceptance of such theorizing. Parents have not only witnessed their child's personality distorted and his or her ambitions destroyed by illness, they have felt blamed, directly or indirectly, for causing the condition. Family members may carry the burden of living with someone whose actions can be unpredictable and distressing, and whose emotional responses are un-rewarding, but they may also receive little empathy and support from therapists who are liable to censure and distrust them. The reactions of society to the schizophrenic person and his or her relatives may be sufficient, of themselves, to produce distorted patterns of family interaction.

Domestic and non-domestic stress

If we study the family, not for formative influences building a vulnerability to schizophrenia, however, but for current household stresses influencing the course of an already established illness, a far more clear-cut picture emerges. Schizophrenic people living with relatives (by birth or marriage) who are critical or smothering have a much higher relapse rate, according to research from several countries and cultures, than those who return to relatives who are less hostile or intrusive.[74] Further studies have shown that relatives who are less critical and involved exert a positive therapeutic effect on the schizophrenic person – their presence leading to a reduction in the patient's level of arousal.[75] In the same vein, schizophrenic people who see their parents as being affectionate and undemanding have a low relapse rate if they are in contact with their parents, but tend to do poorly and relapse more often if they are not.[76] The benefits of a low-stress household on the relapse rate of schizophrenic people appear to be equally as strong as the effect of antipsychotic drug treatment.[77]

There is no indication that the more critical and overinvolved relatives are at all abnormal by everyday Western standards. It appears, in fact, that the households where there is more criticism and intrusiveness are those with patients who have personality attributes which make them difficult to live with.[78] The evidence suggests that the families in which schizophrenic people do well have adapted to having a psychotic person in the household by becoming unusually low-key and permissive.[79] In the developing world the picture is different. A study conducted in Chandigarh, India, reveals that few relatives of schizophrenic people in this Third World city show the same high levels of criticism and overinvolvement found to be common in the West.[80] These Western responses to mentally disordered family members may be a product of emotional isolation engendered by nuclear-family life, or the result of high achievement expectations placed on the psychotic. The decline of extended-family living is largely a consequence of industrialization, and educational and occupational achievement standards are higher in our advanced technological society. Through such family dynamics as these, political economy may affect the course of schizophrenia.

It is also clear that other forms of stress in the lives of schizophrenic people trigger psychotic relapse and influence the course of the illness. In a study conducted in London, 46 per cent of a group of schizophrenic patients experienced a stressful life event which was clearly not a consequence of the illness in the three-week period preceding a psychotic relapse. By contrast, only 12 per cent of a matched group from the general population had experienced such stress. The life events noted included role changes (such as leaving school), change of living arrangements, development of illness, and other disappointments and crises. When life events were included which may not have been independent of the individual's own actions or illness (events such as job loss), nearly two-thirds of the schizophrenic people reported experiencing such stress compared with less than a fifth of the general population sample.[81] Subsequent research,[82] including a nine-country WHO study,[83] has confirmed that stress, particularly in the preceding two or three weeks, can precipitate episodes of schizophrenia. The research also shows that severe stress provokes more intense symptoms of schizophrenia.[84] Major life-event stress is particularly likely to precipitate relapse in patients who are taking medication:[85] it appears that patients who are not using medication are more susceptible to relapse with minor stress and that antipsychotic drugs benefit the patient by raising the threshold of response to all but major stresses.

It is unclear whether stress can create a vulnerability to schizophrenia during an individual's development[86] (levels 1 and 2 of Figure 1.2) but it is clear that stresses of various kinds play a part in triggering psychosis in those who are already vulnerable and in shaping the course of a manifest schizophrenic illness (levels 3 and 4 of Figure 1.2). At these later stages – influencing the vulnerable individual and those already schizophrenic – we may also perceive the prominent effect of political and economic forces. Much that is stressful in life is not covered by such concepts as family hostility or recent life changes. We all need to have the respect of others, for example. Finding value and meaning in life and having a sense of belonging to one's own kind and community are omnipresent existential concerns. Problems arising from these concerns commonly emerge in the lives of schizophrenic people – problems (it will be argued here) produced or exacerbated by the political and economic dimensions of the society.

The following chapters will attempt to show that political economy assumes a hitherto underemphasized importance in the production and perpetuation of schizophrenia. Specifically, it not only determines mental-health policy and legislation, it also molds public reaction to insanity and even shapes psychiatric ideology. Political and economic factors influence the social status, social role and social integration of the psychotic – his or her sense of worth, meaning and belonging. Just as the destinies of all in society are shaped by political and economic forces, so too is the course of schizophrenia.

SUMMARY

- Schizophrenia, originally termed dementia praecox, is a functional psychosis with some unifying features but several distinctly different forms.
- In defining dementia praecox, Emil Kraepelin saw poor outcome as a central feature of the condition.

- Although Eugen Bleuler found outcome from the illness to be good in a majority of cases, Kraepelin's original pessimism has been more widely accepted.
- Bleuler's good results may have been a consequence of his enlightened treatment approach.
- Scandinavian psychiatrists have adopted a narrow diagnostic approach to schizophrenia, emphasizing poor outcome.
- Russian psychiatrists use a broad diagnostic concept which includes patients who would not be considered psychotic elsewhere.
- American psychiatry switched from a similarly broad diagnostic approach to a narrow definition of schizophrenia in 1980.
- The course of schizophrenia is quite variable; the outcome can be mild in half the cases.
- The prevalence of schizophrenia varies widely (partly because of diagnostic differences) but it is often close to 1 schizophrenic person for every 200 adults in populations in the industrial world.
- Schizophrenia appears to be universally distributed.
- Multiple social and biological factors interact to produce a vulnerability to schizophrenia, to trigger an episode of psychosis and to shape the course of the illness.
- Genetic predisposition contributes to the vulnerability to schizophrenia but does not alone account for its occurrence.
- An overactivity in tracts of neurons in which the neurotransmitter is dopamine may be one of the underlying biochemical deficits in schizophrenia.
- Some schizophrenic people appear to suffer from mild cerebral atrophy.
- The underlying functional deficit in schizophrenia may be an inability to discriminate relevant from irrelevant environmental stimuli.
- Theories which suggest that family communication patterns produce a vulnerability to schizophrenia remain unverified.
- Evidence that family stresses trigger relapse in schizophrenia, on the other hand, is strong.
- Political economy refers to the part of the social structure that regulates labor, energy, production and reproduction in groups larger in size than the family.
- Political and economic factors, it is argued, are important in influencing the course of schizophrenia.

Chapter 2

Health, illness and the economy

How far do economic factors influence our birth and death, control our health, mold our behavior and identity and affect our sanity? We may look for the answer to these questions by two methods – by studying the differences between social classes and by calculating the human effects of fluctuations in the economy.

SOCIAL CLASS, ILLNESS AND DEATH

Lower-class people in industrial society die younger. This much was clear to the statisticians of the nineteenth century and continues to be true today. In 1842, the average age of death for different classes in various British centers of trade and manufacturing was estimated to be as follows:

	Gentry	Tradesmen	Laborers
Bethnal Green	45	26	16
Leeds	44	27	19
Liverpool	35	22	15
Manchester	38	20	17

The well-to-do classes enjoyed a lease of life more than double that of the working classes.[1] The dramatic difference was largely accounted for by high infant mortality in the poorer classes and by deaths among adults from consumption, pneumonia, infectious diseases and other conditions associated with poverty, malnutrition and overcrowding.[2]

Class differences in life span persist in modern industrial society. According to the British Registrar General's figures, there is a clearly defined social-class gradient in mortality rates. British working-class citizens run a greater risk of death at all ages. In adults the difference in death rates is apparent over a wide range of causes from malignancy to heart disease. Where the cause of death is accidental or from respiratory or infectious disease, lower-class mortality rates are most dramatically elevated – from 3 to 5 times greater than for the highest social class.[3]

Throughout the Western world there is a similar relationship between social class and life expectancy. In nineteenth-century America, as in Britain, the ratio of the death rates in the highest and lowest classes was around 2:1. By the 1940s the class gap had closed to 1.4:1 or 1.3:1, but in more recent decades no further progress has been made towards narrowing the class difference.[4] The differential is greatest in the middle years of life and includes deaths from stress-related causes. Several studies have shown, for instance, that sudden death from heart attack is more common in people with lower levels of education. Some researchers attribute this finding to the stress of living in or near poverty.[5]

Sickness rates follow the same pattern as mortality. British unskilled working men, aged 45–64, report four times the number of days of acute sickness as men of the same age in professional jobs, and twice the rate of chronic sickness.[6] In the United States illness of all kinds is more common among the poor. Forty-one per cent of all low-income Americans aged 45–64 have a chronic illness which limits their activity – only 14 per cent of high-income Americans are so afflicted.[7] Multiple studies have reported a close association between high blood pressure and lower-class status,[8] and a county-wide survey of risk factors for illness in Florida found socioeconomic status to be the social factor most strongly affecting the incidence of psychosomatic illness.[9]

While material factors such as poor nutrition and poor housing contribute to high rates of illness and death in the lower classes, environmental stress is also important. Migration, unemployment, job turnover, divorce and separation are all more common among the poor.[10] A survey of the Toronto Borough of East York found symptoms of physical and emotional distress to be from 3 to 5 times more common among the poorly educated and low-income residents. The presence of these symptoms, in turn, was found to be associated with the person's exposure to a recent stressful life event, particularly demotion or job loss.[11] Two studies conducted in New Haven, Connecticut, and another carried out in Manhattan, New York City, have yielded similar results – substantially higher levels of psychological symptoms in working-class subjects than in the upper class. The difference in symptom levels in these studies, as in Toronto, was explained by the larger number of unpleasant life events affecting the working-class members. This finding held true (in the New York City study) when only those life events were counted that were independent of the person's own actions – suggesting that it was indeed the stress that precipitated the symptoms and not the psychological disturbance that led to the stressful events.[12]

A large-scale survey of drinking habits among residents of suburban Chicago offers similar evidence of links between social class, stress and symptoms. Low-income residents and those who reported more economic strain were more likely to have symptoms of anxiety. Lower-class members were also more likely to have low self-esteem and a sense of limited personal control over events. Operating together, these three factors – heightened anxiety, low self-esteem and a limited sense of mastery – were found to increase the individual's inclination to use alcohol to relieve distress.[13] Class status may thus mold personality, coping strategies, emotional symptoms and alcohol use, and indirectly influence physical health.

SOCIAL CLASS AND MENTAL ILLNESS

The evidence is strong that stresses are greater among the lower working class and that increased ill health and emotional distress are, to a certain extent, a consequence of these stresses. It is also clear that schizophrenia and other mental disorders are more common in the lower classes. In the Great Depression sociologists Robert Faris and Warren Dunham found that the highest rates for treated schizophrenia were concentrated in Chicago's slum areas. From a rate of over 7 cases per 1,000 adults in these central districts the prevalence of treated schizophrenia declined gradually through the more prosperous sections of the city to the lowest rates of below 2.5 per 1,000 adults in the most affluent areas.[14] Since the publication of this pioneer work, a number of other epidemiological studies have confirmed that high rates of mental disorder, particularly schizophrenia, are concentrated in centrally located, low socioeconomic districts in many American and European cities – Peoria, Illinois; Kansas City, Missouri; St. Louis, Missouri; Milwaukee, Wisconsin; Omaha, Nebraska;[15] Worcester, Massachusetts;[16] Rochester, New York;[17] Baltimore, Maryland;[18] Oslo, Norway;[19] and Bristol, England.[20]

Sociologist Robert Clark demonstrated in the 1940s that Chicago residents in low-status and low-income occupations had a higher incidence of treated schizophrenia than higher-status workers.[21] This observation has also been confirmed by a number of studies. In their survey of New Haven, Connecticut, in the 1950s, August Hollingshead and Frederick Redlich revealed a gradient of progressively greater prevalence of treated schizophrenia in the lower socioeconomic classes. The prevalence of the illness was 11 times greater in the lowest class compared with the highest class.[22] Leo Srole and his associates, in a community survey of midtown Manhattan in New York City, which located both treated and untreated cases, found mental disorder to be more common in the lower classes than in the upper classes and more prevalent in those who remained at the same socioeconomic level than in the upwardly mobile.[23] Dorothea Leighton and her colleagues, again, found mental disorder to be most frequent in the lowest social class in their comprehensive survey of Stirling County, Nova

Scotia.[24] Social psychiatrist Örnulv Ödegard demonstrated that first admissions for schizophrenia to all psychiatric hospitals in Norway were most common among low-status workers, such as ordinary seamen and farm laborers, and one-third as frequent among the owners and managers of businesses and others in high-status occupations.[25] In London, Lilli Stein showed that there existed a social-class gradient in the incidence and prevalence of mental illness (with the highest rates in the lowest classes) which was particularly marked for schizophrenia.[26] Reviewing these data, epidemiologist William Eaton concludes that, if we divide the population into three social classes, it is common to find a three-to-one difference in rates of schizophrenia between the lowest and highest classes.[27]

SOCIAL DRIFT OR SOCIAL STRESS?

A reasonable explanation for the social-class gradient in schizophrenia, and one which is commonly given, is that people with the greatest risk of developing the illness drift into lower-status occupations and low-income city areas as a result of their marginal, pre-psychotic levels of functioning. This is known as the social-drift hypothesis. An alternative explanation would be that the stresses of lower-class living, including labor-market stresses and class-related effects on foetal development and birth complications, increase the risk of developing schizophrenia. A final theoretical possibility is that there exists an increased genetic predisposition towards schizophrenia in the lower classes. When we come to look at the prevalence of schizophrenia in the Third World (in Chapter 9), we will find that the relationship between class (and caste) and schizophrenia is reversed. In the developing world it is the *upper*-class, *better*-educated individuals who are more at risk from schizophrenia. As industrialization advances, moreover, this inverted social-class gradient switches around to conform to the pattern found in the West. These phenomena clearly defy explanation by either the social-drift or genetic hypotheses and they invite speculation about possible socioeconomic and socially determined obstetric causes.

The shifts in the occurrence of schizophrenia that accompany the advance of industrialization may be a result of class-related changes in nutrition, obstetric complications and survival of the newborn (as we shall see in Chapter 9). In the modern industrial world, both social drift and class-related obstetric factors could be producing the class gradient for schizophrenia; the two theories are not mutually exclusive. Support for the social drift theory comes from a study conducted in Britain in 1963 which demonstrates that, although schizophrenic males are overrepresented in the lowest socioeconomic class, the social class of their fathers and other male family members is distributed much as in the general population.[28] Similar findings have come from the United States.[29] Sociologist Melvin

Kohn, who has reviewed the published research on this topic, however, argues that the thesis has not been decisively proven. The studies conducted so far offer conflicting results. Dr. Kohn concludes:

> The weight of evidence lies against the drift hypothesis providing a sufficient explanation of the class–schizophrenia relationship. In all probability, lower class families produce a disproportionate number of schizophrenics.[30]

The view that schizophrenia may be provoked, even partially, by factors related to lower-class living, however, is not well accepted by the mainstream of psychiatric writers. Psychiatrist Robert Cancro argues in the American *Comprehensive Textbook of Psychiatry* that such a conclusion is 'premature,' but, he concedes, not yet 'definitively rejected.'[31] In the same textbook, psychiatrist Herbert Weiner contends that 'no simple [causal] relationship between social class and schizophrenia exists.'[32] With such cautious opinions as these, the role of social causation is widely discounted in the day-to-day practice of psychiatry.

Why have the findings on social class and schizophrenia had so little impact on psychiatry? American psychiatrists John Strauss and William Carpenter suggest that this neglect

> may . . . reflect the fact that influential research and clinical writing and teaching most often come from persons and institutions with predominantly upper and middle class orientations, while a large number of schizophrenic patients are lower class and unemployed.[33]

To acknowledge that class-related factors provoke the development of schizophrenia is not to deny that social drift is also important. Indeed, it is not unusual to find schizophrenic people who have had marginal levels of social functioning for some years before their first, clear psychotic break. In such cases, downward mobility is unavoidable, and this, in itself, becomes an additional source of stress.

An interesting observation emerges from the research on the social mobility of schizophrenic people. While many patients may not show a decline in occupational status to a level lower than that of their fathers, the occupational level of the general population is sometimes found to have risen around them.[34] Relative to the rest of the population the schizophrenic people have lost ground. What is happening, then, is not exactly social *drift* but social *stagnation*. This is what one might expect to see in a group of people who are not high in drive and ambition. For individuals living in some settings this would not be a great weakness. In modern industrial society, however, where to stay at the same level is to lose status, the pre-schizophrenic person may be at a disadvantage in comparison to more driven individuals and under greater pressure than he or she would experience in a non-industrial setting.

The link between social class and mental disorders such as schizo-phrenia, interestingly, has been conclusively demonstrated only for city dwellers. Strongest in large cities, it becomes weaker in smaller cities and most rural areas. In the small town of Hagerstown, Maryland, for example, the prevalence of schizophrenia was not related to social class.[35] Dorothea Leighton and her co-workers did detect a social-class gradient for mental disorder in rural Nova Scotia, but not in rural Sweden.[36] In two British studies, one comparing London women with women in the crofting and fishing community of North Uist in the Outer Hebrides and another comparing women in London with women living in the rural Isle of Wight,[37] the prevalence of mental disorder was found to be highly influenced by class in the urban setting but not at all in the rural communities. On the rural Danish island of Samsö, although mental disorder in general was more frequent among the lower social classes, the prevalence of psychosis in particular was unrelated to class.[38]

The absence of a social-class gradient for schizophrenia for most rural areas can be explained in two ways. Schizophrenic people may migrate away from rural areas and become part of the urban underclass. This explanation is a variation of the social-drift hypothesis. Alternatively, the conditions of rural working-class life may be less likely to create a vulnerability to schizophrenia than urban lower-class existence. We shall see shortly, when we look at the effects of the business cycle, that there is also a rural–urban difference in the effect of fluctuations in the economy on symptoms of mental disorder, just as there is a rural–urban variation in the influence of social class. The rural–urban difference in the effect of economic change cannot be explained by social drift, and if the differential is the result of similar factors in each case (which is possible), then we should look for real differences in the impact of economic and class-related stress between cities and country towns.

This, then, may be a convenient point to begin to examine the effects of the business cycle on health, illness and mortality.

BUSINESS CYCLES

The economy rises and falls with a variety of rhythms. Since the Industrial Revolution, capitalist development has advanced in long phases of growth, interrupted every few decades by great, global depressions marked by industrial stagnation and high rates of unemployment. Each newly industrialized nation joins in synchrony with the economic pulse of the more developed societies. In Britain, the 'hungry forties' of the last century were followed by the Great Victorian Boom (1850–73). The industrialized economies of Europe and North America all felt the impact of the protracted Great Depression of the late nineteenth century (1873–96) and reeled again in the 1920s and 1930s.[39] Faced with this pattern it hardly seems surprising that we are again struggling with a protracted global economic recession in the 1990s. Superimposed on the long waves are shorter business cycles of varying amplitude – about two a decade may be identified, for example, in the period since the Second World War.

The social effects of both the long and short business cycles as well as of briefer economic fluctuations have been studied. Researchers have looked for correlations between economic indicators and illness, mortality rates and such social events as marriage, divorce and crime.

As early as 1893, for example, it was noticed that divorce became less common in the depression and more common in the boom.[40] (This phenomenon, which continues to hold true today, may well be a consequence of the greater degree of individual economic independence which becomes possible when more employment – especially women's employment – is available.) By 1901 another researcher identified an increase in marriage rates with periods of prosperity in trade.[41]

More elaborate social studies of the impact of fluctuations in business were carried out in the 1920s. Statisticians William Ogburn and Dorothy Thomas found that the boom brought with it high rates of marriage, divorce, birth, infant mortality and general mortality. Only suicide and (possibly) criminal convictions were found to increase in the depression.[42] A few years later, Dorothy Thomas confirmed these findings (except for divorce and crime) and expanded on them. She noted that beer and spirits consumption, arrests for drunkenness and alcohol-related deaths all increased in the boom. The only social phenomenon clearly tied to economic recession was suicide.[43]

Recent studies of the business cycle have applied advanced statistical techniques and have concentrated not just on the effects of the boom or bust but also on the impact of *any* economic change, up or down, reasoning that any change can be stressful.

Every week for 16 months from 1971 to 1973, researchers conducted surveys of samples of the population of Kansas City to gather information on recent events in people's lives and to evaluate their mood and stress symptoms. Ralph Catalano and David Dooley subsequently looked for correlations between these survey results and measures of local economic fluctuations. They found that both the local unemployment rate and absolute economic change (up or down) were linked to increases in the number of life events reported by the respondents and to their physical and emotional symptoms of stress. The unemployment rate alone was most closely associated with an increase in reports of depressed mood. The researchers noted that the changes in mood and stress symptoms were sometimes immediate but usually followed the economic change with a lag of 1–3 months.[44] People with low income responded much more severely to economic change than did city residents in the middle-income bracket. The poor, Catalano and Dooley reason, have the smallest economic resources with which to cushion any short-term economic setbacks . . . .When the economy improves it may be the low-income group which disproportionately has to pay the psychological price of adapting to new jobs in new locations with new colleagues.[45]

RURAL–URBAN DIFFERENCES

From the large metropolitan area of Kansas City, Catalano and Dooley and their co-workers next turned their attention to small-town Hagerstown, Maryland, and the surrounding rural Washington County. Hagerstown, it will be recalled, was the site of an earlier study which revealed no association between social class and mental illness. At the time of both studies the town population was close to 36,000. For 32 months from 1971 to 1974, the researchers conducted surveys of the small-town and rural residents, collecting the same information as in the Kansas City study. The survey of Hagerstown and district, however, revealed none of the associations between economic change, stress and pathology that had been found in Kansas City.[46] The small-town and rural residents appeared to be protected against the psychological impact of both social class and economic change. Why was this so?

The contrast was not due to differences in economic stress, for the local economy of Hagerstown was *less* stable than that of the large city. The difference, report the researchers, may have been a result of the fact that the small-town residents started from a lower baseline of stress. Respondents from the Hagerstown area reported fewer life events and stress symptoms than Kansas City residents, and showed less fluctuation in these variables. The small-town residents, furthermore, may have enjoyed more social support, which acted as a buffer against stress. The Hagerstown residents were more satisfied with their neighborhoods, friendships and marriages than were big-city dwellers, and they were more likely to have multiple social roles beyond marriage and employment.[47] Being an amateur baseball coach or a volunteer fireman, for example, may have minimized the impact of unemployment or demotion.

Another report confirms that rural residents may be protected by social support from some of the health hazards of economic change. Comparing the impact on manufacturing workers of plant closings in two areas – one rural and one urban – Susan Gore found that rural workers enjoyed more social support than urban employees. Unemployed workers who rated their wives, relatives and friends as unsupportive had more severe psychological problems and symptoms of ill-health. They blamed themselves more for being unemployed and felt more economically deprived. Those who feel unsupported, argues Gore, are more dependent on their jobs for self-esteem, and when unemployed they are more likely to lose their sense of worth.[48]

BOOM OR BUST?

The early studies of the business cycle, we have seen, implicated the boom in the production of most social pathology, with one clear exception being suicide. Catalano and Dooley's analysis of short-term economic fluctuations in Kansas City points to absolute economic change (up and down) as a source of stress and stress symptoms and to a link between unemployment and depressed mood. When the news media cite research on the effect of the economy, however, it is always the harmful impact of the depression and deepening unemployment that we hear about – never the boom. Why is this so?

The commonly cited research that links economic recession to multiple social problems is the work of Harvey Brenner, an American statistician. Using complex statistical techniques, Dr. Brenner has pursued the hypothesis that the increase in problems during the boom is, in fact, a delayed response to the business decline that precedes it. Thus when the U.S. Congress asked for a report, in 1976, on the *Social Costs of National Economic Policy*, Brenner was able to supply them with a document, more than 200 pages long, which pointed to unemployment as having a profound impact on health and crime.[49] A sustained 1 per cent increase in unemployment, claimed Brenner, has the following effect:

Social phenomenon	% Increase
Suicide	4.1
State mental hospital admissions	3.4
State prison admissions	4.0
Homicide	5.7
Cirrhosis of the liver mortality	1.9
Cardiovascular-renal disease mortality	1.9
Total mortality	1.9

The figures have since been widely quoted and widely accepted. But can they be taken at face value? At the crux of this issue is Brenner's heavy reliance on the supposed lag between the initial stress of unemployment and the subsequent appearance of social pathology. Cerebral strokes, for example, are linked to the economic recession, Brenner argues, with a lag of 6–9 years; cardiovascular-renal disease with a lag of 3–6 years.[50] When the length of the business cycle being studied is only 3–5 years, the use of lags such as these becomes difficult to comprehend. So, too, is a lag of two years behind the recession for arrests for drunkenness.[51] "The inclusion of a minus one year lag borders on the incredible," protests epidemiologist Stanislav Kasl about one of Brenner's pieces of research. "Surely that must undermine and ridicule the investigator's own efforts to suggest unidirectional causal interpretations."[52]

The problem with Brenner's use of the lag is not merely that a number of absurd and inexplicable correlations is offered (some of the lagged correlations, properly explained, might be reasonable) but that the optimal lag is determined *post hoc* by scanning the data. If a lagged effect is expected, it should be possible to predict in advance roughly what the lag period will be, so that a clear hypothesis may be tested. Brenner does not attempt to do this, however, and little pattern or consistency emerge from the lagged correlations.

Does it matter whether it is the boom or bust that brings more problems? To anyone interested in politics and political theory it does, for it is an issue at the heart of a debate between radicals and liberals. To the Marxist it is capitalism which is pathogenic; the business cycle is an inherent element of the capitalist economic system – an unavoidable consequence of the production of goods for the market and of the resulting crises of overproduction.[53] The liberal economist sees the business cycle as an unfortunate feature of the industrial economy, but one which can be controlled.[54] He or she favors fiscal and monetary policies which will stimulate the economy and turn away the ugly face of unemployment. Sustained economic growth is seen as feasible and necessary to minimize human suffering. The Marxist does not regard the upsurge in commodity production and consumption and the accompanying mobilization of labor which marks the boom as necessarily beneficent. One cannot imagine, however, even the most liberal wing of the U.S. Congress calling for a report on the harmful social effects of the economic recovery.

Congress, for example, would not be likely to call upon Joseph Eyer. Unlike Brenner, radical social analyst Eyer sees much social pathology and mortality as a direct consequence of the boom. Less than 2 per cent of the death rate in the United States – that for suicide and homicide – varies directly with unemployment, he argues. The general death rate, including such stress-related causes as coronary heart disease, alcoholic cirrhosis and perforated gastric and duodenal ulcers, rises during the boom. Eyer attributes some of the excess mortality of the boom to change in diet, alcohol consumption and cigarette-smoking, but he considers social stress to be the most important cause. Among the stresses of the boom he identifies are social-relationship changes such as rising marriage and divorce rates, fragmentation of the community due to increased migration and such job-related factors as overwork, alienating work processes and industrial disputes. The lag between these stresses and the development of pathology, argues Eyer, pointing to research on the impact of life events, would not be years, as Brenner suggests, but a few days, weeks or months – if the impact were not immediate.[55]

Observing that industrialization brings about an increase in mortality in younger adults at the age of labor-market entry, Eyer sees the development of wage work as central to the disease-producing stresses of our society. He argues, moreover, that the deleterious impact of modern labor conditions may be seen in the high mortality that affects those cohorts of workers who enter the U.S. labor market during the boom to a greater extent than those who enter during the depression.[56]

That this type of cohort analysis may lead to more than one interpretation is evident from economist Alfred Bunn's study of heart-disease mortality in Australia. Bunn traces an epidemic increase in coronary heart disease back to a point source in the Great Depression. Each cohort of Australian citizens born in successive decades experienced a dramatic increase in mortality during the 1930s – an increased risk which was sustained throughout the lives of surviving members of these cohorts. The decline in the death rate from heart disease after 1968 – a phenomenon which has not otherwise been adequately explained – is due, Bunn argues, to the eventual death of most of the population who had been of working age during the Great Depression. Immediate and late effects of unemployment and economic stress, suggests Bunn, contribute to heart-disease mortality; the more recent recessions of the early 1960s and late 1970s add their own lesser waves of increased mortality to the epidemic initiated by the Great Depression. Bunn, like Brenner, finds an association between high annual unemployment rates and fluctuations in mortality from coronary heart disease.[57]

Bunn disagrees with Eyer's claim that high mortality is closely related to *low* unemployment and the boom, and there is evidence to support each side of the argument. Regardless of which view is correct, both researchers agree on a principle which will become important later in this book: circumstances early in life prime an individual to respond to environmental stimuli later in a way which can promote ill health. According to Eyer, for example, entering the labor force during the boom increases the individual's susceptibility to the effects of economic stress; according to Bunn, working through the Great Depression produces a permanent increase in the risk of heart disease. When we discuss factors promoting the occurrence of schizophrenia in Chapter 9, this idea will emerge again. There it will be suggested that, if a woman's nutrition changes later in life in response to economic change, migration or class-related factors, her risk of obstetric complications will increase and so will her child's risk of schizophrenia.

Which is more harmful to one's health – the boom or the slump? Both have been incriminated. The case of infant mortality gives us the opportunity to pursue the question further and to see if prosperity may indeed bring undesired consequences.

INFANT MORTALITY

Nowhere is the issue of the pathogenic effect of the boom *versus* the bust better illustrated, and nowhere is the question of the use of the lag as a statistical device more central, than when we look at infant mortality. The early studies of the business cycle, as we have seen, found infant deaths to increase in the boom. Predictably, however, when Brenner studied this relationship he found increases in infant mortality to be a response to economic downturn after a lag of varying numbers of years. The death rate of infants aged one month to one year (postneonatal mortality), for example, is said to be related to increases in unemployment with a lag of 3–5 years.[58] Figure 2.1, which is taken from Brenner's article on the topic, illustrates this point. In the figure, percentage changes in postneonatal mortality occurring over five-year intervals are plotted annually for half a century. Brenner has advanced the infant-mortality graph by four years, to match the lag which his statistical analysis reveals, and to show a mirror-image relationship between the lagged graph of infant mortality and an inverted graph of unemployment (i.e. unemployment and lagged infant mortality rise and fall together).

There are problems with this analysis, however. In the first place, if we do away with Brenner's lag and put the graph of postneonatal mortality back where it started, four years later – as in Figure 2.2 – we see that there is a respectable fit between the mortality graph and the inverted unemployment rate. In other words, it seems that postneonatal mortality rises when unemployment *falls*. This picture suggests that we should at least look to see if such an inverse correlation is statistically significant – but Brenner does not do so.

In the second place, there is no logical explanation for a four-year lag in postneonatal mortality. Deaths in this age group – one month to one year – are typically related to the immediate environment and are due to such causes as intestinal and respiratory disease, infections and accidents. One would predict a lag of no more than a month behind an economic change in most cases. Even if one hypothesized that the infant was at increased risk of death due to economic influences working throughout the mother's pregnancy and delivery, then the maximum lag period in those instances would be less than two years. A four-year lag makes no rational sense.

Finally, there exist excellent *a priori* grounds for assuming a direct link between high infant mortality and the boom. Victorian observers were well aware that infant mortality in Britain decreased during crises in trade.[59] Figure 2.3 demonstrates that the contemporary commentators were correct: infant mortality rose and fell with the industrial growth rate through the latter half of the last century.

The reason for this effect, maintained the philanthropists and physicians of the time, was the employment of mothers. In the industrial areas of Victorian England a very large proportion of young married women were employed in the factories from dawn to dusk – or longer. Female factory hands returned to work within two weeks of the birth of a child, frequently

Figure 2.1 Five-year changes in the U.S. unemployment index (inverted) and the neonatal mortality rate per 1,000 live births. Neonatal mortality is moved forward four years to show the relationship with a four-year lag
Source: Reproduced from Brenner, M. H., "Fetal, infant and maternal mortality during periods of economic instability," *International Journal of Health Services*, 3: 145–59, 1973, by permission of the publisher.

Figure 2.2 Five-year changes in the U.S. employment index and the neonatal mortality rate per 1,000 live births. Neonatal mortality is not lagged

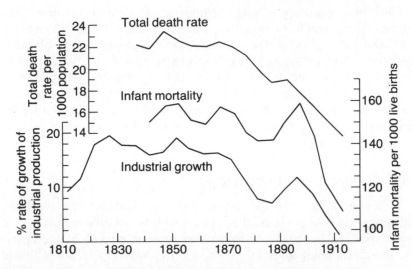

Figure 2.3 General mortality and infant mortality for England and Wales, and industrial growth for the U.K., 1810–1920; expressed as five-year averages
Source: Mitchell, B. R., *European Historical Statistics 1750–1970*, abridged edn., New York: Columbia University Press, 1978.

leaving the infant in the care of elderly childminders or girls as young as seven years of age. Fatal accidents to infants in the care of incompetent minders were not uncommon. Laudanum and other widely available preparations of morphia were freely used to quiet fractious babies. Early weaning was essential and infants were routinely fed with watered-down and often contaminated milk. Deaths from intestinal infection were prevalent.[60]

Physicians pointed out that infant mortality was highest where more women were employed in the factories. Around the Lancashire cotton mills the death rate was particularly high, and the Medical Office of Health for Staffordshire offered the following figures for 1880.[61]

Groups of towns	Rate of infant mortality
Many women employed	195
Fewer women employed	166
Practically no women employed	152

There is another reason – one which is particularly relevant to the topic of this book – why infant mortality may increase during the boom. Women who are raised in poverty have poor nutrition in childhood and are consequently small in stature and likely to have small pelvic cavities and birth canals which are malformed by rickets (vitamin D deficiency). During the boom, their nutrition is likely to improve and, when pregnant, the developing foetus will be larger than usual. As a result, labor will be more difficult and rates of brain damage and infant mortality due to obstetric complications will increase. We will return to this issue in Chapter 9. At that point it will be argued that the risk of obstetric complications and infant brain damage – and thus the risk of later development of schizophrenia – increases in different classes at different phases during the advance of industrialization. The result is a curious changing pattern of occurrence of schizophrenia.

WORK STRESS AND ALIENATION

One source of interest in the debate over the harmful effects of the boom versus the bust is the attempt to evaluate the relative importance of two potential health hazards – the stresses of working and of unemployment. The direct link between the working environment and ill health and death is evident in the statistics on industrial accidents and disease. One estimate reveals that each year in Britain two thousand workers die from an injury sustained on the job, another thousand die from an industrial disease and a million take sick leave because of an industrial illness.[62] Less commonly recognized, women performing housework have a high injury rate, thousands dying in Britain each year as a result of domestic accidents.[63] Not so straightforward to evaluate, however, is the importance of workplace stress in the production of mental and stress-related illness.

We may find evidence of the hazards of work stress in the research on heart attacks. Psychological stress and significant life changes increase the risk of myocardial infarction and sudden cardiac death.[64] A thirty-year follow-up study of healthy Canadian men found that sudden cardiac death was much more common on the first working day of the week. Thirty-five per cent of such deaths in previously healthy men, and 75 per cent of the deaths at work, occurred on a Monday. The researchers point to "reintroductions to occupational stress, activity or pollutants after a weekend respite" as likely precipitants.[65] A study conducted in the United States similarly has revealed a higher death rate from coronary heart disease on Mondays than on other days of the week.[66]

Pointing to the same source of stress, one study has demonstrated that overwork increases the risk of heart attack in young men more than any of the standard risk factors.[67] Several other pieces of research have shown overtime and increased work load to be correlated with changes in serum cholesterol, cardiac arrhythmias and an elevated frequency of myocardial infarction.[68] American tax accountants, for example, approaching the tax deadline of April 15, show changes in blood-clotting and serum cholesterol which increase their risk of heart attacks and strokes.[69] A study comparing heart-attack victims and a matched control group of healthy people, all of whom were employed in the same Swedish nationwide chain, found that workers suffering heart attacks had experienced many more stressful life events before falling ill – but the events that were more common in the heart-attack victims were all job-related. The stressful events included major changes in working schedule or conditions, undertaking more responsibility at work or having trouble with the boss.[70] The same research group studying members of the Swedish construction workers" trade union found that increased responsibility at work was the only life-change measure among dozens examined that predicted an increased risk of heart attack in this sample.[71]

One important piece of research, the Framingham (Massachusetts) study of risk factors in coronary heart disease, found no correlation between job-related stress and the presence of angina pectoris and other indications of heart disease. This finding may well be due to the fact that all of the heart patients in this study suffered from relatively chronic illness and were heart-attack survivors: sudden-death victims were automatically excluded.[72] On balance, the evidence is strong that the stresses of working are important precipitants of heart attack.

One of the most widely embraced of Karl Marx's theories is his concept of alienation. The concept is well enough accepted, in fact, that the U.S. Senate in 1972, concerned about the apparent spread of job dissatisfaction among workers and the threat of falling productivity, commissioned a study of alienation in the workplace.[73] Illustrated in the popular imagination by the assembly-line worker who is so disgusted and bored that he willfully damages the car on which he is working, Marx's theory of alienation covers this phenomenon and more. Marx described the estrangement of the worker from the creative process and from the product of his or her labor, an alienation from his or her essentially human characteristics, and from his or her fellow human beings. This condition, argued Marx, is the inevitable consequence of commodity production, wage work and the division of labor – a result of converting labor into a commodity.[74]

The experience of working-class men and women offers numerous examples of what Marx meant. Many auto workers despise the cars they build. "What'd you buy this piece of shit for?" demands a young General Motors worker of author Barbara Garson, kicking her car – a machine he might have helped build himself.[75] The work process may be regarded with derision. "There's a lot of variety in the paint shop," reports another Lordstown worker. "You clip on the color hose, bleed out the old color, and squirt. Clip, bleed, squirt, think; clip, bleed, squirt, yawn; clip, bleed squirt, scratch your nose."[76] The boredom can be dehumanizing – "You forget you're not a machine,"[77] says a copy typist; the close supervision oppressive – a steelworker complains, "I would rather work my ass off for eight hours a day with nobody watching me than five minutes with a guy watching me."[78] Job-status differences estrange co-workers. "What is this *'Yes, sir'* bullshit?" yells the same steelworker at his foreman. "I came here to work, I didn't come here to crawl."[79]

The problems, moreover, are not to be found only in the industrial workplace. Writes Lillian Breslow Rubin:

> There is, perhaps, no greater testimony to the deadening and deadly quality of the tasks of the housewife than the fact that so many women find pleasure in working at jobs that by almost any definition would be called alienated labor – low-status, low-paying, dead-end work made up of dull, routine tasks; work that often is considered too menial for men who are less educated than these women.[80]

The effort to enforce household labor may distort domestic relations. A working-class husband insists angrily:

> A wife's got to learn to be number two. That's the way it is, and that's what she better learn. She's going to stay home and take care of the family like a wife's supposed to do.[81]

How widespread is worker alienation? A large majority of workers in many industrialized countries express satisfaction with their work when polled; the size of this majority is always greater in higher-status jobs and older age groups. When asked whether they would prefer another occupation, however, as many as 60 per cent of American workers say yes.[82] Arthur Kornhauser, in his study *Mental Health of the Industrial Worker*, sees the expression of satisfaction with fundamentally unfulfilling jobs as an adaptive response on the part of the workers – a consequence "of their dwarfed desires and deadened initiative, reduction of their goals and restriction of their efforts to a point where life is relatively empty and only half meaningful."[83] The extent of alienation, therefore, is hard to measure. Reviewing the research, Marie Jahoda and Harold Rush can conclude only that

> there exists a stratum of society – its size is hard to determine – of degraded, frustrated, unhappy, psychologically unhealthy people in employment whose personal morale is as low as their productivity, who are unable to provide a constructive environment for their families, [and] whose lack of commitment in employment colors their total life experience.[84]

Can we estimate the psychological impact of alienating work? In his study of Detroit factory workers, Arthur Kornhauser found a clear correlation between the mental health of the worker and the skill of his job. Feelings of inadequacy, anxiety, depression and hostility were greater in those who performed the most routine, repetitive work. These symptoms, Kornhauser demonstrated, were not related to the worker's pre-employment characteristics but were a product of the job itself.[85] More than one study has shown that restricted independence at work is related to poor mental health. A large survey of American men representing a broad range of civilian occupations found low work complexity and close supervision to be associated with the worker's low job satisfaction, low self-esteem and raised level of anxiety.[86] A more recent survey of adults living in Oslo, Norway, extends these findings. The degree of close supervision on the job was found to be correlated with a variety of psychiatric symptoms – a link which was not explained independently by social and demographic factors.[87]

Reviewing the literature widely, Stanislav Kasl concludes that the correlation between measures of mental health and job satisfaction is not a particularly powerful one, though, as we have seen, expressed job satisfaction may not be a good reflection of the actual qualities of the work environment. Kasl finds that the evidence is clearest for the heightened prevalence of mental disorder among those performing the most routine, unskilled factory work.[88] For some workers, it is clear, we should not necessarily expect unemployment to be psychologically damaging – it may be a welcome release for those in the most alienating occupations.

UNEMPLOYMENT

Though the majority of the research points to serious adverse consequences from unemployment, there are indications that job loss for some workers under certain circumstances may not be distressing and may even be a positive experience. Blue-collar workers laid off by plant closings showed few lasting psychological or stress-related problems over the two-year period of displacement, unemployment and re-hiring through which they were followed by research workers Stanislav Kasl and Sidney Cobb. The working men in this study generally showed brief, initial responses to stress – increased depression, anxiety and raised blood pressure – most evident during the phase of anticipation prior to unemployment. Kasl suggests that these men showed few damaging effects from unemployment because many had given up the idea that their monotonous jobs were meaningful or important.[89]

Researchers Ramsay Liem and Paula Rayman counter with the suggestion that Kasl and Cobb's findings were undramatic because the unemployment circumstances of the men in their sample were not severe. In his own study of blue-collar and white-collar families in which the husband lost his job, Liem found significant increases in psychiatric symptoms in both the men and their wives and signs of mounting family distress. Symptoms increased as unemployment continued but receded after re-employment. The response to job loss was greater in this sample than in Kasl and Cobb's study, argues Liem, because the period of unemployment was much longer, the local economy was severely depressed and job prospects were poorer. Plant closings such as Kasl and Cobb studied, furthermore, may create a type of unemployment in which self-blame is less prominent.[90]

Liem's interpretation of these findings is borne out by a study of middle-class, unemployed men conducted by sociologist Craig Little. Nearly half of the men in this sample had a somewhat more positive response to unemployment; these were more likely to be the men who were optimistic about re-employment, had not been out of work long and were in a better financial situation. Kasl's point is also supported, however, since the more positive responses came from men whose prior job satisfaction had been low.[91]

The context in which job loss occurs clearly affects the response of the unemployed. Acknowledging this point, we may also recognize that the consequences of unemployment are usually distinctly harmful. Evidence on the damaging effects of unemployment began to accumulate during the Great Depression. Two researchers reviewing the topic in 1938, after compiling more than a hundred reports, observed that unemployment could lead to emotional instability, depression, hopelessness, distrust, domestic problems, narrowed activities and apathy.[92] More refined modern studies confirm these findings; the introduction of higher levels of financial support for the unemployed does not appear to have reduced the impact of joblessness.

Paula Rayman and Barry Bluestone's study of job loss in the American aircraft industry found unemployment to be linked to serious signs of strain such as alcoholism, raised blood pressure, increased smoking and anxiety.[93] Plant closings in Appalachia brought depression and sickness to the redundant employees.[94] A British study notes increasing general symptomatology in unemployed young men.[95] Older American workers laid off after years of stable employment responded with more ill health than those in a control group, a sense of powerlessness and loss of initiative.[96]

As unemployment has spread in the late 1980s and early 1990s, fresh reports have come in from around the world. A survey of Finnish manufacturing workers demonstrated a strong link between unemployment and mental ill health.[97] German furniture factory employees who lost their jobs were eight times more likely to report poor psychological health if they remained unemployed for a year.[98] Scottish school leavers who became unemployed showed intellectual, emotional and behavioral deterioration whereas those who went on to a job or training improved or were stable.[99] A recent series of British studies indicates that unemployed people are more depressed and anxious and have less self-esteem and self-confidence; the worst affected are middle-aged men, middle-class people, those who live in low unemployment areas and people with a strong work ethic.[100] A study conducted in Michigan finds that unemployment may lead to depression, anxiety and poor physical health via two routes – increased financial strain and an increased vulnerability to life event stress.[101] A Swedish study reveals a physiological basis for the increased vulnerability to stress: unemployment is associated with changes in the person's immune system and dramatically elevated levels of the hormone cortisol.[102]

Some studies point to harmful effects from both job stress and unemployment. The survey of members of the Swedish construction workers' union, mentioned above, found joblessness and dissatisfaction with work to be associated with an increased accident rate; unemployment and changes at work increased the risk of neurosis.[103] In the study of Toronto residents, job loss and demotion at work combined were major risk factors for ill health.[104] We may safely conclude that modern labor dynamics can be unhealthy for both employed and unemployed workers.

SUICIDE

Analysis of suicide patterns yields more evidence of the destructive effect of labor dynamics and especially of unemployment. All authorities are agreed that suicide rates peak during economic recessions and have done so throughout the century.[105] The unemployment index is the strongest predictor of changes in the suicide rate, having a greater impact on male suicide rates[106] and on older people of working age.[107] One researcher, Albert Pierce, has asserted that suicide statistics show an increase whenever the economy fluctuates up or down,[108] but later attempts to replicate his work have found unemployment to be more important than absolute economic change.[109] The view of Emile Durkheim, the early French sociologist, that "fortunate crises . . . affect suicide like economic disasters"[110] has not been borne out. His claim, however, that work protects against suicide does appear to be supported by the data.

Throughout the industrial world suicide is more common in the elderly[111] and is higher in retired men than in working men of the same age.[112] The pattern of increasing suicide with age holds true for white Americans; but for blacks and especially American Indians, who experience high levels of unemployment early in life, the suicide rate shows a peak in the young-adult years (see Figure 2.4). The Indian reservations with the highest suicide rates are those with the most severe problems of unemployment, alcoholism and traditional family disintegration.[113] Suicide is more common among those in the lower-income, lower-status jobs where employment is least secure.[114] Economic stress could account for many of these findings, or the absence of a

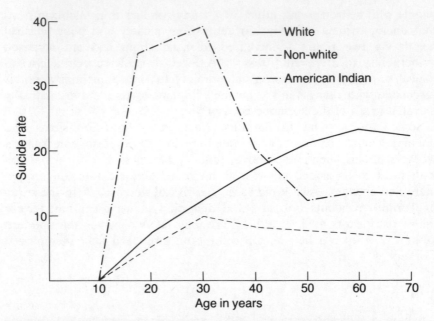

Figure 2.4 Age-specific suicide rates per 100,000 population for white, American Indian and other non-white groups in the U.S.A., 1969 and 1971 average
Source: National Institute of Mental Health, *Suicide, Homicide and Alcoholism among American Indians*, Washington D.C., Department of Health, Education and Welfare, 1973.

socially endorsed useful role (in middle-class whites, a problem most common in late life) could be an important precipitant of suicide. That the current picture is a response to changes accompanying the growth of wage work is supported by a study of suicide in Hong Kong. Before industrialization, Chinese suicide was more common in younger adults; industrial development has brought declining prestige, changed roles and a steep rise in suicide to the elderly of the modern city.[115]

The circumstances of individual suicide victims suggest that jobless-ness, work problems and economic difficulties may all be critical stresses. Studies have generally found around a quarter to a third or more of suicide victims to be unemployed – a substantially higher rate than in the general population or in control groups.[116] For example, a large-scale study of bricklayers and carpenters in Denmark found more unemployment in the recent background of workers suffering violent deaths from both accident or suicide.[117] In addition, a pattern of frequent job changes, job dissatisfaction and downward mobility is often uncovered in the history of suicide victims.[118] Which comes first – the emotional problems or the work difficulties? Two controlled studies have tried to tackle this question by examining unemployment rates in psychiatric patients who committed suicide versus those who did not: both studies found an association between unemployment and suicide for men.[119] In many cases it is clear that unemployment and job instability are a result of poor physical or mental health;[120] but we should not expect a simple one-way relationship. Impaired performance or loss of work role may well damage self-esteem and increase hopelessness and depression. The central role of the workplace in this relationship for those who are employed is revealed by the repeated finding that suicide (like sudden cardiac death) is most common on Mondays, declining in frequency as the week progresses.[121]

It is clear that the job market and the economy have a direct and decisive impact on our patterns of living, our view of ourselves and our emotions. Since this is so, we might reasonably expect the economy to influence the onset of serious mental illness and to affect the rate of admission to psychiatric hospital.

MENTAL HOSPITAL ADMISSIONS

The first comprehensive attempt to estimate the effect of the economy on mental hospital admissions was Harvey Brenner's *Mental Illness and the Economy*, published in 1973.[122] Earlier researchers had studied the variations in hospital admissions over relatively short periods of time, and some had pointed out that rising admission rates during the Great Depression appeared to correspond to increasing unemployment figures.[123] Brenner's work went a great deal further, however, and is still the most important study of the topic.

Brenner analyzed admissions to New York state mental hospitals from the mid-nineteenth century to the late 1960s, looking for correlations with measures of economic activity and employment. From 1910 the data included admissions to public and private hospitals; for the earlier period admissions to one state hospital were examined. Admission rates regularly increased during economic decline. This relationship was particularly clear for patients with functional psychosis. For schizophrenic people from childhood up to the age of around 60 years the relationship was strong, and the finding held true for first admissions and readmissions. The effect of economic change appeared to be more or less immediate; the correlation occurred with no lag but was strengthened by the addition of a (theoretically acceptable) one-year lag.

In select groups of patients the relationship between admission rates and the economy was found to be reversed. Elderly patients with senile brain disease were more commonly admitted during the boom, as were female patients with late-onset involutional psychosis.[124]

Brenner's work on mental hospital admissions has been subject to close scrutiny and has survived the challenge largely undamaged.

Statisticians James Marshall and Donna Funch criticized Brenner for his use of statistical detrending procedures and for his failure to make allowances for changes in hospital capacity. Their replication of Brenner's work, taking into account these technical points, essentially confirmed the original findings. The state of the economy, they found, was closely tied to the admission of working-age men and women; but for the young and the aged, hospital capacity was a better predictor of admission rates.[125]

Brenner's principal finding of a link between the recession and mental hospital admissions has since been confirmed by a number of other studies. In Ontario, admissions to a provincial psychiatric hospital for the period from 1960 to 1977 were found to exceed discharges during economic slumps; during the boom the reverse held true.[126] Readmissions to state inpatient and outpatient mental health facilities in Missouri from 1971 to 1979 correlated with the unemployment rate.[127] Community mental health center outpatient admissions in Denver, Colorado, in the 1970s were also linked to the unemployment rate.[128]

What could explain these findings? Brenner examines three theories. Firstly, the tolerance for the dependent mentally ill might decrease as families encounter greater economic stress. The data do not support this hypothesis, for the most dependent – the young and the aged – tend to be hospitalized in the boom and not the recession. It seems likely, in fact, that increased mobility during the boom and expanding employment opportunities outside the home for potential care-givers may be stronger factors leading to rejection of the mentally disabled.

A second possibility is that financial destitution may lead patients to seek the shelter of hospital as an almshouse. Again, the explanation is not supported by the statistics. Economically comfortable patients show the same increase in admission rates during the slump as do marginal patients. Admissions to costly private hospitals also increase during recessions – an economic burden rather than a means of support.[129]

We are left with one likely explanation – economic stress and unemployment lead to a true increase in symptoms of psychiatric illness. Much of the research cited in this chapter supports the notion that the economy can lead directly to such changes in psychological symptoms. Why should the impact on hospital admissions occur more in the recession than in the boom? Perhaps because those who are susceptible to serious mental illness are most likely to be functioning marginally on the job and are most likely to be laid off when the economy takes a downturn. The fact that it is principally working-age men and women who show increased hospital admissions during declines in the economy favors this idea. Other research has shown that the admission of unemployed patients and those with job-related difficulties does, in fact, increase during recessions.[130] Overall, we have strong evidence that the onset of episodes of mental illness increases with each setback in the economy and with the reduction in the call for labor.

Physical and mental diseases, including schizophrenia, are more common in the lower classes and their occurrence fluctuates with the economy. The effects of economic expansion, economic stress, working conditions and unemployment are involved in the genesis of this ill health, despair and insanity. In the next chapter we will examine the extent to which the economy and the labor market shape the course of schizophrenia and influence whether it emerges as a benign or a malignant condition.

SUMMARY

- Illness and death rates are higher in the working classes.
- Stressful life events are more common in the lower classes and contribute to the raised prevalence of stress-related physical and mental illness.
- Schizophrenia is concentrated in the lower classes in the industrial world and in the upper castes and classes in the Third World – a pattern which only a theory of social causation can explain.
- Social causation and social drift may operate together to account for the social-class gradient for schizophrenia in urban-industrial areas.
- In large cities, fluctuations in the economy are associated with increased changes in people's lives and with symptoms of psychological distress.
- Residents of rural areas appear to be protected from the adverse effects on physical and mental health of low socioeconomic status and fluctuations in the economy.
- Early studies of the business cycle found that most social pathology increased in the boom, except suicide which became more common in the slump.
- Research tying social pathology to rising unemployment can often be faulted for over-enthusiastic reliance on the notion of lagged effects.
- Infant mortality increases during the boom.
- Both the stresses of working and unemployment can create significant health hazards.
- Work problems, economic stress and unemployment appear to be important in precipitating suicide.
- Mental hospital admissions for working-age people increase during the slump, probably in response to economic and labor-market stresses.

Part II

The political economy of schizophrenia

Chapter 3

Recovery from schizophrenia

Few topics in psychiatry have been researched as frequently over as long a period of time as has recovery from schizophrenia. Ever since Emil Kraepelin focused on the deteriorating course of the illness in defining dementia praecox, psychiatrists throughout the Western world have been interested in comparing the recovery rates of their patients with those of other physicians. More than a hundred long-term outcome studies of schizophrenia have been published in Europe and America during this century and several thousand studies of the short-term effect of different treatment methods have been carried out. Despite this volume of work, however, a clear picture of long-term outcome in schizophrenia has not emerged.

Many researchers have formed the impression that recovery rates in schizophrenia have improved in comparison with earlier times. Their optimistic conclusions have not always been disinterested; often they have attributed the improved outcome to new treatment methods – insulin coma, electro-convulsive therapy and psychosurgery[1] or, more recently, community treatment and the antipsychotic drugs.[2] Heinz Lehmann, an American psychiatrist, writing in a major textbook in 1981, endorses the widespread opinion that modern psychiatric treatment has improved the outlook in schizophrenia. The chances for a favorable outcome from a schizophrenic psychosis, he argues, are four or five times better than they were in the early years of the century. He attributes this change to "good follow-up therapy and well controlled maintenance drug treatment."[3] He presents a table of ten follow-up studies of schizophrenia conducted since the 1930s which appear to support his argument and show improving recovery rates.

A number of researchers have arrived at more pessimistic conclusions.[4] Joseph Stephens, a professor of psychiatry at Johns Hopkins University, after reviewing thirty-eight long-term follow-up studies which included data on patients admitted as early as the First World War, remains unimpressed with improvements in recovery rates or the long-term benefits of drug treatment.[5] Swiss psychiatrist Manfred Bleuler (son of Eugen

Bleuler, who coined the term "schizophrenia") has a particularly interesting perspective:

> During the greater part of my life, I have lived in hospitals which cared mostly for severe cases of schizophrenia, and from babyhood on through my whole childhood, gravely sick schizophrenics even lived in my parents' family.[6]

Study of the course of illness in his patients over several decades led him to conclude, in 1968, that little change had occurred in the proportion of patients who deteriorated or who recovered:

> There still exists the sad chronic evolutions to severe chronic conditions, and it is doubtful whether modern therapy has been able much to increase the number of total, lifelong recoveries.[7]

The only improvement Manfred Bleuler could detect was a decrease in the severity of chronic schizophrenic deterioration as a result of a reduction in the mishandling and neglect of hospitalized patients that was common earlier in the century. Although not impressed with the results of treatment, Dr. Bleuler is less pessimistic about the natural course of the illness. He writes:

> Generations of psychiatrists felt that schizophrenia was a process psychosis progressing to complete deterioration, if life was long enough to allow the process to come to an end. . . . I am certain today that the contrary is true.[8]

Dr. Bleuler found that many of his chronic patients improved later in life, rather than deteriorating, and that another 25–35 per cent of his schizophrenic patients before the Second World War recovered from their illness after only acute episodes of psychosis.

Which view is correct: that schizophrenia is an inherently catastrophic illness from which only modern psychiatric treatment can afford relief; or that it is a condition with a considerable, spontaneous recovery rate upon which treatment has little long-term effect? The first point of view, without a doubt, is the opinion of the majority of psychiatrists. Taking a deeper look into the storehouse of information on recovery from schizophrenia in the dusty volumes of psychiatric journals going back to the turn of the century may help resolve this issue. If we analyze this material according to time periods that reflect the major changes in the state of the economy, we may also throw some light on another question: to what extent have changes in the economy during the century influenced the outlook for schizophrenic people?

FOLLOW-UP STUDIES

Unfortunately, there are problems involved in comparing the results of the many long-term follow-up studies of schizophrenic people. As we have seen in Chapter 1, which patients are labeled schizophrenic varies from country to country, from time to time and from one psychiatrist to another. The patients chosen to be followed may be male or female, adolescent or adult, experiencing their first psychotic break or more chronically ill, or selected by any other criteria the researcher chooses. Any of these factors may affect the course of the psychosis. The patients may be followed for any period of time: one year, ten years or until death. If the illness is progressive, this factor could clearly affect the results. These follow-up studies are obviously not strictly comparable. Any attempt to get useful information from them, then, makes the assumption that the differences between the studies balance out when large numbers of them are collected into groups. If significant changes in outcome are uncovered, it will be necessary to calculate whether the variations may be due to differences in diagnosis, patient characteristics or follow-up methods between the groups.

MEASURES OF RECOVERY

One of the crucial variables in these studies is how the psychiatrist chooses to measure the patients' condition at the time of follow-up. The researcher may be most concerned about whether symptoms of the illness are still present but can concentrate on either psychotic features, such as hallucinations or delusions, neurotic symptoms, such as anxiety, or personality defects like withdrawal or eccentric habits. The proportion of patients considered to have recovered will depend on how rigorously recovery is defined. If outcome is measured in terms of social functioning, the investigator may look at any combination of a range of features including the following: working ability, capacity to care for basic needs, abnormal behavior causing distress to others, criminal activity, number of friends or sexual functioning. Social functioning measures are particularly hard to standardize. A fairly unambiguous measure is whether the patient is in or out of hospital at follow-up; but this is not necessarily, as we shall see, a reliable measure of social functioning.

To impose some consistency on the follow-up results, information has been gathered from studies according to predetermined definitions of terms which have been in use throughout this century:

Complete recovery: Loss of psychotic symptoms and return to the pre-illness level of functioning.

Social recovery: Economic and residential independence and low social disruption. This means working adequately to provide for oneself and not being dependent on others for basic needs or housing. This term is the one most open to variations in measurement.

Table 3.1 Recovery and hospitalization rates in 85 outcome studies of schizophrenia

Authors	Country	Years of admission	Median year of admission	Follow-up years later	Original cohort size	Number dead and not followed up
Kraepelin (1919)	Germany	late 1880s	late 1880s	up to 29 or until death	c65	–
Kraepelin (1919)	Germany	late 1880s	late 1880s	up to 29 or until death	c45	–
Kraepelin (1919)	Germany	late 1880s	late 1880s	up to 29 or until death	c97	–
Evensen (1904)	Norway	1888–1897	1892	5–15	182	29
1881–1900		**Percentages derived from totals**				
E. Bleuler (1950)	Switzerland	1898–1905	1901	3–10	515	0
Stearns (1912)	USA	1901–1905	1903	?	395	75
Rosanoff (1914)	USA	1907–1908	1907	5	169	23
Mayer-Gross (1932)	Germany	1912–1913	1912	16–17	328	125
Bond (1921)	USA	1914	1914	5	47	3
Murdoch (1933)	England	1900–1931	1915	1–31	75	11
Müller (1951)	Switzerland	1917–1918	1917	5–30	100	1
Rennie (1939)	USA	1913–1923	1918	1–26 or until death	500	–
Strecker & Willey (1927)	USA	before 1920	before 1920	over 5	186	0
Lemke (1935)	Germany	1918–1923	1920	15	255	24
Freyhan (1955)	USA	1920	1920	13	100	11
Otto-Martiensen (1921)	Germany	before 1921	before 1921	?	527	98
1901–1920		**Percentages derived from totals**				
Jönsson & Jönsson (1992)	Sweden	1925	1925	30 or until death	77	7
Langfeldt (1939)	Norway	1926–1929	1927	7–10	100	0
Braatöy (1936)	Norway	1926–1929	1927	6–7	208	15
Bond & Braceland (1937)	USA	1927–1928	1927	5	116	10
Norton (1961)	England	1928–1930	1929	2	207	–

Complete recovery			Social recovery			Hospitalized			Stage or type of illness	Treatment
Number followed up (+ dead)	Number completely recovered	%	Number followed up (+ dead)	Number socially recovered	%	Number followed up (+ dead)	Number in hospital at follow-up	%		
c65	c12	8							Hebephrenic	
c45	0	0							Paranoid	
c97	c13	13							Catatonic	
			182	27	15				Male, first admission	
207	25	12	182	27	15					
			515	307	60				First admission	Early discharge
315	16	5				315	202	64		
						169	99	59	First admission	
294	89	30	294	103	35	294	56	19		
47	1	2	47	9	19	47	31	66	Women, mixed duration	
75	12	16							Criminal	
			100	28	28	100	33	33	First admission	
456	112	25	456	166	36	456	254	56	Mixed duration	
186	38	20								
			126	43	34	126	35	27	Male	
						100	65	65	Mixed duration	ECT, insulin coma, psychosurgery, psychotherapy
			312	105	34	312	66	21		
1373	268	20	1850	761	41	1919	841	44		
77	0	0							First admission	
100	17	17	100	21	21	100	46	46	Acute onset	
208	40	19	208	62	30	208	97	47	First admission	
113	12	11							Mixed duration	No specific treatment
						207	122	59	Female, mixed duration	

Authors	Country	Years of admission	Median year of admission	Follow-up years later	Original cohort size	Number dead and not followed up
Wooton *et al.* (1935)	England	1928–1931	1929	2–5	104	–
Fromenty (1937)	France	mid-1920s to mid-1930s	1930	up to 15 or until death	271	–
Cheney & Drewry (1938)	USA	1926–1935	1930	1–12	500	50
Hunt *et al.* (1938)	USA	1927–1934	1930	3½–10½	677	69
Rupp & Fletcher (1940)	USA	1929–1934	1931	4½–10	641	89
Horwitz & Kleiman (1936)	USA	1930–1933	1931	1–3	193	8
Gerloff (1936)	Germany	1925–1939	1932	7–11	382	52
Malamud & Render (1939)	USA	1929–1936	1933	2–9	344	21
Müller (1951)	Switzerland	1933	1933	5–18 or until death	100	5
Stalker (1939)	Scotland	1932–1937	1934	1–6	133	0
Fröshaug & Ytrehus (1963)	Norway	1933–1935	1934	6–8	95	3
Briner (1939)	Germany	1933–1936	1934	2–5	267	37
Romano & Ebaugh (1938)	USA	1933–1936	1934	1–4	600	46
Guttman *et al.* (1939)	England	1934–1935	1934	3–4	188	7
Norton (1961)	England	1934–1936	1935	2	224	–
Beck (1968)	Canada	1930–1942	1936	25–35	84	0
Carter (1942)	England	1935–1937	1936	3	47	–
Tsuang *et al.* (1979)	USA	1934–1944	1939	30–40 or until death	200	–
Coryell *et al.* (1986)	USA	1934–1945	1939	40 or until death	93	–
Errera (1957)	USA	1932–1948	1940	8–24	59	2
Johanson (1958)	Sweden	1938–1942	1940	10–18	100	16
Freyhan (1955)	USA	1940	1940	13	100	4

Complete recovery			Social recovery			Hospitalized			Stage or type of illness	Treatment
Number followed up (+ dead)	Number completely recovered	%	Number followed up (+ dead)	Number socially recovered	%	Number followed up (+ dead)	Number in hospital at follow-up	%		
95	18	19				95	64	67	Mixed duration	
271	41	15							Mixed duration	Heavy sedation, "abcès de fixation" or "sulfoidol"
452	51	11	452	112	25	452	197	44	Mixed duration	No specific treatment
604	82	14							First admission	
608	40	7	608	133	22	608	343	56	First admission	
170	9	5				170	89	52		Radiothermy, CO_2 & O_2, and psychotherapy
			341	113	33					
309	53	17	309	94	30	309	155	50	Mixed duration	Psychotherapy or social readjustment
			100	38	38	100	28	28	First admission	
129	15	12	129	26	20	129	91	71	First admission	"Ordinary" methods
			87	16	18	87	32	37	First admission	
			245	111	45	245	64	26	Early	Continuous narcosis or early discharge
442	1	0	442	152	34	442	247	56	Mixed duration	
184	42	23	184	67	36	184	77	42	Early	No drastic treatment
						224	141	63	Female, mixed duration	
84	6	7	84	11	13	84	54	64	First admission	No insulin coma, ECT or psychotherapy
47	10	21	47	14	30				Adolescent	No specific treatment
186	38	20	186	65	35	186	33	18	Mixed duration	
87	27	31	87	42	48				"Schizophreniform" Brief duration	
			54	14	26	54	13	24	Ages 15 to 21	
98	1	1	98	8	8				Males, first admission	No treatment or lobotomy
						100	42	42		

64   The political economy of schizophrenia

Authors	Country	Years of admission	Median year of admission	Follow-up years later	Original cohort size	Number dead and not followed up
1921–1940		Percentages derived from totals				
Hastings (1958)	U.S.A.	1938–1944	1941	6–12	251	9
M. Bleuler (1978)	Switzerland	1942–1943	1942	20–23 or until death	208	–
Masterson (1956)	U.S.A.	1936–1950	1943	5–19	83	–
Holmboe & Astrup (1957)	Norway	1938–1950	1944	6–18	255	0
Astrup et al. (1963)	Norway	1938–1950	1944	5–22	721	32
Eitinger et al. (1958)	Norway	1940–1949	1944	5–15	154	–
Harris et al. (1956)	England	1945–1968	1946	5	126	2
Vaillant & Funkenstein (1966)	U.S.A.	1948–1950	1949	2–14 or until death	72	–
Leiberman et al. (1957)	England	1948–1950	1949	3	156	2
Norton (1961)	England	1949–1950	1949	2	145	–
Niskanen & Achté (1971)	Finland	1950	1950	5	100	4
Huber et al. (1975)	Germany	1945–1959	1952	22	502	–
Kelly & Sargant (1965)	England	1950–1955	1952	2	39	2
Stephens (1970)	U.S.A.	1948–1958	1953	5–16	472	17
Norton (1961)	England	1953	1953	2	129	–
Ackner & Oldham (1962)	England	c1954	1954	3	66	–
Astrup & Noreik (1966)	Norway	1951–1957	1954	5–12 or until death	273	–
1941–1955		Percentages derived from totals				
Brown et al. (1966)	England	1956	1956	5	111	3
Brown et al. (1966)	England	1956	1956	5	228	6
Fröshaug & Ytrehus (1963)	Norway	1953–1959	1956	3–8	103	5

Complete recovery			Social recovery			Hospitalized			Stage or type of illness	Treatment
Number followed up (+ dead)	Number completely recovered	%	Number followed up (+ dead)	Number socially recovered	%	Number followed up (+ dead)	Number in hospital at follow-up	%		
4264	503	12	3761	1099	29	3984	1935	49		
247	68	28	247	103	42				Mixed duration	No "modern" therapies
208	30	14	208	64	31	208	93	45	Mixed duration	
83	15	18	83	27	33				Adolescent	
255	97	38	255	147	58	255	89	35	First admission, acute onset	ECT, insulin coma and psychosurgery
696	131	19	696	248	36	555	118	21	Non-acute	ECT, insulin coma and psychosurgery
154	18	12								ECT, insulin coma and lobotomy
125	37	30	125	61	49	125	42	34	Mixed duration	Insulin coma
			70	19	26	70	17	23	Mixed duration	ECT, insulin coma
154	49	32	154	85	55	154	44	29	First admission, early	ECT, insulin coma
						145	53	37	Female, mixed duration	
100	30	30	100	59	59	100	22	22	First admission	
502	111	22	502	281	56	502	67	13		
39	14	36	39	18	46	39	12	31	Selected	Insulin coma
383	97	25							First admission	
						129	26	20	Female, mixed admission	
66	27	41	66	38	58	66	14	21	Early	Insulin and barbiturate coma
273	16	6	273	92	34				First admission	ECT, insulin coma, leucotomy and psychotropic drugs
3285	740	23	2818	1242	44	2348	597	25		
88	32	36	97	53	55	88	11	12	First admission	Phenothiazines
173	32	18	205	79	39	173	47	27	Previous admissions	Phenothiazines
97	23	24	97	35	36	97	17	18	Female, first admission	

Authors	Country	Years of admission	Median year of admission	Follow-up years later	Original cohort size	Number dead and not followed up
*Wirt & Simon (1959)	USA	c1956	1956	1	80	0
Henisz (1966)	Poland	1956	1956	7	249	22
Mandelbrote & Folkard (1961)	England	1956–1958	1957	2–4	288	8
Kelly & Sargant (1965)	England	1956–1958	1957	2	39	0
Norton (1961)	England	1957	1957	2	189	–
Cole et al. (1963)	USA	1957–1959	1958	3	110	0
Hoenig & Hamilton (1966)	England	1958–1960	1959	4	62	0
Kelly & Sargant (1965)	England	1958–1961	1959	2	45	0
Holmboe et al. (1968)	Norway	1958–1961	1959	5–7	169	0
Engelhardt et al. (1982)	USA	1958–1962	1960	15	670	24
Niskanen & Achté (1971)	Finland	1960	1960	5	100	5
Leyberg (1965)	England	1960	1960	3	81	0
Holmboe et al. (1968)	Norway	1959–1962	1960	5–8	42	0
Levenstein et al. (1966)	USA	1959–1961	1960	2	77	1
Vaillant et al. (1964)	USA	1961–1962	1961	1–2	103	0
Kelly & Sargant (1965)	England	1960–1963	1961	2	48	0
Hall et al. (1966)	USA	1961–1962	1961	1	188	0
Bland et al. (1978)	Canada	1963	1963	11–12	92	0
Bland & Orn (1978)	Canada	1963	1963	14	45	2
Niskanen & Achté (1971)	Finland	1965	1965	5	100	6

Complete recovery			Social recovery			Hospitalized			Stage or type of illness	Treatment
Number followed up (+ dead)	Number completely recovered	%	Number followed up (+ dead)	Number socially recovered	%	Number followed up (+ dead)	Number in hospital at follow-up	%		
79	7	9	79	29	37	79	20	25	First admission	Chiropromazine, reserpine, ECT, insulin coma and psychotherapy
230	30	13	230	73	32				Early	Chlorpromazine, ECT and insulin coma
			230	96	42	288	51	18	Mixed duration	
39	12	31	39	24	61	39	2	5	Selected	Phenothiazines
						189	19	10	Female, mixed duration	
			108	47	43				Male, mixed duration	
62	17	27	53	20	38	62	6	10	First admission, mixed duration	Antipsychotic drugs, ECT and psychotherapy
44	14	32	44	32	73	44	3	7	Selected	Phenothiazines
169	12	7	169	35	21				First admission	
						670	75	11	Mixed duration	Outpatient treatment
100	29	29	100	68	68	100	14	14	First admission	Antipsychotic drugs
81	18	26	81	26	32	81	14	17	Mixed duration	Hospital and community treatment
42	6	14	42	15	36				First admission	
77	9	12	77	30	34				Selected	Antipsychotic drugs and psychotherapy
100	25	25	100	64	64	100	13	13	Mixed duration	Phenothiazines and psychotherapy
48	24	48	48	32	67	48	4	8	Selected, mixed duration	Phenothiazines, ECT and insulin therapy
188	c38	20	188	72	38				Acute, first admission	
88	29	33	88	61	69				First admission	Antipsychotic drugs and ECT
43	7	16	43	27	63	43	2	5	First admission	Antipsychotic drugs
100	21	21	100	64	64	100	10	10	First admission	Antipsychotic drugs

Authors	Country	Years of admission	Median year of admission	Follow-up years later	Original cohort size	Number dead and not followed up
Salokangas (1983)	Finland	1965–1967	1966	7½	100	8
Helgason (1990)	Iceland	1966–1967	1966	20–21	107	23
Cottman & Mezey (1976)	England	1964–1968	1966	4–9	56	1
Marneros et al. (1992)	Germany	before 1967	before 1967	25	148	–
WHO (1979)	Denmark	1968–1969	1968	2	48	–
WHO (1979)	England	1968–1969	1968	2	57	–
WHO (1979)	USA	1968–1969	1968	2	38	–
WHO (1979)	Czechoslovakia	1968–1969	1968	2	53	–
Prudo & Blum (1987)	England	1968–1969	1968	5	100	6
Salokangas (1983)	Finland	1969	1969	8	75	5
Stone (1986)	USA	1963–1976	1969	10–20	c140	–
Harrow et al. (1978)	USA	after 1970	after 1970	2–3	79	4
Munk-Jørgensen & Mortensen (1992)	Denmark	1972	1972			
Möller et al. (1982)	Germany	1972–1974	1973	5–6	103	7
Johnstone et al. (1979)	England	before 1978	before 1978	1	45	1
Marengo et al. (1991)	USA	c1977	c1977	8	111	–
Biehl et al. (1986)	Germany	1978	1978	5	70	3
Jablensky et al. (1991)	Denmark	1978–1980	1979	2	80	–
Jablensky et al. (1991)	Ireland	1978–1980	1979	2	57	–
Jablensky et al. (1991)	USA (Hawaii)	1978–1980	1979	2	29	–
Jablensky et al. (1991)	USA (Rochester)	1978–1980	1979	2	31	–

Complete recovery			Social recovery			Hospitalized			Stage or type of illness	Treatment
Number followed up (+ dead)	Number completely recovered	%	Number followed up (+ dead)	Number socially recovered	%	Number followed up (+ dead)	Number in hospital at follow-up	%		
100	25	25	100	64	64				First admission	
107	3	3	107	27	25				First episode	Hospital and/or community treatment
42	22	52	42	34	81	42	2	5	First admission	Phenothiazines and community care
148	28	19	148	61	41	148	36	24		
48	5	10							Mixed duration	
57	20	35							Mixed duration	
38	8	21							Mixed duration	
53	14	26							Mixed duration	
88	17	19	71	42	59	100	13	13	Mixed duration	
75	16	21	75	38	51				First admission	Hospital and community treatment
72	0	0	72	7	10	72	11	15	Mixed duration	Exploratory psychotherapy
79	13	16	79	33	42	79	14	18	Acute and chronic	Phenothiazines and psychotherapy
53	10	19	53	10	19	53	8	15	First admission	
85	16	19	85	42	49				Mixed duration	Neuroleptics and sociotherapy
			43	15	35				Acute	
			74	38	51				Mixed duration	Hospital and community treatment
						70	3	4	First episode	Hospital and community treatment
80	22	27							First episode	Hospital and/or community treatment
57	21	37							First episode	Hospital and/or community treatment
29	7	24							First episode	Hospital and/or community treatment
31	12	39							First episode	Hospital and/or community treatment

Authors	Country	Years of admission	Median year of admission	Follow-up years later	Original cohort size	Number dead and not followed up
Jablensky *et al.* (1991)	U.S.SR	1978–1980	1979	2	164	–
Jablensky *et al.* (1991)	Japan	1978–1980	1979	2	70	–
Jablensky *et al.* (1991)	U.K.	1978–1980	1979	2	86	–
Jablensky *et al.* (1991)	Czechoslovakia	1978–1980	1979	2	87	–
Breier *et al.* (1991)	U.S.A	1976–1984	1980	2–12	74	4
Shepherd *et al.* (1989)	England	before 1983	before 1983	over 5	121	9
Scottish Schizophrenia Research Group	Scotland	before 1986	before 1986	5	49	1
1956–present	Percentages derived from totals					

Note: * Year of admission unclear: study included in this section as phenothiazine was used.

	Since an important part of the definition is employment status we run a risk of tautological reasoning in correlating social recovery with the unemployment rate.
Hospitalization:	In a psychiatric hospital at the time of follow-up.

Every European and North American follow-up study that was uncovered during a lengthy period of library research and that provided information on one or more of these categories has been included in Table 3.1. A study is included only if it followed a sample of patients selected at the time of admission to treatment: cohorts selected at the time of hospital discharge do not include those who remain in hospital and die there. The list has been updated for the second edition of this book but is certainly not complete; the German literature alone probably contains a great many more suitable studies. The eighty-five studies that are included, however, form a more comprehensive survey than has previously been made; most importantly they give us a good deal of information about recovery rates for patients admitted in every decade since the turn of the century.[9]

Recovery rates during various time periods were figured by the simple method of adding all patients who achieved each level of recovery in one time period and calculating what percentage they formed of the total group

Complete recovery			Social recovery			Hospitalized			Stage or type of illness	Treatment
Number followed up (+ dead)	Number completely recovered	%	Number followed up (+ dead)	Number socially recovered	%	Number followed up (+ dead)	Number in hospital at follow-up	%		
164	30	18							First episode	Hospital and/or community treatment
70	20	29							First episode	Hospital and/or community treatment
86	52	60							First episode	Hospital and/or community treatment
87	58	67							First episode	Hospital and/or community treatment
62	3	5	62	26	42	62	11	18	Chronic	
116	17	15	116	51	44				Mixed duration	Hospital and community treatment
40	7	17	43	8	19				First admission	Antipsychotic drugs and ECT
3715	830	22	3388	1478	44	2827	406	14		

of patients followed up in that period. A point of detail: patients who were dead at the time of follow-up, and for whom there was no information about the state of their illness when they died, could either have been included in the analysis or excluded. In this survey they were included in the total of patients followed up, but, of course, they never contributed to the proportion of recoveries. This tends to reduce the calculated recovery rates for the earlier decades of the century, when institutional death rates were substantially higher, and makes the test of the theory that outcome from schizophrenia was good during those years more severe.

PERIODS OF ANALYSIS

Each study was assigned to a time period according to the median date of admission of the group of patients. Unavoidably, several patient groups were admitted during one time period and followed up in another. Assigning the group to the earlier time assumes that the conditions in force earlier in the illness are more important in shaping the ultimate course. This limitation suggests, however, that the trends in recovery rates should be analyzed only over rather long periods of time.

The periods of analysis selected were as follows.

1881–1900: The Great Depression of the late nineteenth century (1873–96 in Britain) ran through most of this period and was a time of severe unemployment throughout the industrial world. Mental institutions were overcrowded and, particularly in Germany, barren and coercive.[10] An aura of pessimism pervaded psychiatry. Kraepelin's patients were admitted at this time, and since only one other study is available for the period, these results are not included in the formal analysis.

1901–20: The period was characterized by improving employment and included the First World War. More active psychiatric treatment methods were established and, in the United States, the mental hygiene movement developed.

1921–40: This was a time of severe economic depression, beginning several years earlier in Europe than in the United States, with unemployment rising to around a quarter of the work force throughout the industrial world. Electro-convulsive therapy, insulin coma and psychosurgery were introduced in the treatment of psychosis.

1941–55: This period saw the Second World War and, particularly in northern Europe, postwar full employment. A postwar social revolution in psychiatric treatment occurred in northern Europe, resulting in increased rehabilitative efforts for psychotic patients.

1956 onwards: Declining employment and 'stagflation' characterized the economies in most industrial countries. The neuroleptic drugs were introduced into widespread use at the beginning of this period and US community mental health centers began to be established in the mid-1960s. With the addition of recent studies for the second edition of this book, this period has been expanded to be longer than the others; there are not enough new studies to split this period into two, however.

RESULTS

The results of the analysis are shown in Figure 3.1. Average figures for unemployment in the United States and the United Kingdom for each time period are also drawn in (inverted) to allow comparison.[11] The figures from the two outcome studies on patients admitted before 1901 are sketched in dotted lines to emphasize that they are not reliable but merely indicative of the general trend.

The picture that emerges is in conflict with some widely held beliefs in psychiatry. In the first place, *recovery rates from schizophrenia are not significantly better now than they were during the first two decades of the century*. The arrival of the antipsychotic drugs shortly before 1955 appears to have had little effect on long-term outcome. Complete recovery rates remain around 20–25 per cent and about 40–45 per cent of schizophrenics are socially recovered at follow-up.

Second, the state of the *economy appears to be linked to outcome in schizophrenia*. During the Great Depression of the 1920s and 1930s, the

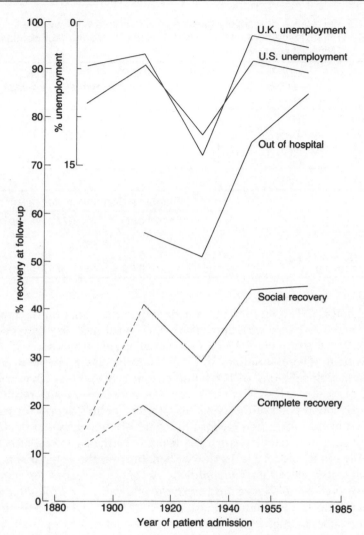

Figure 3.1 Outcome from schizophrenia in Europe and North America as reflected in 85 studies, and average unemployment (inverted) for the U.S.A. and the U.K. for the same time periods

rate of complete recovery was halved at 12 per cent; social recovery fell to less than 30 per cent. An analysis of variance shows that these changes are greater than would be expected by chance. The little information available for patients admitted during the Great Depression of the late nineteenth century shows the same trend toward low recovery rates. There is a statistical correlation between changes in the recovery rates and US and UK average unemployment after 1900 (see Table 3.2), but as we are comparing only four periods we should not attach too much significance

Table 3.2 Correlation of recovery rates in schizophrenia with average
unemployment rates in the U.S.A. and U.K. during four periods of the
twentieth century

Admission period	Complete recovery %	Social recovery %	U.S. unemployment %	U.K. unemployment %
1901–20	20	41	4.7	3.5
1921–40	12	29	11.9	14.0
1941–55	23	44	4.1	1.5
1956–85	22	44	5.9	4.0

	Pearson's Correlation Coefficient			
	U.S. unemployment		U.K. unemployment	
	r	∝	r	∝
Complete recovery	0.95	0.02	0.98	0.01
Social recovery	0.95	0.02	0.97	0.01

to this statistic. The more important finding is the variation of complete,
symptomatic recovery with unemployment; social recovery may fluctuate
with the economy merely because it is itself partly a measure of patient
employment. These variations in recovery rates now allow us to explain
the conflicting opinions of how outcome in schizophrenia has changed
during the century. If we contrast recent rates of recovery with results from
the Great Depression of the 1930s or with Kraepelin's figures for patients
admitted in the 1880s then modern outcome will appear superior. On the
other hand, if we include recovery statistics from the two decades between
the depressions, recent results do not benefit from the comparison.

Finally, it is clear that *schizophrenic people experienced the impact of
deinstitutionalization before the antipsychotic drugs were brought into use.*
The claim which is commonly heard, particularly in the United States, that
the antipsychotic drugs made community treatment of schizophrenic people
possible is brought into dispute. The proportion of schizophrenic people
out of hospital at follow-up increased significantly from around 50 or 55
per cent before 1940 to more than 70 per cent in the immediate postwar
period. After the antipsychotic drugs were introduced, the proportion of
patients out of hospital continued to increase to 86 per cent. One point
stands out with regard to this trend towards community treatment: whereas
the decrease in hospital use in the postwar years before 1955 was associated
with an improvement in the recovery rates of schizophrenic people, after
the advent of drug treatment deinstitutionalization did not bring any
improvement in the symptoms or social functioning of these patients.

Despite the popular view in psychiatry, the antipsychotic drugs have
proved to be a critical factor in neither emptying mental hospitals nor

achieving modern recovery rates in schizophrenia. Other probable causes of the deinstitutionalization movement will be presented in Chapter 4, and political, economic and social explanations for the variations in recovery from schizophrenia will be offered in Chapters 5, 6, 7 and 8. The reasons for the poor showing of the antipsychotic drugs will be discussed in Chapter 10. It will be argued that, rather than psychiatric treatment having a big impact on schizophrenia, both the course of the illness and the development of psychiatry itself are governed by political economy.

Before going on to this analysis, however, we should see if there are reasons to doubt the accuracy of the findings of the survey of outcome studies of schizophrenia.

DIFFERENCES IN DIAGNOSIS

Could differences in the diagnosis of schizophrenia between one country or one time period and another have produced these results? We know, for example, that Scandinavian psychiatrists have a narrow concept of schizophrenia which excludes brief illnesses and emphasizes poor outcome. American psychiatry, on the other hand, until the 1970s employed a broad concept of schizophrenia, which included much of what European psychiatrists call manic-depressive illness and also some conditions which would not be considered psychoses elsewhere (see Chapter 1). If the sample of outcome studies included proportionally more Scandinavian studies and fewer American studies during the Great Depression, then this bias might account for the low recovery rates found for that time period. As Table 3.3 shows, however, this is not the case. In fact the largest proportion of Scandinavian studies in the survey appears during the period 1941–55, when the overall outcome was best; and the largest proportion of American studies comes during the Great Depression, when outcome was worse. These variations, theoretically, would tend to minimize the changes in outcome that were found, not inflate them.

If the studies for the three geographic areas, Great Britain, the United States and Scandinavia, are plotted separately, as in Figure 3.2, we find that recovery rates are, in fact, worse in Scandinavia and better in Britain. If there were a large proportion of British studies during the period 1941–55, this might account for the good outcome noted at that time. Again, this is not the case. The largest proportion of British studies happens to be in the most recent time period – a variation which should have biased the results in favor of antipsychotic drug treatment. It is true that there were no Scandinavian studies included for the years before 1921, and this fact may have boosted the outcome results for those early decades, but this bias should, in theory, have been offset by the small proportion of British studies during the same period.

The most important conclusion to draw from Figure 3.2, however, is

Table 3.3 Recovery rates in the U.S.A., Scandinavia and Britain in 85 outcome studies of schizophrenia. The proportion of total subjects from all countries in each time period upon which the regional recovery rate is based is also shown

	1901–20		1921–40		1941–55		1956–85	
	Recovery rate %	Proportion of total group %	Recovery rate %	Proportion of total group %	Recovery rate %	Proportion of total group %	Recovery rate %	Proportion of total group %
U.S.A.								
Complete recovery	17	73	11	70	25	22	16	20
Social recovery	35	27	29	57	37	14	41	25
Scandinavia								
Complete recovery	–	0	12	12	20	45	18	26
Social recovery	–	0	22	13	41	47	42	25
Britain								
Complete recovery	16	5	19	11	33	12	29	26
Social recovery	–	0	30	10	53	14	46	33

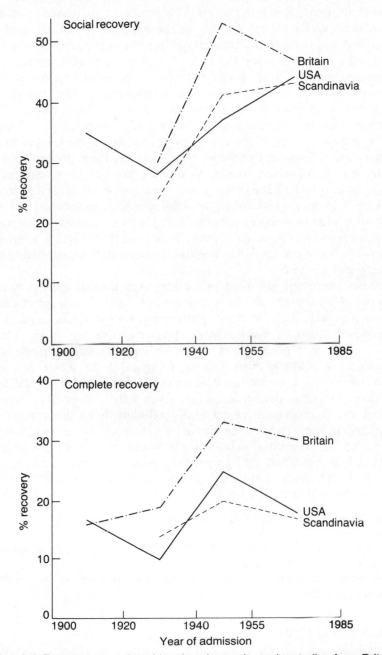

Figure 3.2 Recovery rates in schizophrenia as shown by studies from Britain, the U.S.A. and Scandinavia

that, with some minor exceptions, the same overall pattern of poor outcome in the depression and higher recovery rates during the boom is shown in all three parts of the world. The pattern is not demonstrated for Britain and Scandinavia before 1921, as there is only one British study for that period and none from Scandinavia, but the subsequent relationship to economic fluctuations and the lack of improvement with the arrival of the antipsychotics is clear. Social recovery rates do not appear to have improved as much in the United States immediately after the Second World War as they did in the European countries. This could well be a reflection of the fact that the postwar social psychiatry revolution occurred several years earlier in northern Europe than it did in the United States.

Diagnostic differences from country to country, then, probably do not account for the observed results. Could the findings be an artefact of changes in diagnostic habits over time? One important historical change was Eugen Bleuler's conception of schizophrenia, introduced in 1911, which attempted to escape Kraepelin's emphasis on inevitable deterioration as a central feature of the illness. Bias from this source is averted in the survey of outcome studies by beginning the formal analysis with Eugen Bleuler's own patients.

Another important historical factor has been the changing American diagnosis of schizophrenia. The broadening of the U.S. concept of schizophrenia may have become most evident after 1950 – this is when the incidence of manic-depressive illness appeared to decline in the United States.[12] American psychiatrists began to separate schizophrenia from manic-depressive illness more rigorously again in the mid-1970s, after lithium carbonate was introduced as an effective treatment for the latter condition. American diagnosis became even narrower in 1980, when it adopted the Scandinavian practice of excluding from the category of schizophrenia brief, "schizophreniform" psychoses.[13] These developments suggest that American studies between 1950 and the late 1970s might tend to report better outcome and give a false picture of fluctuating recovery rates. Although this is a reasonable concern it does not appear to be a critical factor in shaping the results of this survey in view of the following:

- U.S. results fluctuate according to the same pattern as European results after 1920.
- British outcome figures are better than U.S. results despite a narrower British diagnostic approach.
- U.S. studies account for a relatively small proportion of the results in this survey after 1950.

PATIENT SELECTION

If more chronic, poor-prognosis patients were included in the cohorts studied in the Great Depression, this bias could account for the worse

outcome noted at that time. This potential problem does not appear to
have occurred. More studies of patients with good prognostic features
were, in fact, included in the series from 1921 to 1940 than were included
in the periods immediately before or after. Good-prognosis patients were
considered to be those designated as "first admission," "early," "acute" or
"selected" (see Table 3.4). An even larger proportion of patients in the
studies after 1956 had good prognostic features; this could conceivably
have led to an over-optimistic estimate of recovery rates since antipsychotic drugs were introduced. Any kind of bias due to patient selection
seems to be less important when we compare the actual recovery rates for
"good-prognosis" patients with the total group. The differences, as shown
in Figure 3.3, are not particularly great. The interesting possibility emerges,
however, that the patients with a potentially favourable outlook achieve
better recovery rates only when the economy is thriving.

Although we have to use caution in interpreting the findings of this

Figure 3.3 Recovery rates for good-prognosis patients designated as "first
admission", "early," "acute" or "selected" among 85 outcome studies of
schizophrenia (solid line). Recovery rates for the total group of patients are added
(dotted line) for comparison

Table 3.4 Recovery rates for good-prognosis patients designated as "first admission," "early," "acute" or "selected" among 85 outcome studies of schizophrenia. The proportion of total subjects with these good-prognosis designations is also shown

	1901–20		1921–40		1941–55		1956–Present	
	Recovery rate %	Proportion of total group %	Recovery rate %	Proportion of total group %	Recovery rate %	Proportion of total group %	Recovery rate %	Proportion of total group %
Complete recovery	–	0	12	51	26	39	24	68
Social recovery	54	33	28	51	49	31	44	58

survey of outcome in schizophrenia, particularly for the early years of the century, the results are by no means invalidated by the limitations of the research material. In fact, most of the possible bias that was detected would tend to downplay the somewhat provocative findings rather than dramatize them.

SUMMARY

An analysis of eighty-five follow-up studies of outcome in schizophrenia conducted in Europe and North America since the turn of the century reveals:

- Recovery rates for patients admitted since the introduction of the antipsychotic drugs are no better than for those admitted after the Second World War or during the first two decades of the century.
- Recovery rates were significantly lower during the Great Depression of the 1920s and 1930s.
- The Great Depression excepted, complete recovery occurs in roughly 20–25 per cent of schizophrenics and social recovery in 40–45 per cent.
- The proportion of schizophrenic patients in hospital at follow-up has declined dramatically through the century, most of the decrease having taken place before the advent of the antipsychotic drugs.
- These findings do not appear to be artefacts of variation in diagnosis or selection of patients.

Chapter 4

Deinstitutionalization

What accounts for the finding arrived at in the previous chapter, that the proportion of schizophrenic patients found to be in hospital at follow-up declined dramatically *before* the advent of the antipsychotic drugs? A widely held belief about modern mental health care is that these drugs, introduced in the mid-1950s, brought a new dawn to psychiatry, making possible effective treatment and community care for psychotic patients. Chlorpromazine, the first of the antipsychotic drugs, initiated a "therapeutic revolution" in the hospital and community treatment of schizophrenia, argues psychiatrist John Davis in the *Comprehensive Textbook of Psychiatry*. He continues:

> Those changes have resulted in a massive reduction in the number of hospitalized schizophrenic patients, a finding all the more remarkable since, up to the introduction of the new drugs, there had been a steady increase in the number of hospitalized mental patients. The shift in the fate of mental patients is the most convincing proof of the efficacy of those agents.[1]

Dr. Davis illustrates the point with a graph showing the rise and fall in the number of residents of U.S. state and county mental hospitals during this century. His graph is essentially similar to the broken line in Figure 4.1, with the addition of the letters CPZ and an arrow pointing to the peak of the graph in the mid-1950s indicating the time chlorpromazine began to be widely used. The observation that the antipsychotic drugs made deinstitutionalization possible has become a truism of modern psychiatric practice. But how accurate is it?

A moment's reflection discloses that the figures relevant to this issue are not the *absolute* numbers of mental hospital residents, but the numbers *as a proportion of the general population*. A graph of the rate of mental hospitalization – the continuous line in Figure 4.1 – reveals a different picture. Whereas the absolute number of mental hospital residents peaked in 1955, the rate of hospital use peaked in 1945 and never climbed as high again. Although there has been a marked decline in the population of

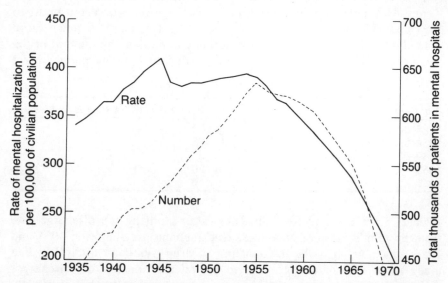

Figure 4.1 Resident patients in U.S. federal, state, county and private hospitals
Source: U.S. Bureau of the Census, *Historical Statistics of the United States: Colonial Times to 1970*, Part I, Washington, D.C., 1975, p. 84.

mental hospitals since the introduction of the antipsychotic drugs, it is clear that something else was happening in the first postwar decade to alter patterns of psychiatric hospital use.

THE IMPACT OF THE ANTIPSYCHOTICS

Several psychiatrists, especially those practicing in northern Europe before and after the Second World War, have remarked that the arrival of the antipsychotic drugs in 1954 had little impact on the discharge rates of many mental hospitals. Örnulv Ödegard studied the figures for patients first admitted to all Norwegian psychiatric hospitals before and after the introduction of the antipsychotics.[2] He found a small increase in discharge rates for patients admitted during 1955–59 compared with those admitted during 1948–52, prior to the use of drugs. But he found a much bigger increase in the discharge rate when he compared the 1948–52 group with patients admitted in the late 1930s. The figures for functionally psychotic patients were:

Admission date	% discharged and not readmitted
1936–40	52
1948–52	63
1955–59	67

In Britain, Alan Norton observed the same pattern at Bexley Hospital in Kent.[3] Although some improvement in discharge rates occurred between 1953 and 1957 with the introduction of drug treatment, a much more dramatic trend of improvement was already under way by the end of the Second World War, as these figures for female schizophrenic people show:

Admission date	% in hospital 2 years after admission
1928–30	59
1934–36	63
1949–50	37
1953	20
1957	10

Michael Shepherd and his colleagues, after studying the discharge rate from St John's Hospital in Stone, Buckinghamshire, between 1954 and 1957, concluded that the introduction of drug treatment after 1954 had made no significant change.[4] Their net release-rate figures (discharges expressed as a proportion of the average number of patients in residence) for schizophrenia were as follows:

Year	Net release rate (%)
1954	18.4
1955	19.5
1956	15.4
1957	18.8

At Mapperley Hospital in Nottingham, the patient population began to decline as early as 1948, from 1,310 patients in that year to 1,060 in 1956, and continued to drop at a similar pace after drugs were brought into use.[5]

Similar examples for the United States are harder to find. The number of patients resident in Massachusetts mental hospitals was already declining in 1954, before chlorpromazine was in use;[6] and at Vermont State Hospital the discharge rate for schizophrenia increased steadily after 1948.[7] Looking only at first-admission, white, male schizophrenic people entering California state hospitals, psychiatrist Leon Epstein found that the discharge rate for such patients was already increasing between 1951 and 1954 (the year when drug treatment was introduced). Furthermore, schizophrenic patients first admitted in 1956 and 1957 who were treated with the new drugs showed a *lower* discharge rate than those who were treated without drugs. The discharge rate for this group of patients as a whole (drug-treated and drug-free) nevertheless continued to increase.[8] Erwin Linn demonstrated that the same phenomenon occurred at St.

Elizabeth's Hospital in Washington, D.C. Although the discharge rate for functional psychotics increased at this hospital between 1953 and 1956, the release rate for those treated with drugs was again lower than for those treated without drugs.[9] (Such a result, however, would theoretically occur if only the patients with the worst prognosis were given drug treatment.) Overall it seems probable that some other influence besides a purely pharmacological effect was operating to stimulate American deinstitutionalization.

Much more influential than these studies, however, were the figures for New York state mental hospitals presented by Henry Brill and Robert Patton. They noted that the residential population of the state hospitals was increasing by around 2,000 patients each year until 1955. In that year 30,000 cases received the new type of drug treatment, and in the following year the upward trend was converted into an annual *decrease* in the residential population of the following approximate magnitude:

1956	500
1957	500
1958	1,200
1959	2,000

The authors concluded that "the abrupt population fall was in material degree due to introduction of the new drugs" because "no other explanation for the statistical changes could be found."[10] They were, however, unable to demonstrate a direct cause-and-effect relation between drug treatment and patient discharge although, as sociologist Andrew Scull points out,[11] and as Davis's view at the beginning of this chapter illustrates, their work is often interpreted as having done so. The New York experience was so close to the pattern for the country as a whole that the use of antipsychotic drugs is now inextricably linked in the minds of most American psychiatrists and mental health professionals with the development of community care for psychotic patients and the radical changes associated with the advent of the deinstitutionalization era. The data from northern Europe, however, make it plain that increased discharge rates, shorter hospital stays and community treatment for people with psychosis were becoming the rule in many areas well before the antipsychotic drugs arrived on the scene.

If not to the new drugs, to what, then, may we attribute these postwar changes in the management of mental patients?

THE SOCIAL PSYCHIATRY REVOLUTION

A revolution in the treatment of people with psychosis was taking place in many parts of northern Europe before drugs were available – a revolution which went largely unnoticed in the United States until it was well under way. Mainstream opinion in American psychiatry to this day, in fact, has overlooked the significance of the European social psychiatry revolution and continues to emphasize the central importance of drug treatment. As expressed by John Davis, the advent of chlorpromazine

> created an atmosphere that emphasized positive treatment and led to the vigorous application of other therapies, such as milieu therapy, psycho-therapy, group therapy and occupational therapy. The greater use of those social therapies was made possible by the effective treatment, through medication, of the disruptive and destructive aspects of the patient's illness.[12]

From the American perspective this association of events appeared to be true, but the evidence from northern Europe demonstrates that social therapies, far from being "made possible" by drug treatment, preceded and rivaled the antipsychotic drugs in their impact on the rehabilitation of psychotic patients.

British psychiatrists at Netherne Hospital, near London, noted a "greatly improved general pattern of care of the severely ill in hospital" during the period from 1945 to 1948 compared with conditions for those admitted a decade earlier. They saw

> the changes for the better being evident from the larger number of open wards, the increased freedom patients are able to enjoy, the abolition of restraint and strong clothing, and the diminution of seclusion, aggression and incontinence.[13]

The psychiatrists associated these improvements with the introduction of physical therapies (insulin coma and electro-convulsive therapy) and with changes in hospital policy and community attitudes.

In 1949 Dr. George Bell unlocked the doors of all the wards of Dingleton Hospital in Melrose, Scotland. In earlier decades physician superintendents of other hospitals had made similar attempts – Rutherford at Lenzie Asylum in 1881, for example, and Saxtby Good at Littlemore Hospital, Oxford, in 1935 – but public pressure had always forced the doors closed again. Bell's success, however, heralded an Open Door Movement in psychiatry which swept the Western world in the years that followed. Mapperley Hospital opened its doors in 1953 and Warlingham Park, South London, soon after. Day hospitals for psychotic patients were used extensively in Great Britain in the 1940s and 1950s, and in Amsterdam, Holland, a comprehensive program was developed for the treatment of the mentally ill in their own homes. Not until 1958, when drug treatment was well established, did St. Lawrence Hospital, New York, become fully open door.[14]

Within the European hospitals, other changes were taking place. Beginning in 1946, British psychiatrists developed new patterns of institutional living. Termed "therapeutic communities" by Dr. Tom Main, groups of therapists and patients worked together to create a hospital environment where traditional models of institutional authority were broken down, patients participated in the government of their hospital community, staff and patient roles were blurred and open communication was highly valued. Initially, this type of treatment setting was not available for psychotic people. Tom Main worked with demoralized ex-soldiers at Northfield Hospital, Birmingham, and Maxwell Jones, foremost in developing the therapeutic community concept, worked with unemployed drifters and, later, patients with character disorders at the Henderson Hospital in South London.[15] In due course the therapeutic community idea was introduced into wards for psychotic patients. At the Littlemore Hospital, Oxford, throughout the 1960s there were therapeutic communities in three different treatment units – for the elderly, for brain-damaged patients and for general adult psychiatric patients. The programs, radical in concept, were established by Dr. Ben Pomryn, who had worked with Maxwell Jones at the Henderson Hospital. On the general adult unit – the Phoenix Unit – staff and some 60 acute and chronic psychiatric patients (i.e. 70 or more people) participated in daily community meetings which established ward policy, evaluated new admissions, held interviews with patients' families, prescribed treatment (including drug treatment and electro-convulsive therapy) and authorized discharges. Maxwell Jones introduced similar changes to Dingleton Hospital and turned it into an innovative model drawing staff and visitors from many parts of the world.

The new hospital activity and therapeutic optimism were geared to early discharge, rehabilitation and treatment in the community. Chronically institutionalized patients developed social competence and were placed in supervised hostels, returned to their families or were set up in houses of their own, living together in family-like groups. Psychiatrists and nurses left the wards to see patients in their homes and in outpatient clinics and to consult with family physicians and community mental health workers. Sheltered workshops prospered, especially in Holland and, after 1960, in Britain, and produced goods competitive in the industrial market-place. Industrial therapy in the United States, meanwhile, lagged a long way behind.[16]

Such radical changes, in several areas pre-dating the introduction of chlorpromazine, explain why drug treatment appeared to have little effect in many hospitals. Professor Ödegard demonstrated that of the seventeen mental hospitals in Norway, those which had previously had a poor discharge record showed the most benefit from the introduction of the antipsychotic drugs; those which already had a higher discharge rate, and were presumably more advanced in social therapeutic techniques, showed no increase in the number of patients discharged and maintained in the community after drugs became available (see Table 4.1). Dr. Ödegard

Table 4.1 Number of patients discharged and not readmitted per 100 admissions for all Norwegian mental hospitals

Hospital	1949–53	1955–9	% change
1	75.7	71.6	−5.4
2	67.1	65.5	−2.4
3	66.5	62.3	−6.3
4	60.2	57.6	−4.3
5	58.4	44.9	−23.1
6	57.0	49.8	−12.6
7	56.6	59.6	+5.3
8	54.4	49.0	−9.9
9	53.8	63.9	+18.8
10	53.6	53.6	0
11	52.0	51.2	−1.5
12	51.1	51.4	+0.6
13	49.1	65.4	+33.2
14	48.7	50.4	+3.5
15	46.7	46.5	−0.4
16	44.4	51.4	+15.8
17	34.2	41.4	+21.0

Source: Ödegard, Ö., "Pattern of discharge from Norwegian psychiatric hospitals before and after the introduction of the psychotropic drugs," American Journal of Psychiatry, 120: 772–8, 1964.

concludes that for hospitals where social *milieu* therapy was not well developed "the drugs were a real blessing," but that

> in the more privileged institutions the drugs simply meant that one form of therapy was replaced by another and equally efficient one.[17]

Similarly, Dr. N. H. Rathod, a psychiatrist at Cane Hill Hospital in Surrey, demonstrated that the effects of the new "tranquillisers" were very limited on wards where particular attention was paid to the creation of a therapeutic environment.[18]

Antipsychotic drugs, then, appear to be more effective for the psychotic patient who is living in an inadequate setting and to be less valuable where the environment is designed for his or her well-being. This is an important point and one which we will return to later in the book. It is a point which is not readily apparent to mental health professionals who were not practicing before the antipsychotic drugs were in use; and because of the peculiarities of deinstitutionalization in the United States, it is a point scarcely recognized in American psychiatry. In practice, drug treatment is all too often used as a cheap substitute for adequate psycho-social care. As concern grows over the harmful side effects of the antipsychotic drugs and over the social plight of large numbers of poverty-stricken psychotic people in the community, this becomes an issue of some consequence.

DEINSTITUTIONALIZATION IN THE UNITED STATES

The antipsychotic drugs had a more revolutionary impact in the United States, where there were relatively more backward asylums in 1955, than in those parts of northern Europe where social therapy prevailed. The subsequent course of deinstitutionalization in America also differed from that in northern Europe. Despite the development in the United States of a network of community mental health centers after 1965, the welfare of the chronically and severely mentally ill has largely been overlooked. A substantial proportion of those discharged from U.S. mental hospitals were merely transferred to another category of institution – nursing homes.

For many patients the switch was to their disadvantage. Nursing-home staff are generally low paid and have no training in mental health, wards are often locked and overcrowded, the environment is frequently shabby, there are generally no attractive grounds for recreation, and psycho-social treatment and activity programs are deficient or absent. In general, the only treatment offered is drugs; and it was the advent of the antipsychotic drugs, facilitating control of the florid features of patients' psychosis even when the patients are in grossly inadequate settings, which allowed huge numbers of the mentally ill to be shunted to cheaper nursing-home care. Thus, although the number of patients in U.S. state and county mental hospitals declined from 504,604 in 1963 to 369,929 in 1969, the number of patients with mental disorders in nursing homes increased to such an extent that the total institutionalized population of the mentally ill was actually *higher* in 1969. Mentally ill residents of mental hospitals and nursing homes combined rose from 726,325 in 1963 to 796,712 in 1969. Many patients were elderly but large numbers of younger adults were also transferred to nursing homes. The number of patients under the age of 65 in state and county mental hospitals fell by nearly 100,000 between 1963 and 1969 but the number of mentally ill patients in this age group in nursing home accommodation increased by more than 25,000 during the same period.[19] Ellen Bassuk and Samuel Gerson point out, however:

> Untherapeutic though many nursing homes are, living conditions in most of them are at least tolerable. Conditions may be worse for discharged patients living on their own, without enough money and usually without any possibility of employment. Many of them drift to substandard inner-city housing that is overcrowded, unsafe, dirty and isolated. Often they come together to form a new kind of ghetto sub-population, a captive market for unscrupulous landlords.[20]

Newspaper reports have exposed the impoverished condition of formerly hospitalized patients leading lives of isolation and fear in the community: 100 discharged patients in Washington, D.C. without therapeutic rehabilitation programs; 200 ex-patients of Agnews State Hospital in California housed in boarding homes in San Jose with no medical care; 300–1,000 patients in rooming houses and hotels in Long Beach, New York, without supervision. A survey of discharged mental patients conducted in 1970 in California's San Mateo County found 32 per cent living in board and care homes.[21] These "small wards in the community" are generally sordid and bare establishments in poor, inner-city areas where theft is rampant. A third of the chronic mental patients in a large sample of residents of board and care homes in Los Angeles had been robbed or assaulted or both during the previous year.[22] Each such establishment houses more than fifty ex-hospital patients, and may accommodate several hundred.[23] The patients often receive no psychiatric treatment other than a supply of drugs and have no employment or worthwhile social activity. A typical boarding home resident, report California psychiatrists Theodore Van Putten and James Spar,

> spends 8.46 hours of the day in bed, a time limited primarily by the sponsor's continual efforts to keep him out of his bedroom, and 1.46 hours at the dining table. He spends the rest of the day in virtual solitude, either staring vacantly at television (few residents reported having a favorite television show; most were puzzled at the question), or wandering aimlessly around the neighborhood, sometimes stopping for a nap on a lawn or park bench.[24]

Patients who suffer a psychotic relapse are likely to be treated briefly in hospital with drugs and may well be discharged again to an inadequate setting or to live on the street. As this cycle repeats itself they become known as "revolving-door patients." About half of the patients released from U.S. psychiatric hospitals in the early 1970s were readmitted within a year of discharge.[25] As public mental hospital beds are cut back, it becomes increasingly difficult for acutely psychotic patients to gain re-admission. For example, in 1981 the state hospital in Denver, Colorado – Fort Logan Mental Health Center – had a waiting list for admission of more than one hundred adult cases. Since the hospital's discharge rate was around one adult every week or two, patients at the bottom of the waiting list could expect admission within two to four years.

In consequence of the nationwide bed shortage and rapid-discharge policy many psychotic people end up in jail, usually charged with offenses associated with trying to survive on the streets without money: trespass (sleeping in the hallway of a public building) or defrauding an innkeeper (eat and run). Around 6–8 per cent of the 147,000 inmates of local jails in the United States are psychotic.[26] Similarly, 8 per cent of a large sample of federal prisoners surveyed in 1969 were diagnosed as psychotic.[27]

Such is the plight of a substantial proportion of the "deinstitutionalized" mentally ill across the United States. It is scarcely surprising that, as revealed in the last chapter, the overall social functioning of schizophrenic people has not improved with the introduction of antipsychotic drugs. But in northern Europe, also, the picture has changed from the early days of the social psychiatry revolution.

PSYCHIATRIC STAGNATION

In Britain, the number of mental patients admitted to hospital who had "no fixed abode" increased threefold between 1959 and 1964. By 1966, 10 per cent of the 30,000 men and women "sleeping rough" in Britain were thought to be suffering from mental illness.[28] More than 20 per cent of the longer-term residents of the Camberwell Reception Centre for the destitute (a converted Victorian workhouse in South London) were considered mentally ill in the early 1970s.[29] At this time, too, concern developed over the increasing numbers of mentally ill criminal offenders who were committed to hospital or incarcerated in prison or borstal, though the proportion of inmates of prison (as opposed to prison hospitals) suffering from schizophrenia is lower in Britain than in the United States.[30]

The Social Services Act of 1970 transferred the responsibility for many aspects of community care for the mentally ill away from local health authorities and placed it in the Social Services Departments. Many professionals feel this has not been a successful move. In 1976 only 43 per cent of the recommended minimum number of places in hostels and group homes had been established and day facilities were equally scarce. Some local authorities had provided none at all.[31] A survey of the social situation of 190 schizophrenic people living in the community in Salford in the late 1970s revealed 30 per cent accommodated in slum housing, 16 per cent with inadequate nutrition and 34 per cent who spent all or most of their time doing absolutely nothing. Among more than 100 largely psychotic patients in the psychiatric wards and day hospital of the London Borough of Camden on a single day in 1976, a half were known to have been living alone before admission, nearly a third in transitory accommodation (such as abandoned homes, doss houses and reception centers) or sleeping on the streets; two-thirds were totally unemployed, most of them for more than a year; and more than a third of the inpatients received no visitors. Many of these patients, clearly, had no worthwhile community links, but despite their obvious social depravation only 6 per cent of Camden's inpatients were subsequently discharged to any kind of supportive setting, like a hostel or group home.[32] Such "rehabilitation" was not what the innovative British community psychiatrists of the 1950s had in mind.

Hospital conditions have also deteriorated in Britain. Government reports, covering the period from 1976 to 1982, record the widespread existence of overcrowding, understaffing and custodial attitudes to patients throughout mental hospitals in many counties. Instances of cruelty and neglect are documented.[33]

Why did the deinstitutionalization movement go sour in Britain? Why was it never particularly sweet in the United States? Or, phrasing the questions differently, why was there a golden era of active social and community psychiatry in northern Europe in the immediate postwar years but not in the United States?

OUTDOOR RELIEF

Sociologist Andrew Scull in his book *Decarceration* attributes the motivating force for the British and American deinstitutionalization movement to the postwar development of welfare programs which enabled the indigent and the disabled to be maintained more cheaply outside an institution.[34] This form of support, known to the Victorians as "outdoor relief," had been drastically reduced in the mid-nineteenth century. The twentieth-century Great Depression increased the pressure for a more comprehensive relief of poverty in the industrial nations, and both Britain and America instituted social-insurance schemes for the totally and permanently disabled in the five years following the Second World War.[35] Scull's analysis has considerable merit. Ödegard has made a similar observation concerning Norway's

> new and improved pension system for persons incapacitated by illness, which was introduced in 1960 and which includes psychotic invalids. . . . This has made possible the discharge of many psychotic invalids and is probably the main reason why the rates of discharge as "not cured" did not show any great increase until after 1960.[36]

It is also clear, as Andrew Scull has argued, that the American switch to the use of nursing homes is attributable to the health-insurance structure. The state governments are responsible for the cost of maintaining patients in state mental hospitals, but care provided in a private nursing home may be billed to Medicaid (for the indigent) or Medicare (for the elderly). Since the federal government pays a large part of these insurance bills, it rapidly became apparent to state legislators after the inception of these programs in 1965 that they could cut the state budget by transferring mental patients to private-sector care.

Reference to disability pensions and health-insurance schemes, however, does not answer all the questions about the early stages of deinstitutionalization. Looking at disability payments, one would have predicted, for example, a late onset for community care in Norway, and an earlier, roughly simultaneous timing in Britain and America. To understand why the postwar social psychiatric revolution took place in northern Europe and not America, and why it subsequently stagnated in Britain, it is necessary to study other political factors.

POLITICS AND INSTITUTIONS

Broadly speaking, one can set down four possible political motives for a deinstitutional trend:

- cost savings;
- a humanitarian concern for the welfare, liberty and human rights of the institutional inmates which outweighs the fear of their liability to the community;
- a need to put the buildings to a new purpose; and
- a need to put the inmates to a new purpose.

Which elements are applicable to the postwar psychiatric deinstitutionalization?

Cost saving, as discussed above, has clearly been an important factor behind the emptying of psychiatric institutions, but it does not explain the differences in the characteristics of the process between countries.

Humanitarian concerns, while usually part of the rhetoric associated with changes in institutional use, are probably never sufficient cause for such changes. The welfare of the mentally ill was the espoused reason for the nineteenth-century movement to institutionalize massive numbers of the insane and for the reverse trend after the Second World War. The humanitarian concerns of the advocates of deinstitutionalization during the late nineteenth and early twentieth century, however, were never sufficient to halt the expansion of hospital care. Why did their views suddenly become effective after the Second World War? Furthermore, humanitarian considerations can scarcely account for the widespread current practice of maintaining psychotic people in poverty, housed in degrading environments in the community, largely without proper care and treatment. On the contrary, it seems more probable that the philosophy of care is a secondary phenomenon, itself shaped by the contemporary patterns of institutional use.

The conversion of old institutions to new purposes historically has been very common. Seventeenth-century French leper hospitals became houses of correction,[37] a nineteenth-century British jail was converted into an insane asylum[38] and Victorian workhouses in the twentieth century became general hospitals or reception centers for the destitute. There is no indication, though, that the mentally ill were discharged from mental hospitals after the Second World War to make way for some urgent new function for the buildings. Many of the old hospital wards have been closed and left vacant. More urgent, perhaps, was the need to avoid the capital outlay required to keep the old, Victorian institutions functional.

We must look, then, to a *change in the perceived value of the institutional inmates* themselves to find the stimulus for deinstitutionalization.

LABOR DYNAMICS

So great was the labor shortage in postwar Britain that *The Times* of January 1947 called for the selective immigration of half a million foreign workers, and economist Lionel Robbins warned that 100,000 foreigners should be recruited to work in the coal mines if the country was not "to lapse into a position of impotence and economic chaos." The government launched an attack on non-productive "spivs and drones," and the *Daily Mail* argued that if Scotland Yard were used "to help to round up the work dodgers" one-and-a-half million workers could be added to the labor force. By September of that year the Cabinet was discussing the possibility of banning the football pools to force the redeployment of the women who processed the coupons into the labor-starved textile industry.[39]

A sustained, peacetime labor shortage of these dimensions had not been seen in Britain, or in those other north European nations which experienced the phenomenon, since employment records began or, quite probably, since the beginning of the Industrial Revolution. It seems reasonable to suppose that such a demand for labor, extraordinary also by recent Western standards, was a major stimulus to the effective rehabilitation of the mentally ill. Contemporary observers confirm this view. British social psychiatrist David Clark identifies as major factors which promoted the European Open Door Movement and deinstitutionalization

> the development of welfare states where the disabled (including the psychiatrically crippled) were supported in their homes, [and] the development of full employment (in northern Europe at least) creating a demand for the labour of impaired people.[40]

Similarly, Professor Ödegard reports of Norway:

> Since the war there has mostly been a certain degree of over-employment, and it has been possible for hospitals to discharge to an independent existence even patients with a borderline working capacity and a questionable social adjustment.[41]

In Massachusetts, one of the few parts of the United States where the mental hospital population began to diminish before antipsychotic drugs were introduced, the decline in hospital use was also seen to be associated with a vigorous demand for labor.[42]

The strategic importance of the rehabilitation of large numbers of the mentally ill should not be underestimated. Between the Great Depression and the 1950s the proportion of schizophrenic people in Britain who were employed may have increased by as much as 20 percentage points: an estimate suggested by the improvement in the social recovery rate of British schizophrenic people revealed in the last chapter. Since 34 people in every 10,000 of the population were schizophrenic, according to a postwar prevalence study conducted in London,[43] one can estimate that the rehabilitation of schizophrenic people alone may have added 30,000 workers to the British labor force.

A number of other reports have confirmed that rehabilitation efforts for the disabled are closely related to the demand for labor. The Heller Committee survey of permanently disabled workers in the San Francisco Bay area in 1942 and 1943 found that wartime labor conditions left virtually none of the disabled unemployed.[44] British and American studies show that the employment of the mentally retarded increased from around 40 per cent in the Great Depression to 80 or 90 per cent during and after the Second World War.[45] Vocational rehabilitation activities were also very highly developed in the full-employment conditions of the Eastern Bloc countries before the dissolution of communism.[46]

Labor dynamics, then, may explain many features of the deinstitutionalization movement. Before the introduction of the antipsychotic drugs, the postwar full employment in northern Europe required the rehabilitation of the marginally employable mentally ill, stimulating the development of more therapeutic styles of hospital care and a policy of early discharge. The move to milieu therapy and community treatment was delayed in the United States, where full employment did not generally develop. The introduction of disability pension schemes made possible the discharge of patients in the absence of employment opportunities, and the advent of the antipsychotic drugs allowed the control of symptoms in patients placed in inadequate and stressful settings. These changes, particularly in the United States, led to a different style of community management – the transfer of patients to low-cost placements, often without genuine attempts at making patients productive, valued and integrated members of society. The steep rise in unemployment in Britain from the late 1960s may go a long way to explain the subsequent stagnation in British psychiatric rehabilitation.

INTERNATIONAL COMPARISONS

The countries that led in the postwar revolution in social psychiatry were, according to Maxwell Jones,[47] Britain, the Netherlands, Norway and Switzerland. Table 4.2 lists postwar unemployment statistics for these countries and other parts of Europe and North America; the unemployment figures have been adjusted[48] to make them reasonably comparable. The four countries that were progressive in psychiatry at that time are among those with low unemployment rates.

Countries like the United States and Italy, where the rehabilitative movement was delayed, had higher rates of unemployment. Open-door policies and the deinstitutionalization movement did not reach Italian mental hospitals until the 1960s, arriving in the wake of an economic boom

Table 4.2 Unemployment rates in northern Europe and North America

	High unemployment						Low unemployment					
	Belgium	Denmark	Germany	Italy	Canada	U.S.A.	France	Netherlands	Norway	Sweden	Switzerland	U.K.
1950	6.3	4.1	7.2	8.7	3.6	5.2	1.4	2.0	2.7	1.7	0.5	2.5
1951	5.7	4.5	6.4	9.2	2.4	3.2	1.3	2.4	3.6	1.6	0.2	2.2
1952	6.8	5.9	6.1	9.8	2.9	2.9	1.3	3.5	2.4	1.7	0.3	2.9
1953	6.8	4.4	5.5	10.2	2.9	2.8	1.6	2.5	3.3	1.9	0.3	2.6
1954	6.2	3.8	5.2	8.7	4.5	5.3	1.6	1.8	2.2	1.8	0.2	2.3
1955	4.7	4.7	3.8	7.5	4.3	4.2	1.5	1.3	2.5	1.8	0.1	2.1

Sources: All unemployment statistics, except those for Norway, have been adjusted to render them comparable, and are taken from Maddison, A., Economic Growth in the West, New York: Twentieth Century Fund, 1964, p. 220. Unadjusted figures for Norway are taken from Mitchell, B. R., European Historical Statistics 1750–1970, abridged edn., New York: Columbia University Press, 1978, p. 68.

which brought many changes in the social and political climate.[49] Italian psychiatrist Franco Basaglia introduced sweeping innovations, after 1961, in the mental hospitals in Gorizia and then Trieste, as unemployment dropped to a postwar low. The subsequent national psychiatric reforms embodied in law 180 (enacted with the support of both the Italian communist party and the right wing) led to a dramatic decrease in the numbers of mentally ill people in hospital. The reforms were implemented with most success in the industrial north of the country where the labor shortage was most apparent.[50]

The number of mental hospital beds in use varies substantially from one industrial nation to another. Sweden, in 1974, provided one psychiatric hospital bed for 250 citizens, for example, whereas in Poland one psychiatric bed served more than 800. A number of economic and political factors might be expected to influence mental hospital use and, if the demand for labor was an important stimulus to deinstitutionalization, then unemployment could prove to be one such influence on psychiatric hospital use. In the mid-1960s, in fact, industrial nations with higher unemployment rates tended to use more mental hospital beds (see Table 4.3). A multiple regression analysis shows that the average national unemployment over a five-year period accounted for 40 per cent of the variance in the provision of psychiatric beds in 1965 in the nine Western industrial nations for which comparable statistics are available (see Table 4.4).[51] This relationship was independent of a number of other economic and demographic variables. After taking into account the influence of per capita gross national product, infant mortality (as an indicator of the national level of health and welfare provisions) and the proportion of elderly in the population, unemployment accounted for 47 per cent of the variance in the use of mental hospital beds. Over the next decade, however, the relationship between mental hospital use and unemployment disappeared. As Table 4.4 shows, by 1974 a combination of two factors – the national infant mortality rate and the proportion of the population over age 65 – predicted 71 per cent of the variance in mental hospital beds provided; unemployment accounted for only 1 per cent of the variance.

The link between unemployment and mental hospital use in 1965 suggests that, until that time, the availability of work may have acted as a control on hospital discharge rates. The correlation disappeared after the 1960s because psychiatric hospital populations continued to shrink in Australia, Canada and the United States in the absence of improvements in employment. Elsewhere mental hospital use increased or remained relatively constant. This divergence may be attributed to the degree to which each country exercised the option, offered by disability benefits and drugs, to maintain mentally ill people in the community regardless of the availability of employment. In addition, in the United States the advent of Medicaid in 1965 led to massive reductions in mental hospital beds as

Table 4.3 Psychiatric hospital beds per 10,000 of the general population, average annual unemployment rates over five-year periods, infant mortality per 1,000 live births, general population over age 65 and per capita gross national product in 1979 U.S. dollars

	1965					1974				
	Psychiatric hospital beds	Average annual unemployment (%) 1961–5[b]	Infant mortality	Elderly population %	Per capita GNP	Psychiatric hospital beds	Average annual unemployment (%) 1970–4[b]	Infant mortality	Elderly population %	Per capita GNP
Western industrial nations										
Japan	13.3	1.3	18.5	6.4	3,633	18.4	1.3	10.8	8.0	7,425
West Germany	17.7	0.5	23.9	12.0	7,908	17.8	1.0	21.1	14.0	10,681
France	20.5	1.5	21.9	12.2	6,304	—	2.8	14.7	13.0	9,508
Italy	22.4	2.9	35.6	9.9	3,568	20.9	3.2	22.6	12.0	5,243
Australia	27.1	2.1	18.5	8.4	5,801	20.7	2.2	16.1	9.0	7,874
U.K.	28.5[a]	2.6	19.0[a]	12.3	5,348	31.9[a]	3.3	16.3[a]	14.0	6,529
U.S.A.	31.1	5.7	24.7	9.5	7,873	14.2	5.4	16.7	11.0	9,577
Sweden	35.4	1.5	13.3	12.8	9,374	40.5	2.3	9.2	15.0	11,835
Canada	35.9	5.4	23.6	7.6	6,070	21.8	5.8	15.0	8.0	8,497
Centrally planned economies										
Hungary	2.4	—	38.8	10.2	2,335	—	—	34.3	13.0	3,039
Romania	3.1	—	44.1	7.6	1,824	7.0	—	35.0	9.0	2,804
Bulgaria	4.2	—	30.8	8.5	1,866	—	—	25.5	11.0	2,645
U.S.S.R.	9.9	—	27.6	7.3	3,354	—	—	27.7	9.0	4,913
Czechoslovakia	11.7	—	25.5	9.9	3,567	11.3	—	20.4	12.0	4,692
East Germany	18.2	—	24.8	14.6	3,412	18.9	—	15.9	16.0	4,558
Poland	—	—	41.7	7.0	2,042	12.1	—	23.7	10.0	3,069

Sources: Psychiatric hospital beds (except U.S.S.R.) and infant mortality: World Health Organization, *World Health Statistics Annuals, 1964 to 1977*, vols. I, III, Geneva: 1967–77; U.S.S.R. psychiatric hospital beds (1962 figure): Field, M. G. and Aronson, J., "Soviet community mental health services and work therapy," *Community Mental Health Journal*, 1: 81–90, 1965; Unemployment: Sorrentino, C., "Unemployment in international perspective," in B. Showler and A. Sinfield (eds.), *The Workless State*, Oxford: Martin Robertson, 1980; Elderly population: World Bank, *World Tables, 2nd edn.*, Baltimore: Johns Hopkins University Press, 1980; Per capita GNP: CIA National Foreign Assessment Center, *Handbook of Economic Statistics 1980*, Washington, D.C.: U.S. Government Printing Office, 1980.
Notes: [a] Figure for England and Wales.
[b] Unemployment statistics are adjusted to U.S. concepts to render them comparable.

Table 4.4 Variance in psychiatric hospital beds provided in nine Western industrial
countries accounted for by different social indicators

		% of variance accounted for	cumulative % of variance
1965	(N=9)		
	Unemployment	40	40
	GNP	25	64*
	Infant mortality	5	70
	Elderly in population	6	75
1965	Entering unemployment as the last step (N=9)		
	GNP	26	26
	Infant mortality	0	26
	Elderly in population	3	28
	Unemployment	47*	75
1968	(N=9)		
	GNP	39	39
	Unemployment	24	63*
	Infant mortality	9	72
	Elderly in population	3	75
1971	(N=9)		
	GNP	37	37
	Unemployment	10	47
	Infant mortality	10	57
	Elderly in population	8	65
1974	(N=8)		
	Elderly in population	34	34
	Infant mortality	36	71*
	GNP	8	79
	Unemployment	1	80

* Significant at the .05 level (two-tailed test).
Note: Variance statistics were obtained by a stepwise multiple-regression method.

patients were transferred to nursing homes. No longer is it essential that
mental hospitals control and sustain a large segment of the surplus
population. Their use has become, to a greater degree, a matter of social
policy. The extent of psychiatric institutional care now appears to be
largely a reflection of two factors. One is the national, political commitment to the quality and universality of health and welfare provisions (of
which infant mortality is an indicator). The other, since the antipsychotic
drugs are of little benefit in the care of senile organic psychosis, is the
proportion of the elderly in the general population.

Deinstitutionalization, in some circumstances a sign of progressive
efforts towards community care and rehabilitation of the mentally ill, may
elsewhere indicate the opposite – abrogation of responsibility for the
welfare of a segment of the poor. In the United States, where health and

welfare provisions for the destitute are not well developed, the small numbers of available mental hospital beds represent a refusal to provide adequate psychiatric treatment for the indigent mentally ill. In Sweden, on the other hand, a political commitment to adequate health and welfare provisions coupled with the existence of a large elderly population leads to a substantially greater use of mental hospitals. Each of the other Scandinavian countries, like Sweden, maintains comprehensive health and welfare services, low infant mortality rates and substantial numbers of psychiatric hospital beds. Of these four countries Denmark and Norway, with the greatest labor shortages until the mid-1970s, preserved relatively low rates of mental hospital use and the most highly developed community treatment programs.[52]

It is evident from the figures in Table 4.3 that it was not only the labor shortage in the Eastern Bloc countries in the 1970s which led to their minimal use of psychiatric institutions but also the underdevelopment of their health services in general (witness their high infant mortality rates) and the low proportion of the elderly in the general population. Nevertheless, we know that the labor shortage in these countries, particularly the U.S.S.R. and Poland, at that time led to a very great emphasis on work therapy, intensive community rehabilitation efforts, greater acceptance of the mentally ill in the community and the workplace and efforts to keep the elderly productive.[53]

Full employment, then, may no longer be a major factor determining the size of mental hospital populations but it could be an important influence on the characteristics of community treatment and the adequacy of rehabilitative efforts. Where the surplus population is large, the conditions established for the person with a psychotic illness tend to be least conducive to his or her recovery. Where the labor of the marginally productive is in demand, there shall we find the most highly developed community treatment programs and the most humane hospital conditions. We shall see to what extent these factors influence the course of schizophrenia.

SUMMARY

- The rate of mental hospital occupancy as a proportion of the general United States population was declining before the introduction of the antipsychotic drugs.
- Revolutionary changes in hospital and community psychiatry in northern Europe preceded the introduction of antipsychotic drug treatment.
- The discharge rates from progressive hospitals, particularly in northern Europe, were not improved by the arrival of the antipsychotics.
- The delay in the introduction of new social and community psychiatry techniques to the United States created the impression there that drug treatment was vital to community care.

- Deinstitutionalization in the United States has relied heavily on the use of drugs and has led to the placement of large numbers of the mentally ill in low-cost, inadequate settings.
- Community care for the mentally ill in Britain stagnated after the 1960s.
- The main political and economic driving forces to deinstitutionalization were (a) cost-saving and (b) in northern Europe, the postwar demand for labor.
- Comparing Western industrial nations in 1965, the number of mental hospital beds in each country was correlated with the national unemployment rate.
- A decade later, mental hospital use appeared to be less influenced by the labor market and more affected by national health and welfare policy.

Chapter 5

Madness and the Industrial Revolution

In the last decade of the eighteenth century a humane method of treating the mentally ill sprang into being in Europe, within a few years came to be adopted in many parts of the civilized world, and after half a century or so faded away. It left in its place restrictive patterns of institutional care of which few people in psychiatry are proud but which persisted until the latter half of the twentieth century. Many psychiatrists have remarked on the common features of moral treatment (as the early movement was called) and the post-Second World War social psychiatry revolution. Were the two movements indeed similar? And, if so, could they have been stimulated by similar political and economic conditions? If not, why did moral treatment come into being when it did? The use of moral management was accompanied by claims of excellent recovery rates in mental illness. Were these claims accurate? If so, why were the methods abandoned and what light does the episode throw on the conventional approach to the history of medicine which shows us always progressing to higher levels of technical achievement through a process of scientific discovery?

THE YORK RETREAT

This house is situated a mile from York in the midst of a fertile and smiling countryside; it is not at all the idea of a prison that it suggests, but rather that of a large farm; it is surrounded by a great walled garden. No bars, no grilles on the windows.[1]

So runs the description of the York Retreat given by a Swiss visitor in 1798. The name, "Retreat," was significant: not a "hospital" nor an "asylum" but "a quiet haven in which the shattered bark might find the means of reparation or safety."[2] Within this house was developing a mode of care for the mentally ill which was to prove as revolutionary as Pinel's action in striking the chains from the inmates of Bicêtre in 1793.

Like Pinel's work, the York Retreat was a reaction against the inhumanity of the contemporary treatment of the insane. It was founded in 1792 and opened in 1796 by the Society of Friends after one of their members, Hannah Mills, died in the York Asylum under circumstances which suggested neglect or ill treatment. Designed for thirty patients and primarily made available to Quakers, the cost of treatment at the York Retreat ranged from eight to fifteen shillings a week. Accommodation for personal servants was provided at a further fee. The establishment was clearly not intended to be for the poor.

Under the direction of William Tuke, a 60-year-old tea and coffee merchant, a style of non-medical care was developed which, like Pinel's approach, came to be called moral treatment. Believing that most deranged people could be rational if not provoked by harsh treatment or cruelty, the Tukes encouraged the exercise of patients' self-control as an alternative to the use of external restraint. Punishment for inappropriate behavior was avoided, but minor privileges were awarded to those who conformed to the attendants' wishes. Chains were never used and straight waistcoats rarely, and then only to prevent a patient hurting himself or herself or other residents. The iron sashes of the windows were disguised to look like wood. Patients were expected to dress in their best clothes and take part in all usual social activities – tea parties, reading, writing, sewing and gardening. Work was felt to be essential in fostering patients' self-control and self-esteem. Drugs were seldom used, and exercise, warm baths and a generous diet of "meat, bread and good porter" were felt to be most useful in quieting patients and ensuring good sleep.[3]

BEFORE MORAL TREATMENT

The revolutionary nature of moral treatment at the York Retreat becomes evident when it is set against conventional care of the time. At the nearby York Asylum, where Hannah Mills had died, abuses were exposed by investigations conducted some years after the opening of the Retreat. "Flogging and cudgelling" were routine, and patients were "verminous and filthy."[4] Behind a partly hidden door, a Swiss visitor in 1814 discovered a series of small cells

> in a very horrid and filthy condition . . . the walls were daubed with excrement; the air-holes, of which there was one in each cell, were partly filled with it.

Upstairs he found a room

> twelve feet by seven feet ten inches, in which there were thirteen women who, [the keeper] told me, had all come out of those cells that morning . . . .I became very sick, and could not remain longer in the room. I vomited.[5]

Charles Dickens characterized asylum care of this period as follows:

Coercion for the outward man, and rabid physicking for the inward man, were the specifics for lunacy. Chains, straw, filthy solitude, darkness, and starvation; jalap, syrup of buckthorn, tartarised antimony, and ipecacuanha administered every spring and fall in fabulous doses to every patient, whether well or ill; spinning in whirligigs, corporal punishment, gagging, "continued intoxication"; nothing was too wildly extravagant, nothing too monstrously cruel to be prescribed by mad-doctors.

Lest we should consider that these practices were enforced through malice, he continues:

In other respects these physicians were grave men, of mild dispositions, and – in their ample-flapped, ample-cuffed coats, with a certain gravity and air of state in the skirts; with their large buttons and gold-headed canes, their hair-powder and ruffles – were men of benevolent aspects.[6]

Frank abuses aside (and psychiatrist William Parry-Jones argues that these may well have been overemphasized by historians[7]), Dickens' point is well taken. We should not assume that the eighteenth-century mad-doctors were morally degenerate; chains and flogging were not necessarily maliciously intended. Even George III during his bouts of insanity was chained, beaten, starved and intimidated with threats.[8] The management techniques were those of animal trainers because the insane were regarded as bestial. At the Bicêtre in Paris and the Bethlem Hospital in London, the inmates were exhibited to the public, for a fee, like zoo creatures.[9] The insane were left naked in the cold and damp because they were believed to possess inhuman resistance to the effects of the elements.[10] Both Andrew Scull and French psychologist Michel Foucault have emphasized that the introduction of moral treatment involved a redefinition of the madman's condition from the essence of bestiality to a degree of human rationality.[11] Now the lunatic becomes a fractious child. As the Swiss doctor commented in the visitors' book at the Retreat:

In moral treatment, one does not consider the insane to be completely deprived of reason, out of reach of the influence of fear, hope, affection and honour. Rather one regards them, it seems, like children who have too much energy, and who put it to dangerous uses.[12]

In this redefinition lay the revolutionary impact of moral management.

THE ORIGINS OF MORAL TREATMENT

Curiously enough, this fundamentally new approach was not only introduced simultaneously by Pinel and Tuke, but similar humane methods of patient care sprang into being independently at the same point in time in other parts of Europe. In Florence, Vicenzo Chiarugi, the physician in charge of the newly open Hospital Bonifacio, published regulations for patient care, in 1789, which eliminated the use of physical force or any type of restraint except for the occasional use of the straightjacket. He specified: "It is a supreme moral duty and medical obligation to respect the insane individual as a person."[13]

Similarly, Joseph Daquin, the physician in charge of the institution at Chambéry in the Savoy region (an independent duchy situated between France and Italy) published, in 1791, a treatise advocating humane care for the mentally ill.[14] Around the same time, Parisian physician and philosopher Georges Cabanis, who arranged Pinel's appointment to the Bicêtre, proposed improved treatment methods for the insane.[15] Physician John Ferriar at the Manchester Lunatic Hospital, although administering such standard medical remedies as blood-letting, blistering and purging,[16] expressed the opinion, in 1795 (the year before the Retreat opened), that the primary goal of treatment lay in "creating a habit of self-restraint," not through coercion, but by "the management of hope and apprehension, . . . small favours, the show of confidence, and apparent distinction."[17]

For each of these independent innovations, local causes may be found. Psychiatric historian George Mora, for example, suggests that Pinel and the French physicians, in liberating the insane, were reflecting the spirit of freedom and equality of the French Revolution (1789–99); Chiarugi's radical reforms were a product of the revolutionary political economic reforms of the rule of the Grand Duke Peter Leopold (1747–92); the philosophy of the York Retreat was based on the contemporary British bourgeois ideal of the family.[18] But these individual influences fail to explain the simultaneous but independent origin of the same notion within a five-year period in different parts of Europe.

To call the phenomenon "a striking example of *zeitgeist* in the history of psychiatry"[19] is to say nothing about causes. To see it as a reflection of the Enlightenment's eighteenth-century ideals of human dignity, worth and freedom is to provide a unifying concept but still only fits one ideology within the broader framework of another. If we examine the political and economic underpinning of Enlightenment thinking, however, we may be in a better position to understand why moral treatment occurred when and where it did. British historian Eric Hobsbawn has this to say about the philosophy of the Age of Reason:

> The Great Encyclopaedia of Diderot and d'Alembert was not merely a compendium of progressive social and political thought, but of techno-logical and scientific progress. For indeed the conviction of the progress of human knowledge, rationality, wealth, civilization, and control over nature with which the eighteenth century was deeply imbued, the "Enlightenment," drew its strength primarily from the evident progress

of production, trade, and the economic and scientific rationality believed to be associated inevitably with both.[20]

Revolutionary to the old social and political order, the Enlightenment ideas were central to the capitalist transformation of production. Leaving aside, for the moment, the American Revolution (1776–83), the culmination of eighteenth-century Enlightenment philosophy and its associated political, economic and technological changes was (what Hobsbawm refers to as) the "dual revolution."[21] This comprised the French Revolution of 1789 and the contemporaneous British Industrial Revolution (which Hobsbawm dates from the 1780s, when the British economy became "airborne"[22]).

> It is significant [writes Hobsbawm] that the two chief centres of the [Enlightenment] ideology were also those of the dual revolution, France and England . . . .A secular, rationalist and progressive individualism dominated "enlightened" thought. To set the individual free from the shackles which fettered him was its chief object . . . .Liberty, equality and (it followed) the fraternity of all men were its slogans.[23]

Enlightenment ideas, then, gave the French Revolution its slogan, the determined capitalist his individualism, and the innovators of moral treatment their philosophical base. Beyond France and England, the sites of the origin of the humane treatment methods were also centers of Enlightenment ideology and progressive politics. Savoy, culturally linked to France, instituted enlightened peasant liberation shortly before the French Revolution;[24] and Chiarugi in Florence was under the influence of one of the most remarkable reforming princes of the eighteenth century, Grand Duke Leopold of Tuscany, a man strongly influenced by Enlightenment ideas. Moral treatment, moreover, was most avidly adopted by another enlightened nation – post-revolutionary, industrializing America.

When moral treatment, then, set the insane "free from the shackles," the movement was a component of the dual revolution that shook the Western world. This is most compellingly revealed in the image of Pinel, at the height of the French Revolution, striking the chains from the insane of Bicêtre and La Salpêtrière. But the essential connection between the Industrial Revolution and the new methods of managing the insane can, similarly, be demonstrated. Central to an understanding of the process are the changes that were taking place in the deployment of labor.

THE GROWTH OF WAGE LABOR

In 1780, on the eve of the dual revolution, France and Britain were the two economic giants of Europe. In volume of trade they were nearly equal. France's foreign trade had increased fourfold in sixty years and her colonial system in some areas was stronger than that of the British.[25] Each of these countries, like the rest of Europe, was experiencing staggering population growth. In the half century after 1750 the population of France rose by 22 per cent, from 22 million to nearly 27 million; in the United Kingdom population increased 60 per cent, from 10 million to 16 million.[26] In each of the two countries the conditions of the rural poor were harsh and worsening. The great majority of French peasants were landless or had insufficient holdings, oppressed by feudal dues, tithes, taxes and inflation.[27] In Britain, the enclosure of common lands in the eighteenth century deprived cottagers of their subsistence and drove increasing numbers into agricultural wage labor which provided meager and intermittent compensation. The result was destitution for many and an increase in applications for poor relief. Taxes for relief – the poor rate – more than tripled between 1760 and 1801 in Britain, and nearly equaled the entire cost of British national government, excluding the army and navy.[28]

Holding back the onset of the Industrial Revolution, argues British historian T. S. Ashton, were social resistance to change and the lack of skill and adaptability of the workers.[29] But as the population grew, the mass of the landless poor swelled and the ranks of beggars, vagrants and unemployed increased, the diversion of laboring men, women and children into industrial wage work became possible.

> It was not the least of the achievements of the industrial revolution [writes Ashton] that it drew into the economic system part of that legion of the lost, and that it turned many of the irregulars into efficient, if overregimented, members of an industrial army.[30]

In France, by way of contrast, the Revolution so far improved the condition of the peasants that the flow of "landless free labourers merely trickled into the cities" and the "capitalist transformation . . . was slowed to a crawl."[31]

Some of the "irregulars" in Britain were less readily "regimented" than others – the insane among them. What was to be done with those who would not, or could not, work? In striving to hold down the cost of poor relief the policy makers of the early Industrial Revolution became obsessed with the need to force "the very great number of lazy People to maintain themselves by their own Industry." Obligating applicants for relief "to submit to the Confinement and Labour of the Workhouse"[32] was one such measure. The number of psychotic and mentally deficient people confined in poorhouses in England and Wales, however, became considerable – 4,000–5,000 by 1789, estimates Kathleen Jones.[33] Many more were confined for vagrancy in jails and Bridewells (houses of correction), and others were maintained on outdoor relief.[34] Hospitals and asylums were few. Bethlem in London had existed since the twelfth century, and two hospitals were opened through voluntary public subscription in the 1750s

– the Manchester Lunatic Hospital and St Luke's in London. In most areas, however, those lunatics who were unmanageable in workhouses and jails were transferred, at public expense, to private madhouses. The number of these private establishments was increasing, and 30–40 licensed houses existed at the end of the eighteenth century.[35] The York Retreat was one such.

THE ASYLUM MOVEMENT

Public responsibility for the care of pauper lunatics could not be avoided, and indeed it became a basic requisite in shaping the new wage labor force (as Andrew Scull has pointed out in his book on this theme, *Museums of Madness*[36]). To separate the employable from the unemployable was essential to the rationalization of poor relief. The able-bodied should not be encouraged to be idle, but the incapacitated had to be accommodated. In an effort to reduce the bill for the care of pauper lunatics in private madhouses, the British County Asylum Act of 1808 recommended the establishment of public specialty hospitals for the insane. The first county asylums to open were in rural districts where pauperism was severe and subsistence farming declining.[37]

Throughout Europe, moral treatment was intimately tied to the development of the new specialty establishments for lunatics. The York Retreat was one of a growing number of private madhouses, and its methods were copied, to a limited degree, by the new county asylums. Bicêtre had become a central institution for the insane alone, only one year before Pinel struck off the fetters. La Salpêtrière was converted to that purpose in the same year. The miscellany of the poor, who had previously been confined there, was released by the revolutionary government "in order to distribute it to the points where the labor force was rarest."[38] Criminals, henceforth, were to be housed separately from lunatics.[39] Chiarugi's humane methods were introduced in a newly erected hospital for the insane in Florence. And in the United States, as the first wave of hospitals for the insane began to be opened, moral treatment was the style of management which the new superintendents studied and aimed to establish in their institutions.

REHABILITATION AND INSTITUTIONALIZATION

One of the attractions of moral treatment was its curative and rehabilitative emphasis. If patients could be cured and discharged to support themselves, they would cease to be a drain on the public purse. The proprietor of the private Whitchurch Asylum in Herefordshire, for example, played up this point in an advertising handbill. Arguing that patients admitted to his establishment recovered in a matter of days, compared with months and years for a cure in the local county asylums, he estimated that the cost of a cure in his private licensed house was a fraction of the cost in the public asylums.[40] Furthermore, the emphasis in moral management on hard work and self-discipline, as Scull has pointed out, reflected the same attitudes required in shaping the new industrial labor force.[41]

Despite the rehabilitative emphasis in moral treatment, however, the increase in asylum care was rapid. With the growth of wage work and the existence of a large, cheap supply of labor, the marginally functional insane were at a considerable disadvantage. Many of those who might have been fairly productive in working subsistence smallholdings were now unemployable. Labor mobility, long working hours and poverty made it harder for families to support their disabled members at home.[42]

When outdoor relief expenditure was severely restricted in the mid-nineteenth century there was a commensurate increase in the outlay on lunatic asylums and workhouses.[43] The proportion of the population of England and Wales officially identified as insane (including those in workhouses and the community, but largely comprising asylum inmates) grew dramatically during the moral treatment era and the period of establishment of county asylums. In 1807, the official count was 2.3 insane people per 10,000 population; by the time moral treatment had faded away in 1870, there were officially 24.3 per 10,000. Nearly all of the increase (at least after 1844 when the available figures allow a distinction to be made) is in the number of pauper lunatics; the number of private patients remained remarkably small and constant throughout the nineteenth century.[44]

There was clearly a growth in the recognition and confinement of the insane, but did the Industrial Revolution also spawn an actual increase in the occurrence of insanity? Contemporary opinion was divided on this question, the majority arguing that the increase was more apparent than real. As we shall see in Chapter 9, however, there is a distinct possibility that psychosis, and particularly schizophrenia, was indeed becoming more prevalent as the nineteenth century advanced.

MORAL TREATMENT OF THE POOR

The treatment methods of the moral-management advocates and of the twentieth-century pioneers of social psychiatry were very similar (see Table 5.1); so, too, was the political function of the movements they created. Just as the post-Second World War social psychiatry revolution legitimized deinstitutionalization, so moral treatment legitimized the growth of institutional care in the nineteenth century. In each case, the ideology of a treatment approach, initially humane and directed towards the patients' benefit, became subtly distorted and was used to serve

Table 5.1 Moral treatment and the post-Second World War social psychiatry revolution compared

Moral treatment	Post-Second World War social psychiatry revolution
Non-restraint	Non-restraint
Non-confinement	Open door
Self-control emphasized	Therapeutic community
Privileges – not punishment	Positive reinforcement
Small treatment settings	Small units
Homelike environment	Less barren wards
Warm baths and generous diet	Patient comforts improved
Work therapy	Vocational rehabilitation
Patients are human	Patients are to be respected
Patient seen as child	Patient seen as adult
Social activities	Social retraining
Drugs seldom used	Drug treatment valued
Early discharge	Early discharge
Community involvement	Community involvement
Legitimized institutional expansion	Legitimized institutional decline
Supposed cost savings	Supposed cost savings

political ends which were not necessarily in the patients' interests. After the Second World War, the effort to rehabilitate patients to decent living conditions and a useful role in the community became translated into a rush to dump patients on the street and in nursing homes in order to save money. Similarly, Samuel Tuke's *Description of the Retreat*, published in 1813, encouraged reformers in the belief that asylums could be curative and hastened the expansion of the county asylum system. Moral treatment, as it was offered to paupers in the public asylums, however, bore relatively little resemblance to moral treatment as it was developed for the middle-class clientele of the York Retreat.

At the Retreat, seven staff cared for thirty patients, and, in addition, personal servants lived on the premises. In the county asylums, the generally accepted ratio was one keeper to thirty patients.[45] The early asylums were overcrowded and staffed by unqualified and untrained keepers. Despite the superintendents' promises of improved cure rates, local authorities were unwilling to pay for a decent standard of care. Consequently, many patients slept on straw, mechanical restraints were commonly used and opportunities for patients to work or enjoy social diversion were restricted.[46] The high annual mortality rates at the asylums of Lancaster and the West Riding of Yorkshire (17 per cent and 18 per cent, respectively, of the resident population) were the result, argued John Thurnam, a physician at the York Retreat, of poor nutrition and hygiene. Even greater mortality rates at the Norfolk County Asylum (19 per cent) and at St Peter's Hospital for paupers in Bristol (20 per cent) were the consequence of lack of adequate medical care and "the want of a proper amount of land for the exercise and employment of the patients."[47]

By the mid-1840s only five of the seventeen county asylums had abandoned mechanical restraint. Foremost among them were Lincoln Asylum, under the direction of Robert Gardiner Hill, and the massive new asylum at Hanwell, Middlesex, where John Conolly was the superintendent. The limited acceptance of moral treatment at that time is illustrated by the fact that Hill was forced to resign his post owing to public opposition; and Conolly was unable to persuade his governing committee to meet the expense of two of his innovative ideas – basic education classes for patients and professional training for the staff. With the restriction of outdoor relief and the great expansion of the asylum system, during the next decade, the situation was reversed. By the mid-1950s, nearly all the thirty county asylums had discarded mechanical restraints and adopted some features of moral management.[48] Staffing patterns, at least in some asylums, improved. At Lancaster Asylum in 1846, on the "tranquil" wards, there was one attendant for twenty-five patients, and on the more disturbed wards, one attendant to fifteen refractory patients.[49] The value of moral treatment in legitimizing social policy is here illustrated – legitimizing, that is, the Poor Law Commission policy of categorizing the destitute, providing poor relief in specialized institutions and cutting back on outdoor relief. The task accomplished, the cost of care per patient was soon reduced through progressive cheeseparing and expansion of the size of the institutions. Mechanical restraints and solitary confinement returned, and by the late 1860s moral treatment in the public asylums had again become a mere facade.[50]

In his description of nineteenth-century private madhouses, *The Trade in Lunacy*, William Parry-Jones highlights the differences in treatment for the poor (paid out of the public purse) and for private patients. He remarks:

> With regard to the maltreatment of lunatics in madhouses, confined under bad, often appalling, physical conditions, the evidence is . . . substantial and refers, especially, to pauper departments during the first half of the nineteenth century.[51]

Again:

> The various factors which operated to keep the charge for paupers as low as possible . . . served to delay the introduction of the non-restraint system and to foster the continuance of the merely custodial confinement of lunatics.[52]

Mechanical restraint was rarely seen in licensed houses receiving only private patients, but was freely used in those houses taking paupers.[53] Some proprietors felt that restraints should not be used on patients from the "respectable class: their feelings are more acute than those of the humbler grade."[54] But the fact that non-restraint treatment required more and better trained staff and led to higher charges was generally recognized.[55] Whereas in the pauper establishments one keeper might care for ten or fifteen patients, in the houses for the wealthy the ratio was one attendant or servant for every one or two patients.[56] Moral treatment in Britain, it is clear, was not generally for the poor. As we have seen, for a few years, from the 1850s to the 1860s, during the expansion of the asylum system, a form of moral treatment was made available to paupers in county asylums; but otherwise, humane care was for those who could afford it.

CURE RATES

Did the class bias in quality of care influence the outcome of insanity? In attempting to answer this question, we have to be very cautious about using the published cure rates of the time. Where one madhouse proprietor talked of patients being "cured" or "discharged recovered" another might have used the term "relieved" or "improved." Again, patients admitted to one establishment might have included more who were young and early in the course of a functional psychosis; on the other hand, many of those admitted to county asylums were chronic patients transferred from workhouses or were elderly people with dementia. Bearing these considerations in mind, the statistics published in 1845 by Dr. John Thurnam (see Table 5.2) are among the most useful. The figures show that institutions receiving paupers consistently reported lower recovery rates and higher mortality rates. Dr. Thurnam argued that these results were not entirely due to the condition of the patients on admission, but were, in part, a consequence of the differences in their management.[57]

The size of the institution may have been an important factor: asylums and licensed houses receiving private patients were generally a good deal smaller. Metropolitan licensed houses for paupers held an average of 400 patients; those for private patients had an average capacity of 23 residents.[58] For this reason, perhaps, at the model pauper asylum of Hanwell in Middlesex – with 1,000 beds, far and away the largest mental institution in the country – the recovery rate was well below average, despite the emphasis on moral management and non-restraint. Daniel Hack Tuke's figures show the recovery rate at Hanwell fluctuating between 25 per cent and 32 per cent of admissions during the first forty-five years of the hospital's operation.[59] At Lancaster Asylum, Britain's rapidly expanding, second largest mental hospital, the introduction of more progressive treatment methods in the early 1840s reduced mortality rates but failed to improve discharge and cure rates; the percentage of recoveries, in fact, declined after the introduction of moral treatment.[60] The social policy which established large, cost-effective asylums and limited expenditure on

Table 5.2 Recovery and mortality rates for British mental institutions, comparing private and pauper establishments before 1845

	Recovery as % of admissions	Mortality as % of number resident
County asylums		
Receiving both private and pauper patients (average of 6 asylums, 1812–44)	46.87	10.46
Receiving paupers only (average of 9 asylums, 1812–44)	36.95	13.88
Metropolitan licensed houses		
Receiving principally private patients (average of 27 houses, 1839–43)	30.87	6.80
Receiving principally paupers (average of 3 houses, 1838–43)	23.74	18.10
Provincial licensed houses		
Receiving principally private patients (average of 41 houses, 1839–43)	43.50	6.57
Receiving principally paupers (average of 44 houses, 1839–43)	41.50	10.56

Source: Thurnam, J., *Observations and Essays on the Statistics of Insanity*, London: Simpkin, Marshall, 1845, Table 12.

patient care reduced the possibility of rehabilitation for the insane poor. The improvements in public mental hospital care made during the expansion of the asylum system in the 1850s and 1860s cannot be shown to have improved cure rates. The smaller size of the private establishments, on the other hand, and the much higher ratio of staff to residents, may well have enhanced the possibility of recovery for wealthier patients.

LABOR IN NINETEENTH-CENTURY BRITAIN

What was the effect of the labor market on policy and practice in nineteenth-century British psychiatry? As we have seen, at no time was there a particularly strong rehabilitative emphasis to public psychiatry. This observation is understandable in view of the exceptionally high levels of unemployment which existed throughout the century. A famous dispute has raged among social historians as to whether living conditions for the working class worsened or improved during the early decades of the British Industrial Revolution.[61] Over one fact, however, there can be little room for debate (although information on the subject is scattered) – prior to 1850 unemployment was substantial. Vagrancy was increasing dramatically, 10 per cent of the population were paupers in the 1840s and, at times, cyclical unemployment reached colossal heights. In the business slumps of 1826 and 1841–42 unemployment in the region of 75 per cent was not uncommon in the hard hit areas of the industrial north and Midlands.[62] A contemporary observer, Henry Mayhew, writing of Londoners in the early nineteenth century, concludes:

> In almost all occupations there is . . . a *superfluity of labourers* . . . . In the generality of trades the calculation is that one-third of the hands are fully employed, one-third partially, and one-third unemployed throughout the year.[63]

Although the availability of employment increased after 1850,[64] unemployment continued to be considerable throughout the Great Victorian Boom (1850–73) and may well have been only moderately better than during the subsequent Great Depression (1873–96).[65] That the heyday of moral treatment in the county asylums occurred in the boom years of the 1850s and 1860s is perhaps not especially relevant (except insofar as improved institutional conditions allowed an increased strictness in the limitation of outdoor relief[66]). There is no evidence, on the one hand, of a labor shortage at that time or, on the other hand, of a stronger rehabilitative effort or increase in discharge rates from the institutions. What is relevant is that the one clearly rehabilitative movement in psychiatry in Britain since the beginning of industrialization and the development of asylums occurred during the only period of significant labor shortage in two centuries – the years immediately following the Second World War.

The labor history of nineteenth-century America is substantially different from that of Britain. How did it influence psychiatry in the United States?

INDUSTRIALIZING AMERICA

Labor was in short supply in industrializing and expanding America during the first half of the nineteenth century.[67] Historian Daniel Boorstin writes:

> English observers in the mid-nineteenth century admired the ease with which American labourers moved about the country, from one job to another. They were amazed at the general freedom from fear of unemployment. . . .[68]

Real wages, in consequence, were higher in the United States than Europe.[69] The members of the Yates Committee to the New York legislature in 1824 reported:

> In this country the labor of three days will readily supply the wants of seven, while in Europe the labor of the whole week will barely suffice for the maintenance and support of the family of an industrious laborer or peasant.[70]

Pauperism was exceedingly rare by European standards, and what there was existed largely in the maritime cities, where newly arrived immigrants congregated. Less than 1 per cent of the population of Philadelphia were paupers in the 1820s and less than 2 per cent of the population of New York State.[71] Unemployment remained low during much of the antebellum period, becoming more significant from the 1850s onward.[72] Population increase and the late Victorian depressions of 1873, 1884 and 1893, however, brought high unemployment and poverty.[73] Peacetime labor shortage of early nineteenth-century dimensions has not been seen since in the United States.

Was American psychiatry more rehabilitative in its emphasis in the early nineteenth century, in response to the heavy demand for labor? It is certainly true that moral treatment was vigorously adopted by the first corporate asylums which were established (by public subscription) in those years. The founders of these New England hospitals were much influenced by the examples and writing of Tuke and Pinel and applied their methods from the moment the doors were opened – at the Friends' Asylum, Frankford, Pennsylvania (1817), Bloomingdale Asylum, New York (1821), McLean Hospital, Boston, Massachusetts (1818), and the Retreat at Hartford, Connecticut (1824). The independent Pennsylvania Hospital in Philadelphia, which established a separate branch for the insane in 1841, was also a model of progressive care. These hospitals, many of them established by Quakers, were, like the York Retreat, primarily intended for the treatment of private patients. Some, however, like the Hartford Retreat and the Bloomingdale Asylum, took substantial numbers of paupers in return for public funding. As in the best British private establishments, staffing was comfortably high – one attendant to six patients at the Pennsylvania Hospital – one attendant to two patients at other hospitals. Restraints were very rarely used, and a full, if somewhat overregimented, schedule of social and work activities was established for all inmates. Such was the success and public good favor of these progressive institutions that they were a major influence in the development of public hospitals for the insane.[74]

AMERICAN PUBLIC HOSPITALS

Discussions of this era in American psychiatry often make the point that moral treatment was not generally made available to the poor or that it existed more in the pious mouthings of hospital superintendents than in the actual condition of patients in the public institutions.[75] This point of view deserves some debate, however, especially if we restrict ourselves to a study of the earliest decades of operation of the public hospitals. George Mora writes, in the *Comprehensive Textbook of Psychiatry*, for instance:

Among the earliest state-supported institutions were the Eastern State
Hospital at Lexington, Kentucky, opened in 1824; the Manhattan State
Hospital in New York City, opened in 1825; the Western State Hospital
in Staunton, Virginia, opened in 1828; and the South Carolina State
Hospital in Columbia, South Carolina, opened in 1828. In contrast with
the private or corporate hospitals, in which moral treatment was
applied, those state institutions remained largely custodial.[76]

Of the four examples chosen by Dr. Mora, two might reasonably be
described as "largely custodial." The performance of the state asylum in
Lexington, Kentucky, was less than creditable. Historian David Rothman
considers that it "had . . . become a custodial institution" by 1845;[77] the
figures supplied by Gerald Grob in his review of *Mental Institutions in
America* suggest that this may have been true as early as 1840 (see Table
5.3). Yet even this institution had high ideals in the early years – the
directors insisted, for example, that no restraints be used.[78] In using
Manhattan State Hospital as an example, Mora is presumably referring to
the New York City Asylum on Blackwell's Island which actually opened
in 1839. This institution, as we shall see later, was also clearly custodial,
but for special reasons. At the Western Virginia State Hospital, however
(according to Norman Dain's study of that state's mental hospitals), moral
treatment was introduced in 1836 by an enthusiastic young superintendent
who so upgraded the quality of the hospital that he was able to attract
private, upper-class, white patients, who accounted for a third of the
admissions.[79] Social reformers visiting the hospital in 1842 regarded it as
excellent, and reported:

> The employments, recreations, amusements, instructions, and influ-
> ences are very various, and well fitted to soothe the excited, cheer the
> desponding, guide the erring, check the vicious, raise the fallen, and
> restore the insane. The restraints are very few.[80]

Treatment at each of the two Virginia state hospitals was reportedly
comparable, and benefited from an exceptionally good level of staffing –
one staff member (including slave attendants) for every three patients.[81]
South Carolina State Hospital, the last of Dr. Mora's examples, far from
being custodial had a high patient turnover. From data provided by Gerald
Grob, we can calculate that from 1845 (when records became available)
to 1865 the number of patients discharged as recovered (and not merely
improved) was regularly around 50 per cent of admissions (as shown in
Table 5.3) or 20 per cent of the total hospital population.[82]

As we survey the fourteen or so public hospitals which were in operation
in the United States by 1845, and recall that non-restraint management had
established itself in fewer than a third of the ill-staffed British county
asylums by the mid-1840s, it appears possible that the pauper lunatic in

Table 5.3 Patients discharged "recovered" expressed as a percentage of admissions in selected years for American asylums open before 1845[a]

	1820	1825	1830	1835	1840	1845	1850	1855	1860	1865	1870	1875
Corporate and private hospitals												
Hartford Retreat, Connecticut	–	23	55	50	60	43	47	43	41	37	33	40
McLean Asylum, Massachusetts	22	36	41	54	48	62	45	46	32	43	42	19
Bloomingdale Asylum, New York	–	46	43	42	53	44	51	49	33	43	39	30
Friends' Asylum, Pennsylvania	20	–[b]	44	22	46	52	52	40	40	28	42	32
Pennsylvania Hospital	–	–	–	–	–	45	51	57	46	44	36	42
State and city hospitals (northern)												
Maine Insane Hospital	–	–	–	–	28	39	60	32	46	33	37	36
Boston Insane Hospital, Mass.	–	–	–	–	7	24	51	29	41	25	26	30
Worcester State Hospital, Mass.	–	–	–	46	51	42	52	55	60	48	41	25
New Hampshire Asylum	–	–	–	–	–[b]	42	44	53	45	39	28	44
New York City Asylum, Blackwell's Is.	–	–	–	–	–[b]	–[b]	–[b]	–[b]	–[b]	–[b]	27	31
Utica State Asylum, New York	–	–	–	–	–	46	47	47	31	32	32	31
Central Ohio Asylum	–	–	–	–	52	29	51	63	49	41	–	–
Vermont Asylum	–	–	–	–	45	29	53	48	41	38	29	25
State hospitals (southern)												
Kentucky Eastern Asylum	–	44	–[b]	–[b]	8	37	34	35	46	44	28	60
Maryland State Hospital	–	–	–	9	38	44	35	37	50	65	83	16
Tennessee State Hospital	–	–	–	–	–	–[b]	34	46	47	–[b]	41	44
South Carolina Asylum	–[b]	–	–	–	–	57	50	31	54	70	29	29
Virginia Eastern Asylum	–	–[b]	–[c]	–[b]	–[b]	–[b]	–[b]	–[b]	–[b]	–[b]	–[b]	46
Virginia Western Asylum	–	–	–[b]	–[b]	–[b]	–[b]	–[b]	–[b]	–[b]	–[b]	44	40

Source: Percentages calculated from data in Grob, G. N. I., *Mental Institutions in America*, New York: Free Press, 1973, pp. 374–93.

Notes: [a] These figures, being calculated on statistics for a single year, are substantially less accurate and more subject to fluctuation than if based on longer time periods.
[b] Hospital open but figures not available.

America at this time was the more fortunate. Unsatisfactory hospital conditions were primarily to be found in New York City and in some institutions in the non-industrial South. Besides the two state hospitals in Virginia, we know that progressive and humane measures were practiced in Worcester State Hospital, in Massachusetts; at Utica, in upstate New York; and at the Vermont Asylum, in Brattleboro. The Maine Insane Asylum was in the hands of Isaac Ray, a prominent psychiatrist and moral-treatment advocate.[83] If Worcester State Hospital is a fair illustration, staffing patterns were excellent by contemporary British asylum standards – one attendant to twelve or fifteen patients during the 1830s and 1840s.[84]

Mortality rates (the measure which Dr. Thurnam considered the best standard of comparison of the quality of asylum care) were considerably better in American state hospitals than in British county asylums in the 1840s (see Table 5.4). These differences were not due to the admission of more elderly patients to British hospitals – the age distribution of admissions to British and American asylums was quite similar.[85] Since acutely ill patients tended to have a higher death rate, the low mortality might theoretically have been a result of the admission of more chronic patients to the American hospitals. Equally, the lower death rate in the American institutions may well have reflected better conditions for American insane paupers.

In general, David Rothman feels the American public asylums tried to emulate the private institutions but were not able to achieve quite the same standards:

> There were lapses and failures, but in the first few years of the asylums they were not gross ones. Most mental hospitals in the 1830s and 1840s abolished the whip and the chain and did away with confinement. . . . And often they accomplished more, treating patients with thoughtfulness and humanity.[86]

Charles Dickens, in his *American Notes*, though critical of much that he saw in the New World of 1842, was very favorably impressed by the Boston Insane Hospital for paupers, and devotes several pages to a description of his visit. He was particularly struck by the dignity with which the patients were treated, their freedom from restraint or restrictions in the use of potentially dangerous instruments, their provisions for work and social activity (including sewing circles, balls and carriage rides) and the intimate involvement of the superintendent and his wife in the daily life of the hospital:

> It is obvious that one great feature of the system, is the inculcation and encouragement, even among such unhappy persons, of a decent self-respect.[87]

The Boston Hospital, aside from this report, has never been heralded as an outstandingly progressive hospital by the standards of the times.

Table 5.4 Mortality rates in British and American pauper asylums as a percentage of the number resident

British county asylums		American state and city hospitals		
	Mean annual mortality % 1939–44		Annual mortality %	
			1840	1845
Receiving paupers only		*Northern states*		
Bedford	10.5	Maine	10.4	8.7
Dorset	12.2	Boston, Mass.	6.2	5.8
Kent	10.7	Worcester, Mass.	6.6	7.6
Lancaster	13.2	New Hampshire	–	7.9
Middlesex	9.1	Utica, New York	–	7.9
Norfolk	19.1	Central Ohio	10.7	10.8
Suffolk	10.8	Vermont	7.4	7.6
York	13.6			
Receiving private and pauper patients		*Southern states*		
Chester	11.8	Maryland	10.0	9.3
Cornwall	7.7	South Carolina	–	8.4
Gloucester	10.7	Eastern Virginia	–	9.4
Leicester	11.3			
Nottingham	9.2			
Stafford	13.7			

Sources: British asylums: Thurnam, *Observations and Essays on the Statistics of Insanity*, Table 13. American asylums: mortality rates calculated from statistics in Grob, *Mental Institutions in America*, pp. 374–93.

Dickens also found the private Hartford Retreat to be "admirably conducted,"[88] but he was severely critical of the recently opened New York City Asylum on Blackwell's Island. At the latter institution:

> I saw nothing of that salutary system which had impressed me so favourably elsewhere; and everything had a lounging, listless, madhouse air.[89]

At last Dickens had come upon an American asylum as depressing as he was to find St Luke's in London a few years later.[90] And the reason for the melancholy conditions at the New York City Asylum? Perhaps, as he says,

> New York, as a great emporium of commerce, and as a place of general resort, not only from all parts of the States, but from most parts of the world, has always a large pauper population to provide for; and labours, therefore, under peculiar difficulties in this respect.[91]

The New York *State* Hospital, over 200 miles north at Utica, escaped the problem of overcrowding with foreign-born paupers from which the city hospital suffered,[92] and became recognized as a model state institution. The rare instance of unenlightened hospital conditions was to be found where poverty and unemployment were beginning to appear within the shores of the United States.

REHABILITATION

Not only were conditions generally humane in the public institutions, they were also genuinely rehabilitative. Work therapy was strongly emphasized at such state hospitals as Worcester, Massachusetts; Utica, New York; and Brattleboro, Vermont.[93] Patients were released on parole from the Eastern Virginia Asylum to seek work in local towns, and some were also boarded out with families in order that "the accustomed life of the lunatic shall be less essentially at variance with that pertaining to persons generally of sound mind."[94] Several hospitals, including Utica, instituted the measure for which Conolly in England was unable to obtain funding – classes for patients. A variety of subjects was taught, including music and drama. Most hospitals had libraries for the patients. In addition, links with the community at large were strengthened by encouraging the participation of teachers, ministers and other visitors in the day-to-day operation of the hospitals.[95]

The rehabilitative emphasis appears to have been associated with reasonably high discharge rates. As Table 5.3 shows, the proportion of patients discharged "recovered" from public hospitals in different years compared quite well with figures for private hospitals. (No doubt, of course, hospital superintendents attached different meanings to "recovered," but there is no reason to believe that public hospital doctors were particularly optimistic in this respect.) We see very respectable recovery rates not only at South Carolina Asylum, as previously noted, and at such hospitals of repute as Worcester and Utica, but also at the New Hampshire Asylum, the Central Ohio Asylum and the Vermont Asylum. Recovery rates at these hospitals through the 1850s were at least equal to those (given by Thurnam) for the best British county asylums. Table 5.5, drawn from Thurnam's statistics, shows that recovery rates at the American corporate hospitals and at the Worcester Asylum (admittedly the best of the state hospitals) all exceeded average cure rates at British institutions through the mid-1840s. Such direct comparison of overall recovery rates, however, can yield only very crude impressions in view of the probable differences in the patient populations and in measures of recovery. Cure rates in the United States, for example, might have been boosted if many chronic psychotic people, especially black, were not admitted to the state hospitals but languished in jails and workhouses. It is not apparent, however, that this occurred more in the United States than in Britain; and, as we have seen, the lower mortality rates in American institutions suggest that the American hospitals were receiving their fair share of chronic patients. Higher discharge rates from American institutions might

Table 5.5 Recovery and mortality rates in British and American mental institutions before 1845

	Recovery as % of admissions	Mortality as % of number residents
Britain		
Private and charitable asylums (average of 8 asylums, 1766–1843)	40.94	8.93
Metropolitan licensed houses (average of 30 houses, 1839–43)	25.65	14.68
Provincial licensed houses (average of 85 houses, 1838–43)	42.24	9.85
County asylums (average of 15 asylums, 1812–44)	40.25	12.79
United States		
Corporate hospitals		
Bloomingdale Asylum, New York, 1821–41	46.18	10.32
Friends' Asylum, Frankford, Penn., 1817–42	44.38	10.64
Hartford Retreat, Conn., 1824–43	56.29	–
McLean Asylum, Boston, Mass., 1818–43	44.95	11.07
(average of 4 corporate asylums)	47.41	10.65
State hospitals		
Worcester State Hospital, Mass., 1833–43	44.56	6.76

Source: Thurnam, *Observations and Essays on the Statistics of Insanity*, Table 12.

partly have reflected a policy of early discharge rather than a real difference in patient outcome. Nevertheless, such figures would still have been an accurate reflection of a greater rehabilitative emphasis in American psychiatry of the period.

THE "CULT OF CURABILITY"

Some contemporary observers formed the impression that American mental hospital treatment and cure rates were superior to those that existed in Britain. Like Dickens, Captain Basil Hall was a British visitor whose impressions of America were generally somewhat uncomplimentary. In the published account of his travels, however, he waxed lyrical over the patient management at the Hartford Retreat, which he witnessed in 1827, and contrasted the high recovery rates at that hospital with current British results. During the previous year, 25 of the 28 "recent" cases admitted to the Hartford Retreat – 89.2 per cent – had recovered, he reported, but "at two most ancient and celebrated institutions" of the same type in Britain only 25.5 per cent of "recent" (acute) cases were cured.[96] Hall's claims attracted a great deal of attention on both sides of the Atlantic and were widely quoted in the press. Soon, other

American hospital superintendents reported similar rates of success. Samuel Woodward at the Worcester State Hospital claimed recovery rates for "recent" (acute) cases of 82–91 per cent for the early years of the hospital's operation between 1833 and 1840. John Galt, superintendent at the Eastern Virginia Asylum, announced, in his report of 1842, 92 per cent recovery in acute cases and 53 per cent recovery overall in new admissions. Around the same time, William Awl, superintendent of the Ohio State Asylum, reported cure rates of 80–100 per cent for cases of recent onset, and 48 per cent recovery for all cases of up to ten years' duration admitted over a four-year period.[97] Heads of corporate and public asylums alike argued that recovery from insanity was the rule, incurability the exception. As stated by Amariah Brigham of Utica State Hospital: "No fact relating to insanity appears better established than the general certainty of curing it in its early state."[98]

It is easy to dismiss such claims as American bombast and typical of the entrepreneurial audacity of the New Republic. The claims were, indeed, extravagant and clearly motivated, in part, by a wish to impress state legislators with the value of investment in hospital care. Dorothea Dix used these reports of the benefits of modern treatment in her successful campaign to establish public mental hospitals throughout the United States. The episode in American psychiatry has subsequently been disparaged as the "Cult of Curability."[99] Obviously, statistics may have been molded somewhat to improve the effect. Galt's 92 per cent recovery figure was, like many other reports, based on a small sample – 13 admissions. Criteria for defining "recent" cases and "recovery" were subject to manipulation; and patients who relapsed, were readmitted and subsequently discharged again, might be counted as "recovered" more than once.[100] Despite such statistical flaws, nevertheless, we cannot rule out the possibility that cure rates were outstandingly good at the time. Indeed, it seems quite possible that recovery rates for acutely ill patients admitted to American public and private mental hospitals throughout the first half of the nineteenth century were distinctly better than in the decades that followed or in contemporary Britain. Two points emerge clearly from the reports of the period. The emphasis on curability was largely an American phenomenon, and it pervaded public psychiatry as extensively as it did the private institutions. In Britain, George Burrows reported similarly high recovery rates in 1820 for "recent" cases admitted to his madhouse, as did the proprietors of other private establishments.[101] The same degree of universal optimism, however, did not develop in British public hospitals of the period.

The enthusiasm of the American hospital superintendents was, in fact, based upon the observation of distinctly superior rates of recovery. Table 5.6 allows us to compare separately the cure rates for acute and chronic patients admitted to several British and American hospitals before 1842.

The American recovery rates for acute patients were substantially better than the British. It may reasonably be assumed that these figures for recent cases are more comparable than those for total admissions. Undetermined numbers of chronically psychotic and demented patients, epileptics and mentally retarded among the general admissions largely determined the overall recovery rate, which, as we may see in Table 5.6, bore little relationship to the cure rate in acute illness. Significant differences in the causes of acute mental illness, however, could conceivably have accounted for the disparity in recovery rates. Thurnam argued, for example, that more of the American hospital admissions were suffering from alcohol-related psychoses and delirium tremens, which ended either in early recovery or death.[102] If this opinion were correct, we would expect to find higher death rates in the American asylums (in fact, as we have seen, they were lower) and higher recovery rates in male patients (which was true at Bloomingdale Asylum, but not at Worcester[103]). Whatever the causes, it

Table 5.6 Percentage of admissions discharged "recovered" from British and American asylums according to duration of illness

	Less than 12 months duration	More than 12 months duration	All cases
Britain			
Private hospitals			
York Retreat, 1796–1843	61.87	18.88	46.94
Asylums for private and pauper patients			
Bethlem Hospital, 1827–39	52.38	12.50	50.96
Dundee Asylum, 1820–40	59.06	13.71	42.36
Lincoln Asylum	50.95	9.62	40.10
St. Luke's Hospital, 1751–1834	39.71	–	–
County asylums for paupers only			
Maidstone Asylum, Kent	49.26	4.84	20.68
Wakefield Asylum, Yorkshire	53.74	11.50	44.18
United States			
Corporate hospitals			
Bloomingdale Asylum, New York, 1882–41[a]	74.85	11.57	47.19[a]
Friends' Asylum, Frankford, Penn., 1817–38[b]	58.23	25.20	45.11
State hospitals			
Worcester State Hospital, Mass., 1833–40	82.78	14.40	42.30
Central Ohio Asylum, 1838–42	79.53	20.20[c]	47.70[d]

Sources: Thurnam, *Observations and Essays on the Statistics of Insanity*, p. 57. Statistics for Ohio Asylum are added from Grob, *Mental Institutions in America*, p. 182.
Notes: [a] Private patients only.
    [b] Private and pauper patients.
    [c] Cases of 1–10 years duration.
    [d] Cases of up to 10 years duration.

is clear that there was a distinctly better course and outcome to acute mental illnesses in early nineteenth-century America, which needs to be explained.

THE COVER-UP

Few physicians care to believe that their methods are not as successful as those of others and, still less, that the achievements of their profession are following a progressively downhill course. Such concerns may well explain the intensity and somewhat derisory air with which later American psychiatrists have attempted to refute the curability claims of the moral-treatment era. They have been anxious to see the errors in these reports but less keen to validate any truth within them. Most vigorous and influential of these critics was Pliny Earle, and his work *The Curability of Insanity*, published in 1876, is frequently cited as the definitive debunking of the "myth of curability."[104] Dr. Earle contended that the excellent recovery rates recorded by Samuel Woodward during the earliest years of the Worcester State Hospital were grossly exaggerated by statistical juggling. He made much of the fact that the same patient might be counted as "recovered" after every relapse and that percentages of recoveries were calculated on the basis of those discharged, not on the numbers admitted. His conclusion, much more in keeping with the figures for his own institution, late in the century, was that insanity was, in fact, far less curable than had been supposed.

Pliny Earle's attempt to rewrite psychiatric history, however, has itself been exposed as a cover-up. Dr. Sanbourne Bockoven, who has reanalyzed Dr. Earle's figures and uncovered more material on Samuel Woodward's patients,[105] concludes that Earle himself was guilty of statistical juggling. Dr. Earle knew, for example, that the counting of repeated recoveries, which he so criticized and which has been raised by every critic since, made almost no difference to the overall recovery rate of Worcester State Hospital patients – a difference of less than a quarter of a percentage point. Dr. Earle also knew of the existence of a comprehensive follow-up study of Samuel Woodward's discharged patients, conducted by Dr. John Park, a later superintendent of Worcester State Hospital – a study which showed that outcome was, indeed, so superior in the early decades of the hospital's operation that Dr. Park judiciously withheld the results from publication.

At Dr. Earle's suggestion, Dr. Park had compiled a retroactive review of admissions and discharges since the opening of the hospital in 1833, employing his own criteria for "recovery," not Dr. Woodward's. His results (continued up to 1950 with modern data), showing the changes in the percentage of admissions discharged as recovered from Worcester State Hospital, are displayed in Figure 5.1 (taken from Dr. Bockoven's book). Dr. Park, who was as keen as Dr. Earle to demonstrate that the early recovery rates were artificially inflated, was unable to reduce Dr.

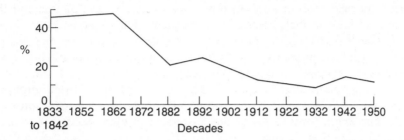

Figure 5.1 Percentage of admissions discharged as "recovered" from Worcester State Hospital over successive decades
Note: Reprinted by permission of the author. From Bockoven, J. S., *Moral Treatment in Community Mental Health*, New York: Springer, 1972, p. 56, © 1972 J. Sanbourne Bockoven.

Woodward's figures by more than 2 or 3 per cent. Overall recovery rates of 45 per cent in the moral-treatment era, as we can see, fell to 20 per cent in the late Victorian Great Depression and to 10 per cent in the 1930s.

David Rothman has criticized Dr. Bockoven's work on two counts. Rothman argues, in the first place, that the revised recovery rates for Dr. Woodward's patients "are considerably lower than the claims for the 1830s and 1840s." Here Rothman makes the error of confusing the claimed recovery rates for "recent" (acute) cases (which were over 80 per cent) with general admissions (45 per cent recovery). Secondly, Rothman claims that Bockoven "makes no attempt to question just what 'recovery' meant in the original records."[106] But Rothman is incorrect here, also. Bockoven demonstrates exactly what "recovery" meant for Woodward's patients by presenting the results of Dr. Park's follow-up, 36–60 years after discharge, of all of Woodward's patients who left the hospital, "recovered," prior to 1847. There were 1,173 such patients, and information was collected on the condition of 984 of them. This project was both ambitious and successful, and took Dr. Park ten years to complete. The study showed that an extraordinary 58 per cent of the patients followed-up never had another relapse in the rest of their lives or until the time of follow-up. Another 8 per cent had relapsed but were well at follow-up. Dr. Bockoven draws the conclusion that, during the moral-treatment era,

> the natural history of psychosis in general (including cases due to organic changes of the central nervous system) was such that a large proportion of patients were able to leave the mental hospital, and only a small proportion, perhaps 20–30 per cent, were destined to die in a mental hospital. Favorable outcome was, of course, even more frequent in the functional psychoses considered alone.[107]

A contemporary of Pliny Earle, Isaac Ray, a psychiatrist of equal stature and experience, rebutted Earle's views in 1879. Dr. Ray argues that the early statistical reports were no more biased than recent figures and that recoveries had, in fact, become less frequent. The reasons, he believed, for the decline in recovery rates included a failure to provide an adequate trial of moral treatment to many patients. Latter-day psychiatric historians, however, have generally ignored Dr. Ray and repeated Pliny Earle's rather self-serving opinions as accurate.[108] They have, thereby, buried important information – the course of functional psychoses in patients admitted to early nineteenth-century American hospitals was more benign than in the hundred years that followed.

THE DEMISE OF MORAL TREATMENT

It is possible, then, that the labor shortage in the first half of the nineteenth century in America influenced rehabilitative efforts for the insane and elevated recovery rates in psychosis. This notion, however, reverses some of the orthodox explanations for the demise of moral management in the latter part of the century. Thus, it was not so much that the failure of promises of curability led legislators to demand cost-cutting in the institutions; it may have been the diminished need for manpower which reduced the incentive to fund vigorous treatment programs and caused a reduction in cure rates. It was not just a build-up of chronic patients and an increase in hospital size and overcrowding which caused the deteriorating institutional conditions; it was the decline in rehabilitative efforts which created the build-up of chronic patients. And the foreign paupers who filled the asylums and so outraged the sensibilities of the psychiatrists and middle-class clientele – the Irish "clodhoppers" with their "filthy habits" – they were not incurable because they had "scarcely an idea beyond that of . . . manual employment," as Isaac Ray claimed.[109] They were stuck because there was no employment outside the hospital, and no longer any work therapy within the hospital.[110] (Inmates' work had become too competitive to be tolerated by the unemployed beyond the institutions' walls.) If funding cuts and overcrowding with chronic patients and paupers were the problems, then the affluent private hospitals which selected more "recent" cases and excluded paupers – Pennsylvania Hospital, the Friends' Asylum, McLean Hospital, Bloomingdale Asylum (which excluded paupers after 1857) and the Hartford Retreat (after 1866)[111] – should have experienced few difficulties. As Table 5.3 shows, however, recovery rates deteriorated in these institutions also after 1870. Public and private asylums alike declined from curative to custodial institutions.[112]

Moral treatment reached its zenith in labor-starved, early nineteenth-century America for two reasons. Firstly, given a demand for labor, moral management was a truly rehabilitative measure which could restore the maximum level of functioning to the marginal psychotic patient. Secondly, as in contemporary Britain, it legitimized the establishment of specialized institutions for confining the unemployable insane. With the inevitable disappearance of the labor shortage, the social-control functions of the institutions overcame their rehabilitative purpose. Where environmental factors had previously been seen as important in causing psychosis, the emphasis now was on heredity. Prevailing concepts of prognosis were pessimistic.[113] At this point in history, in the coercive, prison-like environment of a German asylum[114] during the universal, late nineteenth-century Great Depression, dementia praecox was defined as a progressively deteriorating and all but incurable illness.

When moral treatment returned, a century and a half after its original appearance, its objectives and ideology were similar but the locations were switched. This time it was in labor-short northern Europe that it served (at least initially) a genuinely rehabilitative purpose, but in America it was largely used merely to legitimize the deinstitutionalization movement – the transfer of the indigent mentally ill from indoor to outdoor relief, and from state budget to federal. Both the concept and management of psychosis appear to have been influenced by political and economic factors. Ideology and practice in psychiatry are to a significant extent at the mercy of material conditions.

SUMMARY

- Moral treatment was a humane and non-restrictive method of management for people with psychosis which came into being simultaneously in several parts of Europe in reaction to the eighteenth-century concept of madness as bestial.
- The origins of moral treatment were also those of the French Revolution and the English Industrial Revolution – Enlightenment thinking, dramatic changes in population and labor patterns, and the capitalist transformation of production.
- The treatment method was inextricably tied to the development of mental institutions, and it helped legitimize the public asylum movement.
- A function of the new asylums was to enact the social policy of providing poor relief to the unemployable in institutions and cutting back on outdoor relief to the employable.
- Moral treatment was little used in British public asylums except for a brief spell during the boom years of the 1850s and 1860s when the asylum system was being expanded.
- Private patients in Britain enjoyed more humane care and better recovery rates than paupers.
- The high levels of unemployment in Britain throughout the nineteenth century may well have limited rehabilitative efforts for the insane poor.

- The labor shortage in early nineteenth-century America was associated with more intense rehabilitative efforts and higher cure rates, especially in acute mental illness, in public asylums.
- Later American psychiatrists attempted to obscure the fact that recovery rates were higher during the moral-treatment era.

Chapter 6

Labor, poverty and schizophrenia

Why did fewer schizophrenic people recover during the twentieth-century Great Depression? It is, of course, scarcely surprising that social recovery rates in schizophrenia declined at that time since employment is a large part of the measure of social functioning; but why was there a drop in the rate of complete, symptom-free recovery (as revealed by the analysis of follow-up studies in Chapter 3) from an average of 20 per cent to 12 per cent? Which of the following possible explanations is most applicable?

- Government spending on psychiatric treatment decreased during the Depression, resulting in hospital overcrowding and poor quality care.
- The stresses of the Depression, including economic hardship and unemployment, affected patients and their families and prevented recovery or precipitated psychotic relapse.
- The reduced demand for labor led to diminished rehabilitative and reintegrative efforts for schizophrenic people, resulting in changes in mental-health policy, psychiatric ideology and social tolerance of the mentally ill.

GOVERNMENT SPENDING

Mental hospital admissions, especially for schizophrenic patients and other functional psychotics, increase during an economic recession (as Harvey Brenner's work, *Mental Illness and the Economy*, has shown). If legislators cut back on funding during the Great Depression, at a time of increasing demand, the result would, presumably, have been overcrowding, deteriorating care and non-therapeutic hospital conditions. Is this what happened? The evidence suggests it is not.

The annual expenditure on psychiatric hospitals in the state of Colorado, for example (as can be seen in Figure 6.1), increased considerably between 1913 and 1955, even after allowance has been made for inflation and state population growth. During the decade of the Great Depression, however, expenditure was consistently well *above* the general trend. Before the

1930s, two other spikes of increased spending are evident during the recessions of 1914–15 and 1920–22. Hospital spending was less than usual during the Second World War, but returned to the general trend after the war. (Spending on mental health services after 1955 is not presented here because of the added complications of alternative sources of revenue – such as federal funding, social security benefits and public health insurance – which became important after the onset of deinstitutionalization.) In this state of the union, at least, psychiatric funding did not decrease during the Depression but, rather, increased at a faster rate than usual in an effort to meet the increased demand for care.

The same spending pattern has held true for England and Wales since

Figure 6.1 Annual expenditure in Colorado state psychiatric hospitals in constant (1967) dollars per 1,000 population
Source: Expenditure: "State of Colorado Budget Reports, 1923–24 to 1955–56;" inflation factor: "Bureau of Labor Statistics Wholesale Price Index, All Commodities;" population of Colorado: Decennial U.S. Census with interval year estimates.
Note: Capital outlay is included.

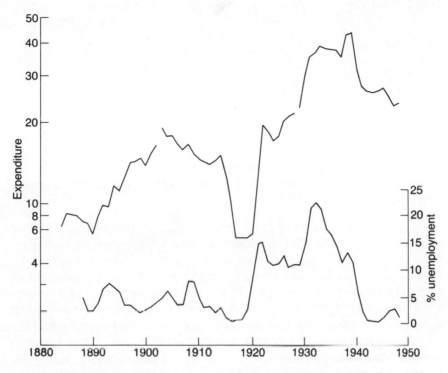

Figure 6.2 Annual expenditure on "lunacy" and lunatic asylums in England and Wales in constant (1871) pounds per 100 population; annual unemployment for comparison

the late Victorian era, as Figure 6.2 shows. Here the rate of expenditure on "lunacy" and lunatic asylums increased during the nineteenth- and twentieth-century Great Depressions, decreased slowly during the relatively full employment years after the turn of the century and after the Second World War, and dropped sharply during the two world wars.

It is possible, of course, that the increased use of mental institutions in the Depression outstripped even these inflated hospital expenditures, in which case overcrowding and poor care would still have occurred. This does not seem to have happened, however. Brenner reports, for example, greatly increased capacity at New York state public hospitals during the Great Depression – a 73 per cent increase in available beds between 1929 and 1938. Overcrowding was common at these hospitals before, during and after the Great Depression, but was apparently no worse during the early years of the economic downturn than in the late 1920s and mid-1950s.[1] Figures for the percentage occupancy of Canadian mental hospitals between 1934 and 1960 draw the same picture (see Figure 6.3). Overcrowding in these hospitals was at its lowest in the 1930s and at its highest in the 1950s.

Figure 6.3 Percentage occupancy of Canadian mental institutions
Source: Urquhart, M. C. and Buckley, K. A. H., *Historial Statistics of Canada*, Cambridge: Cambridge University Press, 1965.

Decreased government spending and hospital overcrowding, it seems, are not the explanation for the poor outcome in schizophrenia during the Great Depression. Similarly, there is no sign of increased spending after the Second World War to account for the improved recovery rates at that time. The switch to community care was, in fact, considered to be a cost-saving measure. Whether, in actuality, community treatment was cheaper is hard to determine. An analysis of the real cost of such care would have to include the expense of social services provided through several agencies, and of supportive accommodation and disability payments. No such study appears to have been done in Britain. Some American cost and benefit studies of deinstitutionalization were made available in the 1970s. Their value for our purpose is somewhat reduced by unsophisticated analytic methods, small sample size or the inclusion of unrealistic projections of savings and benefits attributed to the patients' employability. All of these studies, however, show community treatment to be significantly cheaper than state hospital care.[2]

It seems that, during the Great Depression, more money was spent on buying more hospital care for schizophrenic people and the result was, for whatever reasons, lower recovery rates.

ECONOMIC STRESS AND UNEMPLOYMENT

Stress may provoke a psychotic relapse in someone with schizophrenia (as discussed in Chapter 1). Both the boom and bust parts of the business cycle bring their own varieties of stress. In the depression they include loss of status, self-worth and independence for the unemployed, a sense of failure for those who slip down the social ladder, and economic hardship for many. Schizophrenic people in the community are exposed to all these possible stresses and those with marginal levels of functioning are particularly at risk when jobs are in short supply.

Clinical experience shows us that economic uncertainty is a serious stress for many patients. As social security regulations were tightened during the early years of the Reagan administration, for example, many patients with a stable psychotic disorder whose disability payments were abruptly terminated suffered relapses of their illness. The mental condition of many people with psychosis similarly becomes worse when their most basic needs are not provided for. In the United States, homeless, male schizophrenic patients are frequently admitted to hospital, hungry, dirty, sleepless and floridly psychotic. When, after some meals and a good night's sleep, their mental state dramatically improves, hospital staff claim that the patient has "manipulated" his way into free board and accommodation. More benign observers argue that the patient's improvement is evidence of the efficacy of the dose of the antipsychotic medication which he received on admission. In fact, such patients often improve as readily without medication. The florid features of their psychosis on admission are an acute response to the stress of their poverty and deprivation.

We can estimate from the social recovery rates in Chapter 3 that 70 per cent of schizophrenic people were unemployed at follow-up during the Great Depression – significantly more than after the Second World War. In recent years, again, it has become so common for schizophrenic people in the community to be out of work that mental health professionals rarely consider unemployment a significant stress for their patients. For many of these people with psychotic illness, however, the dreary round of days without purposeful activity, lives devoid of meaning and a social existence stripped of status are a constant strain. British unemployed men complain:

'You're a drag on everybody else really.'
'Sometimes I get to walking up and down on the carpet.'
'. . . cannot be bothered to dae nowt, just feel like stopping in bed all day.'
'When you're out of work you worry and don't feel like eating.'
'I go for a walk and try to do some reading if I can, but it's very hard for me to get the brain functioning properly.'
'I'm so *moody* you know.'
'I thought, "'What's the bloody point of it all, anyway? What's the reason for it all?'" Then you start to become, well, deranged.'
'I think you start to lose your identity in yourself. . . . There's times when, well "'What's . . . what am I?'"'[3]

Such responses are those of unemployed men who are not particularly susceptible to psychosis. The impact on schizophrenic people can scarcely be less severe, and could well affect their recovery and relapse rates.

Indeed, the similarity of many features of chronic schizophrenia to the psychological effects of extended unemployment is striking. Anxiety, depression, apathy, irritability, negativity, emotional overdependence, social withdrawal, isolation and loneliness, and a loss of self-respect, identity and a sense of time – all these are common among the long-term unemployed.[4] Compare these features, and the words of the British unemployed quoted above, with this description of the chronic schizophrenic person:

> Anergy, or disturbances of volition, have at times been incorrectly described as apathy. . . . Patients may be abnormally tired, fatigue easily, and experience clinical depression. The chronic schizophrenic may sit blankly for long periods, unaware of the passage of time. . . . He may remain in bed when he intended to look for a job, avoid or put off without reason any activity that is new, unfamiliar or outside of his routine. . . . Life is routine, constricted, empty. He may sleep most of the day, be awake most of the night. The chronic schizophrenic in the community may fear contact with strangers. . . . He may be unable to cope with . . . the complex demands of welfare departments.[5]

Although many of these "negative" features of schizophrenia are known to be made worse by the social deprivation of institutional care, they are nevertheless seen by psychiatrists as inherent aspects of the illness. (Hence the emphasis on the biological concept of "anergy" rather than the psychological attribute of "apathy.") Mental health professionals become frustrated by, and sometimes critical of, their chronic psychotic patients' dependency, incompetence and unreliability. To label such problems as biological deficits helps the professional cope with his or her frustrations, but it also increases the pessimism regarding treatment and the stigma which attaches to the patient. That such deficits are, to a large extent, socially induced becomes apparent, however, when we read the words of this unemployed (non-psychotic) teenager:

> I feel outside of it . . . [unemployment] just makes me feel different. I really admire these guys who can get up and shave, and have breakfast, and make a journey to work, and come home again, and have meals – guys who can do all that in one day! I don't know how they can manage it. When I've got to sign on, or anything like that, just do the one thing, it bugs me all day. . . . Or if I've got anything to do . . . say to catch a bus to go somewhere, it's a real drag. We can't seem to get with it.[6]

The similarity in the emotional reactions of the unemployed and of psychotic patients was highlighted by a study conducted in the Great Depression. The level of negativity and pessimism about the future in large samples of the Scottish and Lancashire unemployed was found to be greater than that of groups of psychotically depressed and schizophrenic patients.[7] If the unemployed are as distressed as hospitalized psychotic patients, how can we hope that the unemployed psychotic people will return to normal during hard times? In fact we may ask, as does the author of the study of the Scottish and Lancashire jobless, "why mentally distressed unemployed . . . do not become psychotic."[8]

The answer is, of course, they may well do so. Brenner found that it was precisely that segment of the population that suffers the greatest relative economic loss during a depression – young and middle-aged males with moderate levels of education – that showed the greatest increase in rates of admission to New York mental hospitals for functional psychosis during an economic downturn. Prominent among these patients were first admissions for schizophrenia.[9] We saw in Chapter 2 that the likeliest explanation for this effect was a true increase in the occurrence of psychosis secondary to the stresses of the economic recession and unemployment. In Chapter 9 we shall explore in more detail whether labor dynamics significantly affect the rate of occurrence of schizophrenia. Here we shall concentrate on how far the labor market influences the course and outcome of the illness.

Unemployment may exert an indirect influence on some psychotic patients in the community. One stress factor known to be associated with poor outcome in schizophrenia is the effect of living with hostile, critical or emotionally overinvolved relatives. The greater the proportion of time a schizophrenic person spends in the company of such a relative, the greater is his or her chance of relapse.[10] During a depression, both the relative and the patient are more likely to be unemployed and at home together. For the minority of schizophrenic people who live with such a relative, this may be a serious stress. A successful treatment program which has been developed to reduce the high risk of relapse for such patients uses as one of its techniques efforts to increase the separation of patient and relative by getting one of them out of the house and at work.[11]

On the other hand, the home environment for the unemployed patient may be too understimulating. It was found in one five-year follow-up study of schizophrenic people in London that for patients who were unemployed and living at home, the length of time spent doing absolutely nothing was similar to that of patients in backward asylums.[12] Such poverty of daily existence is known to be closely allied to the clinical poverty of institutionalism and the negative features of schizophrenia.[13]

To emphasize, thus, the stresses of unemployment for schizophrenic people is not to overlook the fact that, for many of these individuals, the stress of employment is also a major difficulty. Schizophrenic people experience severe problems, argues psychiatrist Hans Huessy, as a consequence of the "fabulously highly developed division of labor in industrial society."[14] Work-related stress is certainly important for these patients. In one group of schizophrenic people, for example, 60 per cent had experienced a stressful life event in the three weeks before their psychotic breakdown; of these, the stress for one-third had been related to stopping or starting work, completing job training or changing hours of employment.[15] Starting work, however, is an acute stress which, if weathered, may lead the psychotic person to higher functioning. Unemployment, on the other hand, brings the chronic strain of low status and purposelessness, which may prevent recovery. Whichever part of the picture we study, nevertheless, it seems likely that the labor market is closely involved in the social production and perpetuation of psychosis.

THE INDUSTRIAL RESERVE ARMY

Unemployment, argued Friedrich Engels, is not an aberration but an unavoidable component of capitalist production:

> It is clear that English manufacture must have at all times save the brief periods of highest prosperity, an unemployed reserve army of workers, in order to be able to produce the masses of goods required by the market in the liveliest months.[16]

Karl Marx, like Engels, maintained not only that "a surplus labouring population is a necessary product of accumulation . . . on a capitalist basis" but that it is also

> a condition of existence of the capitalist mode of production. It forms a disposable industrial reserve army, that belongs to capital quite as absolutely as if the latter had bred it at its own cost.[17]

Marx developed this concept in some detail in *Capital* and distinguished various components of the reserve army of labor. The segment which he labeled the "stagnant" category of the "relative surplus population" would these days be called the secondary labor force. It is characterized by

> extremely irregular employment. Hence it furnishes to capital an inexhaustible reservoir of disposable labour-power. Its conditions of life sink below the average normal level of the working class.[18]

Even the most poverty-stricken among them are "in times of great prosperity . . . speedily and in large numbers enrolled in the active army of labourers."[19] Many of the marginally functional mentally ill are to be found in this group and in the related category of

> those unable to work, chiefly people who succumb to their incapacity for adaptation, due to the division of labour; . . . the victims of industry, . . . the mutilated, the sickly, the widows, &c.[20]

The size of the industrial reserve army in modern times is considerable. The ranks of the officially unemployed have to be multiplied several times to include discouraged workers, housewives who wish to work, the underemployed and the disabled (who could be rehabilitated).[21] The true United States unemployment rate during the early 1970s, according to political scientist Charles Anderson, might be realistically estimated at 25 per cent.[22] Since then it has become considerably greater. In the 1980s official unemployment in the United States exceeded 10 per cent, and in Britain ran close to 14 per cent. These figures conceal even more massive wastage of human power in certain segments of the population. Official unemployment among adult black men in the United States rose to 45 per cent in the 1980s; and if black men not counted by the census-takers were included, the figures would indicate that fewer than half of adult black males are employed. Increasingly, U.S. workers are employed in low-paid jobs – in 1990 a fifth of American workers, a third of Hispanic-Americans, earned too little, working full-time, to keep a family out of poverty. With the definition of "full employment" being adjusted upwards with some regularity – most recently to 6.5 per cent in the United States; with poverty increasing – nearly a sixth of American families, a third of black families, living in poverty in 1992; it cannot be argued that the industrial reserve army has been demobilized.[23]

REHABILITATION AND REINTEGRATION

Marx's analysis suggests that the treatment of the great majority of the mentally ill will reflect the condition of the poorest classes of society. In the absence of a powerful political counter-force the outlook in schizo-phrenia is unlikely to get better. Despite the fact that an improvement in conditions of living and employment for people with psychotic disorders may yield higher rates of recovery, this consideration will remain secondary. Significant treatment efforts will be expended only on those skilled workers who are acutely mentally ill and whose disappearance from the work force involves the loss of a substantial investment in training. Efforts to rehabilitate and reintegrate the chronically mentally ill will only be seen at times of extreme shortage of labor – after the other battalions of the industrial reserve army have been mobilized. At other times, the primary emphasis will be one of social control. The rate of recovery of those who have an "incapacity for adaptation" will, then, be a barometer of the extent of unemployment.

There is evidence to support this interpretation. In earlier chapters, for example, we have seen that successful rehabilitation and social reintegration of the mentally ill are related to the demand for labor and, in many instances, this success appears to be a reflection of the intensity of the rehabilitative efforts. To recapitulate:

- Rehabilitation of the mentally and physically disabled is more successful in wartime and during periods of labor shortage.
- Deinstitutionalization began, before the introduction of the antipsychotic drugs, in those north European countries that had low unemployment rates.

- The number of mental hospital beds provided in the industrial nations in 1965 was related to the national unemployment rate.
- The proportion of schizophrenic people in hospital at follow-up increased during the Great Depression.
- Discharge and recovery rates in labor-starved, early nineteenth-century America may have been higher because of the availability of moral treatment in the public asylums.
- Recovery rates and treatment efforts declined as pauperism and unemployment became more common in the new republic.

Just how does the labor market influence approaches to the mentally ill? Rehabilitative and reintegrative efforts for psychiatric patients are composed of three inter-related elements:

(1) political consensus, or state mental health policy;
(2) professional consensus, or psychiatric ideology; and
(3) social consensus, or tolerance of the mentally ill.

A speculative attempt to illustrate how these components may vary with the business cycle is set out in Table 6.1. At any one time, opposing sets of attitudes may be encountered, but as the economic climate changes so does the balance of opinion.

Table 6.1 Differences in rehabilitative and reintegrative efforts for the mentally ill during the depression and the boom

Depression	Boom
Political consensus	
Custodial care is necessary to protect the community	Community care is preferable
Hospital expansion is required	A cost-benefit analysis of psychiatric rehabilitation must include savings resulting from patients'' increased productivity
Professional consensus	
Schizophrenia is incurable	Schizophrenia is curable
Genetic and biological factors are important causes of psychosis	Social factors are important causes of psychosis
Hospitals are therapeutic	Mental institutions are harmful
Early discharge is dangerous	
Physical, surgical and pharmaceutical treatment methods are most valuable	Psychosocial treatment is valuable in psychosis
Neurotic patients are more treatable than psychotic	Treatment efforts should be directed towards the severely mentally ill
Social consensus	
The mentally ill are dangerous and should be locked up	Anybody can become mentally ill
I would not want to work with/live next to/marry a mental patient	

It becomes clear from this formulation that psychiatric ideology may be influenced by changes in the economy – a notion which implies a rejection of the conventional concept of scientific progress inherent in mainstream medical history. There are certainly grounds for this position. As we have seen, when recovery rates and treatment standards declined at the end of the moral-management era, and at the onset of the Great Victorian Depression, psychiatric philosophy became pessimistic and turned from an interest in social causes of illness to biological and hereditary factors. Kraepelin defined schizophrenia as an incurable disease. Early discharge was considered dangerous. Eugen Bleuler reformulated the concept of schizophrenia as a condition from which many recovered without defect in the sunnier economic climate of Switzerland before the First World War. At this time, he and his colleagues at Burghölzli Hospital in Zurich – Carl Jung and Adolf Meyer – developed psychodynamic theories of schizophrenia. Bleuler encouraged the early discharge of his patients to avoid the dangers of institutionalism. During the twentieth-century Great Depression, physical treatment methods and psychosurgery were emphas- ized. Psychosis was neglected and psychiatry, especially in America, concentrated upon the long-term, dynamic treatment of less severely disturbed, middle-class and upper-class, neurotic patients. Widespread interest in social factors in mental illness, in the understanding of psychosis and in community care were not to return until 80 or 90 years after moral treatment disappeared – until the boom decades after the Second World War. By contrast, psychiatry in post-revolutionary Russia during the early twentieth century pursued a different course – a method of psychological and social reintegration which evolved from the work of Ivan Pavlov.[24]

Ideological views which emerge counter to the mainstream of psychiatric thought make no headway in the face of a contrary political and social consensus. Critics, in the mid-Victorian era, who objected to the expansion of asylums into mammoth institutions where individual treatment was impossible were ignored by local authorities and a tax-conscious populace concerned to maximize cost-efficiency.[25] Hospital superintendents who attempted to establish open-door policies before the advent of the postwar social psychiatry revolution were defeated by public opinion.[26] Alfred Adler, in the 1930s, gained little recognition for his views on the import- ance of social factors in psychopathology; and the work of American social scientists in the 1930s on the interaction of culture and mental disorder did not influence psychiatric theory or practice to an appreciable degree.[27]

A recent example further illustrates how psychiatric philosophy is molded by the politics of the period. In 1981, as part of a nationwide trend towards budgetary cuts in human services, the City and County of Denver, Colorado, sharply reduced its allocation to Denver General Hospital. The administrators of the community mental health center, which formed a part of the hospital, responded by drastically cutting their services to their most severely disturbed clients – money-losing outreach services to hundreds of ex-state hospital clients in boarding homes, including a day-care program, alternative supportive housing, sheltered employment and vocational training. A number of these chronically ill clients brought a class action suit against the hospital and its funding agencies, demanding reinstatement of these essential services. The psychiatrists and admini-strators of the mental health center entered the following defense: there was no evidence to show that the type of community services they had been providing to the chronic psychotic patients were at all effective.[28] Their view was incorrect,[29] but this is incidental. The point of interest here is that less than a decade earlier the Colorado state legislators had been assured that such community treatment methods were so superior that the state hospitals could be run down and the funds diverted to community mental health centers. The change from buoyant optimism to the depths of pessimism had taken less than ten years – from legitimizing the last stages of deinstitutionalization to legitimizing the final abandonment of the same patients to poverty and neglect in their inner-city ghetto. The story of moral treatment is, here, being repeated under similar economic conditions. The cause for mounting pessimism appears the same in each case – governmental indifference leaves the patients stranded in sordid environments, without adequate treatment and without a purpose in life. The victims are blamed each time, however; it is, supposedly, the inherently incurable nature of the patients" condition which indicates that we should not waste time and money treating them.

SOCIAL TOLERANCE

Can it be shown that public tolerance of the mentally ill is similarly affected by the economic climate? In general, discrimination, prejudice and nega-tive stereotyping are known to increase sharply as competition for scarce jobs increases. Negative attitudes towards ethnic minority groups become more common during hard times.[30] But information about the effect of the economy on attitudes toward the mentally ill is limited. In Britain, many observers noted an improvement in public attitudes towards mental patients at the time of the postwar social psychiatry revolution.[31] As Professor Morris Carstairs wrote in 1961:

> Few would claim that our current 'wonder drugs' exercise more than a palliative influence on psychiatric disorders. The big change has been rather one of public opinion.[32]

In America, in line with the higher unemployment, the later onset of deinstitutionalization and the less intense rehabilitative and reintegrative thrust of that movement, public attitudes were slower to change. Com-munity studies from the 1950s reported that attitudes towards the mentally ill were characteristically negative and rejecting.[33] By the 1960s there were indications that the general public was becoming more accepting,[34] but there was no subsequent demonstrable improvement in the status of the mentally ill during the economic stagnation of the 1970s.[35]

REHABILITATION EFFORTS – CAUSE OR EFFECT?

Having seen that both recovery rates in schizophrenia and rehabilitative efforts expended on the mentally ill tend to diminish during the depression, the question of cause and effect remains to be addressed. Do the patients fail to get better because nobody bothers to treat them, or does nobody bother to treat them because they fail to get better? Earlier in this chapter it was suggested that unemployment has a direct psychological impact on those who are out of work, including the mentally ill, and could thus stand in the way of recovery from psychosis. Can we rule out the additional possibility, implicit in Marxist theory, that a labor glut so diminishes the political incentive to rehabilitate the mentally ill that treatment efforts and community integration are discouraged, thereby worsening recovery rates?

Like most "chicken and egg" questions, this one is probably unanswerable. The events occurring at times of major policy change are so tightly intertwined that no one factor can be recognized as causative. Kathleen Jones, for example, sees three components to the postwar British social psychiatry revolution – the open-door movement, the introduction of the antipsychotic drugs and legislative developments:

> From the point of view of therapy or of public policy, the coincidence of these three movements was fortunate, since each reinforced the other. From the point of view of social analysis, it was less so, since it made it impossible to trace cause and effect with any confidence. The three strands of development crossed and re-crossed, becoming so interwoven that it will probably never be possible to determine what influence each had.[36]

Certainly there is no indication, in the case of postwar Britain, that psychiatrists, noting greater success rates, dragged politicians unwillingly along. As early as 1948, the National Health Service Act established local authority mental health departments which assumed responsibility for community care for the mentally ill; in 1954 a parliamentary bill pushed for further modernization of mental health services and hospitals; and, in the same year, a Royal Commission was formed to consider legislative reforms which would facilitate community care.[37] All this occurred before the widespread introduction of the antipsychotic drugs and contemporaneous with the earliest moves to open the doors of the psychiatric wards. It seems probable that the political incentive to put into practice advances in psychiatric care and to increase the rehabilitation of the mentally ill was already there – stimulated by the urgent need for labor.

The question of cause and effect has a practical aspect. If it were possible to maintain employment for the mentally disabled artificially during hard times, would recovery rates improve (and admission rates and treatment costs decline), or would the social and political consensus existing during the depression limit the potential for improvement in the course of psychosis? It seems quite possible, in fact, that the effect of the social and political forces would be to obstruct the development of preferential employment for mental patients. Since the earliest days of institutions, workers in the regular labor force have objected to the unfair competition of inmates' labor during periods of unemployment. Charles Dickens illustrates this point by contrasting the prisons of labor-starved America in the 1840s with those of Britain, where a surplus of workers existed:

> America, as a new and not over-populated country, has, in all her prisons, the one great advantage, of being able to find useful and profitable work for the inmates; whereas, with us, the prejudice against prison labour is naturally very strong, and almost insurmountable, when honest men who have not offended against the laws are frequently doomed to seek employment in vain. Even in the United States, the principle of bringing convict labour and free labour into a competition which must obviously be to the disadvantage of the latter, has already found many opponents, whose number is not likely to diminish with access of years.[38]

Here, in a nutshell, is the antagonism between unemployment and rehabilitation and recovery in mental illness.

More recent examples may readily be found. In the 1930s, efforts were made to introduce into British psychiatric hospitals methods of work therapy designed (by Dr. Herman Simon of Gütersloh, Germany) to discourage "idleness or fatuous madness." The failure of these efforts is explained by David Clark:

> The world-wide depression of the 1930s may have made it difficult to justify diverting work to hospital patients when fit men outside were unemployed.[39]

In modern times, sheltered workshops in the United States, which generally provide employment for the disabled by contracting for piece-work with industry, face similar difficulties. During a business recession, fewer contracts are available and disabled workers have to be laid off. Alternatively, the workshops can bid to complete contracts for less than the actual cost. This makes them reliant upon government subsidies which are liable to be cut back as the depression deepens. Some workshops go bankrupt, others find that their attempts to subsidize their programs and under-bid for contracts are opposed by labor unions. Government-sponsored job programs, furthermore, tend to concentrate on finding work for higher functioning workers as unemployment mounts. All in all, it seems likely that, despite the best efforts and intentions of mental health professionals, it may not be possible completely to overcome the negative effects of the business slump on the course of schizophrenia.

LABOR DYNAMICS

Recovery from schizophrenia may worsen in the depression, it seems, because unemployment directly affects schizophrenic people and because the reduced demand for labor results in a deterioration of rehabilitation and reintegration efforts. Economic hardship in the depression may also affect psychotic individuals. We can explore just how powerful is the effect of labor dynamics on the course of schizophrenia by looking beyond the effects of the business cycle to broader relationships between the utilization of labor and outcome in schizophrenia. Specifically, we may predict:

• If one sex is less severely affected by labor market forces, members of that sex will tend to achieve better outcome in schizophrenia.
• If one social class is more affected by the rigors of the labor market, that class should experience poorer outcome in schizophrenia.
• Schizophrenic outcome will be better in industrial nations with continuous full employment unaffected by cyclical changes.
• Outcome in schizophrenia will be better in non-industrial societies where wage labor and unemployment are uncommon.

These predictions allow us to discriminate, to a certain extent, between the effects of the labor market and of economic hardship – only in some of these instances can we expect economic hardship to produce the same direction of change in the course of schizophrenia. Let us see how accurate are these predictions.

SEX DIFFERENCES IN RECOVERY FROM SCHIZOPHRENIA

Despite the fact that the level of female unemployment is often higher than that for males in the United States, for most of this century men have suffered more from the fluctuations of the labor market than have women. In general, substantially fewer women have been involved in wage work than men, and women are more likely to have a valued social role when not earning a wage. One could argue that patients who return to an assured role as a homemaker will experience less difficulty than those who must re-enter the competitive labor market. Furthermore, as Brenner[40] has pointed out, men are more adversely influenced by a recession than women. During the Great Depression and subsequent business downturns, male unemployment increased more than female unemployment and often surpassed it. From this, one might reasonably predict that the course of schizophrenia in women in Western industrial society will be milder than in men.

"That the probability of recovery is greater in women than in men . . . may now be regarded as established,"[41] wrote Dr. Thurnam in his *Observations and Essays on the Statistics of Insanity*, as early as 1845. His analysis showed that the proportion of patients discharged as recovered from the asylums of his day was consistently higher for female than for male admissions. In more recent times Professor Ödegard, in studying all first admissions to Norwegian psychiatric hospitals from 1936 to 1945, found a higher early discharge rate for female schizophrenic patients than for male.[42] Two follow-up studies of schizophrenic patients who entered hospital in Finland in the 1960s show that women patients were more likely to be symptom-free, working and functioning independently.[43] Psychiatrist James Beck has noted that outcome studies often demonstrate that male schizophrenic patients do worse than female but that women are never found to fare worse than men.[44] Similarly, in two different WHO international follow-up studies of schizophrenia, proportionally fewer women subjects were in the worst outcome group at follow-up, and more were in the best outcome category. In the industrial countries, in particular, women tended to have shorter episodes of schizophrenic psychosis.[45] In addition, Brenner's data show that female patients with functional psychosis are less likely than men to be admitted or readmitted to psychiatric hospital when unemployment increases.[46] These sex differences confirm the impression that labor dynamics may influence outcome in schizophrenia. The gap may narrow, however, as the proportion of women in the labor force in Western industrial societies continues to increase and the proportion of men falls.

SOCIAL CLASS

Some social scientists have argued that the social groups that suffer the most stress during the depression are those that suffer the greatest *relative* decline in status – the unemployed among the middle classes, for example.[47] On this basis Brenner has explained the particularly heavy impact of the depression on the mental hospital admission rate of more highly educated male patients.[48] This is as may be; but the business cycle aside, the social classes that come off worst in the competition for jobs are, clearly, the poorest. Black unemployment in the United States, for example, is regularly twice that of whites, in good times or bad. Unskilled workers in the secondary labor force have the least job security of any group, and the lowest status. Their work is often casual, menial, highly routine and, always, poorly paid. Alienation from the creative process is greatest, in general, in the working class. Clearly, if any group were to experience constant difficulty in gaining and holding wage work and in deriving self-esteem and gratification from their employment it would be those in the lowest social classes.

It comes as no surprise to find that recovery from psychosis is worst in the lower socioeconomic groups. Admission rates were higher for pauper lunatics in Victorian Britain and, as we saw in Chapter 5, their recovery rates were lower. Similarly, in modern times, not only is the incidence of serious mental disorder greater in the lower classes (as we saw in Chapter 2), but the outcome from psychosis is distinctly worse. A study conducted in Bristol, England, of male schizophrenic patients first admitted in the early 1950s found that patients from the lower social classes had longer hospital stays, were much less likely to be improved or recovered at the time of discharge, were liable to be readmitted earlier and were very much more likely to become chronically institutionalized than were upper-class patients. The lower-class patients in the community, moreover, were less likely to be employed and showed worse overall social adjustment.[49] The author of this study, Dr. B. Cooper, concludes:

> It seems most likely that clinical condition and economic status are mutually related and interacting, and that the patient who fails to return to useful work is more prone to schizophrenic relapses.[50]

Other investigations have produced similar results. Another British study of male schizophrenic patients from the 1950s found that lower-class patients had longer admissions.[51] In New Haven, Connecticut, August Hollingshead and Frederick Redlich in the 1950s showed that lower-class patients spent longer in hospital and were more likely to be readmitted.[52] Repeating that study a decade later, Jerome Myers and L. L. Bean also found that lower-class patients were more likely to be kept in hospital and more likely to be readmitted. In the community, the patient of low social class had a worse work record (except for homemakers, where ex-patients performed as well as healthy people), and was more socially isolated and stigmatized.[53] A 1974 follow-up study of schizophrenic patients from the eastern United States demonstrated that social class was strongly related to symptomatic outcome. Lower-class patients had more psychotic symptoms when interviewed 2–3 years after discharge from hospital.[54] Finally, the WHO international follow-up study of schizophrenia found that having a higher-status occupation was one of the best predictors of good outcome for patients living in cities in the developed world (London, Moscow, Prague, Washington, D.C. and Aarhus, Denmark).[55]

Three studies do *not* show a significantly longer duration of hospital stay for lower-class schizophrenic people. Two of these, however, were conducted in Britain during the early 1950s, when there was full employment.[56] Under such conditions, one might expect some improvement in schizophrenic outcome in the lower classes (although Cooper's contrary findings for schizophrenic patients in Bristol were also from this period). Ödegard's study of Norwegian hospital admissions from 1936 to 1945 failed to show a consistent pattern of longer hospital stay for patients from lower-status occupations. Ödegard recognized that his results did not conform to the usual pattern found in other countries, and he attributed the findings to the fact that some of the lower-status occupations in Norway, such as public service employment, carried better economic job security, which resulted in the unusually high discharge rates for patients from these groups.[57]

Overall, it is apparent that the majority of studies, and the more comprehensive among them, point to worse outcome in schizophrenia for the lower classes. A number of factors might explain this phenomenon – economic hardship, different levels of tolerance in the family or in the community, or even, as some American researchers have argued, "more limited and rigid concepts of social reality" and poorer "drug compliance" in the lower-class patients.[58] In conjunction with the other material in this chapter, however, the finding may be taken as further support for a link between labor dynamics and the course of schizophrenia.

FULL EMPLOYMENT

Professor Luc Ciompi argues that the benign course of schizophrenia in Switzerland may be a result of the "exceptionally favorable socioeconomic conditions which prevail" in that country. He followed up more than 1,600 schizophrenic patients admitted throughout the century to the University Psychiatric Clinic in Lausanne until they passed the age of 65. Twenty-seven per cent had completely recovered and a further 22 per cent were only mildly disturbed. Thus, about half of the patients had a favorable ultimate course of their illness.[59] Such results are better than average for the Western nations. Are they a result of the full employment that has long existed in Switzerland? Unemployment, there, has rarely reached 1 per cent since the Second World War, and through the 1960s and early 1970s was generally around a tenth of that figure. Even during the Great Depression Swiss unemployment did not scale the heights common throughout the rest of Europe.[60] As Professor Ciompi remarks:

> If the socioeconomic condition is Switzerland did indeed exert a favorable influence on outcome, that would certainly be a highly significant finding. It would suggest that under favorable circumstances schizophrenia may run a predominantly favorable course.[61]

It would be equally significant if it could be shown that a benign course to schizophrenia was a by-product of the full employment that used to exist in planned socialist economies. The job security and the lower-intensity, slower-paced labor process that were usual under socialist central planning[62] could have been particularly suitable for the rehabilitation of schizophrenic patients. In the U.S.S.R., continuous full employment existed from 1930 until the collapse of the communist regime. A right to work was recognized, and workers could expect jobs to be found for them even if they were barely productive.[63] As the mayor of Moscow pointed out on a visit to London in 1983, "It might be difficult for you to understand, . . . but one of the main issues we face in Moscow is the lack of labor hands in the city."[64] In Moscow, Leningrad and other large cities at that time, vocational rehabilitation programs for the mentally disabled were highly developed and psychiatrists gave a great deal of attention to patients' optimal work placement.[65]

In fact, outcome from schizophrenia in Moscow in the late 1960s was shown to be better than for patients in Western industrial countries. The WHO International Pilot Study of Schizophrenia is a large-scale, cross-national, collaborative project which was conducted simultaneously in nine countries in the West, in the Eastern Bloc and in the Third World. (This study will be discussed in more detail in the next chapter.) Schizophrenic patients were selected from among those admitted to psychiatric centers in 1968 and 1969. On initial evaluation (as mentioned in Chapter 1) the groups of patients in most centers appeared to be comparable, but a standardized evaluation procedure showed that psychiatrists in Moscow and Washington, D.C. were using a broader, more inclusive diagnostic concept of schizophrenia. At two-year follow-up, overall outcome for the schizophrenic patients in Moscow was found to be better than for those admitted to the Western centers in London, Washington, D.C., and Aarhus (Denmark). Although relatively few of the Russian patients made a rapid and complete recovery (as can be seen in Table 7.1 in the next chapter), nearly half of these patients had favorable outcome – that is, they had been non-psychotic for less than a year or had, at least, shown no serious social impairment for longer than four months during the two-year follow-up period. By the same standardized follow-up criteria, only slightly more than a third of the patients in the centers in Britain, America and Denmark showed as great a degree of overall improvement. Substantially fewer of the Russian patients, furthermore, were in the worst outcome category at follow-up.[66] The superior recovery rates for schizophrenic patients in Moscow may have been an artefact of the broader diagnostic approach there; yet a similarly inclusive diagnostic concept in Washington, D.C. does not seem to have led to better outcome for the American schizophrenic patients.

Recovery from schizophrenia in the WHO study was, however, no better in Prague (Czechoslovakia) than in the West, despite a labor shortage in Prague at that time. This difference between outcome in Moscow and Prague is difficult to explain. We can only say that the data so far available from full-employment societies are ambiguous, but that there is some evidence that such societies benefit from a more benign course to schizophrenia than is found in industrial nations with significant levels of unemployment.

We have gone a long way towards demonstrating that socioeconomic conditions shape the course of schizophrenia. Outcome data on schizophrenia in the Depression, in the two sexes, in different social classes and in different political-economic systems all tend to support the notion that the effects of the labor market and, possibly, economic hardship are critical. In all of these instances the observed differences in the course of schizophrenia may be explained by either a direct effect of unemployment on the psychotic individual or by the influence of the demand for labor on rehabilitative and reintegrative efforts. In all these instances except one – the difference in recovery patterns for men and women – economic hardship may also be an important stress leading to relapse or poor outcome.

One further prediction remains to be examined – that if labor-market conditions can adversely affect the course of schizophrenia, the illness should be more benign in non-wage-labor settings. In the next chapter we will examine this possibility and also use the opportunity to study how major differences in political and domestic economy may affect the schizophrenic person.

SUMMARY

- Spending on psychiatric hospital care increases during a depression.
- The effect of both economic stress and unemployment on patients in the community could account for the decreased recovery rate from schizophrenia during the twentieth-century Great Depression.
- Many of the negative features of chronic schizophrenia are identical with the psychological sequelae of long-term unemployment.
- Rehabilitative and reintegrative efforts for the mentally ill fluctuate with the business cycle and may contribute to changes in schizophrenic outcome.
- Female schizophrenic patients achieve better outcome than male.
- Schizophrenic patients of lower social class achieve worse outcome than higher-class patients.
- Schizophrenic outcome in full-employment societies may be better than in other industrial nations.

Chapter 7

Schizophrenia in the Third World

Two to four billion dollars were spent on the treatment of schizophrenia in the United States in 1971[1] – about 0.5 per cent of the gross national product. This figure excludes social security benefits for schizophrenic patients and other indirect costs. Such a substantial investment should surely have yielded Americans significantly better rates of recovery than in less affluent parts of the world. By contrast, psychiatric care is very low on the list of priorities in developing countries. Despite this fact, the evidence points overwhelmingly to a much better outcome from schizophrenia in the Third World. It is worth looking at this evidence in some detail.

BRIEF PSYCHOSES IN THE THIRD WORLD

There are numerous reports that psychoses have a briefer duration in the Third World, and virtually none to indicate that such illnesses have a worse outcome anywhere outside the Western world. Transitory delusional states (*bouffées délirantes*) in Senegal, for example, with such typical schizophrenic features as "derealization, hallucinations, and ideas of reference dominated by themes of persecution and megalomania"[2] occasionally develop the classic, chronic schizophrenic course, but generally recover spontaneously within a short period of time. Acute paranoid reactions with a favorable course and outcome are common in the Grande Kabylie of northern Algeria[3] and throughout East Africa.[4] Acute psychotic episodes with high rates of spontaneous remission are frequent in Nigeria,[5] and brief schizophrenia-like psychoses are reported to account for four-fifths of the admissions to one psychiatric hospital in Uganda.[6] Indistinguishable from schizophrenia, acute "fear and guilt psychoses" in Ghana manifest hallucinations, inappropriate emotional reactions, grotesque delusions and bizarre behavior. Under treatment at local healing shrines, such illnesses are generally cured within a week or so, although they may occasionally progress to chronic schizophrenia.[7] Doris Mayer, a psychiatrist, also found typical schizophrenic states to be more readily reversible in the Tallensi of northern Ghana.[8] Many more examples could be given of the prevalence of such brief psychoses in Singapore, Papua and other developing countries.[9] "Acute, short lasting psychoses," according to Dr. H. B. M. Murphy, a Canadian psychiatrist with much research experience in cross-cultural psychiatry, "form a major part of all recognized mental disorders . . ." in the Third World.[10]

NOT REALLY SCHIZOPHRENIA

But are they schizophrenia? Some psychiatrists would argue that these acute psychoses are indeed schizophrenia in view of the typical schizophrenic features such as hallucinations, delusions, bizarre behavior and emotional disturbances. They would also point to the minority of cases, initially indistinguishable, which develop the chronic schizophrenic picture. Others would deny that any brief psychosis can be schizophrenia precisely because schizophrenia, by definition, is a chronic illness. According to the American Psychiatric Association's most recent *Diagnostic and Statistical Manual (DSM-III-R)*,[11] a psychosis must last six months to be labeled schizophrenia. This is a terminological issue which must not be allowed to obscure the point of logic. If schizophrenia has a more benign course in the developing world (and there is considerable evidence to show that this is the case), then we might well find many schizophrenic episodes in these societies which are of a shorter duration than six months. To argue that these are not schizophrenia is to prejudge the issue.

Could these be cases of organic psychosis? Certainly, some could be. There is a high prevalence in Third World countries of trypanosomiasis, pellagra and related parasitic, nutritional and infectious disorders which may develop into psychotic states. Malaria, in particular, is often associated with acute psychotic episodes.[12] It is unlikely, however, that all brief episodes in the Third World are organic in origin. In conducting their social psychiatric survey of four aboriginal tribes in Taiwan, two psychiatrists, Hsien Rin and Tsung-Yi Lin, were particularly concerned about the diagnosis of organic and functional psychoses. They carefully separated schizophrenia from malarial psychosis, drug-induced psychosis and un-classifiable cases. Although skeptical at the outset of the study, after cross-checking their information and cross-validating their diagnoses they were forced to conclude that psychoses in general, and schizophrenia in particular, had a notably benign course among these Formosan farmers and hunters. Of ten confirmed cases of schizophrenia, only two had been active for more than two years, and five had been ill for less than a year.[13] More recent data, presented below, from the WHO ten-country study confirm the impression that the superior outcome in Third World cases is not due to the inclusion of acute psychotic episodes of organic origin.

CONFLICTING REPORTS

Some reports fail to show better outcome for schizophrenia and other psychoses in the Third World. They are relatively few and deserve a closer analysis. Dr. J. De Wet, the assistant physician superintendent of a South African mental hospital, concludes that the recovery rate from schizophrenia is no greater in his Bantu patients than is reported for Europeans. His observations were made, however, on patients treated in what appears to have been a particularly traditional and restrictive Western-style hospital setting, which we now know can have a profoundly deteriorating effect on the course of schizophrenia. Only a handful of patients in his 1943 sample were ever discharged from hospital, and these only after several months of confinement. Those who were discharged were the patients who "completely recovered": ten years later they were still doing well at home. None of the patients who remained in hospital regained anything but an indifferent functioning level or worse. The patients in De Wet's 1953 sample all received 15–30 electro-convulsive treatments and none "was discharged until two months after ECT in order that sudden relapses did not take place at home."[14] Again the results were not good. By contrast, others who are familiar with the Bantu have described excellent recovery from schizophrenia-like psychoses in their own communities.[15] Dr. De Wet's report demonstrates what happens to the usually excellent course of schizophrenia in Africans when they are managed in a traditional European hospital setting. The report is not evidence, despite De Wet's claims, of generally poor outcome from psychosis among the Bantu.

Another study which finds poor outcome from schizophrenia in a Third World peasant society comes from psychiatrist Joseph Westermeyer. Dr. Westermeyer has published an interesting series of articles on 35 psychotic subjects whom he located in 27 villages of Ventiane province, Laos. The cases were selected by asking villagers if any of their neighbors were considered *baa* or insane. Nine of the subjects so identified were rated as suffering from organic psychoses and 24 as having functional psychoses, mostly schizophrenia. Only 2 teenagers were considered no longer psychotic. The group of subjects was clearly very actively disturbed; only 2 were working and only 5 were lucid enough to provide useful information about themselves. Dr. Westermeyer compares the current functioning of these disturbed people with their pre-illness state and concludes, not unreasonably, "that severe social dysfunction was associated with psychosis in a peasant society."[16] He goes on to argue, however:

> These findings are in contrast to the social functioning of psychotic patients who are receiving psychiatric care. Follow-up studies of psychotic persons receiving psychiatric care in North America and Europe have shown that many return to economic productivity (about half of schizophrenics do so) and make a fair to good social adjustment.[17]

The problem with this conclusion is not difficult to detect. Dr. Westermeyer is comparing Lao cases who are, by virtue of the selection technique, currently highly disturbed, with Western psychotics who are followed up some time after their acute episode. Later in this chapter we shall see that many people suffering from psychosis in Third World societies are never labeled insane. Dr. Westermeyer himself, in an earlier paper, emphasizes that

> folk criteria for mental illness are determined primarily by the persistence of social dysfunctional behavior rather than by disturbances in thought and affect.[18]

Cases which are psychotic but not disruptive are overlooked by this study, as well as those who were psychotic and who have recovered. Drs Rin and Lin, in their community survey, located subjects who had been psychotic previously and had become well. They found three times as many of these individuals as active cases. Rin and Lin's technique provides something close to lifetime-prevalence data; Westermeyer, whose method detected only those who had been psychotic in the past year, provides period-prevalence data. As Dr. Westermeyer confirmed when questioned about this issue, his method has "a built-in bias for prolonged cases."[19] It gives us no indication of true recovery rates.

Follow-up studies can give us a more definitive picture of recovery from schizophrenia in the Third World. Several such reports are available, and only one, the first listed here, fails to reveal substantially better recovery rates for schizophrenic people in the developing world.

Chandigarh, India

P. Kulhara and N. N. Wig, British-trained psychiatrists, report that the outcome for schizophrenic patients treated by the Department of Psychiatry in the Postgraduate Institute of Medical Education and Research of Chandigarh, India, is no better than for schizophrenic patients in a previous study in London.[20] Modern inpatient and outpatient services were offered to the Indian schizophrenic patients admitted in 1966 and 1967 and followed up $4\frac{1}{2}$–6 years later. A criticism of this study is that of 174 cases admitted, only 100 could be found for follow-up. These included, of course, all the patients who remained in hospital but excluded those who had moved away and others who might have been expected to show a good outcome.[21] This problem may explain why Drs Kulhara and Wig report a much less impressive recovery rate for India than that found in the WHO study to be described later.

Mauritius

A follow-up study of African and Indian schizophrenic patients twelve years after their first admission to hospital was carried out in Mauritius, an island in the Indian Ocean, by the Canadian social psychiatrist Dr. H. B. M. Murphy and the superintendent of the hospital, Dr. A. C. Raman. They found that although the incidence of schizophrenia was close to the British rate, the recovery rate was outstandingly better. Sixty-four per cent of the patients had maintained a complete, symptom-free recovery, and over 70 per cent were functioning independently. The patients were initially treated in hospital without the use of antipsychotic drugs. Strenuous efforts were made to trace as many as possible for follow-up, with the result that all but 2 per cent were found.[22]

Sri Lanka

Very similar results were obtained in Sri Lanka by anthropologist Nancy Waxler, who followed up patients five years after their first admission to hospital in 1970 with schizophrenic episodes. Some of these patients had been ill for as long as five or ten years before admission. Most of the sample came from rural areas, generally from families of farmers and laborers. All but one of the 44 schizophrenic patients were traced. At follow-up, 45 per cent of the patients complained of no symptoms at all and 69 per cent had no psychotic symptoms; half of the patients were rated by a psychiatrist as having made a normal adjustment and 58 per cent were considered normal by their families. Clearly, these people were not merely well by virtue of the tolerance of their family members, they were well by a number of standards.[23]

Hong Kong

Psychiatrists W. H. Lo and T. Lo attempted to follow up, after an interval of ten years, all of the schizophrenic patients who lived on Hong Kong Island and had first attended the Hong Kong Psychiatric Centre in 1965. They were able to evaluate only 82 out of the original 133 patients. Their outcome results for this densely urbanized manufacturing center are intermediate between those for European patients and those for schizophrenic patients in Mauritius and Sri Lanka. A substantial number of their subjects had a relapsing course to their illness, but at follow-up 65 per cent were free of psychotic symptoms and a similar proportion had achieved good social recovery.[24] The outcome for these patients compares favorably with the estimated 45 per cent social recovery rate for Western schizophrenic patients (see Chapter 3).

Singapore

In a study conducted by three British-trained psychiatrists, Drs Tsoi, Kok and Chew, an effort was made to trace all 637 patients with a diagnosis of schizophrenia who were admitted for the first time to Woodbridge Hospital in Singapore during 1975. Five years after admission, 424 were located and reexamined. Despite the fact that many cases could not be traced, and that those who were reassessed included the patients who fared poorly and required readmission to hospital, the outcome results were very favorable. Complete recovery was observed in 35 per cent of cases and only minimal illness in a further 28 per cent. These results are very similar to those for Hong Kong, both sites being densely populated cities. Nearly two-thirds of the patients in the Singapore study were working, since at the time of the study labor was in short supply and jobs for patients were easy to come by.[25]

Three Indian cities

A team of psychiatrists, headed by Dr. Verghese, conducted a five-year follow-up study of all of the patients attending three Indian clinics, in Lucknow, Vellore and Madras, in 1981–82 who suffered from schizophrenia of less than two years' duration. Out of 386 patients identified, 323 were successfully traced and interviewed. Sixty-six per cent of the patients displayed a favorable overall outcome on a combination of measures: 64 per cent were free of psychotic symptoms and 40 per cent showed no deficits in working ability. The patients from rural areas did better than those from the cities.[26]

WHO PILOT STUDY OF SCHIZOPHRENIA

A problem with attempts to compare recovery rates in different parts of the world is that research studies vary in the way in which patients are selected and diagnosed and in the criteria used for measuring outcome. To clarify this picture the World Health Organization's international, collaborative follow-up study of schizophrenia[27] has brought standardized methods of diagnosis and follow-up to the analysis of outcome for psychotic patients from nine countries in the industrial and non-industrial world. Patients admitted to psychiatric centers in Aarhus (Denmark), Agra (India), Cali (Colombia), Ibadan (Nigeria), London (England), Moscow (Russia), Prague (Czechoslovakia), Taipei (Taiwan) and Washington, D.C. (U.S.A.) were evaluated according to a standardized procedure and categorized by a computerized diagnostic scheme – the CATEGO system. By this method, groups of very similar acute and chronic schizophrenic patients were selected in each of the nine centers from among those patients applying for treatment during 1968 and 1969. In seven of the centers (as mentioned in previous chapters) the patients labeled schizophrenic were found to be essentially similar, but in Moscow and Washington, D.C. the diagnosis of schizophrenia was distinctly broader. At a two-year follow-up the

Table 7.1 Percentage of schizophrenic patients in different overall outcome
groups in the *WHO International Outcome Study*

Centers	Best-outcome group	Two best-outcome groups combined %	Two worst-outcome groups combined %	Worst-outcome group %
Aarhus	6	35	48	31
Agra	48	66	21	15
Cali	21	53	28	15
Ibadan	57	86	7	5
London	24	36	41	31
Moscow	9	48	20	11
Taipei	15	38	35	15
Washington	23	39	45	19
Prague	14	34	39	30
Developed nations	15	39	37	28
Developing nations	35	59	23	13

researchers were taken by surprise at the marked variability in the course
and outcome of schizophrenia in the different centers. Patients in the
developing world showed strikingly better results.

Combining various factors, patients were categorized into five groups
according to overall outcome. As may be seen from Table 7.1, the best-
outcome category includes 35 per cent of patients from centers in the Third
World in comparison with only 15 per cent from centers in the industrialized world. These patients were psychotic for less than four months of the
two-year follow-up period and developed a full remission with no social
impairment. The two best-outcome categories combined embrace 59 per
cent of patients from the developing world but only 39 per cent of those
from industrial nations. More than a quarter of patients from the developed
world were in the worst outcome category at follow-up, twice the proportion of those from the developing nations. These patients were psychotic
for more than eighteen months of the follow-up period and were severely
socially impaired. Nigeria and India, where the catchment areas were
largely rural and most of the population was engaged in agriculture,
recorded the best overall outcome. Urbanized Cali, where unemployment
was significant, showed somewhat less satisfactory outcome. In Taipei, the
most industrially developed of the Third World centers and with serious
levels of unemployment, the outcome was little better than in the industrial
West and less good than in Moscow. Although few patients in Moscow
were in the best-outcome group, a large proportion was in the best two
groups combined, and few were in the worst categories; these results place
Moscow in an intermediate position between centers in the developed and
developing worlds.

Could patient selection have influenced these results? It is possible that the schizophrenic people presenting for treatment at Third World centers, while appearing comparable with those in the Western samples, were in fact not representative of all the schizophrenic people in the community. It seems unlikely, however, that those who were admitted for treatment would be predominantly people with less severe forms of the illness, and a more recent WHO study allows us to be certain about this point.

WHO TEN-COUNTRY STUDY

Beginning in 1978, WHO conducted another international follow-up study of people suffering from psychosis,[28] using the same standardized diagnostic procedure as in the earlier research. The study, conducted at twelve locations in ten countries around the world, aimed to include every person at each location who made contact with any helping agency because of psychotic symptoms for the first time in his or her life during the study period. The sites for the study were Aarhus, Denmark; Agra and Chandigarh, India; Cali, Colombia; Dublin, Ireland; Honolulu and Rochester, U.S.A.; Ibadan, Nigeria; Moscow, Russia; Nagasaki, Japan; Nottingham, England; and Prague, Czechoslovakia. At the Third World sites, a variety of traditional and religious healers was contacted to identify subjects – herbalists, Ayurvedic practitioners and yoga teachers in India, for example, and *babalawo* and *aladura* healers in Nigeria. This wide-ranging effort to identify every new case of psychotic illness at each location virtually eliminated the chance that the cases in any area were biased by the selection procedure.

Again, the outcome for Third World cases was substantially better, indicating that the results in the earlier WHO study were probably not a result of a selection bias. Nearly two-thirds (63 per cent) of the subjects in the developing-world sites experienced a more benign course leading to full remission compared to little more than a third (37 per cent) in the developed world. Similarly, a smaller proportion of Third World cases suffered the worst type of outcome: only 16 per cent of developing-world cases were impaired in their social functioning throughout the follow-up period compared to 42 per cent in the developed world. The superior outcome for Third World subjects was certainly not a result of more intensive treatment: more than half (55 per cent) of the developing-world cases were never hospitalized, in contrast to a mere 8 per cent in the developed world; and only 16 per cent of developing-world subjects versus 61 per cent of cases in the developed world were taking antipsychotic medication throughout the follow-up period.

Did the Third World cases experience a milder course because more of them were, in reality, suffering from some good-prognosis condition which mimics schizophrenia – an acute atypical psychosis or an organic disorder caused by an infectious agent? If this were the case, we would expect there to have been more acute atypical psychoses in the Third World sample and for the good-outcome cases to be clustered among these subjects. In fact, this was not the case. The proportion of acute illnesses and of the more atypical, broadly defined cases, it is true, was greater among the Third World subjects; but outcome was better in Third World subjects regardless of whether they were acute or insidious in onset, or whether they were "core" schizophrenic cases, diagnosed according to the most restrictive criteria, or broadly diagnosed cases.

The general conclusion is unavoidable: schizophrenia in the Third World has a course and prognosis quite unlike the condition as we recognize it in the West. The progressive deterioration which Kraepelin considered central to his definition of the disease is a rare event in non-industrial societies, except perhaps under the dehumanizing restrictions of a traditional asylum. The majority of Third World schizophrenic people achieve a favorable outcome. The more urbanized and industrialized the setting, the more malignant becomes the illness. Why should this be so?

WORK

It was argued in earlier chapters that the dwindling cure rates for insanity during the growth of industrialism in Britain and America, and the low recovery rates in schizophrenia during the Great Depression, were possibly related to labor-force dynamics. The apparently superior outcome for schizophrenia in Russia in the WHO Pilot Study, if it were not a consequence of diagnostic bias, may have been a result of full employment and an emphasis on work rehabilitation in the country at that time. The picture which has now been drawn of schizophrenia in the Third World gives more support to the notion that the work role may be an important factor shaping the course of schizophrenia.

In non-industrial societies that are not based upon a wage economy, the term "unemployment" is meaningless. Even where colonial wage systems have been developed, they frequently preserve the subsistence base of tribal or peasant communities, drawing workers for temporary labor only.[29] In these circumstances, underemployment and landlessness may become common but unemployment is rare. Unemployment may, however, reach high levels in the urbanized and industrial areas of the Third World.

The return of a person suffering from psychosis to a productive role in a non-industrial setting is not contingent upon his actively seeking a job, impressing an employer with his worth or functioning at a consistently adequate level. In a non-wage, subsistence economy, people with mental illness may perform any of those available tasks that match their level of functioning at a given time. Whatever constructive contributions they can make are likely to be valued by the community and their level of disability will not be considered absolute. Dr. Adeoye Lambo, a psychiatrist well known for developing a village-based treatment and rehabilitation program in Nigeria, reports that social attitudes in Nigerian rural communities permit the majority of those with mental disorders to find an appropriate level of functioning and thus to avoid disability and deterioration.[30] In India, research workers for the WHO follow-up study of schizophrenia encountered difficulty in interviewing their cases as the ex-patients were so busy – the men in the fields and the women in domestic work.[31] The more complete use of labor in pre-industrial societies may encourage high rates of recovery from psychosis.

But what of the nature of the work itself? John Wing, a British social psychiatrist who has done a great deal of research on schizophrenia, identifies two critical environmental factors which lead to optimal outcome from the illness. The first of these, which we will return to later, is freedom from emotional overinvolvement – smothering or criticism – from others in the household. His second criterion, which is relevant here, is that there should be stable expectations precisely geared to the level of performance that the individual can actually achieve.[32] Industrial society gives relatively little leeway for adapting a job to the abilities of the worker. High productivity requirements and competitive performance ratings may be particularly unsuitable for a rehabilitating schizophrenic person. In a peasant culture he or she is more likely to find an appropriate role among such tasks of subsistence farming as livestock management, food- and fuel-gathering or child-minding. As the authors of the WHO pilot study of schizophrenia comment about life in the countryside of India

> work in the rural setting is mostly collective, agricultural, and often does not require particular skills. Many occupations are passed from father to son. Thus, competitive situations seldom exist. The occupational pursuits do not usually require fine skill and adaptability and often do not demand much effort or strain. . . . Employment conditions in the country usually do not have any untoward effects on most patients.[33]

Many clinicians in the West have noticed that the demands of a full 40-hour week are overly taxing for psychotic clients. In hunter-gatherer and peasant societies, the distinction between work and non-work may be hard to make (in some cultures it is not linguistically possible to differentiate "work" from "ritual" or from "play"[34]), but the demands of subsistence are unlikely to be burdensome. !Kung Bushmen work no more than two to three (6-hour) days a week in hunting and food-gathering for themselves and their dependants, and about two hours further each day are spent on food preparation and "housework."[35] Slash-and-burn agriculture, for example among the Bemba of north Zimbabwe or the Toupouri of north Cameroon, calls for only three or four (5-hour) working days a week.[36]

Plough agriculture commonly requires a 30- to 35-hour work week.[37] Estimates of labor requirements for irrigation agriculture vary. In Yunnan Province in pre-revolutionary China, the working day was seldom longer than 7–8 hours, including frequent rest periods, even at the busiest time of year; during the slack months, there was virtually no farm work to be done. Elsewhere a demanding 50- to 70-hour work week has been recorded, but both of these examples of irrigation agriculture involve market production, not just local subsistence needs.[38] Where production is for use and not for exchange, labor needs tend to be low.[39]

In each setting there is wide individual variation. In pre-revolutionary Russia, for example, peasant farmers in Volokolamsk were found to work between 79 days a year in the least industrious households and 216 in the most industrious.[40] This compares with an expectation of around 230–40 working days a year for employees in modern industrial society. Work demands in many cultures are particularly low for young, unmarried adults[41] (who may be at higher risk of developing schizophrenia), but whatever the usual pattern, work-load expectations are more readily adjusted to meet the capacities of the marginally functional individual in a village setting than in the industrial labor market. There can be little doubt that it is simpler for a schizophrenic person to return to a productive role in a non-industrial community than in the industrial world. The merits of tribal and peasant labor systems are apparent: as in the West during a period of labor shortage, it is easier for family and community members to reintegrate the sick person into the society, and the psychotic person is better able to retain his or her self-esteem. The result may well be not only better social functioning of the psychotic person but also more complete remission of the symptoms of the illness.

OCCUPATION AND OUTCOME

In searching for predictors of good outcome in schizophrenia, the WHO pilot study examined a number of patient characteristics. We may look at these data for evidence of an association between occupation and outcome in schizophrenia but, in so doing, we encounter difficulties presented by the variety and complexity of work and subsistence patterns in the developing world. Poverty can be extreme in the urban slums of the Third World, where many eke out an existence by self-employment in street-vending and similar activities or with low and irregular earnings from work in the formal and informal segments of the urban labor market. Outright unemployment, however, is often most severe in the upwardly striving, urban middle classes. In rural areas, this reversal of the usual Western pattern is even more marked, with unemployment among the aspiring educated at times being severe, while those working the land are largely outside the labor market.[42]

In rural districts, therefore, we should look for a reversal of the usual Western pattern of outcome from schizophrenia and for superior outcome in the less educated – the subsistence farmers with limited exposure to Western acculturative forces. A mixed recovery picture might be expected to occur in those urban areas where economic development is incomplete and is creating stresses for the new managerial and professional classes. In the most highly developed cities of the Third World we should expect a pattern of recovery similar to the West with the best outcome in the high-status occupations. In general, we might anticipate outcome to be better in villages, where more of the population is outside the wage-labor market, than in the cities.

In fact the WHO data show neither rural nor urban living to be strong predictors of good outcome.[43] The information on residence, however, was gathered at intake rather than at follow-up. The lack of association between residence and outcome, therefore, may merely reflect what several authors have noted – that migrant laborers who fall ill while working in the industrial areas return to the village to recuperate.[44] Urban psychotic people may benefit from this return to traditional village roles.

Other WHO pilot study data more clearly document an association between occupation and outcome. Farmers were more likely than patients in any other occupation to experience the most benign pattern of illness – full remission with no relapses – and the unemployed were least likely to experience such a mild course to the psychosis. In urbanized Cali and Taipei patients from high-status professional and managerial occupations were found to achieve good overall outcome, while this was not the case in the largely rural catchment area around Agra, India.[45] This pattern confirms the impression that schizophrenia may be more benign in the successful upper classes in the industrialized setting, but more malignant among the better educated in India who are known to suffer rates of unemployment several times greater than the poorly educated and illiterate.[46] The data from Nigeria do not fit as neatly. Even though many patients in the sample appear to have come from rural districts, Nigerian schizophrenic people in managerial jobs experienced good overall outcome.[47] This could be explained by a strong local demand for educated labor at that time or, again, the high mobility of the migrant labor force may confuse the picture; patients who were unable to continue in managerial positions could return to a less demanding role in their farming community.

Migrant-labor practices allow Third World schizophrenic people to change occupation and residence after developing psychotic symptoms. Level of education, however, is less easily changed. It is therefore interesting to note that a high level of education is one of the few strong and consistent indicators of poor outcome in the Third World,[48] thus standing in contrast to Western patterns of recovery. This point, then, may be one of the most useful pieces of evidence in the WHO study, pointing to a link between good outcome for schizophrenia in the Third World and the maintenance of traditional occupational roles.

STRESS

Unemployment on the one hand and intensified work demands on the other are special stresses of modern industrial society. Are there other increased stresses of life in the fast-paced industrial world which might account for the poor prognosis for schizophrenia in the West? It depends what we mean by stress. Urban overcrowding, job insecurity, productivity pressure and alienation from the creative process are all chronically stressful facets of industrial life. Those who live in peasant communities, however, must face equal levels of domestic discord and often suffer problems of poor health, high infant mortality and inadequate housing, clothing, food and water. With the development of state-level societies and colonialism come increasing difficulties with authority, status disparity, poverty and starvation. To passing tourists, the palm-studded fishing village near Mazatlan on the west coast of Mexico might seem a subtropical paradise; but when Russell McGoodwin, an anthropologist, asked the inhabitants what caused them most suffering they listed many complaints including poverty, family problems, the burden of work, inadequate water supplies and poor clothing. In response to the question, "What do you enjoy?" nearly half answered, "Nothing."[49] Life in non-industrial societies is not low in stress. Rousseau's 'noble savage' leading a life of peace and perfect order in 'the state of nature' cannot be found. But some features of tribal and peasant life might well improve the social integration and the outlook for those who suffer from a psychotic episode.

A PSYCHOTIC EPISODE IN GUATEMALA

Maria, a young Indian woman living in a village on Lake Atitlan in Guatemala, alienates her close relatives and the people of the community by her irresponsible behavior before finally suffering a full-blown psychotic episode. She hallucinates, believing that spirits are surrounding her to take her to the realm of the dead, and she walks about the house arguing with ghosts. A local shaman perceives that she is *loca* (crazy) and diagnoses her as suffering the effect of supernatural forces unleashed by the improper behavior of certain relatives. He prescribes a healing ritual which calls for the active participation of most of her extended family. Her condition requires her to move back to her father's house, where she recovers within a week. Benjamin Paul, the anthropologist who describes Maria's case, points out several features of interest. Maria is never blamed for her psychotic behavior or stigmatized by her illness, because her hallucinations of ghosts are credible supernatural events and she is innocently suffering the magical consequences of the wrong-doing of others. The communal healing activities lead to a dramatic reversal of Maria's course of alienation from family and community. In the West, a psychotic episode is likely to lead to increased alienation. In the case of Maria, conflict resolution and social reintegration are central to her recovery and result from the folk diagnosis and treatment of her symptoms.[50]

THE FOLK DIAGNOSIS OF PSYCHOSIS

Throughout the non-industrial world, the features of psychosis are likely to be given a supernatural explanation. The Shona of southern Rhodesia, for example, believe visual and auditory hallucinations to be real and sent by spirits.[51] In Dakar, Senegal,

> one can have hallucinations without being thought to be sick. A magical explanation is usually resorted to and native specialists are consulted. There is no rejection or alienation by society. The patient remains integrated within his group. As a result, the level of anxiety is low.[52]

The psychiatrist who gives this report claims that 90 per cent of the acute psychoses in Dakar are cured because the patient's delusions and hallucinations have an obvious culturally relevant content, and he or she is not rejected by the group.

Similarly, in the slums of San Juan, Puerto Rico:

> If an individual reports hallucinations, it clearly indicates to the believer in spiritualism that he is being visited by spirits who manifest themselves visually and audibly. If he has delusions . . . his thoughts are being distorted by interfering bad spirits, or through development of his psychic faculties spirits have informed him of the true enemies in his environment. Incoherent ramblings, and cryptic verbalizations indicate that he is undergoing a test, an experiment engineered by the spirits. If he wanders aimlessly through the neighborhood, he is being pursued by ambulatory spirits who are tormenting him unmercifully.[53]

In many cases where a supernatural explanation for psychotic features is used, the label "crazy" or "insane" may never be applied. I once remarked to a Sioux mental health worker from the Pine Ridge Reservation in South Dakota that most Americans who heard voices would be diagnosed as psychotic. Her response was simple. "That's terrible."

NIGERIAN ATTITUDES TO MENTAL ILLNESS

Urban and rural Yoruba with no formal education, from the area of Abeokuta in southwestern Nigeria, were asked their opinions about descriptions of typical mentally ill people. Only 40 per cent of those questioned thought that the paranoid schizophrenic person described was mentally ill.[54] (Some 90–100 per cent of Americans labeled the subject of this vignette as mentally ill.[55]) Only 21 per cent of the uneducated Yoruba considered the description of the simple schizophrenic person to be that of a mentally ill person. (Some 70–80 per cent of American respondents called this hypothetical case mentally ill.[56])

What is perhaps even more impressive than the details about labeling psychosis in this Nigerian study is the very high level of tolerance revealed. More than 30 per cent of the uneducated Yoruba would have been willing to marry the paranoid schizophrenic person described and 55 per cent would have married the simple schizophrenic person. In contrast, when skilled workers from the area of Benin in midwestern Nigeria were asked their opinions about someone specifically labeled a "nervous or mad person," 16 per cent thought that all such people should be shot and 31 per cent believed that they should be expelled from the country. These educated Nigerians conceived of mad people as "senseless, unkempt, aggressive and irresponsible."[57]

MALAYA

In Nigeria it appears that the label "mad," "crazy" or "mentally ill" is applied only to highly disruptive individuals and brings with it harsher treatment. The same pattern has been observed in a Malay village in Pahang state. Here the term for madness, gila, is applied only to violent people. "Madmen" are always handed over to authorities outside the village for permanent banishment. Within the community of over 400 people, however, are many probable psychotic individuals who have never been labeled mad – twelve who are "eccentric," including senile elderly people and marginally functional hermits; and one "person with less than healthy brains" who spends a good deal of time praying and reading in solitude. Five people exhibiting latah – a so-called culture-bound psychosis – were also identified;[58] but this condition may not be a psychosis in the proper sense of the term.[59]

LAOS

Although Dr. Westermeyer in some of his publications disputes that psychotic people often escape being labeled baa (insane) in Laos, his own observations are very close to the findings in Nigeria and Malaya. Lao villagers are apparently slow to apply the term baa, and a person so labeled tends to have a chronic illness, usually of several years' duration, and to be highly disruptive, assaultive or bizarre. Hallucinations are never mentioned by the villagers as a feature of insanity. Unless there are local conditions restricting the development of brief psychoses so common elsewhere in the Third World, then one must assume that the reason there are so few acute cases in Dr. Westermeyer's Lao sample is that they are not considered by the villagers to be *baa*. Interestingly, the severely psychotic *baa* individuals in Laos are not exiled or assassinated but continue to receive food, shelter, clothing and humane care, and are restrained and incarcerated only as long as their violent behavior requires.[60] It is apparent that labeling is an important issue only insofar as it affects management. As we shall see in the next example, it is the concept of illness that lies behind the label that is also critical in determining care and treatment.

FOUR EAST AFRICAN SOCIETIES

Anthropologist Robert Edgerton, describing attitudes to psychosis among tribesmen of four East African pastoral and farming societies, confirms that violence and destructiveness are emphasized in descriptions of psychosis (*kichaa*) and hallucinations are virtually never mentioned.[61] Most commonly reported features of psychosis include murder, assault, arson, abuse, stealing and nakedness. The pastoralists whose homesteads are more widely dispersed and who are more free to move away from disagreeable circumstances are less concerned than the farmers about the social disruption of psychotic people.[62] The intriguing conclusion of Edgerton's survey is that the tribal view of the cause of psychosis determines not only the manner of treatment but also the level of optimism about recovery.[63] The Pokot of northwest Kenya and the Sebei of southeast Uganda have a naturalistic conception of the cause of psychosis. They implicate a worm in the frontal portion of the brain and are very pessimistic about the possibilities of cure. The Kamba of south-central Kenya and the Hehe of southwest Tanzania, on the other hand, attribute the cause of psychosis to witchcraft or stress and are optimistic about curing such disorders. The two tribes which are most unsure about their respective theories of causation, the Pokot and the Hehe, also tend to be more ambivalent about the curability of the condition. The Kamba and the Hehe, holding a supernatural theory for the cause of psychosis, favor the use of tranquilizing herbs and ritual in treatment. The pessimistic Sebei and Pokot, with the naturalistic belief system, are much more inclined to treat psychotic people harshly, as illustrated by the remarks of a Pokot shaman:

> I am able to cure mads. I order the patient tied and placed upon the ground. I then take a large rock and pound the patient on the head for a long time. This calms them and they are better.[64]

The Pokot and Sebei recommend that psychotic people should be tied up forever, allowed to starve, driven away to die or killed outright.

STIGMA

Life for some psychotic people in the Third World, according to a few of these reports, is not a bed of roses. But we should not allow reports of harsh treatment of the most severely disturbed psychotic people in some areas to obscure the central facts. Many people who would be considered psychotic in the West are not so labeled in the Third World, especially if their condition is brief or not disruptive. Many more, though labeled "crazy" like Maria the Guatemalan Indian woman, are treated vigorously and optimistically with every effort to reintegrate them rather than reject them.

Psychiatrists working in the Third World have repeatedly noted the low level of stigma which attaches to mental disorder. Among the Formosan tribesmen studied by Rin and Lin, mental illness is free of stigma.[65] Sinhalese families freely refer to their psychotic family members as *pissu* (crazy) and show no shame about it. Tuberculosis in Sri Lanka is more stigmatizing than mental illness.[66] The authors of the WHO follow-up study suggest that one of the factors contributing to the good outcome for schizophrenic people in Cali, Colombia, is the "high level of tolerance of relatives and friends for symptoms of mental disorder" – a factor which can help the "readjustment to family life and work after discharge."[67]

The possibility that the stigma attached to an illness may influence its course is illustrated by research on Navajo epileptics conducted by anthropologist Jerrold Levy in cooperation with the Indian Health Service. Sibling incest is regarded as the cause of generalized seizures, or Moth Sickness, in Navajo society, and those who suffer from the condition are highly stigmatized for supposed transgressions of a major taboo. It is interesting to learn that these individuals are often found to lead chaotic lives characterized by alcoholism, promiscuity, incest, rape, violence and early death. Levy and his co-workers attribute the career of the Navajo epileptic to the disdain and lack of social support that he or she is offered by the community.[68] To what extent, we may wonder, can features of schizophrenia in the West be attributed to similar treatment?

HIGH STATUS IN PSYCHOSIS

It seems strange in retrospect that tuberculosis should have been such a romantic and genteel illness to eighteenth- and nineteenth-century society that people of fashion chose to copy the consumptive appearance.[69] Equally curious, the features of psychosis in the Third World can, at times, lead to considerable elevation in social status. In non-industrial cultures throughout the world, the hallucinations and altered states of consciousness produced by psychosis, fasting, sleep deprivation, social isolation and contemplation, and hallucinogenic drug use are often a prerequisite for gaining shamanic power.[70] The psychotic features are interpreted as an initiatory experience. For example, whereas poor Puerto Ricans who go to a psychiatric clinic or insane asylum are likely to be highly stigmatized as *locos* (madmen), schizophrenic people who consult a spiritualist may rise in status. Sociologists Lloyd Rogler and August Hollingshead report:

> The spiritualist may announce to the sick person, his family, and friends that the afflicted person is endowed with *facultades* (psychic faculties), a matter of prestige at this level of the social structure.[71]

The study indicates that Puerto Rican schizophrenic people who consult spiritualists may not only lose their symptoms, they may also achieve the status of mediums themselves. So successful is the social reintegration of the male Puerto Rican schizophrenic people studied that, after some readjustment of family roles, their wives found them more acceptable as husbands than did the wives of normal men.

Similar folk beliefs exist in Turkey. Dr. Orhan Ozturk, a psychiatrist in Ankara, writes:

> A person may be hallucinated or delusional, but as long as he is not destructive or very unstable he may not be considered insane. . . . Such a person may sometimes be considered to have a supernatural capacity for communication with the spirit world and may therefore be regarded with reverence and awe.[72]

Ruth Benedict tells us that Siberian shamans who dominate the life of their communities

> are individuals who by submission to the will of the spirits have been cured of a grievous illness. . . . Some, during the period of the call, are violently insane for several years; others irresponsible to the point where they have to be constantly watched lest they wander off in the snow and freeze to death. . . . It is the shamanistic practice which constitutes their cure.[73]

Several other writers have suggested that indigenous healers who have suffered psychotic episodes may find their elevated status and well-defined curing role to be a valuable defense against relapse.[74] Psychiatrist Fuller Torrey argues, however, that few shamans can be psychotic. The role is too responsible and demanding, he claims, for a schizophrenic person to manage.[75] While, no doubt, many healers are not psychotic, Dr. Torrey underestimates the importance of features of psychosis as an initiatory experience. He is neglecting, on the one hand, the heightened possibility of complete remission for Third World psychotic people and, on the other hand, the capacity of schizophrenic individuals to be completely functional in some areas of their lives despite islands of illogical thinking. One well-known North American Indian medicine man with whom I am familiar would doubtless be diagnosed schizophrenic by a Western psychiatrist by virtue of his extremely tangential and symbolic speech, which is often incomprehensible, his inappropriate emotional responses and his halluci- nations. This man, however, is highly respected by his community and often travels the country on speaking engagements. The psychotic individual may be able to function well as a shaman, argues anthropologist Julian Silverman of the U.S. National Institute of Mental Health, because

> the emotional supports. . . available to the shaman greatly alleviate the strain of an otherwise excruciatingly painful [schizophrenic] existence. Such supports are all too often completely unavailable to the schizo- phrenic in our culture.[76]

HEALING CEREMONIES

Being thought of as a spiritualist or healer is not the only way Third World psychotic people may gain status. Curing rituals for those with mental disorders may also enable the individual to increase his or her social status and redefine his or her social role. Anthropologist Ralph Linton observes that low-status individuals among the Tanala of Madagascar, such as second sons and childless wives, may rise in status as a result of the elaborate healing rite for mental illness.[77] Patients who participate in the curing possession cults in Trinidad,[78] among the Yoruba of Nigeria[79] and in the Zar cult of northern Ethiopia[80] have all been observed to achieve an elevation of social status as a consequence of their membership.

Initiation into these cults also provides new friends, ongoing group support and the opportunity for social involvement, and similar benefits appear to result from other healing rites. Robin Fox, a British anthropol- ogist, gives a detailed account of a clan cure for a 40-year-old woman with a chronic mental disorder in the Pueblo Indian community of Cochiti in New Mexico. The woman is a member of the Oak clan by birth, but by undergoing a healing ritual which entails adoption also into the Water clan, she acquires additional supportive relatives, a new social role and a new home. She subsequently shows complete recovery.[81]

GROUP PARTICIPATION

The process of curing in pre-industrial societies, it is clear, is very much a communal phenomenon tending not only to reintegrate the deviant individual into the group but also to reaffirm the solidarity of the community. Thus, the N'jayei secret society of the Mende tribe in Sierra Leone, which aims to treat mental illness by applying sanctions to those who are presumed to have committed a breach of social rules, provides members with a mechanism for social reintegration and, simultaneously, reinforces the integrity and standards of the culture.[82] Such a dual process of unification of the group and integration of the individual is seen to result from the great public healing ceremonies of the Zuni medicine societies[83] or from the intense communal involvement and dramatic grandeur of a Navajo healing ceremony. The Navajo patient, relatives and other participants alike take medicine and submit to ritual procedures in a symbolic recognition that illness is a problem for the community as a whole.[84]

Nancy Waxler, in her research on people suffering from psychosis in Sri Lanka, was impressed with the way in which the intense community involvement in treating mental illness prevents the patient from developing secondary symptoms from alienation and stigma and results in the sick person being reintegrated into society. She writes:

> Mental illness is basically a problem of and for the family, not the sick person. Thus we find among the Sinhalese that almost all treatment of mental illness involves groups meeting with groups. When a mad person is believed to have been possessed by a demon the whole family, their relatives and neighbors, sometimes the whole village, join together to plan, carry out and pay for the appropriate exorcism ceremony. The sick person is usually the central focus, but often only as the vehicle for the demon, and during some parts of these ceremonies the patient is largely ignored.[85]

The importance of this process of social reintegration is confirmed by data from the two WHO outcome studies. In both the developed and developing worlds, social isolation was found to be one of the strongest predictors of poor outcome in schizophrenia.[86] Several other researchers have found this factor to be important in the genesis and outcome of schizophrenia.[87]

SOCIAL CONSENSUS

There is some anthropological evidence that broad group participation in healing not only aids the reintegration of the patient but is also a necessary and powerfully effective element in the treatment of emotional illness. The French anthropologist Claude Lévi-Strauss, for example, analyzes the effectiveness of a highly respected Kwakiutl shaman from British Columbia who is skeptical of his own healing powers. Levi-Strauss concludes that the shaman is effective despite his cynicism because "the attitude of the group" endorses his treatment. The social consensus is more important than the attitude of the healer or even of the patient.[88]

A related example of the importance of social consensus in the outcome of mental illness is provided by anthropologist Lloyd Warner's discussion of the role played in the voodoo death of an Australian aborigine by his own social group after he has been "boned" by an enemy. First the victim's kin withdraw their support and he becomes an isolated and taboo person.

Then the community conducts a mourning ritual to protect the group from the soul of the "half dead" man. Unless the group attitude is reversed by the performance of a counter-ritual, the victim shortly dies.[89] These examples illustrate, on the one hand, the powerful effect of social rejection and stigma on the course of emotional illness and the importance of social acceptance and reintegration; on the other hand, they suggest that any form of treatment which does not receive full community endorsement (and much of institutional psychiatry in the West falls into this category) has a limited chance of success. This analysis, for example, would predict that the Kamba and the Hehe of East Africa who are optimistic about the treatment of mental illness would have better recovery rates from psychosis than the Pokot and Sebei who have no confidence in the ability of their doctors to effect a cure. Edgerton's study presents no evidence, unfortunately, to indicate whether or not this is the case.

Understanding the potential of social consensus to affect outcome allows us to explain why even those individuals who are treated in modern Western-style hospitals and clinics in the developing world rather than by indigenous therapists may experience a higher recovery rate from psychosis. It is not the specific treatment technique that is critical (as long as it is not too regressive) but the social expectations that are generated around the episode of illness. The treatment approaches of the psychiatric clinic may well be supplemented by community diagnosis, rediagnosis and indigenous healing ceremonies which facilitate social reintegration of the sick person. Even among relatively Westernized city-dwellers, according to a report from Senegal, traditional cultural beliefs persist which help to alleviate psychological distress and mental disorder.[90] The existence of a social consensus for recovery and the willingness and capacity of the community to reintegrate the psychotic person are, no doubt, strongly influenced by whether he or she can serve a useful social role. The benefits of traditional community life for the psychotic person are less likely to persist in the face of changing patterns of labor use which increase the risks of unemployment and dependency.

THE FAMILY

One of John Wing's criteria for good outcome in schizophrenia mentioned earlier in the chapter was freedom for the patient from excessive emotional demands or criticism within the family. His recommendation is backed up by a good deal of social psychiatric research from the Medical Research Council in London, which was outlined in Chapter 1. The extended family structure, which is more common in the Third World, allows a diffusion of emotional overinvolvement and interdependence among family members. In Qatar, on the Persian Gulf, for example, schizophrenic patients in extended families show better outcome at follow-up than those who return to nuclear family households.[91] The emphasis on community involvement in the treatment of mental illness in non-industrial societies similarly tends to reduce family tensions. Responsibility is shared broadly and the patient often escapes blame and criticism, allowing the family to be more supportive. According to recent research, for example, relatives of schizophrenic people in Chandigarh, north India, are much less likely to be demanding or critical of their psychotic family member than are the relatives of schizophrenic people in the industrial world. In London, nearly a half of schizophrenic people have such emotionally stressful relatives; in Rochester, New York, the proportion is similar; but in north India, fewer than a fifth of schizophrenic patients were found to have critical and demanding relatives.[92] As mentioned in Chapter 1, this difference might be a consequence of the higher achievement expectations placed on Western psychotic people or of the emotional isolation so common for families of schizophrenic people in the West but so much rarer in the developing world.

In the Third World, it appears, the psychotic person is more likely to retain his or her self-esteem, a feeling of value to the community and a sense of belonging. These are things which, as we shall see, four billion dollars do not buy the schizophrenic person in the United States or elsewhere in the Western world.

SUMMARY

- Brief psychoses clinically indistinguishable from schizophrenia are a common occurrence in the Third World.
- Outcome from schizophrenia is better in the non-industrial world than in the West.
- Intermediate levels of outcome from schizophrenia have been found in the more industrialized parts of the Third World and in the pre-*peristroika* U.S.S.R.
- Third World schizophrenic people are more readily returned to a useful working role.
- In the developing world, outcome from schizophrenia is worse among the better educated – a finding which may be explained by the greater labor market stresses affecting the educated.
- The folk diagnosis of insanity stresses violence and disruption, and many psychotic people from the developing world escape this label.
- Many people with psychosis in the Third World are not stigmatized and some may even rise in status.
- Although some people suffering from psychosis in non-industrial societies may be brutally treated, in the majority of cases vigorous and optimistic efforts are made to achieve a cure.
- Curing rituals encourage broad community involvement and aid the social reintegration of the mentally ill.

- The optimistic social consensus mobilized by the curing ceremony may aid recovery from emotional disorders.
- Family patterns of support in the Third World are better suited to the rehabilitation of schizophrenic people.

Chapter 8

The schizophrenic person in Western society

What is it like to be schizophrenic in Western industrial society? For Mary Byrd in New York City, according to one newspaper report, it is an unbelievably bitter experience:

> One night last week . . . when the air felt like ice and half a foot of snow sent thousands of New Yorkers home early . . . Charlie, Mary Byrd and Frank Jarnot went home to a cluster of IBM cartons, covered with mailing labels and stamped: "Handle With Care". . . . By day, Mary huddles outside a subway entrance. There she stays until Frank comes to lead her the 50 paces to a choice spot alongside the bank building. . . . Taking care of Mary is almost a full-time job for the men, who call the 23-year-old "just a baby," and who take turns leaving hamburgers, coffee and cakes outside her box. . . . "She's living in a fantasy world," Frank says.[1]

An extreme case? Not at all. According to one estimate, roughly half of New York City's 36,000 homeless are thought to be mentally disabled.[2] According to another, there are 25,000 chronically mentally ill in New York living on the street, in missions, public shelters, flophouses and cheap hotels.[3] Of 1,235 men sleeping at a public shelter on New York's Bowery on a night in 1976, 50 per cent showed signs of obvious mental illness, excluding alcoholism; many of these men were former state hospital residents. At the Women's Shelter in New York City more than three-quarters of the women admitted in 1971 were suffering from a psychosis.[4] The degree of mental disturbance among such down and out New Yorkers is by no means slight. Mental health professionals who interviewed 100 long-time residents at the same Men's Shelter on the Bowery in 1965 found 50 per cent of the men to be psychotic and diagnosed 36 per cent of the whole group as schizophrenic. They compared this group of 100 Bowery men with a large sample of recently admitted inpatients at five local psychiatric hospitals. Startlingly enough, the residents of the Men's Shelter were found to be *more* disturbed than the inpatients according to several measures in a standardized evaluation procedure.[5]

Researchers who conducted an ethnographic survey of New York City's homeless in 1981 concluded that the ranks of the destitute on Skid Row had been greatly swollen over the prior fifteen years by large numbers of former state hospital patients. They report:

> By a stroke of grim irony, some of these ex-patients had come full circle back to the institution that had originally discharged them – this time for shelter not treatment.[6]

As the result of a class action suit filed on behalf of the city's homeless, the municipal government had been forced to open an empty state hospital building on Ward's Island as an emergency shelter.

This time around, though, conditions were far worse than when the facility had been staffed as a hospital. Now the building was crammed full of cots and there was no type of treatment or recreational activity. Infestation, disease, violence and fear were pervasive. In consequence, staff pushed and prodded the residents with nightsticks to avoid contact and to maintain order. They dealt with the men in rough language and through barked orders. One feature had not changed since the days when the building was a hospital, however – the characteristics of the residents. Eighty-four per cent of the men seeking shelter there in May 1980 were mentally ill; 60 per cent were found to be moderately or severely disturbed – mostly psychotic.[7]

There can be little doubt that patients are ending up on the streets because of the deficient aftercare planning and services of the mental health system. Nearly a quarter of the patients discharged from New York state psychiatric centers were released to "unknown" living arrangements. From one hospital, nearly 60 per cent of patients were released to an "unknown" address.[8]

This state of affairs is not confined to New York. In a random sample of 50 men on Chicago's Skid Row in the late 1960s, Robert Priest, a British psychiatrist, found 25 per cent to be certainly or probably schizophrenic.[9] Only a decade earlier, however, in 1957 and 1958, before deinstitutionalization was far advanced, an American researcher, Donald Bogue, found a mere 9 per cent of men on Skid Row in the same city to have mental illness. At that time, Bogue reported, "mentally unsound persons . . . are picked up rather promptly by the police, and . . . institutionalized."[10] A survey in Los Angeles found 50 per cent of 7,000–15,000 people living on Skid Row in 1983 to be incapacitated by chronic mental illness – 40 per cent of the men and 90 per cent of the women.[11] In Philadelphia, according to another report, 44 per cent of the Skid Row homeless, and at least a quarter of the people living on the streets and in the shelters of Washington, D.C., are schizophrenic.[12] Forty-seven per cent of the emergency shelter users in St. Louis suffer from a functional psychosis.[13] In Denver in 1981, the judge who heard most of the cases related to the mental illness statute remarked that the primary residential care provider for mental patients was the city bus company. When they stopped offering free rides on the buses "the mentally disabled people who had found a home on the Ride (the bus system) hit the streets again."[14] Up to 600,000 men and women are living on Skid Row in the major cities of the U.S.A.;[15] if we conservatively estimate that a quarter of this population are schizophrenic people, it becomes clear that lives such as Mary's are to be counted in the tens of thousands.

The dimensions of the problem are similar in other countries. Twenty-seven per cent of a sample of men sleeping in a Skid Row mission in Toronto in the 1970s were found to be psychotic; 20 per cent of all the men were suffering from schizophrenia or a paranoid state.[16] Twenty-four per cent of the men who booked into the Camberwell Reception Centre in London on a night in 1965 had previously been admitted to a psychiatric hospital for reasons other than drinking.[17] Another survey of the same shelter in the 1960s found 22 per cent of the longer-term residents to be mentally ill, mostly with schizophrenia. It was apparent that their destitution was a consequence of their illness – 90 per cent had been living in settled homes before they fell ill.[18] In two Salvation Army hostels in Central London in the late 1960s, 15 per cent of a sample of residents were "gross and unequivocal cases" of schizophrenia.[19] Robert Priest found that 32 per cent of the men in his random sample of residents of Edinburgh doss houses in the late 1960s were definitely or probably schizophrenic.[20] A 1989 survey of long-stay users of government resettlement units in Britain revealed that up to 25 per cent were suffering from schizophrenia.[21] At least a tenth of Britain's 30,000 homeless[22] were suffering from psychosis in the 1960s,[23] and in the deepening economic gloom of recent times these figures have become considerably greater. A tenth of all the schizophrenic people seen at the emergency psychiatric clinic of the Maudsley Hospital in south London during six months in 1978 and 1979, for example, were homeless; few were offered any ongoing treatment.[24] British people who suffer from a psychosis are increasingly leading lives of vagrancy and neglect.

JAILS AND PRISONS

To escape hunger many of the destitute and homeless people with psychosis steal or eat meals for which they cannot pay; to avoid cold, damp and the discomforts of homelessness many sleep in public buildings or empty houses and are arrested. As described in Chapter 4, around 6–8 per cent of the inmates of local jails in the United States suffer from psychosis; but as they account for only 2–5 per cent of jail admissions,[25] it is clear that they are detained longer than other offenders. Being destitute, they cannot bail themselves out, and judges hesitate to release the unemployed, homeless and mentally disturbed on their own recognizance.

Some of the psychotic individuals in jail are being held on serious charges, such as burglary, assault, sexual assault and arson – their crimes often a product of their mental illness. Substantial numbers of these inmates have proven too dangerous to be treated effectively in the community, but no long-term hospital care can be found for them.[26] Whatever the type of crime, in fact, many people suffering from psychosis remain in U.S. jails because hospital care or effective community care is not available. In 1991, the jail in Flathead County, Montana, held 82 mentally ill people because local psychiatric hospitals would not take them.[27] Even non-criminal mental patients are housed in jail for the sake of mere convenience. In Kentucky in 1987, 1,417 people were jailed, merely awaiting a court hearing for involuntary hospitalization,[28] and three-quarters of a random sample of admissions to Bryce Hospital in Alabama were confined in jail while awaiting admission.[29]

In U.S. state and federal prisons a similarly large proportion of the inmates suffer from psychosis:[30] in one study, 5 per cent of Oklahoma state prisoners were found to be schizophrenic;[31] 10 per cent of admissions to the Washington state prison system were psychotic, in another;[32] and 7 per cent were psychotic among Michigan prison inmates, in a third.[33] A recent review concluded that 6–8 per cent of people in U.S. prisons were seriously mentally ill and that the number is increasing.[34] In some states, psychotic patients are even sent from mental hospitals to prison for treatment; in Massachusetts, according to a 1979 report, approximately one patient every four days is transferred to prison because mental hospital staff consider the person unmanageable. Judges, furthermore, send severely mentally ill offenders to prison in preference to hospital because they find that mental health facilities frequently fail to provide adequate long-term hospital or community care for dangerous and highly disruptive patients.[35] The number of inmates of U.S. prisons and local jails in 1991 was close to 1.2 million,[36] and a modest estimate would allow that four out of every hundred of these prisoners are schizophrenic and more suffer from other psychoses. Thus, there may be as many as 50,000 schizophrenic prisoners in the United States. But if only 2 per cent of the 20 million U.S. jail *admissions* a year are schizophrenic (probably an underestimate), then hundreds of thousands of such psychotic people spend some time behind bars annually (even allowing for the repeated admission of many).

What are conditions like for the imprisoned mentally ill? Large jails and prisons in the United States generally have so many such inmates, often acutely disturbed, that they establish cell blocks as "hospital" units. In one such unit in the Baltimore city jail, mental patients may be seen sitting on their beds in a large, bare, unpainted cell gazing blankly into space. In the old asylums, conditions as bankrupt and deadening as these were rare. When I visited this jail, in one part of the unit I saw a psychotic person locked in a darkened linen closet which had been converted to a "seclusion room" by affixing a wire mesh window to the door. This patient was being detained on a misdemeanor charge but was not released to the city psychiatric hospital because, argued the staff, care was no better at the hospital.

Similar conditions have been described on the "mental ward" of a large midwestern city jail. There iron mesh had to be fixed over the inside of the barred doors "because," reported a deputy, "inmates kept running headfirst into the bars trying to injure and kill themselves."[37] In the same jail, one overtly psychotic woman who had been detained for four months was found lying in her own trash and excrement. Jail staff had not attempted to bathe her, but had instead sprayed her with disinfectant.[38] The disruptive behavior of the mentally ill in jail is routinely regarded as a "disciplinary problem;" such individuals are often held in bare cells of solitary confinement, shackled to the wall if necessary. Staff of an Illinois jail even reported "calming down" psychotic inmates with a jet of cold water from a fire hose borrowed from the neighboring fire department.[39]

Psychiatrist Edward Kaufman criticizes the violation of standards of care in the psychiatric units of U.S. prisons. One such unit in a western penitentiary

> consisted of 8 barred cells with no windows. This unit did not permit more than 1 patient out of his cell at a time. There was no television or recreational activity of any kind because the ward psychiatrist did not want a "country club atmosphere" that would attract patients to make them want to stay.[40]

In another prison psychiatric unit, the ward psychiatrist ordered the use of a "stun-gun firing rubber bullets to control threatening behavior." In a third,

> inmates who were "suicidal" were strapped nude to the bars of their cells for 48 hours before they were given a psychiatric evaluation.[41]

An administrator of the U.S. Department of Justice states:

> Jails are without question, brutal, filthy cesspools of crime – institutions which serve to brutalize and embitter men to prevent them from returning to a useful role in society.[42]

Open toilets in overcrowded cells, vermin, filth, dilapidation, brutality, homosexual rape and lack of medical care, of hygiene or constructive programs have all been documented as existing widely in U.S. jails and prisons.[43] To attempt to treat psychotic patients in such settings by the mere addition of antipsychotic drugs is scarcely calculated to improve their chances of recovery.

What accounts for such treatment of the mentally ill in a civilized society? In a word, money. State governments have drastically cut back the funding for psychiatric hospitals and have failed to maintain community mental health services at an adequate level. Police and judges have responded as they feel they must to protect the community from the crime, disruption and violence that result from the lack of support and treatment of psychotic people. State legislators do not counter this problem by boosting mental health funding because, in the first place, prison care is cheaper than hospital treatment (about four times cheaper in Colorado) and, in the second place, the expense of law enforcement and the upkeep of local jails is borne, not by the state government, but by the counties and municipalities.

In the broadest sense, however, the mentally ill are incarcerated in these degrading conditions because, where there exists a massive reserve army of unemployed, the concern to establish social control over the deviant takes precedence over the concern to provide effective rehabilitation. The same is true of sane offenders – incarceration rates rise during an economic recession (but are unrelated to crime or conviction rates),[44] and jail and prison populations tend to be greater in those Western industrial nations with the highest rates of unemployment.[45] The larger the surplus population, the greater the extent of confinement and the worse the conditions of the poor – the mentally ill among them.

WHERE ARE AMERICAN SCHIZOPHRENIC PEOPLE?

The plight of the chronically mentally ill who lead a barren existence in America's boarding homes and nursing homes has been described in Chapter 4. Here we may attempt to estimate the number of these patients who suffer from schizophrenia. Some 300,000–400,000 chronic mental patients reside in board and care homes in the United States according to the 1981 report of a committee of the Department of Health and Human Services which investigated the conditions of the chronically mentally ill.[46] The large majority of these are chronic schizophrenic patients: probably 60 per cent of this number could be so diagnosed.[47]

The same government report indicates that there are 250,000 patients in nursing homes with a primary diagnosis of mental illness, excluding elderly patients with non-psychotic, senile mental disorder. One hundred thousand of these patients were transferred directly into nursing home care from state mental hospitals; more were admitted there after an interim period in another nursing home, in hospital or in the community.[48] Only 38,000 of the mentally ill in nursing homes are under age 65. We might conservatively estimate that half of this number are schizophrenic people. Perhaps 20 to 25 per cent of the 200,000 elderly mentally ill in nursing homes suffer from schizophrenia as many of this number are afflicted with organic psychoses of late life. An estimate, therefore, of from 60,000 to 70,000 schizophrenic people in U.S. nursing homes may be reasonable.

Table 8.1 Crude estimates of the location of schizophrenic people in the U.S.A. in the 1980s

Location	Total population	% schizophrenic	Number schizophrenic	% of all U.S. schizophrenic people
Skid Row homeless	500,000–600,000	25	125,000–150,000	10–12
Jails and prisons	1,200,000	4	50,000	4
Boarding homes	300,000–400,000	60	180,000–240,000	14–19
Nursing homes	–	–	60,000–70,000	5–6
Hospitals	–	–	200,000–250,000	16–20
Totals in non-domestic setting			490,000–635,500	39–51

Note: See the text for an explanation of the derivation of these estimates.

If we add to these numbers another quarter of a million schizophrenic people resident in state, county, private and Veterans Administration hospitals,[49] and if we accept the estimate that there are around 1.25 million schizophrenic people in the United States,[50] we are forced to the discomforting conclusion that more than half of American schizophrenic people are to be found in institutions, in inadequate community settings, in jail, prison or on the streets (see Table 8.1). Fewer than 5 out of 10 schizophrenic people in treatment in the United States are likely to be living in anything resembling a family home or domestic environment. These figures alone might be considered sufficient explanation for the poor outcome from schizophrenia in America.

RESTRAINTS AND SECLUSION

We should not assume that the patients who are in hospital are necessarily in ideal therapeutic environments. Their conditions of confinement may be quite harsh. Although both restraints and seclusion, for example, have proved to be largely unnecessary in British practice, their use is still commonplace in hospitals in the United States. One report indicates that 44 per cent of patients on an acute admission unit in California are locked up in seclusion for varying periods of time.[51] The seclusion room experience often colors and dominates the psychotic person's view of his or her illness. When 62 patients at a major U.S. psychiatric hospital were asked to draw pictures of themselves and their psychosis, over a third spontaneously drew a picture of the seclusion room. Even a year after the hospital stay, the experience of seclusion, with its associated feelings of fear and bitterness, symbolized for many patients the entire psychiatric illness.[52]

It is also common for patients to be tied down to their beds with restraints in U.S. hospitals. During one month in the 1980s, a quarter of all patients evaluated in a psychiatric emergency room in Cincinnati, Ohio, were placed in restraints.[53] Mechanical restraints are frequently used on psychiatric wards, the commonest reasons being not violence but "non-conformity to community rules"[54] and "behavior disruptive to the thera-peutic environment."[55] Understaffing and overcrowding may also force the use of such measures. The Colorado Foundation for Medical Care found that the overuse of both restraints and seclusion at Fort Logan Mental Health Center in Denver, Colorado, in 1981 was the result of a shortage of direct care staff. At the Colorado State Hospital in the same year, overcrowding on the forensic unit was so severe that patients were transferred to the surgical ward and shackled to their beds in order to accommodate the overflow.[56] Such are the human consequences of cost-cutting in public psychiatric services.

STIGMA

There is more to the degradation of being schizophrenic in Western society, however, than harsh treatment and inadequate living conditions. An American schizophrenic woman explains:

> Let's just say I have a case of shame – I really do. When I look at some of the things I've really gone through – some of the things I've done, some of the things I've said – my father's feeling of shame for me does not equal my own.[57]

Another patient writes:

> I have often been fraught with a profound guilt over my diagnosis of schizophrenia . . . . I had little idea how dehumanizing and humiliating the hospital would be for me. . . . I felt that I had partly lost my right to stand among humanity . . . and that for some people I would be forevermore something of a subhuman creature. . . . Mental health professionals often treated me . . . as if I were a stranger or alien of sorts, set apart from others by reason of my label.[58]

In contrast to Maria, the Guatemalan Indian woman whose episode of psychosis was described in the last chapter, these American schizophrenic individuals must accept blame, and must blame themselves, for their condition. They feel estranged from others; the stigma of their illness obstructs their social reintegration.

With the growth of interest in community psychiatry, considerable attention was focused on the question of the stigma of mental illness in the 1950s and 1960s. Shirley Star, using a series of vignettes depicting people with psychiatric symptoms, conducted a nationwide survey of members of the American public in 1950 and found the general reaction to the mentally ill to be negative and poorly informed.[59] Elaine and John Cumming, using the same techniques, uncovered essentially similar attitudes among residents of a rural town (which they called Blackfoot) in Saskatchewan, Canada, in 1951, and found that the negative attitudes towards the mentally ill were untouched after a six-month psychiatric educational campaign.[60] After a six-year survey of residents of the Champaign-Urbana area of Illinois in the 1950s, J. C. Nunally concluded that the insane are viewed by the general public with "fear, distrust, and dislike."[61] He reported:

> Old people and young people, highly educated people and people with little formal training – all tend to regard the mentally ill as relatively dangerous, dirty, unpredictable and worthless.[62]

They are considered, in short, "all things bad."[63]

In more recent years a dispute has arisen over whether the initial impressions of high levels of stigma attached to mental illness continue to hold true. A number of researchers in the 1960s concluded that the public tolerance of the mentally ill had improved.[64] In the late 1970s, twenty years after Nunally's original survey, William Cockerham again analyzed public attitudes towards the mentally ill in Champaign-Urbana and found them to be somewhat more tolerant.[65] But other researchers have found no improvement in popular mental health attitudes between the 1960s and 1970s;[66] and a second survey of public tolerance of the mentally ill in Blackfoot, Saskatchewan, twenty-three years after the Cummings' original study, revealed that virtually no change had occurred.[67]

It is possible that gains were made in public acceptance of the mentally ill in the 1960s but that, as the consequences of the abandonment of the psychotic people in the community have become apparent, no further progress has taken place. Whatever the truth of the matter, it is obvious that mental patients are still highly stigmatized. Branded as "psychos" in popular parlance, they encounter great hardship in finding employment[68] and generate fear as to their dangerousness. Citizens fight to exclude psychiatric treatment facilities and living quarters for the mentally ill from residential neighborhoods.[69] The status afforded the mentally ill is the very lowest – lower than that of ex-convicts or the retarded.[70] Even after five years of normal living and good work, according to one survey, an ex-mental patient is rated as less acceptable than an ex-convict.[71] Usually indigent and unemployed, the chronic mental patient does not have a valued social role. He or she rarely possesses any of the indicators of mainstream social status: if working, the job is likely to be the most menial available; he or she generally has no decent housing, no yard, no family, and no car. Such patients rarely have social or sexual contact with any but other mental patients. The chronic mental patient in our society truly has pariah status.

Even the agencies serving the mentally ill are tainted by association.

Mental health professionals often disdain chronic psychotic patients, preferring to work with "good therapy cases" closer to their own class and interests.[72] Psychiatrists may avoid such patients – in one sample, only 5 per cent of private psychiatric patients were schizophrenic[73] – and community mental health centers often fail to address their needs. Mental health professionals are likely to hold attitudes towards mental patients which are similar to those of the general public; they may even be *more* rejecting. In one study, mental hospital staff were considerably less likely than members of the public to take the trouble to mail a sealed, addressed letter which they believed to have been accidentally lost by a mental hospital patient.[74]

Most tragic of all, the mentally ill themselves accept the stereotype of their own condition. Young patients in rural Ireland viewed their "spending time in the 'madhouse' . . . as a permanent 'fall from grace' similar to a loss of virginity."[75] A number of studies have shown that mental patients are as negative in their opinions of mental illness as the general public.[76] Some reports, indeed, indicate that mental patients are *more* rejecting of the mentally ill than were their family members or the hospital staff.[77]

LABELING THEORY

Research on the stigma of mental illness has been fueled by interest in labeling theory. Once a deviant person has been labeled "mentally ill," argues sociologist Thomas Scheff, society responds in accordance with a pre-determined stereotype and the individual is launched on a career of chronic mental illness from which there is little opportunity for escape.[78] There is evidence to support Scheff's position. A study of the attitudes of residents of a small New England town, published in 1963 by Derek Phillips, shows that a normal person of an "ideal type" who is described as having been in a mental hospital is socially rejected to a much greater degree than is a simple schizophrenic person who seeks no help or who instead consults a clergyman.[79]

In David Rosenhan's well-known study, normal volunteers presented themselves for voluntary admission to a dozen different psychiatric hospitals with complaints of auditory hallucinations. Every pseudo-patient was admitted, and although they reverted to normal behavior and denied psychotic symptoms immediately upon admission, each one was labeled schizophrenic at the time of discharge. Staff described the reasonable actions of the pseudo-patients as if they were pathological. None was discharged in less than a week – one was detained for almost two months.[80] One might reasonably conclude from studies such as these that pressures to conform to stereotypic expectations may well influence hope of recovery and the features of schizophrenia.

Critics of labeling theory argue that the approach understates the importance of the initial deviance and of the inherent pathology of mental illness in causing a label to be attached, and that it minimizes the capacity of mental patients to shake off the harmful effects of stigma.[81] Such criticisms may be valid, but they fail to refute the possibility that labeling may have a significant effect on shaping the features of mental illness once established – an effect which may be substantial in many cases. John Strauss and William Carpenter, American psychiatrists who are authorities on the outcome of schizophrenic illness, conclude that:

> Labeling is an important variable affecting the course, and perhaps the onset of schizophrenia. . . . Who can doubt the devastating impact on a fragile person of perceiving that the entire social milieu regards him (wittingly or not) as subhuman, incurable, unmotivated, or incompetent to pursue ordinary expectations. . . ? Can we doubt that a deteriorating course of disorder is fostered when fundamental roles are changed by social stigma and employment opportunities become limited?[82]

HOW STIGMA INFLUENCES THE COURSE OF ILLNESS

Exactly how could the stigma and degradation of mental illness affect the symptoms of schizophrenia and shape the course of the illness? Cognitive dissonance theory helps explain this process. In outline this social psychological theory states that:

(a) pieces of knowledge or ideas (cognitions) are dissonant if one contradicts the other;
(b) dissonance is psychologically uncomfortable and motivates a person to resolve the contradiction; and
(c) the person will actively avoid situations which increase the dissonance.

For example, if a woman smokes two packs of cigarettes a day, believes herself to be reasonably strong-willed and sensible but knows that cigarettes cause lung cancer, she may reduce the level of dissonance between these ideas by quitting cigarettes, coming to see herself as weak-willed and foolish, or minimizing the evidence that links smoking with cancer.

Experiments have shown the following consequences of cognitive dissonance theory to hold true:

(a) After a change in opinion has been made with the aim of reducing dissonance, the person will select from available information evidence to confirm his or her decision, and will tend to overvalue this evidence.
(b) In the face of contradictory evidence which increases dissonance the individual will become *more* active in defense of his or her belief.
(c) If a person is obliged to state a public opinion which is contrary to his or her privately held opinion (thus creating dissonance), there is a

tendency for the opinion to change to conform more closely with the public statement: the smaller the external pressure to make the public statement, the greater is the opinion change.[83]

Faced with the need to accept a diagnosis of major mental illness (and its associated stigma and debased status), anyone with an internal sense of relative worth and competence will experience dissonance (see Figure 8.1). In fact, those who accept a diagnosis of mental illness tend to be people with a sense of ill-being (dysphoria) and a poor self-image: the grandiose and euphoric reject the illness label.[84] Cognitive dissonance theory predicts that those who choose to accept the diagnosis of mental illness will attempt to resolve their sense of dissonance by conforming to their new outcast status and to the stereotype of worthlessness; they will become more socially withdrawn and adopt a disabled role. In seeking to confirm the incurable and incapable features of their role, their psychotic symptoms will tend to persist and they are likely to become dependent on the treatment agency and others in their lives.

Such patterns will be even more exaggerated if the patient's stigmatized status is made evident by discernible physical traits; at worst these may be the shuffle, rigid facial expression and drooling secondary to the use of high doses of antipsychotic drugs; at the least they may include the slow gait of the unemployed, devalued individual with nowhere to go and nothing to do.

Under pressure to return to adequate functioning, symptoms of illness will tend to recur as a defense against mounting dissonance. However, gentle and gradual efforts which lead such individuals to demonstrate publicly that they can function at a more adequate level may result in a change in their self-concept and a movement towards labeled but competent status. Cognitive dissonance theory thus helps explain the precarious balance of functioning which is found in rehabilitating the chronic mental patient. High expectations for his or her level of achievement can lead the patient to a higher level of functioning and decreased segregation and stigma, but they can also create an increased risk of psychotic decompensation and hospitalization.[85] We may now see why success is so often frightening and stressful to psychotic patients.

In contrast, those who initially reject the label and status of mental illness (and psychiatric treatment) will usually attempt to maintain their previous occupational and social status. Any social rejection they experience is likely to result in an increase in grandiosity and even more aggressive avoidance of treatment. Strong efforts to compel such individuals to accept a diagnosis of mental illness may result in superficial compliance but little genuine change in their privately held opinion; consequently they are likely to attempt to evade treatment at every opportunity. However, gradually increasing involvement in a non-debasing

FEATURES OF
COGNITIVE
DISSONANCE
THEORY

Dissonance
established

Motivation to
reduce dissonance

Avoidance of
situations which
increase dissonance

INDIVIDUAL RESPONSE

DEPENDENCE ──────── COMPETENCE ──────── RESISTANCE

Individual is confronted with need to accept
diagnosis of mental illness with consequent
debased status despite an internal sense
of relative worth and competence

(Individual with poor self
concept and dysphoria)

(Individual with
grandiosity and euphoria)

Choose label of mental
illness with debased status

Rejects label of mental illness
and retains sense of worth

Withdraws socially
and becomes disabled

Spontaneous
recovery

Rejects
psychiatric treatment

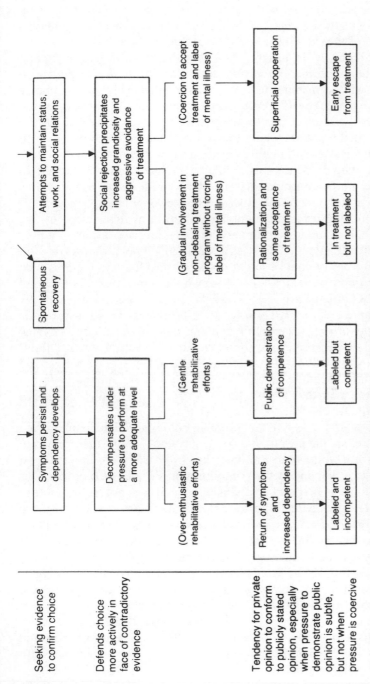

Figure 8.1 Impact of labeling individual "mentally ill" as predicted by cognitive dissonance theory

treatment program, coupled with a high degree of rationalization, may lead these people to a limited compliance with treatment, provided a dissonant label of mental illness is not forced upon them.

Thus, the patient with "insight" will tend to function less well than expected and may become excessively dependent, while the patient who functions well will be inclined to reject treatment. Cognitive dissonance theory gives the mental health professional an explanation of the common observation that he often seems to be encouraging each patient to do the opposite of what the patient wants to do – a situation which can lead to "burn-out" among staff and punitive attitudes towards patients. A reduction in stigma should reduce this conflict and, more directly, result in improved outcome in schizophrenia. If schizophrenia were a high-status illness (as it is in some cultures), it would be less debilitating.

If we were looking for experimental verification of this viewpoint, we would expect to find, counter-intuitively, that patients who accept that they are mentally ill will have the worst course to their illness, that those who reject the label from the outset might do better and that the patients who show the most improvement will be those who accept the label of mental illness but subsequently are able to shake it off. This is, in fact, the finding of Edmund Doherty's study of self-labeling by 43 psychiatric inpatients. Patients who accepted throughout their hospital stay that they were mentally ill were rated as showing the least improvement; those who consistently denied that they were mentally ill did slightly better; and the patients who began by accepting that they were mentally ill but subsequently rejected that notion showed the greatest gains. All three groups were equally disturbed at admission.[86]

My colleagues and I tested the same hypothesis – that labeling and stereotyping are so damaging that patients who accept that they are mentally ill have a worse outcome than those who deny it – in a study of 54 psychotic patients living in the community in Boulder, Colorado. Our results provide some support for this view but do not fully confirm Doherty's findings. Patients who accept that they are mentally ill, we found, have worse self-esteem and lack a sense of control over their lives. Those who find mental illness most stigmatizing have the worst self-esteem and the weakest sense of mastery. Neither rejecting the label of mental illness nor accepting it, by itself, leads to good outcome, it emerges: patients can benefit from accepting they are ill only if they also have a sense of control over their lives. Such patients are few and far between, however, since a consequence of accepting the illness label is loss of a sense of mastery. This is the Catch 22 of being mentally ill in Western society – in the process of gaining insight one loses the very psychological strength that is necessary for recovery.[87]

A conclusion we can draw from this research is that it is equally important for therapists to assist patients in developing a sense of mastery as it is to help them find insight into their illness. This is not what conventional treatment programs do, however. Ordinarily, a good deal more effort is expended on persuading patients that they are ill than on finding ways to put them in charge of their illness. Some of the programs which are most successful at keeping patients out of hospital are unfortunately quite controlling rather than empowering (see "Intensive community support" in Chapter 12). To achieve real empowerment we have to turn to programs that are run or co-run by consumers of mental health services themselves. Some ventures of this type will be described in Chapter 12.

SOCIAL ISOLATION

As might be expected from the humiliating living conditions of the majority of mentally ill people and from their pariah status, Western schizophrenic people lead lives of social isolation. Many studies have shown that such patients have networks of social contacts which are much more restricted than is usual in our society. Schizophrenic people are found to have close contacts with a third to a fifth of the number of people which is average for healthy members of the community. A third of the chronically mentally ill have no friends at all. Schizophrenic people's relationships tend to be more one-sided, dependent and lacking in complexity of content and diversity of interconnections. Although family relationships deteriorate less than contact with friends, a considerable disintegration of family ties does occur.[88] The collapse of the patient's social network appears to be a consequence of the illness, for it occurs after the first hospital admission.[89]

The social isolation of the Western schizophrenic person stands in contrast to the effective social reintegration of the psychotic person in the Third World. Although disruptive and violent individuals living in peasant villages who have been designated "mad" do have restricted social networks,[90] the same problem does not apply, as we saw in Chapter 7, to less chronic and severely disturbed people with psychosis in the Third World. It was pointed out in that chapter, furthermore, that social isolation in both the developed and developing world has been repeatedly shown to be associated with poor outcome. The recent reports on the social networks of schizophrenic people confirm this pattern. One study of schizophrenic people housed in New York hotels demonstrated that, regardless of the severity of the patients' symptoms, those with broader and more complex social networks were less likely to be readmitted to hospital.[91]

FAMILIES OF SCHIZOPHRENIC PEOPLE

The contrast between the social reintegration of people with psychosis in the developing world and the isolation of the mentally ill in Western

society is highlighted by the plight of the families of Western schizophrenic individuals. The stigma that attaches to mental illness also taints
the relatives. Some react by talking to no one about the illness for years,
not even to close friends. Those who do discuss the matter openly may find
themselves snubbed by acquaintances. "Some old friends quit talking to
us," described the mother of a schizophrenic client. "They absolutely
dropped us." Other families respond by withdrawing socially. "We haven't
done much entertaining because of this," commented the parent of
another schizophrenic youth. "I'm never quite sure . . . he's so up and
down." A third of the wives in an American study followed a course of
aggressive concealment including dropping and avoiding friends or even
moving to a new residence. Another third of the wives discussed their
husbands' illness with only a select few friends or relatives.[92] Although
there is a marked tendency for family members to deny the stigma, their
concealment and withdrawal point to an underlying sense of shame and
lead them into social isolation.[93]

In a survey of relatives of schizophrenic people in Washington, D.C.,
Agnes Hatfield observed "a picture of unremittingly disturbed family life
marked by almost constant stress"[94] as the consequence of caring for a
patient at home. She noted that marital disruption, blame, grief and
helplessness were common results. In a study of British families in which
a schizophrenic individual was living at home, half of the family members
reported severe or very severe impairment of their own health as a
consequence of their relative's psychiatric condition.[95]

All of the parents of the mentally ill in a discussion group at the
Massachusetts Mental Health Center "to a greater or lesser extent saw
themselves and the others as ogres responsible for the misfortune that
befell their children."[96] The burden of guilt that such relatives carry
is the result of the popular conception that mental illness is a product
of faulty upbringing. Mental health professionals, adopting this same
attitude, may see the family members as adversaries and add to their
estrangement. Carried to its logical extreme the notion of the "schizo-
phrenogenic" family led to the bizarre occurrence in a Colorado court of
a 24-year-old man, with the support of his psychiatrist, suing his parents
for "malpractice" which supposedly caused his schizophrenia.[97] Isolated
and guilt-ridden as they are, it is not surprising that the families of
schizophrenic individuals sometimes become overinvolved with their sick
relatives.[98] Seeing this interaction, mental health professionals may try to
separate them, encouraging the patient to move away from home and
minimize contact with his or her relatives. This step completes a process
of social disintegration: the patient is separated from almost everyone
except other stigmatized patients; the family members are socially isolated
and feel banished not only from the social mainstream but also from their
affected relatives.

ALIENATION

Where pre-industrial cultures offer social reintegration with maintenance of social status and provision of a valued social role for many of those suffering from psychosis, Western society leaves schizophrenic people in a state of social disintegration with pariah status and a disabled role. In the non-industrial world, communal healing processes operate within a social consensus which predicts recovery and minimizes blame, guilt and stigma; whereas in Western society schizophrenia is treated through marginal institutions with a social expectation that all concerned are to blame and that the condition is incurable. These differences in the status, integration and role of the mentally ill may well account for the distinctly worse outcome for schizophrenia in industrial societies.

This constellation of problems has been described before, however: it is encompassed by the concept of alienation. Marx writes of people in industrial society becoming alienated from the process of working and the product of their work, from other people and from their own human qualities.[99] Modern psychologists emphasize that alienation includes a profound sense of meaninglessness and powerlessness.[100]

How does this apply to the schizophrenic individual? In the stigma of mental illness, the most debased status in our society, we see the utmost in painful estrangement of one human from another; and in the schizophrenic person's own acceptance of this same dehumanized stereotype we witness the loss of his or her sense of fully belonging to humankind. It is in the menial jobs which the mentally ill are most likely to find – dishwashing, envelope-stuffing, day-laboring – that work is most dehumanizing and alienation is most severe. But the more common fate of the schizophrenic person – unemployment – is even worse. To stand bored and idle, to be unable to provide for oneself, to fulfill no useful social function, to be of little value to oneself or others – these are the ultimate in alienation: a confrontation with the existential concern of meaninglessness.

In one recent study, when people in community treatment for psychosis in Boulder, Colorado, were interviewed about their lives, their principal complaints were of boredom and (among the men) unemployment – both rated as much more problematic than symptoms of mental illness.[101] Psychotic patients, in fact, score lower than any other group on the Purpose-in-Life Test[102] – a psychological measure used to detect alienation and meaninglessness. Many professionals suspect that the high prevalence of drug and alcohol abuse among the mentally ill – 30 to 40 per cent of most samples[103] – is in part a consequence of the empty lives which many psychotic patients lead. In a study of substance use among the mentally ill in the Boulder community, we found that those with the fewest planned activities were the heaviest marijuana users, giving "boredom" as the primary reason for drug use.[104]

Decades ago, when we were shifting the locus of care from the hospital to the community, we found ways to combat what we called at that time the institutional neurosis – the posturing, the restless pacing, incontinence and unpredictable violence which were bred by the restrictions, regimentation and emptiness of hospital life. Humanizing the hospital wards and establishing "therapeutic communities", which changed the power relationships between staff and patients and involved patients in ward management (as described in Chapter 4), led to a reversal of this institutionally ingrained behavior. It now appears that we have traded the earlier *institutional* neurosis for a new *existential* neurosis which may similarly stand in the way of recovery from the original psychotic illness. It seems likely, however (and I will discuss this in greater detail in Chapter 12), that the same active ingredients which proved successful in reversing the institutional syndrome – normalizing the environment and engaging the patient in his or her own treatment – are also effective in relieving the effect of the existential neurosis.

ORIGINS OF ALIENATION

The schizophrenic person, it appears, is among the most alienated of industrial society, and it is in this condition that one may perceive the causes of the malignancy of the illness. Looking beyond this, the origins of the schizophrenic person's alienation are to be found in the political and economic structure of society – in the division of labor and development of wage work. For it is these aspects of production that have rendered the schizophrenic person – with his or her limited ability to withstand stress, limited productive capacity and limited drive – marginal to the industrial work force, marginal members of (what anthropologist Jules Henry terms) "the driven society."[105]

Caste systems do not perpetuate themselves. Continued enforcement of discriminatory economic and physical sanctions is necessary to maintain the existence of a pariah group.[106] Similar political and economic pressures are necessary to restrict the interclass mobility of members of U.S. ethnic minority groups.[107] The same is true of the low status of the mentally ill in the West. The postwar drive to influence public opinion and increase the community acceptance of mental patients was equivalent to earnest attempts to adjust the status of a caste. The political motivation in some areas, at that time, was to bring the mentally ill into the work force, in other areas, to transfer the responsibility for their care from the state to the community. These efforts have decreased as the political motivation recedes. Now public policy has created the poverty, unemployment and squalid conditions in which the mentally ill live in much of the Western world and, indirectly, has inflamed the pessimism and alienation that are to blame for the malignant course of schizophrenia in our society.

SUMMARY

- Five out of every ten U.S. schizophrenic people are living in boarding homes or nursing homes, in hospital, on Skid Row or in jail or prison.
- The stigma of mental illness in Western society continues to be great.
- A combination of labeling theory and cognitive dissonance theory allows us to explain how the stigma of mental illness can lead to poor outcome from psychosis.
- Schizophrenic people in Western society have restricted social networks and they and their families become relatively estranged from society.
- The social plight of the Western schizophrenic person is encompassed by the single concept of alienation, and has its roots in the division of labor and the development of wage work.

Chapter 9

The incidence of schizophrenia

Does political economy influence the rate of occurrence of schizophrenia? Could factors related to social class and caste or the prevailing mode of production determine how many people develop the vulnerability to schizophrenia? Could labor conditions, unemployment and other socio-economic stresses trigger the onset of the disorder? Up to this point we have concentrated upon the *course* of schizophrenia – recovery from the illness and the level of functioning achieved by chronic sufferers. The course of schizophrenia, it has been argued, is strongly influenced by the utilization of labor, a factor which affects the social role, status and integration of people suffering from psychosis. At this juncture it may be valuable to make a diversion and to examine the *frequency of occurrence* of the illness and the extent to which it is affected by social, political and economic factors.

For social factors to affect a person's vulnerability to illness or the course of the disorder there must be a mediating biological mechanism which converts the social influence into a bodily response. Stressful labor dynamics, for example, can have an impact on the course of schizophrenia because increased stress worsens the dopamine supersensitivity which is believed to underlie the disease (see Chapters 1 and 10). Influences on the occurrence of schizophrenia are likely to be different from those affecting the course of the illness. If social factors are to have an impact on the individual's vulnerability to schizophrenia they might do so by influencing the development of the foetal brain or the occurrence of brain damage later in life – they might affect such factors as maternal and foetal nutrition, maternal drug and alcohol use, infections during pregnancy, delivery complications and childhood infections and head trauma.

INDUSTRIALIZATION AND ILLNESS

Patterns of interaction between socioeconomic factors and the occurrence of illness over time can be complex. Some diseases are worsened by affluence and tend to grow in frequency with industrial progress;

others are a response to poverty and tend to decrease in incidence with the advance of industrialization. A number of diseases associated with Western industrial growth, however, are influenced both by affluence *and* poverty, and have been found to rise in incidence early in the process of development and to fall in frequency later. These illnesses are initially more common among the rich and, later, become more common among the poor. Such diseases include thyrotoxicosis, peptic ulcer, poliomyelitis, appendicitis and coronary artery disease (see Figure 9.1).[1] The reasons for the rise and fall in incidence vary from condition to condition but, in general, they are related to a change in hygiene or diet which acts in childhood to modify individual susceptibility and to the same factor, or a different one, exerting an effect later in life to produce illness. For example, people whose dietary iodine is deficient in youth are less able to adapt to an increase in iodine intake later in life and tend to develop thyrotoxicosis.[2]

The frequency of a mental disorder can vary in a similar way. Emil Kraepelin, in 1926, described a pattern of changing occurrence for a brain disease caused by syphilitic infection, general paralysis of the insane, pointing out that it "was formerly uncommon, underwent a progressively rapid increase from the beginning of the last century and for some time now has been gradually diminishing."[3] Has schizophrenia undergone a similar increase in prevalence followed by a decline? Does the illness first become more common among the upper classes and then among the lower? There is some evidence, in fact, for each element of this pattern. We can look at this evidence in detail shortly, and examine what these curious changes in the occurrence of schizophrenia tell us about the origins of the illness. First, however, it is necessary to define some of the terms which will be used.

INCIDENCE AND PREVALENCE

The *incidence* of an illness is the rate at which new cases occur in a given period of time (usually a year). The *prevalence* of an illness is the total number of cases, new and old, known to exist. The number in existence at any one point in time is the *point prevalence;* the number observed in a given period (say a year) is the *period prevalence;* and the number of people in the population who have suffered from illness at any time in their lives gives us the *lifetime prevalence*. Whereas the lifetime prevalence is unaffected by the rate at which people recover, the point prevalence for schizophrenia will tend to be lower in those areas, such as parts of the Third World, where outcome from the illness is better.

Incidence data are difficult to gather by any method other than by counting the number of referrals to treatment agencies. Such information on schizophrenia is therefore hard to obtain in much of the Third World,

Figure 9.1 Average annual mortality rate from selected diseases in England and Wales from 1901 and numbers of poliomyelitis notifications: five-year periods

Source: Reprinted by permission of the author. From Barker, D. J. P., "Rise and fall of Western diseases," *Nature*, 338: 371–2.

where health services are not comprehensively available. In U.S. studies the annual incidence rate for treated schizophrenia is close to 0.5 per 1,000 of the general population; in Britain the figure is in the region of 0.2 per 1,000.[4] The difference between the incidence in the two countries is largely a reflection of the broader diagnosis of schizophrenia which, until the 1970s, was applied in the United States.

True *prevalence* may be assessed by conducting a community survey of all the households in a given area and detecting all current cases, treated and untreated. In carrying out such a survey the researchers may plan to interview every person in the community or, to save time and expense, they may evaluate only those people who are identified by key informants (such as tribal chiefs or general practitioners) as possibly suffering from the illness. An approximation to prevalence can also be calculated from the number of cases in treatment at hospitals and clinics during a given period. Again this method, which assumes that virtually all cases of a disorder are in treatment, is inapplicable to the study of schizophrenia in most of the Third World. Prevalence data for schizophrenia vary more widely than incidence data – from 0.3 to 4.7 per 1,000 of the population in studies of the United States, from 1.8 to 17.0 per 1,000 in Europe, from 1.9 to 17.9 per 1,000 in Japan and from 0.4 to 7.0 per 1,000 in the developing world.[5]

While we may use incidence data to draw conclusions about what causes the appearance of an illness, strictly speaking, we should not use prevalence data in the same way. Prevalence figures for schizophrenia are the product of three processes – the rate of appearance of the illness (the incidence), the death rate of schizophrenic people (which may well be greater in the Third World) and (except in the case of lifetime prevalence) the rate of recovery.

A problem with comparing different studies of the occurrence of schizophrenia, especially for Third World peoples, is that to draw an accurate picture it is necessary to know the age distribution of each population. Where a large proportion of the population is below age 15, for example, and not at risk of developing schizophrenia, one should expect a spuriously low prevalence of the illness. This source of error would be particularly evident in the Third World, where birth rates tend to be higher and life expectancy shorter than in the West, or in assessing changes in the same culture over a long period of time. In order to correct for this effect it is necessary to calculate a standardized, age-corrected prevalence figure.

Clearly, there are difficulties associated with assessing changes in the frequency of an illness over time or comparing rates between different parts of the world – incidence versus prevalence, point prevalence versus lifetime prevalence, community survey versus treatment statistics, narrow versus broad diagnosis and age-correction differences. It is not surprising that the statistics vary substantially and it is clear that we have to be cautious in interpreting the available data.

Bearing this point in mind, we may return to the issue of variations in the occurrence of schizophrenia over time and what they tell us about links between the illness and society.

WAS SCHIZOPHRENIA RARE BEFORE THE EIGHTEENTH CENTURY?

Is schizophrenia, like death and taxes, an unavoidable part of human existence? Psychiatrist Fuller Torrey argues that it is not: he suggests that schizophrenia may not have existed prior to the eighteenth century.[6] Several other authors disagree, however.[7] There is evidence, for example, that the inhabitants of ancient India and Rome distinguished conditions like schizophrenia from those resembling mania, depression, catatonic stupor and delirium.[8] It is an open question, however, whether schizophrenia was *less common* before the eighteenth century.

The records of Richard Napier, an English mediaeval physician who specialized in the care of the mentally ill, suggest that the condition closest to our modern category of schizophrenia, "mopishness," was not common in his day.[9] British psychiatrist Edward Hare argues that there was a real increase in the occurrence of schizophrenia during the nineteenth century. Not only did the total number of the insane occupying the asylums increase throughout the Victorian era, but so did admission and first-admission rates. First admissions more than tripled between 1869 and 1900.[10] As an editorial in the London *Times* of 1877 quipped,

> if lunacy continues to increase as at present, the insane will be in the majority, and, freeing themselves, will put the sane in asylums.[11]

Many of the Victorian asylum superintendents, caught, as it seemed, in an upward spiral of lunacy, were at pains to point out that this trend was an artefact of increasing recognition of those in need of treatment, and not an indictment of their attempts at prevention. Others, like Daniel Hack Tuke, believed that there was an actual increase in mental disorder brought about by the spread of poverty.[12] Dr. Hare, like Dr. Tuke before him, argues that increased recognition of insanity cannot explain a sustained growth rate on such a scale over several decades. If increasing numbers of mild cases were being admitted to the asylums, he contends, one would expect to find decreasing death rates and increasing recovery rates, and this was not the case. Hare points out, moreover, that the greatest increase was in "melancholia," the nineteenth-century condition which most closely matches the modern diagnosis of schizophrenia.[13]

In a recent article, Dr. Hare argues that it was primarily the early-onset type of schizophrenia which increased during the nineteenth century. He suggests that some new biological factor, such as the mutation of a virus or a change in the immunological defenses of the general population, occurred and caused an increase in schizophrenia around 1800.[14]

Even at the end of the nineteenth century, schizophrenia appears to have been relatively rare. Psychiatrist Assen Jablensky reports that only 9 per cent of men and 7 per cent of women first admitted to the University Psychiatric Clinic in Munich in 1908 were diagnosed as suffering from dementia praecox (the contemporary term for schizophrenia). Since Emil Kraepelin himself (the psychiatrist who defined dementia praecox) evaluated some of these cases, it is unlikely that missed diagnosis accounts for the low prevalence of the disorder among the admissions. The occurrence rate for the diagnostic categories most likely to have included schizophrenia was low among other nineteenth-century asylum populations, also. The greatest increase in institutionalized cases of schizophrenia, Dr. Jablensky suggests, may well have occurred in the present century.[15]

We have to be cautious, however. Historical information faces the same problem as present-day Third World data – the low incidence rates, in each instance, may be a result of restricted access to treatment, and the low prevalence rates may be due to the same problem and to higher death rates and more rapid recovery of people with the illness. They may bear relatively little relationship to the actual occurrence of new cases during the period in question. On balance, though, it seems probable that schizophrenia did become more prevalent during the nineteenth century, presumably in response to socio-environmental changes associated with the Industrial Revolution; possible biological mediating mechanisms include nutritional, immunological and infectious causes.

IS THE INCIDENCE OF SCHIZOPHRENIA ON THE DECLINE?

A number of researchers have pointed out that the incidence of schizophrenia appears to be on the decline. The studies which examine changes in the incidence of schizophrenia since 1960 are listed in Table 9.1.[16] About three-quarters of these studies indicate a decrease in the incidence of the illness since 1960, and about a quarter reveal no change or an increase. All of the studies rely upon data gathered from treatment services, counting patients diagnosed as suffering from schizophrenia who are admitted or making treatment contact for the first time; the figures are age-standardized in only a few instances. The observed changes could be artefacts, therefore, rather than true changes in the occurrence of schizophrenia.

It is possible, for example, that a diagnostic shift from schizophrenia to another diagnostic category could account for a decrease in the observed occurrence of schizophrenia.[17] Australian psychiatrist Gordon Parker and his co-workers found that the decrease in the treated incidence of

Table 9.1 Changes in the incidence of schizophrenia since 1960

Author(s) and year	Country	Period	Measure	Change in frequency
Eagles & Whalley (1985)	Scotland, U.K.	1969–78	Age-standardized first-admission rate	40% decrease
Parker *et al.* (1985)	New South Wales, Australia	1967–77	Number of first admissions	9% decrease
Dickson & Kendell (1986)	Scotland, U.K.	1970–81	Number of first admissions	48% decrease
Hafner & an der Heiden (1986)	Mannheim, Germany	1963–80	First-contact rates	18% increase
Munk-Jorgensen (1986)	Denmark	1970–84	Age-standardized first-admission rates	37% decrease
Munk-Jørgensen & Jørgensen (1986)	Denmark	1970–84	Age-standardized first-admission rates	44% decrease (female)
Joyce (1987)	New Zealand	1974–84	Number of first admissions	37% decrease
Eagles *et al.* (1988)	Aberdeen, U.K.	1969–84	Age-standardized first-contact rates	54% decrease
de Alarcon *et al.* (1990)	Oxford, U.K.	1975–86	Age-standardized first-contact rates and first-ever diagnosis rate	50% decrease (males & females)
Der *et al.* (1990)	U.K.	1970–86	First-admission rates	40% decrease (males) 50% decrease (females)
Folnegović *et al.* (1990)	Croatia	1965–84	First-admission rates	No change
Bamrah *et al.* (1991)	Salford, U.K.	1974–84	Age-standardized first-contact rates	64% increase
Castle *et al.* (1991)	Camberwell, U.K.	1965–84	Age-standardized first-contact rates	25% increase (ICD diagnosis) 40% increase (RDC diagnosis) 38% increase (DSM-III)
Harrison *et al.* (1991)	Nottingham, U.K.	1975–87	Age-specific first-contact rates	No change
Munk-Jørgensen & Mortensen (1992)	Denmark	1969–88	First-ever admission rates	50% decrease

Note: The references cited in this table are listed in note 16.

schizophrenia in New South Wales was accompanied by an increase in the diagnosis of manic-depressive illness following the introduction of lithium carbonate.[18] Some other studies show a similar increase in the prevalence of affective psychoses,[19] but many do not. A recent study provides quite strong evidence suggesting that the changing incidence of schizophrenia is an artefact of a diagnostic shift. Researchers in Edinburgh, Scotland, have found that the proportion of patients who were diagnosed as schizophrenic by hospital psychiatrists at the time of first admission decreased by 22 per cent between 1971 and 1989. When diagnoses for these patients were made according to a computer algorithm, however, there was no such decline; in fact there was a small increase in the proportion diagnosed with schizophrenia.[20]

Another source of error may arise from an increase in the number of cases missed by traditional treatment-based statistics.[21] It is likely that the increased use of antipsychotic drug treatment has led to a greater number of psychotic patients in Europe and elsewhere being treated successfully by general practitioners. These people, consequently, may never be referred to any type of psychiatric treatment agency or included in service-based incidence statistics.[22] Similarly, more psychotic people these days may escape any kind of treatment and, instead, lead eccentric, seclusive lives, live as vagrants, stay in shelters for the homeless or get arrested and jailed. An incidence study of schizophrenia in Nottingham, England,[23] for instance, found that 10 per cent of the sample of cases which were ultimately detected were missed by the original screening procedure as they were only fleetingly in contact with the treatment facilities; further cases with no contact at all with the formal psychiatric treatment system would have escaped detection altogether.

If there is, in fact, any true decrease in the incidence of schizophrenia, the finding could give us important clues as to the causes of the illness. Possible biological mechanisms would include a decrease in the fertility of people with schizophrenia, a change in the population's immunity to an infectious agent and a decrease in brain damage resulting from improvements in obstetric care.

It is not likely that there has been a recent decrease in the fertility of people with schizophrenia. For the incidence of schizophrenia to decrease throughout the 1970s, it would have been necessary for a change in the fertility of schizophrenic people to be in effect through the 1950s. The decrease in the use of hospital confinement for the mentally ill since the mid-1950s makes it more likely that fertility has been increasing rather than decreasing among schizophrenic people. The fertility of schizophrenic patients, moreover, is unlikely to have a major impact on the incidence of the illness because only 11 per cent of people with schizophrenia have a schizophrenic parent.[24]

Changes in hygiene have produced changes in the general population's immunity to various infectious agents. Poliomyelitis is an example of an illness whose prevalence increased with industrialization as a result of changes in hygiene (see Figure 9.1): improvements in sanitation delayed exposure to the poliovirus until later in life, when the virus is more dangerous.[25] Similar changes in immunity or exposure to viral infection might account for the reported changes in the prevalence of schizophrenia.

Developments in obstetric practice may similarly account for the observed changes in the incidence of schizophrenia. The postwar decline in early neonatal mortality rates in England and Wales is paralleled by the subsequent fall – twenty years later – in the first-admission rate for schizophrenia in the 1960s and 1970s.[26] This possibility is discussed at greater length below.

In summary, schizophrenia may or may not be on the decline in Western industrial countries. If it is, possible underlying biological mechanisms would include changes in immunity to an infectious agent or improvements in obstetric care. Next we should look at the remaining element of the complex pattern of changing occurrence of the illness over time – changes in the rate of occurrence of the illness in different social classes.

CASTE AND CLASS

As with thyrotoxicosis, poliomyelitis, coronary artery disease and certain other illnesses, schizophrenia may initially increase in incidence among the upper classes as industrialization progresses and then switch to being predominantly a lower-class disease.

The evidence for the increased rate of schizophrenia in the lower classes in cities of the industrial world was presented in Chapter 2. At that juncture it was pointed out that the social-class gradient for schizophrenia was rarely found in rural areas, a fact which eliminated the likelihood of a selective, genetic cause. The drift of schizophrenic or pre-psychotic individuals into lower-status occupations might partly explain the concentration of schizophrenia in the poorer classes, but there is an important observation which forces the conclusion that some class-specific stress must additionally be at work – the social-class gradient for schizophrenia appears to slope in the reverse direction in peasant cultures and in non-industrialized parts of the world.

The province of Lazio in Italy in the early 1950s, for example, although it included the city of Rome, sustained a largely rural population, many of whom were peasant farmers. An analysis of all reported cases of mental illness in the province between 1951 and 1955 revealed that schizophrenia was most commonly reported in the better educated, clerical workers and professionals.[27] One must expect, however, significant underreporting of psychosis in peasant communities and this factor may account for the observed findings in Lazio. A similar pattern, though, has been noted in other economically underdeveloped areas.

Several studies from India have made the observation that schizophrenia is more common among high-caste members than among the lower castes. First admissions for schizophrenia to the only public mental hospital in Bihar state in 1959 and 1960, according to psychologist Sharadamba Rao, were much higher among the rich Bania merchant caste, the urbanized and upwardly mobile Kayasthas (many of whom are in managerial and government jobs) and the educated Brahmin and Rajput landowners than among the lower-caste peasants who work the land themselves – the Kurmis, Goalas and Koiris – or among the low-caste Telis and the untouchable scheduled castes. The incidence of treated schizophrenia was nearly fifty times greater among the Banias in this study and more than ten times greater among the Kayasthas than in the lowest castes.[28]

These differences might be explained by a greater tendency for the more educated castes to refer their relatives for Western-style psychiatric treatment. That this explanation is not sufficient is shown by three door-to-door psychiatric surveys which confirm the greater prevalence of schizophrenia among the higher castes in India. The field survey of villages in West Bengal conducted by D. N. Nandi and his colleagues found the prevalence of schizophrenia among Brahmins (at 7.2 per 1,000) to be four times greater than among the untouchable scheduled castes (1.8 per 1,000) or the non-stratified Munda and Lodha tribesmen (1.3 per 1,000).[29] In a house-to-house survey of rural, semi-rural and urban inhabitants of the Agra region of Uttar Pradesh, conducted by K. C. Dube and Narendra Kumar, schizophrenia was shown to be three or four times more prevalent among the high-caste Brahmins and Vaishes than among the lowest castes.[30] The field survey of M. N. Elnagar and his co-workers in rural West Bengal revealed that schizophrenia was more common in the high-caste *paras* (neighborhoods) of the village. The *para* occupied by high-caste Singha Roys, where a large proportion of the residents were well educated and worked in business and professional occupations, had the highest prevalence of schizophrenia. In the *para* for low-caste Mahisyas, where the proportion of people working in agriculture was highest, no schizophrenic people could be found.[31]

The Third World inverted social-class gradient appears to switch to the usual Western pattern of occurrence as the society becomes industrialized. In studies of the Chinese in Taiwan conducted between 1946 and 1948 by psychiatrist Tsung-Yi Lin and his associates the prevalence of schizophrenia was high in the upper classes and merchants and increasingly prevalent with higher levels of education. By 1961–63, however, after a period of dramatic growth in urbanization, industrialization and education and during a spell of economic prosperity, the patterns of illness had switched to mirror those of the West.[32] These changes are detailed in Table 9.2.

Table 9.2 Prevalence of schizophrenia per 1,000 of the Taiwanese Chinese population in 1946–8 and in 1961–3

	1946–8	*1961–3*
Social class		
Upper	3.5	0.8
Middle	1.2	1.1
Lower	4.5	2.1
Occupation		
Professional	0	0
Merchant	3.6	0.9
Salaried worker	0.9	0.4
Laborer	1.7	1.9
Farmer and fisherman	1.7	1.1
Unemployed	3.8	5.5
Education		
College	18.2	0.0
Senior high school	13.0	1.9
Junior high school	5.7	0.0
Elementary education	1.1	1.2
No formal education	3.8	3.7

Source: Lin, R., Rin, H., Yeh, E. *et al.*, "Mental disorders in Taiwan, fifteen years later: A preliminary report," in W. Caudill and T. Lin (eds.), *Mental Health Research in Asia and the Pacific*, Honolulu: East-West Center Press, 1969, pp. 66–91.

The high prevalence rates among higher-caste Indians and the well educated in the earlier Taiwanese study could be due to a number of factors, but they cannot be due to the drift of pre-schizophrenic or schizophrenic people into a different social stratum. People cannot change their caste, nor would they drift into higher education. Many of the studies are field surveys and, therefore, would not be influenced by differences between groups in treatment-seeking behavior. As we shall see shortly, however, changes in maternal nutrition and foetal and neonatal health in response to changing social conditions could produce this pattern through a neurodevelopmental effect.

It seems likely that the occurrence of schizophrenia in the West increased during the last century and possible that it has peaked and has been decreasing during the past two or three decades. In preindustrial settings the illness is more prevalent in the upper castes and classes, but in the postindustrial West the illness is more common in the poorer classes. Can we explain this pattern of occurrence?

INDUSTRIALIZATION AND THE HAZARDS OF CHILDBIRTH

Obstetric complications are related to the subsequent development of schizophrenia.[33] The risk of schizophrenia in people who suffer obstetric complications at birth has been estimated to be two to three times greater than those who have normal deliveries.[34] Some researchers argue that those who become schizophrenic following obstetric trauma tend to be people without a genetic vulnerability to the illness.[35] Others suggest the reverse – that people with a genetic predisposition to schizophrenia inherit a nervous-system fragility which renders brain tissue more sensitive to the effects of oxygen deprivation or intracranial bleeding. In the latter case, the combination of genetically based neural developmental abnormality and subsequent nerve tissue damage leads to the development of the illness.[36] It is likely, in fact, that obstetric complications are a risk factor for people with or without a genetic vulnerability to the illness.

Changes associated with industrialization alter the risk of obstetric complications differentially in the various classes. For example, obstetric complications include problems with delivery caused by narrowing of the pelvic birth canal. A significant proportion of women with poor nutrition have pelvic contraction due to childhood rickets resulting from vitamin D deficiency. Improvements in nutrition during industrial development reach the upper classes first, but the first generation of women who gain this benefit are relatively small in stature and at risk of bony deformities because, as children, their nutrition was inferior. Their children, however – the first generation to have better nutrition from the outset – are bigger. Consequently, this first generation of more affluent women will have relatively small pelvic dimensions and, when pregnant, will carry large, well-nourished foetuses. The result will be more difficult deliveries and more brain damage in the new generation of infants.

The result may also be increased infant mortality. As we saw in Chapter 2, even though infant mortality has decreased with industrialization, it rises during the *boom* (see Figure 2.3), confirming that it can be a complication of affluence. Increased obstetric difficulties, then, are likely to lead to increased numbers of neonatal deaths as well as increasing numbers of surviving brain-damaged infants. If neonatal care improves, the proportion of brain-damaged infants which survives will increase; infant mortality, however, may continue to be above average.

Improvements in neonatal care, in the early phase of industrialization, become available sooner to the upper classes. This bias increases the tendency for children born with obstetric complications to higher-class women to survive infancy with brain damage and for similar lower-class children to die earlier in life. Both the increased rate of brain damage and the increased survival rate could, in turn, lead to higher schizophrenia rates in the upper classes.

In the later phases of industrial development upper-class women with good nutrition from birth will have relatively large and well-formed pelvic cavities. Further advances in obstetric care, such as Caesarean section, which decrease the risk of foetal brain trauma, also tend to be selectively available to the upper classes; both of these factors will eventually lead to *lower* brain-damage rates and a subsequent decrease in the incidence of schizophrenia in the upper classes. Lower-class women do not realize the benefits of improved obstetric care as soon. At the present time, for example, low birthweight, an indicator of delayed intrauterine development, premature delivery and other obstetric complications, is more common in black infants in the United States than among white newborn infants.[37] These infants are at greater risk of schizophrenia: studies have found that low-birthweight infants have more damage around the ventricles of the brain (characteristically found in schizophrenia)[38] and that schizophrenic people tend to have lower birthweights than their healthy siblings.[39] The risk of schizophrenia in the lower classes is no longer moderated by poor survival rates of infants at risk, moreover. The black low-birthweight infants have higher survival rates than white low-birthweight infants.

This analysis helps explain why the recent apparent decrease in the incidence of schizophrenia has been greatest in the most prosperous regions of the United Kingdom,[40] why the districts which show no decrease in schizophrenia have large immigrant populations with high rates of poverty[41] and why Western schizophrenia rates are higher among the poor. Differences in intrauterine development, delivery and infant survival may contribute to the increased risk of schizophrenia in the upper classes in the industrializing world and, conversely, to the high risk in lower social classes and (as we shall see shortly) among the children of immigrants in the post-industrial world.

IMMIGRANTS

Information about the occurrence of schizophrenia in immigrants provides a test of the theory that obstetric complications arising from social change affect the rates of the illness. Immigrants to the industrial world from less developed parts of the globe have a higher incidence of schizophrenia than native-born citizens. Some studies demonstrate that the high rates of the illness are also greater than in the immigrants' countries of origin. The common explanations for these observations are that (a) there is a selective tendency for individuals to emigrate who are constitutionally predisposed to develop schizophrenia and (b) the stress of migration or living in an alien culture increases the risk of developing the illness.[42]

Another possibility is that the pattern of occurrence is a response to the same factors that appear to explain the fluctuation in occurrence with the advance of industrialization – immigrants from poorer countries entering the developed world encounter greater obstetric difficulties due, in part, to changes in maternal nutrition but their infants receive better perinatal care, resulting in the survival of increased numbers of offspring with a heightened risk of schizophrenia. If this explanation is accurate:

- The frequency of schizophrenia will be elevated only in immigrants from countries where nutrition and perinatal care are worse than in the new country.
- The incidence of schizophrenia will be greater in immigrants than in the population of their country of origin.
- The rate of obstetric complications will be elevated among immigrants but neonatal survival rates will also be high.
- The incidence of the illness will be greater in second-generation immigrants than the first generation.

There is no shortage of evidence to demonstrate that immigrants from poor countries to rich show high rates of schizophrenia; the data on this point are clear. In the United States and Canada, numerous studies have shown that successive waves of poor migrants in the first half of the twentieth century, many of them fleeing starvation at home, exhibited first-admission rates for schizophrenia considerably higher than those of the general population – these included Greeks, Poles, Irish, Russians and Swedes.[43] Refugees entering Norway were ten times more likely than the native population to suffer from psychosis.[44] Afro-Caribbean immigrants living in the London boroughs of Lambeth and Camberwell in 1961 were three times more likely (after a correction for the age distribution of the population) than native-born residents to be admitted to hospital with schizophrenia,[45] and many studies since that time have confirmed that the Afro-Caribbean rate of the illness is substantially elevated in Britain.[46] Hospital statistics for England and Wales show that Afro-Caribbean immigrants and (to a lesser degree) Asian immigrants from India and Pakistan had higher rates of admission for schizophrenia than the general population.[47]

Reports of immigrant groups from more affluent countries stand in contrast. British immigrants to Victoria, Australia, in 1959 and 1960, for example, demonstrated an incidence of treated schizophrenia which was similar to the native-born rate but was only a quarter of the incidence among immigrants from southern and eastern Europe.[48] European Jews settling in Israel in the 1950s had a lower incidence of schizophrenia than Jewish immigrants from the Middle East.[49] American-born residents of England and Wales experienced rates of hospitalization for schizophrenia in 1971 which were lower than those for most other immigrants and close to those for native-born residents.[50] English-born immigrants to New York State between 1949 and 1951 exhibited a strikingly lower first-admission rate for schizophrenia than immigrants from other nations or even native-born, white Americans.[51] Immigrants were not overrepresented in a sample of Canadian schizophrenics unless they were coming from eastern Europe and entering a disadvantaged minority population.[52] When Irish-born patients admitted to treatment from Camberwell in 1966–67 and in

1970 were compared with a class-matched group of British-born patients
the prevalence of schizophrenia was found to be no greater in the Irish.[53]
These observations confirm the impression that the occurrence of schizophrenia among immigrants from countries with similar nutritional and
health care standards is not elevated.

Most researchers have emphasized that the elevated incidence of schizophrenia among immigrants from poor countries is greater than among the
population of their countries of origin. Psychiatrist Silvano Arieti points
out that in 1949 the treated incidence rate among Italian immigrants to
New York was three times greater than the highest incidence in Italy.[54]
(Diagnostic variations may account for part of this difference.) Örnulv
Ödegard found that treated schizophrenia among Norwegian immigrants
to Minnesota, prior to the 1930s, was twice as common as among native-
born Americans or among the general population of Norway.[55] The
incidence of schizophrenia in Jamaica appears to be substantially lower
than among Afro-Caribbeans in Britain.[56] On the other hand, immigrants
to London from Ireland, where nutrition is no worse, do not show an
increased prevalence of illness when compared to the Irish who remain in
Eire.[57]

If obstetric complications account for the elevated incidence of schizophrenia among poor immigrants, we should expect to find high rates of
these complications of pregnancy and delivery among immigrant women.
This is, in fact, the case. Afro-Caribbean and Asian women in England
and Wales are more likely to die from complications of childbirth than
women in the general population.[58] Asian-born women in Bradford,
England, are shorter in stature, receive less prenatal care and suffer
more complications of pregnancy than British-born women;[59] and Afro-
Caribbean babies are two or three times more likely than European
infants to have a very low birthweight (indicating possible obstetric
complications).[60]

The infants of immigrants, nevertheless, have high rates of survival,
perhaps because of advanced obstetric care. The children of black women
in one British study did not have higher perinatal mortality rates than those
born to white mothers, but the black mothers required more emergency
Caesarean sections.[61] Although perinatal mortality in the Caribbean is
about five times greater than in Britain,[62] perinatal death rates are no
higher for the Afro-Caribbean infants in Britain than for European
babies.[63] As with black low-birthweight infants in the United States,
neonatal survival for Afro-Caribbean low-birthweight infants in the U.K.
is actually *higher* than for white low-birthweight infants.[64]

An increase in obstetric complications and infant survival in immigrant
women would explain an elevation in the occurrence of schizophrenia
among *second-generation* immigrants, but would not contribute at all to
the rate of the illness among the first generation to arrive. The theory that

obstetric complications are implicated in the occurrence of the illness, therefore, is strongly supported by the finding that the rates of the illness are higher in the second generation than the first. A number of studies have shown that second-generation Afro-Caribbean immigrants have higher rates of schizophrenia than those who emigrated from the home country. One study, which demonstrated the incidence of carefully diagnosed schizophrenia among Afro-Caribbeans in Nottingham, England, to be at least six times greater than among the indigenous population, found that the vast majority of these cases were second generation.[65] A study in Birmingham, England, showed that the schizophrenia rate was substantially greater in *British-born* Afro-Caribbeans than among first-generation immigrants or non-Caribbeans.[66] A study of Afro-Caribbeans in south London[67] confirms that the risk of schizophrenia is substantially greater in second-generation immigrants.

The most recent study of this issue, and one which takes particular care to differentiate between first- and second-generation immigrants, has established important findings: (1) the rate of first admission for schizophrenia among young second-generation Afro-Caribbeans in Manchester was nine times greater than among Europeans, and (2) the rate of first admission for mental disorder in the same age group of *first-generation* Afro-Caribbeans was no greater than among the native British population – in fact the rate was a quarter of that found for Europeans.[68] The implication of these observations is that the process of immigration itself does not increase the risk of schizophrenia: it is the process of being born in the new country which presents increased hazards.

The earlier studies described above, however, did find some increase in the rate of occurrence of schizophrenia in first-generation Afro-Caribbeans over that of the local population. It will be important to see if this proves to be true in the future when careful efforts are made to distinguish first- and second-generation immigrants. If it does, we will need to locate another cause for the increased rate of schizophrenia in immigrants in addition to obstetric difficulties. Some researchers have argued that exposure to a novel virus in the host country may be implicated;[69] a similar explanation has been advanced for the elevated rates of infantile autism[70] and multiple sclerosis[71] in immigrant groups.

Others argue that social stress increases the risk of new immigrants developing the illness. The data presented above make it clear that it is only immigrants who come from poor countries and enter the lowest classes of society in the host country who experience elevated rates of schizophrenia. Do the stresses of urban poverty, menial employment and unemployment provoke the development of the illness? The main problem with this explanation is that, although we know that stress can influence the *course* of schizophrenia, we cannot explain how it can *cause* the illness. Stress increases the release of dopamine and, by exacerbating dopamine supersensitivity, could increase the symptoms of schizophrenia; but there is no known biological mechanism which would allow stress to cause new cases of the illness. While there is good evidence that stress can trigger the onset of an episode of schizophrenia and influence the *timing* of its onset, there is no good reason to believe that it will bring on the illness in someone who would otherwise have stayed healthy.

CROSS-CULTURAL COMPARISONS OF INCIDENCE AND PREVALENCE

If, for example, the stresses of unemployment and wage labor could precipitate a schizophrenic illness in predisposed individuals who would not otherwise have fallen ill we would expect the incidence of schizophrenia to be lower in those parts of the Third World where patterns of wage labor have not developed. In fact, this is not the case.

It is true that the *prevalence* of schizophrenia is significantly lower in the Third World. Age-corrected point prevalence or one-year prevalence rates for studies with comparable research characteristics from the developing world average 3.4 per 1,000 (ranging from 0.9 to 8.0 per 1,000) compared to an average of 6.3 per 1,000 (1.3 to 17.4 per 1,000) in Europe and North America.[72] The *incidence* of schizophrenia, however, is not lower in the Third World.

The recently published WHO study of the incidence of schizophrenia conducted at twelve sites in ten different countries was described in Chapter 7. The findings of the study are striking. The rate of occurrence of narrowly defined "core" schizophrenia, it emerges, is very similar at all the sites studied, varying from a low figure of 0.07 per 1,000 in Aarhus, Denmark, to a high of 0.14 in Nottingham, England. More variation is apparent when a broader diagnostic approach is used, from 0.16 per 1,000 in Honolulu, Hawaii, to 0.42 per 1,000 in the rural area around Chandigarh, India.[73] Even so, this range of variation is far less than would be expected based on the earlier, non-standardized prevalence studies. The gradient of occurrence – from the highest rate in a rural Third World setting to the lowest rate in a large American city – is the exact opposite of what would be expected if labor market stress directly influenced the occurrence of schizophrenia.

Other studies conducted in Ireland[74] and Germany[75] using the same standardized approach applied in the WHO study have found narrowly defined schizophrenia to occur with incidence rates which are very close to those identified in the WHO report. It is difficult to explain why new cases of schizophrenia should occur at such similar rates around the world. One thing, however, is clear – that the wide range in prevalence rates identified in the earlier studies is probably not due to variations in the rate of development of the disorder; it is better explained by differences in case finding, diagnostic approaches, research methodology and death and recovery rates of schizophrenic people. The apparently lower prevalence of schizophrenia in the Third World is almost certainly due to the fact that people suffering from schizophrenia are more likely to recover quickly or to die young in developing countries than they are in the developed world.

DOES LABOUR MARKET STRESS TRIGGER THE ONSET OF SCHIZOPHRENIA?

It seems unlikely that the stresses of the labor market directly affect the rate of occurrence of schizophrenia. If such stress affects the *timing* of onset of schizophrenia, however, we would predict:

● First-time admissions to hospital for schizophrenia will increase in times of high unemployment.
● The age of onset of the illness will be earlier in the sex which is most adversely affected by the labor market.

The first of these predictions has been shown to be true – the evidence was presented towards the end of Chapter 2. We may turn now to the issue of gender differences.

GENDER DIFFERENCES

In Chapter 6 it was argued that the more benign course of schizophrenia in women when compared with men may be a result of the fact that fewer women participate in the labor force and that, overall, women are less severely affected by labor market forces. There are no significant differences, however, in the rate of occurrence of schizophrenia in the two sexes in the industrial world. As the age-specific incidence rates for schizophrenia in Monroe County, New York, indicate (see Figure 9.2), however, this overall similarity in the rates masks the fact that there are wide differences between the sexes in the incidence of the illness at different ages.

The incidence of schizophrenia is roughly twice as great for men aged 15–24 years than for women of the same age. As psychiatrist John Strauss argues, this peak may reflect the intense career and work-related stress upon men at this stage of their lives.[76] Unemployment among adolescents is generally three times the rate for adults[77] and more severely affects males, whose participation in the labor force is substantially greater than females at all ages.[78]

In the next decade of life, from ages 25 to 34 years, the incidence of schizophrenia in women peaks. For black women the rate substantially exceeds that of black men. While labor market stresses may play a part in

Figure 9.2 Treated incidence rates for schizophrenia in 1970 in Monroe County, New York
Source of statistics: Barfigian, H. M., "Schizophrenia: Epidemiology," in H. I. Kaplan, A. M. Freedman and B. J. Sadock (eds.), *Comprehensive Textbook of Psychiatry – III*, Baltimore: Williams & Wilkins, 1980, pp. 1113–21.

shaping this pattern (the rank ordering of the incidence of schizophrenia at this age, with black women highest and white males lowest, precisely matches the unemployment rates for these groups), it is likely that other life stresses are important. These are years of child-bearing and child-rearing, when women are called upon to make stressful role adjustments equivalent to the occupational demands placed upon men. They are also years when many women are required to make major career changes, to enter the labor force for the first time or to re-enter after a long absence.

CONCLUSION

As with any illness, the relationship between the changing dimensions of society and the occurrence of schizophrenia is not simple. Labor market stress probably does not affect the occurrence of schizophrenia directly except, perhaps, to influence the timing of episodes and the age of onset. Nevertheless, until a good explanation emerges for the increased occurrence of schizophrenia in *first-generation* immigrants, socioeconomic stress must remain a possible explanatory factor. The transformation of daily life which accompanies the development of industry, on the other hand, may well affect the rate of occurrence of schizophrenia over time in the different castes and classes by bringing about changes in maternal nutrition and the survival of infants. These same influences can explain the elevated incidence of schizophrenia in second-generation immigrants. For the past century or more we have witnessed a tidal wave of schizophrenia sweep over the industrial world; now, unless this is wishful thinking, it may be passing us by. Those who have recently migrated to the West, however, are still being carried along by the swell.

SUMMARY

- Some diseases rise in incidence early in the process of industrial development and fall in frequency later; they are initially more common among the rich and, later, become more common among the poor. Schizophrenia seems to fit this pattern.
- The Industrial Revolution appears to have been accompanied by an increase in the occurrence of schizophrenia.
- Schizophrenia may be becoming less prevalent in the industrial countries in recent decades.
- In preindustrial settings schizophrenia is more prevalent in the upper castes and classes, but in the West the illness is more common in the poorer classes.
- These shifts in the occurrence of schizophrenia may be a result of changes in nutrition, obstetric complications and neonatal care which accompany the advance of industrialization.
- The risks of developing schizophrenia are greatest for the children of those who migrate from poor countries to rich.
- Labor market stress may influence the timing of the onset of schizophrenia but not the incidence.

- Although the prevalence of schizophrenia is lower in the Third World than in the West, the incidence is not.
- Women in the industrial world show a peak incidence of schizophrenia a decade later in life than men.

Part III

Treatment

Chapter 10

Antipsychotic drugs: use, abuse and non-use

---

f

Hundreds of double-blind studies of the efficacy of the antipsychotic (or neuroleptic) drugs have now been conducted. The large majority of these studies suggest that these drugs are significantly more effective than inactive placebos in improving the condition of people with acute and chronic schizophrenia.[1] Time after time, in many thousands of treatment settings, clinical experience has shown that the antipsychotic drugs can bring dramatic relief from psychotic symptoms in most schizophrenic patients. Long-term use of these medications appears to help forestall relapse. Twice as many schizophrenic patients will relapse if placebos are substituted for their active medication than if they continue to take a neuroleptic drug.[2] Yet the overall outcome in schizophrenia, as shown by the analysis of dozens of follow-up studies in Chapter 3, has not improved since the introduction of the antipsychotic drugs in 1954. How can this be?

The issue is a complex one, and we may begin to tackle it by first addressing a related question.

WHICH PEOPLE WITH SCHIZOPHRENIA SHOULD NOT BE TREATED WITH ANTIPSYCHOTIC DRUGS?

The antipsychotic drugs have emerged as a routine, almost automatic, remedy in psychosis and relatively little effort has been made in psychiatry to use these medicines selectively. One might search a long time to find a diagnosed schizophrenic individual who has never been treated with a neuroleptic drug. It may be better, however, to avoid the use of antipsychotic drugs in the care of substantial numbers of these patients, but the existence of such subgroups of schizophrenic patients has not been well recognized.

Misdiagnosed patients

Among any large group of patients labeled schizophrenic there will be several for whom an alternate diagnosis is more appropriate. This is particularly true for chronic patients in the United States who received their diagnosis before the mid-1970s, when American psychiatrists began to distinguish manic-depressive illness from schizophrenia according to European criteria. The history of some patients diagnosed as schizophrenic may reveal clear evidence of the mood swings characteristic of manic-depressive psychosis. Others may be in treatment for schizophrenia although their hallucinations and other symptoms are more suggestive of hysteria. In all such cases a regular review of the history and diagnosis is warranted with a view to changing or discontinuing the medicine for a trial period.

Drug refusers

Many schizophrenic people prefer not to take drugs. Some have grandiose delusions and fail to recognize that they have an illness. Others dislike the unpleasant effects of the antipsychotic drugs and would rather suffer their psychotic symptoms. U.S. courts have recognized the right of psychiatric patients to refuse medication even while they are detained involuntarily under the state's mental illness statute. Such rulings have established that the patient's lack of competence to make a decision about his or her own treatment must be demonstrated (over and above the grounds for involuntary detention) before he or she may be medicated unwillingly.[3]

Seen initially by psychiatrists as "the profession's dark hour"[4] and leading to patients "rotting with their rights on,"[5] the legal constraints placed upon physicians in the use of involuntary medication have not proved as harmful as feared. Psychiatrists and patients alike have been forced to weigh more carefully the benefits and disadvantages of drug treatment in psychosis. While there are occasions when the local court must be asked to rule whether a client is competent to refuse drug treatment, in the majority of cases the patient and physician come to an agreement. The psychiatrist may accept that the patient's refusal is appropriate, or the patient may be persuaded to accept his or her doctor's advice. There is now clear recognition that, for some patients, the course of the schizophrenic illness is not so severe as to require the involuntary use of antipsychotic drugs.

Tardive dyskinesia

The same necessity to weigh the costs and benefits of drug treatment has resulted from the appearance of delayed neurological side effects from the use of the neuroleptic drugs. Tardive dyskinesia comprises involuntary movements of the lips, tongue, jaw and other parts of the body, which may appear after a patient has been taking antipsychotic drugs for several months or years. If the medicines are not discontinued promptly, the condition may become irreversible. As many as a third of outpatients taking antipsychotic drugs have been found to suffer from these symptoms, though they are mild in the vast majority of cases.[6] Patients taking high doses of medication are at greater risk of developing the disorder. In some cases in which tardive dyskinesia has developed, the patient and the doctor may conclude that the disability from the psychosis is less severe than the possible disfiguration due to the drug-induced neurological disorder. In these cases neuroleptics are to be avoided.

Non-responders

Ironically, among the patients who are most likely to develop tardive dyskinesia are those for whom the antipsychotic drugs have proven *least* beneficial.[7] This may well be a result of the understandable tendency for psychiatrists to give ever-increasing doses of medicine to patients who are functioning poorly and who are not responding adequately to the usual drug dosages. Each new crisis or relapse may lead to another dosage increase. Unfortunately, many such patients may find themselves taking very substantial – even incapacitating – amounts of medication to no real benefit.

Interestingly enough, it may be possible to predict which schizophrenic patients will respond poorly to treatment with the neuroleptics. Different groups of researchers have independently shown that patients who find the first dose of these drugs particularly unpleasant are most likely to show little benefit from their use and to relapse early. Such "dysphoric responders" react to a small amount of the drug with depression, anxiety, suspiciousness and immobilization – symptoms which are not alleviated (in one study, at least) by the usual antidotes to the extrapyramidal side effects of the neuroleptics.[8] (Extrapyramidal side effects – rigidity, tremor and restlessness – mimic the symptoms of Parkinson's Disease and may be relieved by the drugs used to treat that condition.)

What proportion of schizophrenic patients are unresponsive to antipsychotic drug treatment? In one British study 7 per cent of a large group of schizophrenic patients showed no improvement with drug treatment and a further 24 per cent relapsed within a year despite such therapy.[9] In a large study conducted by the U.S. National Institute of Mental Health, 5 per cent of the acutely ill schizophrenic patients failed to show improvement with drug therapy,[10] and a number of American studies have found that 10–20 per cent of schizophrenic patients relapse within six months while in treatment with antipsychotic drugs.[11] All those patients who show no short-term benefit from drug treatment, and many of those who relapse despite taking them, might reasonably be considered for treatment with clozapine (a new type of neuroleptic with hazardous side effects) or with no medication.

Good-prognosis schizophrenia

There remains a further subgroup of people with schizophrenia as large as all of the categories above combined, for which there are grounds to believe that the usual drug treatment is unnecessary or even harmful in the long run. These are the people with good-prognosis schizophrenia – the patients who show some indication that the course of their illness will be benign. Generally speaking, these are people whose psychotic illness began with sudden onset later in life than is usual in schizophrenia, whose previous work history and social functioning have been good and whose illness has not yet become long-lasting. To understand why the antipsychotic drugs may be contraindicated for such patients, however, we must review some of what is known of the neurochemistry of schizophrenia and of the action of the antipsychotic drugs.

THE DOPAMINE HYPOTHESIS

Messages flow through the central nervous system as impulses in the nerve cells, or neurons. Where neurons link up, at the synapse, a chemical mediator is released from one cell which transmits the impulse to the next cell by its influence on a specific receptor. A number of these neurotransmitters have been identified. Some, because of their particular importance in areas of the brain concerned with the emotions, have been quite intensively studied and have been implicated in the origin of various neurological and psychiatric disorders. Deficiencies of norepinephrine (noradrenalin) and serotonin at brain synapses, for example, are thought to underlie the development of depressive illness. The predominant theory for a neurochemical deficit in schizophrenia is that the illness is a result of a relative overactivity of certain tracts of neurons in which the chemical mediator is dopamine (dopaminergic tracts).

The dopamine hypothesis of schizophrenia[12] is based upon two main pieces of evidence:

(1) The antipsychotic drugs block the ability of dopamine receptors in the synapse to respond to dopamine and thus reduce the activity in dopaminergic tracts. The relative antipsychotic potency of the different drugs, furthermore, appears to be directly proportional to the capacity of each drug to block dopamine receptors.
(2) The stimulant drug, amphetamine, which increases the release of dopamine and other catecholamines in the brain, will produce in humans an acute psychosis which is very similar to schizophrenia if it is taken in sufficient amounts. The drug will also bring about an exacerbation of psychotic symptoms in schizophrenic patients.

Dopaminergic fibers are to be found in a number of major tracts in the central nervous system. Two of these pathways, the mesolimbic and the mesocortical tracts, are considered to be possible sites of defective dopamine activity in schizophrenia. A disturbance in the mesolimbic system, in particular, can result in an inability to filter out multiple environmental stimuli – a characteristic disorder in schizophrenia.[13] Damage to the limbic system, or electrical stimulation of this pathway, can result in a number of other schizophrenia-like symptoms, including hallucinations, disturbances in thinking and emotion, paranoia, depersonalization and perceptual distortion.[14]

DOPAMINE SUPERSENSITIVITY

The dopamine hypothesis must accommodate itself to the repeated finding that the amounts of the breakdown products of dopamine (homovanillic acid and 5–hydroxyindolacetic acid) leaving the brain in the cerebrospinal fluid are no higher in schizophrenic than in normal people.[15] In fact, one well-designed study demonstrated that the release of dopamine products was *reduced* in schizophrenic people with the worst prognostic indicators. This observation is the reverse of what might be expected from the hypothesis that dopamine activity is elevated in schizophrenia.

Malcolm Bowers, a researcher in neurochemistry, has neatly explained this paradox by arguing that the elevated dopamine activity in schizophrenia is a result not of an excess of dopamine at the synapse, but of a supersensitivity of dopamine receptors to the effects of the neurotransmitter. Consequently, the dopaminergic neurons are more readily stimulated but, through a negative feedback process, the neuronal system attempts to minimize the defect through a reduction in dopamine turnover.[16] Bowers' hypothesis gains support from the observation, made by several groups of researchers, that dopamine receptor binding capacity is increased post-mortem in the mesolimbic tract of schizophrenic people. (Although some of these reports indicate that this finding is restricted to schizophrenic patients who were taking neuroleptics, a larger number of studies has shown that it holds true also for drug-free patients.[17])

If the basic neurochemical deficit in schizophrenia is a dopamine receptor supersensitivity, it would still be possible for sudden increases in dopamine turnover to lead to an acute exacerbation of the psychosis. Recurrent exposure to stress in mice leads to an increase in dopamine turnover.[18] If humans respond similarly, then stress-induced episodes of psychosis in schizophrenic people could result from the effect of an acute increase in dopamine turnover on the chronic receptor supersensitivity.

How do the antipsychotic drugs fit into this scheme? Clearly, by blocking the hypersensitive dopamine receptors they diminish the activity of the neurons and reduce the symptoms of psychosis. The dopamine-blocking action, however, eliminates the feedback process which has been keeping dopamine turnover at a low level. With the administration of these drugs dopamine turnover promptly increases.[19] This is not an immediate problem, as the receptors are blocked by the neuroleptic drugs and the increase in neurotransmitter can have little effect. There is a potential, however, for serious long-term effects.

Chronic dopamine receptor blockade by the administration of the neuroleptic drugs, and the consequent elevation in dopamine turnover, have been found to produce a substantial increase in the number of binding sites for dopamine in the brains of rats.[20] That is, the drugs create an artificial dopamine supersensitivity. There is strong evidence that the same process occurs in humans. It is believed, for example, that tardive dyskinesia – the delayed neurological side effect of chronic neuroleptic drug use which occurs in a large proportion of patients – is a dopamine supersensitivity phenomenon. Dopamine receptors in the nigrostriatal tract overcompensate for the chronic blockade by becoming hypersensitive. The symptoms of tardive dyskinesia (involuntary muscle movements) usually appear after a reduction in the dose of the neuroleptic drug, as this change exposes some of the previously blocked, supersensitive receptors to the action of the neurotransmitter. An increase in drug dosage, on the other hand, will block the receptors and mask the symptoms of the disorder.

A potential hazard of the neuroleptic drugs should now be apparent. An important neurochemical deficit in schizophrenia may well be supersensitivity of dopamine receptors. The immediate action of the neuroleptic drugs is to minimize the effects of that deficit; on this basis rests the great value of these drugs in psychiatry. The long-term effect of the neuroleptics, however, may be *a worsening of this crucial neurochemical defect in schizophrenia*. As in tardive dyskinesia the supersensitivity effect may be temporary, gradually disappearing over the course of weeks or months after drug withdrawal, or – if drug treatment continues long enough – it may become permanent. Herein may lie one reason for the failure of the antipsychotic drugs to produce improvements in the long-term outlook for schizophrenic people.

For the neuroleptics to present a risk of worsening the schizophrenic defect they would need to produce a dopamine supersensitivity not just in the nigrostriatal tract (where they cause tardive dyskinesia) but also in the mesolimbic pathway. Several studies now indicate that they accomplish just this. There is an increase in dopamine binding sites in the mesolimbic region of the brains of schizophrenia patients which is related to the extent of their prior treatment with neuroleptic drugs.[21] Clearly, this formulation, if correct, has serious implications for drug treatment in schizophrenia.

IMPLICATIONS OF DRUG-INDUCED DOPAMINE SUPERSENSITIVITY

We may predict that certain consequences will flow from the tendency of the neuroleptic drugs to produce dopamine supersensitivity if they are, in fact, worsening an underlying defect in schizophrenia. These include:

• Psychotic symptoms will rebound after the withdrawal of antipsychotic drug treatment to a higher level than would have been the case without treatment. Drug-withdrawal studies which evaluate the efficacy of neuroleptic drugs by substituting a placebo for the active drug will therefore give an over-optimistic impression of the value of the drugs.
• The adverse long-term effects of the antipsychotic drugs will be most evident in the case of people with schizophrenia who would otherwise have had a good prognosis. As illustrated in Figure 10.1, the outcome for *poor-prognosis* schizophrenic people is likely to be so serious that a worsening due to drug withdrawal would be difficult to detect and the continuous use of drugs will still offer distinct advantages for these patients. In the case of *good-prognosis* schizophrenic patients, on the other hand, drug withdrawal may worsen the course of an otherwise benign condition and drug maintenance therapy may increase the risk of psychosis, cause side effects or, at best, prove worthless.

We may examine the evidence relating to these predictions in turn.

IMMEDIATE ASSIGNMENT STUDIES

Drug-withdrawal (placebo substitution) studies may exaggerate the long-term benefits of the antipsychotic drugs on the course of schizophrenia. In particular, they may give a spurious impression of the value of drug treatment for good-prognosis patients which is the reverse of their real long-term effect (see Figure 10.1). Accordingly, the only drug studies which would be expected to give an accurate reflection of the efficacy of the neuroleptic drugs in schizophrenia are those which:

(a) assign patients to drug or placebo treatment at the beginning of the study (immediate assignment studies) and do not withdraw neuroleptic treatment part-way through the study; and which also
(b) distinguish between good-prognosis and poor-prognosis patients.

Such studies are few.

Rosen and associates

Psychopharmacology researchers Bernard Rosen and David Engelhardt and their co-workers followed a group of over 400 schizophrenic out-patients of a New York clinic for between four and eight years. They divided the group into good- and poor-prognosis categories on the basis of their own "Hospital Proneness Scale" which measured the patients' prior social attainment, the extent of their previous treatment and their

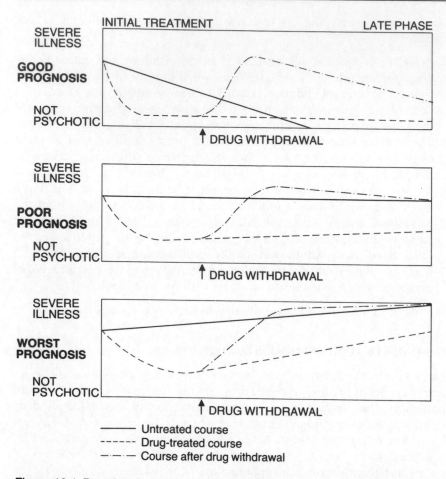

Figure 10.1 Postulated course of illness in good-, poor- and worst-prognosis schizophrenic people with and without neuroleptic drug treatment and after drug withdrawal

performance in psychological tests. The patients were randomly assigned at the very outset of the study to treatment with either a placebo or one of two antipsychotic drugs, chlorpromazine or promazine. The subsequent hospital admission rate indicated that the neuroleptic drugs were effective in keeping the poor-prognosis schizophrenic people out of hospital:

	Hospital admission rate of poor-prognosis patients
Patients taking chlorpromazine	35.7%
Patients taking promazine	29.4%
Patients taking placebo	61.5%

For good-prognosis patients, however, drug treatment appeared to be unhelpful or even harmful:[22]

	Hospital admission rate of good-prognosis patients
Patients taking chlorpromazine	12.2%
Patients taking promazine	28.4%
Patients taking placebo	7.7%

Subsequently these researchers followed up the 129 patients who had been hospitalized to see which schizophrenic patients were hospitalized for a second time. The results were even more striking. Drug treatment proved effective in keeping poor-prognosis patients out of hospital longer:

	Average time before rehospitalization of poor-prognosis patients
Patients on chlorpromazine	14 months
Patients on promazine	16 months
Patients on placebo	6 months

But good-prognosis patients treated with chlorpromazine were hospitalized significantly sooner:[23]

	Average time before rehospitalization of good-prognosis patients
Patients on chlorpromazine	6 months
Patients on promazine	14 months
Patients on placebo	30 months

University of California Group

In a study at Camarillo State Hospital, California, psychologist Michael Goldstein and his associates divided a group of 54 newly hospitalized, male schizophrenic patients into good- and poor-prognosis cases (using a scale devised by Leslie Phillips). The patients were randomly assigned to treatment with a placebo or an antipsychotic drug soon after admission. After three weeks of treatment the poor-prognosis patients appeared to benefit from taking active medication. The good-prognosis patients, however, did better if they were taking a placebo – they improved more rapidly and were discharged sooner. This finding was particularly true for non-paranoid, good-prognosis patients.[24] The researchers uncovered a similar pattern of response when they repeated their study with a new sample of 24 good-prognosis, male schizophrenic patients – neuroleptic drugs failed to benefit the non-paranoid, good-prognosis patients in three weeks of treatment.[25] Unfortunately, no long-term follow-up of the patients in either of these studies was done.

Interestingly enough, this research group obtained analogous findings when they compared the effect of high versus low doses of antipsychotic drugs treatment on a group of 104 young, acute schizophrenic patients. The good-prognosis patients – particularly males – showed a negligible rate of relapse and had fewer symptoms at the end of six months on the *lower* dose of medication. (Female good-prognosis patients in this study only did well on a low dose of medication when they were also receiving adequate family-oriented psychosocial treatment.)[26]

Rappaport and associates

Eighty young, male, acute schizophrenic patients admitted to Agnews State Hospital in California were randomly assigned on admission to chlorpromazine or placebo treatment by Maurice Rappaport and his co-workers. After discharge from the hospital the patients were treated with or without active medication depending, presumably, on their clinical condition and their compliance with the psychiatrist's recommendation. Patients who did well on placebo treatment in hospital tended to be treated without medication after leaving hospital and to be good-prognosis schizophrenic people with a history of good functioning before admission. Placebo treatment failures were likely to be given active medication after discharge. At three-year follow-up the patients who took a placebo in hospital and were off medication as outpatients showed the greatest clinical improvement and the lowest levels of pathology and functional disturbance. They also had the lowest rate of rehospitalization:

Hospital/outpatient treatment	Rehospitalization rate
Placebo/no medication (N=24)	8%
Chlorpromazine/no medication (N=17)	47%
Placebo/neuroleptic (N=17)	53%
Chlorpromazine/neuroleptic (N=22)	73%

The superiority of the placebo/no medication group to the chlorpromazine/ no medication category is particularly worth noting, although part of this difference in outcome may be due to there being a greater proportion of good-prognosis patients in the former group. The authors of the study conclude:

Antipsychotic medication is not the treatment of choice, at least for certain patients, if one is interested in long-term clinical improvement.[27]

Carpenter and associates

Good-prognosis schizophrenic patients with adequate records of prior work and social functioning and a short history of illness were selected for a study conducted at the U.S. National Institute of Mental Health by William Carpenter and his associates. The 49 patients were treated with or without neuroleptic medication at the discretion of their psychiatrists – the assignment to drug treatment was fairly arbitrary but not random. The two groups were equivalent in their prognostic ratings and had similar initial clinical characteristics. At one-year follow-up the patients in the drug-free treatment group demonstrated a more benign course in a number of ways:

	Drug-free	Drug-treated
Average length of hospital stay	108 days	126 days
Rehospitalization rate	35%	45%
Outpatient neuroleptic drug treatment	44%	67%

Patients receiving drug treatment in hospital were also significantly more likely to suffer a postpsychotic depression.

The research team who conducted this study

raise the possibility that antipsychotic medication may make some schizophrenic patients more vulnerable to future relapse than would be the case in the natural course of their illness. Thus, as with tardive dyskinesia, we may have a situation where neuroleptics increase the risk of subsequent illness but must be maintained to prevent this risk from becoming manifest.[28]

Klein and Rosen

One study alone which fits the criteria of (a) immediately assigning patients to a drug-free or drug-treatment category and (b) distinguishing good-prognosis patients fails to support the picture drawn by the research cited so far. Donald Klein and Bernard Rosen randomly assigned 88 schizophrenic inpatients of the Hillside Hospital, New York, to chlorpromazine or placebo treatment. The researchers differentiated good- and poor-prognosis patients by means of the Premorbid Asocial Adjustment Scale. On rating the patients after six weeks of treatment the investigators found that chlorpromazine was more beneficial for the *good*-prognosis than for the poor-prognosis patients.

From the standpoint of this analysis, however, the Klein and Rosen study has two flaws. In the first place, it is not a follow-up study. It gives the outcome of only six weeks of treatment and has no bearing on whether drug-induced dopamine supersensitivity has a detrimental effect on the long-term course of schizophrenia. It therefore stands in contradiction to Goldstein's short-term studies only, and is unrelated to the findings of the research teams of Rosen and Engelhardt, Rappaport and Carpenter. Secondly, the research design itself was biased against recovery in the good-prognosis patients. The research sample was composed of patients who were referred to the drug study after they had failed to improve in milieu (drug-free) treatment and psychotherapy. This selection procedure would automatically weed out the patients who could be expected to do well in drug-free treatment.[29]

Goldberg and associates

The authors of another study of the effect of drug treatment in schizophrenia – Solomon Goldberg and his associates – have also claimed to refute many of the findings presented above. "We find no evidence," they argue, "that patients with good signs are not in need of drugs; instead they profit most from drug treatment."[30] Goldberg's research, however, is a drug-*withdrawal* study; as such, it may be expected to demonstrate a benefit for drug treatment in good-prognosis patients – but, according to the supersensitivity psychosis hypothesis, the benefit is spurious.

May and associates

A number of studies may be found in the literature which, while not precisely fitting the criteria established for this analysis, nevertheless yield useful information. Philip May and his colleagues, for example, in a four-year follow-up of over 200 first-admission schizophrenic patients showed that 59–79 per cent of patients recovered in various drug-free treatments (including psychotherapy and electroconvulsive therapy) and that the successes from such treatment (presumably good-prognosis patients) did as well in the long term as patients who were initially treated with neuroleptics.[31]

Schooler and associates

Nina Schooler and her co-workers made a similar finding in another immediate assignment drug study of a large sample of schizophrenic people conducted through the U.S. National Institute of Mental Health. In a follow-up of the discharged patients one year after leaving hospital the researchers were surprised to find that "patients who received placebo treatment in the drug study were *less* likely to be rehospitalized than those who received any of the three active phenothiazines."[32]

Pasamanick and associates

We should recognize, however, that there is another immediate assignment study which does not discriminate good- and poor-prognosis patients – Benjamin Pasamanick's comparison of outcome of drug-treated and placebo-treated patients in home care – and that this report does *not* show a long-term benefit to placebo treatment.[33] Why should the placebo-users in Schooler's NIMH study have had a superior outcome? One possibility is that there were more good-prognosis patients admitted to that study than to Pasamanick's. The subjects in the NIMH study typically had a number of good-prognostic features – the illness was at an early stage, the onset had been acute and later in life, and many of the patients were currently or previously married.[34]

The Soteria Project

Another immediate assignment study of treatment in schizophrenia well worth examining is the Soteria Project. Under the direction of psychiatrist Loren Mosher (at the time Chief of the Center for Studies of Schizophrenia at NIMH) and social worker Alma Menn, this project set out to compare the effectiveness of a non-medical, psychosocial treatment program for first-break schizophrenic patients with the drug-oriented treatment of a community mental health center. Acutely ill patients who had previously had no more than two weeks of inpatient psychiatric treatment were arbitrarily assigned to treatment in a short-stay inpatient unit followed by outpatient aftercare or to Soteria House, a home for up to six patients in the community staffed by non-professionals. Patients in the standard community mental health center program spent a much shorter time in their initial period of residential (hospital) care – one month compared with five-and-a-half months of residential care for Soteria patients. Whereas all the mental health center patients were initially treated with neuroleptic drugs only 8 per cent of Soteria patients received such therapy.

Follow-up, two years after admission, showed that the outcome for Soteria patients compared quite favorably with that of the schizophrenic patients treated by the community mental health center:

Two-year follow-up Treatment after discharge	Soteria	Mental health center
Readmitted to hospital or Soteria House	53%	67%
Taking neuroleptic drugs continuously or intermittently	34%	95%
Receiving psychiatric treatment	59%	100%
Circumstances at follow-up		
Working (full-time or part-time)	76%	79%
Living independently	58%	33%

The overall levels of psychopathology in the two groups of patients were not significantly different at follow-up.

Mosher and Menn suggest:

> Our data indicate that antipsychotic drugs need not be used routinely with newly admitted schizophrenics if a nurturant, supportive psycho-social environment can be supplied in their stead.[35]

The authors point out that their sample of patients was not composed of particularly good-prognosis cases – they selected individuals who were young and single, generally considered indicators of poor outlook. All patients, however, were at a very early stage of their illness. Patients with the fewest relapses in both treatment programs tended to have good-prognostic features (better prior social competence and a later age of onset), but there is no indication whether good-prognosis patients did better in drug-free care.[36]

Soteria Berne

Soteria Berne, a therapeutic household for the treatment of schizophrenia, borrows many ideas from Mosher and Menn's Soteria Project. Established by psychiatrist Luc Ciompi in a twelve-room house in the middle of Berne, Switzerland, the program can accommodate up to eight patients and two nurses. Like the California-based Soteria, the household in Berne aims to manage people with schizophrenia in a small supportive environment using neuroleptic medication in low doses and only in unusual circumstances. Young people with a first episode of schizophrenia are selected fairly randomly for admission (very agitated or involuntary patients are excluded) from among cases presenting to the local emergency services. Some patients with longer-lasting illness and poor-prognosis features are also admitted.

Twenty-five people treated at Soteria Berne were compared with a matched group of 25 similar patients treated at conventional local hospitals. When the two groups were followed up after two years, conventionally treated and Soteria patients had similar levels of pathology and functioning. Soteria-treated patients, however, had used much lower doses of antipsychotic medication – a quarter as much during the acute treatment phase, and half as much overall. Thus the results at Soteria Berne are very similar to those at Soteria in California.[37]

The weight of evidence in these immediate assignment studies suggests that the neuroleptic drugs are unnecessary or harmful, in the long run, for good-prognosis schizophrenic patients. Taken together with the well-established fact that drug-*withdrawal* studies have consistently shown the neuroleptics to be superior to placebos in preventing psychotic relapse,[38] we now have an indication that the antipsychotic drugs produce a heightened risk of relapse for drug-withdrawn patients. They may do this by worsening an underlying dopamine receptor supersensitivity in schizophrenia. On the one hand, then, we have sound reasons to offer good-prognosis and early schizophrenic patients an adequate trial of drug-free treatment (and in the American and Swiss Soteria projects we have models for doing this cost effectively). On the other hand, we have at least one possible explanation for the failure of the antipsychotic drugs to have a measurable impact on overall outcome in schizophrenia.

If we now look at the interactions between environmental stress and antipsychotic drug treatment in schizophrenia we may find further reasons for the poor showing of the antipsychotics and, in addition, useful indications as to how we can help make low-dose or drug-free treatment effective.

STRESS, SCHIZOPHRENIA AND DRUG TREATMENT

Stress, as noted in Chapter 1, may precipitate a psychotic episode in a predisposed individual.[39] The antipsychotic drugs, moreover, may be less necessary for preventing relapse in schizophrenia for people living under conditions of low social stress, and of greater utility for those in a more harsh and demanding environment. As British social psychiatrist John Wing writes:

> Drug treatment and social treatments are not alternatives but must be used to complement each other. The better the environmental conditions, the less the need for medication: the poorer the social milieu, the greater the need (or at least the use) of drugs.[40]

A number of pieces of research support this point of view.

A series of projects conducted through the Medical Research Council Social Psychiatry Unit in London has shown that the relapse rate is higher in schizophrenic patients who return home to live with critical or over-involved relatives than in those (the majority) whose relatives are more supportive and less smothering. The relapse rate in the patients living in the more stressful households is reduced by two factors: (a) restricting the contact between patient and relatives to less than 35 hours a week and (b) using neuroleptic drugs. For patients living in the low-stress families, however, the relapse rate was found to be low regardless of whether the patients were taking medicine or not. Figure 10.2 illustrates the nine-month relapse rates for 128 schizophrenic patients (71 from low-stress homes and 57 from high-stress families) – the combined subject groups from the two studies.[41] The rate of relapse among patients living in low-stress households and taking no medication can be seen to be several times lower than the rate for those schizophrenic patients who are exposed to a high-stress environment for much of the time even when these patients are protected by medication.

In a later (two-year) follow-up of one of these groups of schizophrenic patients, psychiatrist Julian Leff and psychologist Christine Vaughn found that neuroleptics did eventually appear to be of some benefit to the patients in low-stress homes. The researchers speculated that the drugs were of value in protecting these patients against additional sources of life-event stress (e.g. job loss) to which they were exposed independently of the fact that their home environments were warm and supportive.[42] Dr. Leff and Dr. Vaughn had demonstrated in an earlier piece of research that relapse was unavoidably common in schizophrenic patients living in high-stress homes but that relapse in patients in low-stress homes was only likely to occur if they were subjected to additional independent stressful events.[43] One may conclude from these findings that neuroleptic drugs are less necessary for schizophrenic patients living in environments which are both supportive and also somewhat protective in warding off unpredictable stresses.

The therapeutic effect of a warm and non-critical relative has been

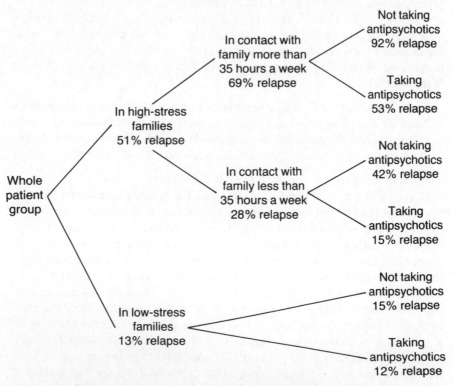

Figure 10.2 Relapse rates of schizophrenic patients in high- and low-stress families
Source: Vaughn, C. E. and Leff, J. P., "The influence of family and social factors on the course of psychiatric illness: A comparison of schizophrenic and depressed neurotic patients," *British Journal of Psychiatry*, 129: 125–37, 1976.

demonstrated in two further studies carried out by the same group of researchers. Heart rate and skin conductance tests showed that schizophrenic people had a higher level of arousal than normal individuals, irrespective of whether the patients were living in high-stress or low-stress households. This heightened level of arousal dropped to normal in a person with schizophrenia when in the company of a non-stressful relative but continued at an elevated rate when in the company of a critical, overinvolved relative. The finding held true for both acutely psychotic patients[44] and those in remission.[45] The neuroleptic drugs similarly are known to decrease the level of arousal in people with schizophrenia – a property which is thought to contribute to their antipsychotic effect. This evidence, then, also implies that the neuroleptic drugs may be less necessary where the social environment is therapeutic and non-stressful.

The level of arousal in schizophrenic patients in hospital or residential treatment can be controlled by creating an environment which is optimally stimulating and supportive. In such a setting drug treatment is minimally necessary. Long-stay hospital patients withdrawn from low-dosage maintenance drugs, according to psychologist Gordon Paul's review of the published research, rarely show harmful effects, and a majority of the relevant studies indicate that drug treatment is not necessary for such patients when they are in a progressive psychosocial treatment program.[46]

One such study is Gordon Paul's own report on a drug-withdrawal project involving 52 severely incapacitated, long-stay schizophrenic patients from an Illinois state hospital. The patients were transferred to two active psychosocial treatment programs and matched groups were assigned to either continuation of their usual drugs or to placebo substitution. Staff and patients were not even aware that a drug study was in process. After four months the drug-withdrawn patients were doing as well as those on drugs (initially, in fact, the drug-withdrawn patients had responded *more* rapidly to the treatment program).[47] By the end of the six-year experimental program, 85 per cent of the schizophrenic patients in psychosocial treatment were still off drugs.[48] Why was drug-withdrawal supersensitivity psychosis not a problem with these patients? Perhaps because, in this instance, they were generally taking only moderate to low doses of medication before withdrawal.

Research cited earlier in this chapter – William Carpenter's study at the National Institute of Mental Health, Loren Mosher's Soteria House and Luc Ciompi's Soteria Berne – has demonstrated that the same observation holds true for young acute schizophrenic patients. Active, individualized, psychosocial treatment programs render antipsychotic drug therapy less necessary for a substantial number of patients.

One prominent, recent study might be seen as conflicting with the general trend of this research. The study, by Solomon Goldberg with his associates in the NIMH Collaborative Study Group, was discussed earlier in the chapter when it was mentioned as showing that the relapse rate of schizophrenic patients withdrawn from antipsychotic drugs was greater than that of patients who continued the drug treatment. Another aspect of the research report is relevant here. At the time of discharge from hospital these patients were randomly allocated to either routine outpatient care or to a more intensive program of sociotherapy – major role therapy, a combination of social casework and vocational counseling. The researchers found that, overall, the intensive sociotherapy was ineffective. This was because the therapy helped some patients and hindered others. Mildly ill patients benefited and more severely ill patients relapsed *sooner* if they were receiving intensive sociotherapy.[49] Patients taking antipsychotic drugs responded well, but those taking placebos had a *worse* community adjustment if they were in major role therapy.[50]

At first glance it appears that these results contradict the evidence for the benefits of psychosocial treatment in schizophrenia, but on closer examination this does not prove to be the case. The psychosocial treatment programs in Gordon Paul's study or on William Carpenter's research ward or at Soteria House were comprehensive attempts to shape a total therapeutic residential environment in such a way as to maximize the psychotic patients' chances of recovery. Major role therapy, on the other hand, consisted of outpatient treatment delivered to schizophrenic patients living in any one of a number of community locations. The patients in this "intensive" therapy program were seen, on average, only twice a month.[51] The main thrust of the therapy was to urge "the patient to become more responsible and to expand his horizons."[52] The authors appropriately conclude that the major role therapy was probably too intrusive and stressful for the marginally functioning patients and that its toxic effect was similar to the influence of the critical and overinvolved relatives in the British studies of the family environment of schizophrenic patients cited above.

By way of contrast, some forms of outpatient therapy which do aim to reduce the stresses in the patients' environment have proved successful. Julian Leff and his co-workers were able to minimize the impact of critical and overinvolved relatives on schizophrenic patients through family therapy and thus to reduce the relapse rate in these patients.[53] New Zealand psychiatrist Ian Falloon in association with a team of researchers in California achieved a similar result working with the families of schizophrenic patients in their homes – family-treated patients showed fewer psychotic symptoms and fewer relapses.[54]

We may conclude that when people with schizophrenia are in an environment which is protective but not regressive, stimulating but not stressful, and warm but not intrusive (whether it be their own family home or a residential treatment unit) many of these patients will need less antipsychotic drug treatment. On the other hand, people with schizophrenia who are exposed to significant stress (whether it be status loss, intrusive relatives, overenthusiastic psychotherapy or hunger, cold and poverty) – such patients will have a high relapse rate and will require substantial doses of neuroleptic drugs to achieve adequate functioning levels.

Many patients, of course, do not choose to be in a highly protective setting – they prefer independence. Life cannot be made stress-free unless one chooses to withdraw from the excitement of daily living. In practice, for most patients drug-free treatment is not feasible. Even in the best community treatment systems there is a place for the judicious use of antipsychotic medication. A reasonable goal for the majority of people with schizophrenia is to use moderate doses of medication which lead to a genuine improvement in quality of life without adding to life's hardships.

In Western society in recent decades, nevertheless, too few schizophrenic people have been placed in reasonably suitable therapeutic settings. With the advent of antipsychotic drugs and the advance of radical deinstitutionalization policies, too many have been thrust into highly stressful environments. As we saw in Chapter 8, around a third of all schizophrenic people in the United States exist in settings which scarcely pretend to be therapeutic – in jail, on Skid Row, in nursing homes or boarding homes. A study of the mentally ill in Utah nursing homes, for example, showed that their use of medication increased with time but that their levels of activity decreased.[55]

Here we find another explanation for the failure of the drug-treatment era in psychiatry to usher in improved outcome in schizophrenia. In the rush to transfer patients to the community – to cut institutional costs regardless of the social costs – the antipsychotics have been used not as an *adjunct* to psychosocial treatment, as John Wing recommends, but as an *alternative* to such care. Too often the psychiatrist is called upon to wedge the schizophrenic patient into an ill-fitting slot because an appropriately therapeutic setting is not available, affordable or even considered feasible. In these circumstances the prescription becomes, in a sense, a political document.

THE REVOLVING-DOOR PATIENT

The ascendancy of psychopharmacology over psychosocial treatment is epitomized by the revolving-door patient. This creation of the neuroleptic era has become a focus of public concern – the central character, for example, in a series of *New Yorker* articles and the subject of a groundbreaking court decision. Sylvia Frumkin's ten admissions to Creedmoor Hospital, New York City, by age 31, her multiple hospital admissions elsewhere, and her family's consequent suffering, all documented in the *New Yorker*,[56] represent nothing unusual. Not uncommonly, several times in one year the same patient will be medicated back to sanity in an American public hospital and discharged to an inadequate environment, placed in an unworkable setting or simply released to live on the street with the full knowledge that readmission will shortly be necessary.

Such a case was Kathy Edmiston. In a hearing concerning her circumstances in the Probate Court of Denver, Colorado, in 1980, Judge Wade commented:

On virtually innumerable occasions respondent has been certified and institutionalized for short periods of time (during which periods her condition has been stabilized by use of medication in a structured setting). She has then been placed either on out-patient status or in a nursing home. She then becomes sufficiently ill that she is picked up or delivered to the emergency room at Denver General Hospital, placed under certification, and the process begins again. Without even a minimally adequate treatment program, respondent and others like her will continue to be victims of their own inadequacies (often including their delusional systems) and will be targets for the influence and exploitation of others. For example, the behavior of this respondent in the community, which is related to the nature of her mental illness, has made her the victim of physical, sexual, and financial exploitation.[57]

The judge ruled that the next time this patient was certified the mental health agency must establish a suitable program for her treatment.

SIDE EFFECTS

There are further reasons why we should not continue to emphasize drug treatment at the expense of environmental considerations – why we should use comprehensive psychosocial approaches to minimize the use of the neuroleptics. Many patients distinctly dislike taking these drugs. One cause of their distaste is the side effects of the medication. Immediate reactions to these medications may include stiffness, shakiness, restlessness or acute muscle spasms. These symptoms may often be controlled by taking anti-Parkinsonian medication. Other adverse reactions to some or all of the antipsychotic drugs are blurred vision, oversedation, blunting of spontaneity, sexual impotence and failure of ejaculation, epileptic seizures and disorders of the eyes, liver, blood and skin.

The long-term risk of developing tardive dyskinesia, a neurological consequence of using neuroleptic drugs, has already been mentioned. Another potential long-term hazard of these medicines has also caused concern – the theoretical possibility that they may promote the development of breast cancer. By blocking transmission in the dopaminergic nerves to the pituitary gland, the neuroleptic drugs cause an elevation in the blood level of prolactin. High levels of this hormone, in turn, are known to induce the growth of breast tumors in mice and rats. Some breast cancers in women appear to respond to prolactin in a similar way. The epidemiological data are not yet sufficient to tell us with any degree of certainty whether women taking antipsychotic drugs are at greater risk of developing breast cancer or not.[58]

Other possible adverse reactions to the antipsychotic drugs – and these are also effects which could help to explain the disappointing influence of these drugs on the long-term outlook in schizophrenia – are an increase in postpsychotic depression and an adverse effect on learning ability. A number of researchers have reported that schizophrenic people treated with neuroleptics may become more depressed after their acute psychosis subsides, possibly as a result of their drug treatment. Some authors have observed that postpsychotic depression is associated with the slowing (akinesia) induced by some antipsychotic drugs.[59] Other reports have disputed that these drugs increase postpsychotic depression;[60] the evidence is not strong either way. (It is possible that some of the observed post-psychotic depression is, in fact, the depressive phase of manic-depressive illness misdiagnosed as schizophrenia.)

The evidence is better, however, that the neuroleptic drugs diminish learning capacity in animals, normal subjects and psychiatric patients.[61] The implication of this side effect is that drug treatment may possibly reduce the capacity of schizophrenic people to benefit from programs of social and vocational retraining and add to their employment difficulties.

The first available example of the so-called "new generation" of anti-psychotic drugs – clozapine – has particularly serious side effects. Most significantly, this drug poses a one-in-a-hundred or one-in-fifty chance of causing a fatal blood disorder in which the patient's white blood cells are suddenly destroyed. To protect against this risk, a patient in the United States and U.K. may collect the medication from the pharmacy each week only if his or her white blood cell count is normal that week. Despite this precaution, there have already been several deaths associated with the use of this drug in the United States in the short time since its introduction (as of writing in 1993). Interaction with other medications can cause sudden fatal respiratory depression. Other important side effects include epileptic seizures, weight gain, sedation, drooling and constipation.[62] Why is such a risky drug in use at all? Because it sometimes works well in reducing the symptoms of schizophrenia when the standard antipsychotics do not. Clozapine has a different mode of action from the standard drugs and probably works by blocking the effects of serotonin and by blocking a different type of dopamine receptor. If someone suffers from severe schizophrenia they may choose to assume the risks associated with this medicine in order to get relief from the illness, but clearly the use of clozapine is not to be undertaken lightly.

There are good reasons, it is clear, to limit the use of the neuroleptic drugs. All patients can benefit from a user-friendly approach which minimizes the dosage of antipsychotic medication, and there is evidence indicating that drug-free treatment can result in good outcome for some people with good-prognosis schizophrenia.

USER-FRIENDLY MEDICATION STRATEGIES

The following strategies are designed to insure that a schizophrenic patient receives the lowest dose of medication which will improve his or her illness and quality of life with the least risk of adverse effects.

When beginning treatment, *start with a low dose of medication and work up gradually*. Blood tests to estimate the serum level of the medication may be helpful. Serum levels are most useful when the patient is getting little benefit from the medication and the level is reported as being low: this lets the doctor and patient know that the poor response may be due to inadequate dosage. If the serum level is high, this suggests that the medication is just not effective for the patient. Therapeutic levels are not well established for the antipsychotic medications, however, so they have to be interpreted with a certain amount of caution.

If antipsychotic medication is ineffective, do not keep increasing the dosage; consider stopping or decreasing it. There is a curious and not very logical difference between the way psychiatrists think about the antipsychotic drugs and other medication they prescribe. The first time a patient tries a medication the psychiatrist is likely to consider this a trial: he or she will increase the medication up to the usual therapeutic range, observe for benefits and, if there are none, stop the drug. But this does not happen with the neuroleptics. The use of antipsychotic drugs is now so routine in schizophrenia that the idea of stopping them if they are ineffective in the usual dosage range is rarely entertained; it is more likely that the dosage will be increased instead. If the antipsychotic medications do not work well, before turning to big doses of these drugs try other supplementary medications, such as lithium carbonate, antidepressants or anticonvulsants. It is especially important to avoid increasing the medication every time the patient has an acute increase in symptoms: there may be many reasons for increasing symptoms, one being that the medication is ineffective. Another possibility is that the symptoms are precipitated by acute stress; in these cases, short-term use of a minor tranquilizer such as Valium (diazepam) is usually effective (see below).

Be cautious about concluding that every exacerbation of the person's condition is due to the schizophrenic illness. Sometimes the underlying problem is that the patient is experiencing severe restlessness as a side effect of the antipsychotic medications. The appropriate way to treat the resulting agitation is by reducing the neuroleptic drug or by prescribing enough side-effect medicine. Sometimes the new symptoms are more psychological in nature and are a result of hysteria or dependency, in which case an increase in antipsychotic medication is not appropriate.

When a patient is in an acute psychotic episode use minor tranquilizers, not heavy doses of antipsychotic medication, to reduce agitation and other acute symptoms (see below). In general, acutely disturbed patients should be given only the dosage of antipsychotic medication that they would ordinarily need as a maintenance dose when they are doing well. In acute treatment in the hospital, however, much bigger doses of the antipsychotic medications are often given, sometimes resulting in severe side effects. The subsequent reduction in dosage when the patient has recovered from the acute episode may take much longer than necessary.

When a patient is stable, *try and establish the lowest dose of medication which keeps the worst aspects of the illness at bay without causing intolerable side effects*. This can be done by cautiously reducing the dosage every few weeks or months. Once this dosage has been established, it may be necessary to stay at that level for an extended period of time.

MINOR TRANQUILIZERS IN SCHIZOPHRENIA

Acutely disturbed schizophrenic patients who are overactive and excited or at risk of hurting others, attempting suicide or running away from treatment may often be helped in the short run by the use of moderate doses of the minor tranquilizers in addition to neuroleptic medication. The belief is widespread in psychiatry that the minor tranquilizers, including the benzodiazepine drugs, diazepam (Valium) and lorazepam (Ativan), are harmful or at best worthless in psychosis. This is not the case. These drugs are often effective in calming agitated psychotic patients – more immediately so, in fact, than the antipsychotic drugs. In some cases they even have a prompt antipsychotic action.

The effectiveness of the benzodiazepines in such cases is probably due to a reduction in the patient's level of arousal. It is also likely that the benzodiazepines exert an antipsychotic effect by their action in blocking dopamine release. They may achieve this effect by stimulating a feedback loop (in which the neurotransmitter is gamma-aminobutyric acid) which damps down the release of dopamine.[63] Several reports have shown that the benzodiazepines in moderate or high doses, alone or in combination with neuroleptic drugs, are effective in controlling psychotic symptoms.[64] Somewhat fewer studies have found them to be ineffective or to produce equivocal results.[65] On balance, it appears that the benzodiazepines are sometimes effective over longer periods of time for people with schizophrenia but, without doubt, they are most useful in calming the acutely disturbed patient and in the acute treatment of the person with catatonic schizophrenia who is immobilized by a high internal level of arousal.[66]

A potential advantage of the minor tranquilizers over the neuroleptics is that, by blocking dopamine *release* rather than dopamine *receptors*, the benzodiazepines should not lead to dopamine supersensitivity, tardive dyskinesia or prolonged withdrawal psychosis. Another advantage is that the minor tranquilizers are much more pleasant to take than the antipsychotic drugs and are generally free from serious side effects. A disadvantage is that tolerance appears to develop to the antipsychotic action of the drugs, rendering them suitable, in most cases, only for short-term use.

Many people with schizophrenia can benefit from a low-dose approach to treatment and some good-prognosis patients may be suitable for drug-free treatment. If we want to consider the latter possibility, two questions remain to be answered: "How should we select schizophrenic patients for treatment without neuroleptics?" and "How is such treatment to be done?"

PROGNOSTIC INDICATORS

In the course of treatment it should become obvious that some patients are appropriate for drug-free management – those with mild psychoses who refuse drugs or who have developed severe tardive dyskinesia, and those who fail to respond significantly to adequate doses of the neuroleptic drugs. If we wish to refrain, however, from using drugs on those schizo-phrenic patients who have not been ill long and whose disorder will be benign without treatment, we have a tricky task on our hands – the task of predicting the future course of the illness. At one extreme we can argue that as many as half of all schizophrenic people, according to a review of drug-withdrawal studies, can survive for a reasonable time in the community without relapse;[67] and, as we saw in Chapter 3, a similar proportion of schizophrenic people achieved good social functioning in the years preceding the introduction of the antipsychotic drugs. How can we predict, though, *which* half will do well?

Efforts to pinpoint indicators of good prognosis have revealed that schizophrenic patients whose illness is more sudden in onset and is a response to a clear life stress, those whose psychosis developed late in life and those who have functioned well before their illness developed (including having good social relationships and getting married) are more likely to improve and recover.[68] The degree of accuracy in using these criteria to predict outcome is not high, however; at best we can correctly sort three out of four patients into good- or poor-outcome groups, but we would be wrong the other quarter of the time.[69]

One point emerges clearly from the research – the symptoms and clinical features of the psychotic episode are of very little value in predicting outcome.[70] Indeed, the diagnosis of schizophrenia itself does not predict an outcome which is necessarily much worse than the prognosis in other psychoses.[71] The best indicator of future functioning, according to two pieces of research, is the patient's functioning before he or she fell ill. The measure of previous competence in any one area, furthermore, is the best predictor of functioning in that same area. Thus, a good work record predicts good vocational functioning, good social relations in the past point to good future social functioning and multiple prior hospital admissions indicate the likely extent of future hospital use.[72]

In practice it is reasonable to assume that a patient who is (a) early in the course of a schizophrenia-like illness and (b) has previously achieved a reasonable level of functioning deserves a trial of treatment without antipsychotic drugs. Many of these patients will eventually improve and do well.

GOOD-PROGNOSIS SCHIZOPHRENIA VERSUS MANIC-DEPRESSIVE ILLNESS

The objection has been raised that many or all so-called "good-prognosis schizophrenic patients" are really misdiagnosed patients with manic-depressive illness. The implication of this view is that we might be better advised to treat such patients with lithium carbonate (a substance which does not cause the same unpleasant side effects as the neuroleptics and which is often highly effective in manic-depressive psychosis) rather than consider drug-free treatment. It is possible that some of these good-prognosis patients are, in fact, suffering from manic-depressive illness. This affective psychosis characteristically begins later in life than schizophrenia and allows patients the opportunity to develop a higher level of social and vocational functioning. It is often difficult to distinguish between episodes of affective illness and schizophrenia, as they share many common features (see Chapter 1).

A number of studies have shown that good-prognosis schizophrenic patients have a high incidence of manic-depressive illness among their relatives – a finding which suggests that they may themselves suffer from an affective illness.[73] Some of these studies are handicapped, however, by using an exceptionally broad concept of schizophrenia, which magnifies the problem of inappropriately incorporating manic-depressive patients under the label "schizophrenia." Richard Fowler and associates, who claim that "most good prognosis cases are variants of affective disorder,"[74] appear to have classified all psychotic patients with good premorbid histories who were not classical examples of manic-depressive illness as "good prognosis schizophrenia." All of these patients had several symptoms of affective illness and some had even suffered prior episodes of clearly defined manic-depressive illness.[75] Michael Taylor and Richard Abrams, who argue that "good prognosis schizophrenia is frequently indistinguishable from manic-depressive illness"[76] also admit that not one of their so-called "good prognosis schizophrenics" earned a diagnosis of schizophrenia according to formal research criteria but that half of them satisfied criteria for a diagnosis of mania. It seems probable, therefore, that many of these patients with good-prognostic indicators would have been readily labeled as manic-depressive by an astute diagnostician and never categorized as schizophrenic.

A more telling piece of research has been carried out by Jack Hirschowitz and his colleagues. They selected ten good-prognosis patients who did meet research criteria for schizophrenia and found that eight of these patients improved during a two-week trial with lithium carbonate. They did not, however, report whether these patients deteriorated again after withdrawal from lithium.[77] Since good-prognosis schizophrenic patients may also improve during two weeks of drug-free treatment, it is not possible to say whether or not the patients' gains were attributable to the medication.

The plainest evidence that there is, indeed, such an individual as a good-prognosis schizophrenic patient (according to standard diagnostic practices) is the mass of research material that forms the basis of Chapter 3. Since the turn of the century in all the developed countries, scores of outcome studies of schizophrenia (often rigorously defined) have shown that there is always a proportion of patients with schizophrenia who recover. The myth that these patients are not really schizophrenic goes back to Kraepelin's original mistake – that dementia praecox was inevitably a deteriorating disorder. As we have seen, Kraepelin's error was forced upon him by the economic and institutional conditions of his place and time.

We may conclude that it is certainly appropriate for the psychiatrist to screen his or her good-prognosis patients closely for evidence of manic-depressive illness. A history of distinct, prior, extended episodes of pathologically elevated or depressed mood is most helpful in this respect. In some instances a clear diagnosis is not possible until the passage of time has revealed a characteristic course of the illness. For some patients a trial of lithium may be in order. In other cases a trial of drug-free treatment is most appropriate.

NEUROLEPTIC-FREE TREATMENT

In modern times, the deliberate treatment of schizophrenia without neuroleptic drugs is seldom practiced outside long-stay, private hospitals which offer psychoanalytic therapy and can only serve the relatively wealthy or well insured. Can such care be offered routinely in community mental health where cost considerations are paramount? The answer is a qualified "yes." Does drug-free treatment necessarily call for intensive dynamic psychotherapy by highly trained therapists? The answer is "no." What must be provided is an opportunity for the acutely ill schizophrenic patient to be cared for in a non-stressful environment which maximizes the chance for a spontaneous remission to occur. In fact the characteristics of drug-free treatment are the same as those of any good low-dosage approach to the care of people with schizophrenia.

The setting

The characteristics of a therapeutic environment for schizophrenic patients have already been set down – warm, protective and enlivening without being smothering, overstimulating or intrusive. In addition, as earlier chapters of this book have indicated, the patients should be allowed to maintain a valued social role, together with their status, dignity and a sense of belonging to the community at large. Patients must be able to stay in residential treatment long enough for their condition to improve and to be free of urgency to move on. With a week's stay in a private psychiatric hospital ward in the United States costing roughly the same as a round-the-world trip, it is clear that extended, low-dosage or drug-free care must be provided in a low-cost, alternative community setting.

Soteria House, when it was in operation, provided a model for such community treatment. A large house in a San Francisco Bay neighborhood, Soteria provided accommodation for six schizophrenic people and two staff. "Recently admitted, very psychotic residents receive a great deal of special one-to-one, or two-to-two attention," wrote Loren Mosher and his associates, "and performance expectations are minimal."[78] As residents became less psychotic they participated more actively in the therapeutic community – planning and performing household tasks and working out interpersonal differences. Each pursued recreational activities of his or her own choice. When compared with the local community mental health center's inpatient ward, Soteria was found to be less orderly and controlling and the staff were more involved, supportive and spontaneous.[79]

Despite the much greater length of residential treatment for the Soteria patients (five-and-a-half months) than for the control group of patients in mental health center care (one month), the average costs of treatment at the end of the first year were almost exactly the same. One reason for this surprising finding may be the Soteria patients' more limited use of outpatient care after discharge. Another reason is that the non-professional Soteria staff were paid distinctly less than the standard salary for mental health professionals. A further explanation is that the average period of in-hospital care for the control group of patients – around one month – was considerably longer than is now usual in cost-efficient, drug-oriented, community mental health center inpatient programs.

The Soteria drug-free treatment may not be cost-effective for community mental health programs. With some loss of therapeutic aptness, however, similar care can be provided in a facility which is cost-efficient – a large (15 beds), well-staffed, community-based, intensive treatment unit. Essentially a low-cost, acute hospital ward in the community, such a facility is described in Chapter 12. While the central purpose of an intensive treatment house of this type is to treat all types of seriously disturbed psychiatric patients in an affordable, non-coercive community setting, it can routinely be used for low-dosage treatment and occasionally for the drug-free treatment of good-prognosis schizophrenic patients who are admitted. Unfortunately, the high turnover of patients in such a unit, the moderate degree of urgency to discharge patients, the large number of residents and the fairly high level of stimulation all detract from the value of this type of facility for treating schizophrenic patients without drugs. It may, however, be the only affordable way that such care can be offered by community-based agencies.

The treatment

The principles of effective care of schizophrenia are the same whether antipsychotic drugs are used or not. If certain good-prognosis patients are selected for drug-free treatment, however, how long should such attempts persist before calling a halt? Patients in the Soteria Project were generally started on an antipsychotic drug if they showed no change after six weeks. Fewer than a tenth of their patients came to require such drug treatment.[80] In other programs the decision as to whether or not to begin neuroleptic treatment will partly depend upon the pressure for quick results in order to make room for new admissions and partly upon the patient's level of agitation and distress. Two or three weeks of drug-free trial, however, may be sufficient for a large proportion of good-prognosis schizophrenic patients to show considerable improvement.

As described above, the minor tranquilizers may be a useful tool in reducing arousal in acutely psychotic patients. Other techniques of stress reduction are equally important. Quiet areas of the treatment facility should be available to allow patients to withdraw from an environment which may be perceived as overstimulating. Close personal contact with staff and other residents, reassurance and the provision of an absorbing activity may also be valuable. Dynamic, "uncovering" psychotherapy is likely to be too stressful and intrusive for many patients and more toxic than beneficial. Along the same lines, expectations for the patient's functioning must be geared to his or her current capability – overenthusiastic exhortations to become more active or sociable may lead to an increase in psychotic symptoms.

Much of the patient's treatment will involve making appropriate plans for his or her life after discharge – finding a place to live and an occupation, neither of which should be too stressful. Some form of supportive but independent living arrangement and supervised or sheltered employment (as described in later chapters) may be appropriate. For all but the most resilient patients a gradual transition into the new living and occupational arrangements will be required. It is useful to minimize the number of changes at any one time and to continue "drop-in" attendance at the residential treatment facility for some time after discharge.

Especially where there is a likelihood that the schizophrenic patient will return to live with his or her family, some meetings with the family members should take place. Where the home environment is accepting, and not stressful, the relatives will learn to be even more helpful if given the advantage of accurate information about the patient's illness and guidance as to reasonable expectations for his or her performance. If the patient's household is found to be highly stressful, family therapy should aim to reduce the relatives' intrusiveness or hostility, and plans may be made to reduce contact between patient and family or to devise alternative living arrangements.

Therapists' respect for the patient's individuality will help meet his or her need for status and independence. Using an unlocked community facility encourages staff to find non-coercive ways to protect the patient and others from hazards arising from psychotic thinking and behavior and poor judgment. These measures may include increased personal contact rather than restraint and distracting recreational activity instead of seclusion. Such methods maintain the patient's own reliance on self-control. Increasing levels of responsibility and involvement in the management of the household and concern for the welfare of other residents gives the patient a useful social role and a sense of personal value to others.

In short, aside from a lessened emphasis on stern paternalism and an increased emphasis on family relations, these treatment approaches attempt to recreate the principles of moral management as practiced in the York Retreat.

SUMMARY

- Antipsychotic drugs may be unnecessary or harmful in the treatment of a proportion of schizophrenic patients; such patients include drug non-responders and good-prognosis cases.
- Long-term treatment with antipsychotic drugs creates dopamine receptor supersensitivity, worsening an underlying biochemical deficit of schizophrenia.
- Withdrawal of antipsychotic drugs may cause a rebound of schizophrenic symptoms to a higher level than would have been the case without treatment.
- Drug-withdrawal studies, consequently, may give an overoptimistic impression of the benefits of the neuroleptic drugs in schizophrenia.
- The majority of non-withdrawal studies indicate that people with good-prognosis schizophrenia do as well or better without antipsychotic drug treatment.
- Stress precipitates psychotic relapse in people with schizophrenia and drug treatment is less necessary for patients in low-stress settings.
- The revolving-door patient has been created by the use of drug

treatment coupled with a neglect of the psychosocial needs of the person with a psychotic illness.

- User-friendly medication strategies promote the use of low doses of antipsychotic medication in schizophrenia.
- The best prognostic measures give a rather crude indication of which patients will recover without drug treatment.
- Some, and only some, people with "good-prognosis schizophrenia" in fact suffer from manic-depressive illness.
- The principles of drug-free treatment are the same as those of any good low-dosage approach to the treatment of schizophrenia.

Chapter 11

Work

"Of all the modes by which the patients may be induced to restrain themselves," wrote Samuel Tuke in his *Description of the Retreat*, "regular employment is perhaps the most generally efficacious."[1] To the moral treatment advocates, in fact, work was not merely a means to occupy and control their charges: it was a central pillar of the moral-treatment edifice. William Ellis, superintendent of the Hanwell Asylum, believed that proper employment "has frequently been the means of the patient's complete recovery."[2] In 1830, Eli Todd wrote to the family of a patient about to leave the Hartford Retreat in Connecticut:

> I cannot too strenuously urge the advantage and even the necessity of his being engaged in some regular employment which shall hold out the promise of some moderate but fair compensation to his industry and prudence.[3]

W. A. F. Browne, superintendent of the Montrose Royal Asylum, had this vision, in 1837, of the perfect asylum of the future:

> The house and all around appears to be a hive of industry. When you pass the lodge, it is as if you had entered the precincts of some vast emporium of manufacture: labour is divided, so that it may be easy and well performed, and so apportioned, that it may suit the tastes and powers of each labourer. You meet the gardener, the common agriculturalist, the mower, the weeder, all intent on their several occupations, and loud their merriment. . . . The curious thing is, that all are anxious to be engaged, toil incessantly, and in general without any recompense other than being kept from disagreeable thoughts and the pains of illness. They literally work in order to please themselves.[4]

Looking back upon such typically Victorian beliefs and dreams we may be excused for doubting the extent to which they were grounded upon accurate observation of the insane and for wondering how far they merely reflected the prominent, middle-class work ethic of the day. Scottish philosopher Thomas Carlyle, for example, made the extravagant claim that

"Work is the grand cure of all the maladies and miseries that ever beset mankind."[5] None the less, we have seen evidence to support the moral-treatment advocates in their emphasis on the importance of work (Browne's fantasies aside). As previous chapters have indicated, unemployment and material circumstances may well be significant in the genesis of insanity, and employment important for recovery. Work may often be crucial for the development of self-esteem and in shaping the social role of the mentally ill person.

RESEARCH ON WORK AND SCHIZOPHRENIA

Up to this point the evidence presented in support of this position has been largely macrostatistical in scale. Such observations have included:

- increasing hospital admissions for schizophrenia during economic slumps (Chapter 2);
- the worsening outcome for schizophrenia during the Great Depression (Chapter 3);
- improved rehabilitative efforts under full-employment conditions (Chapter 4);
- high cure rates for insanity during the labor shortage of industrializing America (Chapter 5);
- better outcome for higher-class and female schizophrenic patients (Chapter 6); and
- superior outcome from schizophrenia in the Third World (Chapter 7).

At this juncture it would be valuable to change the level of magnification and to look for evidence on a smaller scale of the effect of employment and unemployment on the *individual* schizophrenic person. Such evidence, unfortunately, is sparse. Why should this be so?

A clear reason is the difficulty in devising adequate controls for such research. If schizophrenic people who are working do well and those who are unemployed relapse frequently, how can we tell if the unemployment causes a deterioration in the patient's condition or if the patient's severity of illness leads to job loss? When work is scarce and few of the mentally ill are employed, it is difficult to set up an experiment where a group of patients is maintained in employment, and it would not be ethical to keep a control group of patients out of employment if they were able to work.

Such problems are not insuperable, but they are compounded by the general lack of interest within the psychiatric profession in vocational rehabilitation. In the index to the two large volumes of the latest edition of the *American Comprehensive Textbook of Psychiatry*, for example, there are only eleven references to "Work," "Working," "Vocational," etc., but ten times as many references to "Sex," "Sexual" and related items.

Psychiatrists appear to have taken seriously only half of Freud's well-known dictum that the ability to love and to work are central issues in the lives of men and women.[6] That this lack of interest in work is, in large part, a response to the fact that there *is* little work available for schizophrenic people becomes clear when we note that the few pieces of research which are in the literature were almost all conducted two or three decades ago during the postwar years of labor scarcity.

In reviewing these studies, rehabilitation experts have generally concluded that work has a proven benefit on the course of mental illness.[7] To draw this conclusion, however, requires a certain amount of wishful thinking. Working patients *do* fare better, this much is clear. What is less obvious is whether employment leads to clinical improvement or whether higher functioning makes employment possible.

An American psychiatrist, James Stringham, for example, reviewing the progress of 33 older male patients discharged from a large psychiatric hospital in 1947 and 1948, found that 24 were still out of hospital at follow-up; he concluded that having a job had contributed to the successful rehabilitation in half of these cases.[8]

More persuasive evidence for the benefit of work in schizophrenia may be found in a 1955 report by psychologist Leon Cohen of 114 chronic schizophrenic patients discharged from a Veterans Administration hospital. He found that patients who had a job to go to or a definite vocational plan at discharge and those who found employment after discharge were able to stay out of hospital longer. That work was the important element leading to the patients' success is suggested by his additional finding that the severity of the patients' psychosis at discharge was in no way related to the likelihood of rehospitalization.[9]

A British study published in 1958 reports very similar findings. Psychologist George Brown and his colleagues followed for a year 229 male patients (mostly schizophrenics) discharged from seven London area mental hospitals. Over 40 per cent of these patients worked for six months or more and of these nearly all (97 per cent) succeeded in staying out of hospital. Another 43 per cent of the patients never worked at all, and of these fewer than half (46 per cent) succeeded in avoiding rehospitalization. Again there is a suggestion that work was more important than clinical status in determining success, for a full third of the patients who worked for most of the year were rated as moderately or severely disturbed and many more had residual symptoms.[10]

In 1963 Howard Freeman and Ozzie Simmons published *The Mental Patient Comes Home*, a comprehensive report on the fate of 649 psychotic patients discharged in 1959 from nine U.S. state hospitals and three Veterans Administration hospitals. Like the researchers before them, they found that patients who were successful in staying out of hospital were substantially more likely to have been employed than those who were rehospitalized. They also found only a moderate degree of correlation between the patient's working ability and his or her level of psychotic symptoms.[11]

Psychologist George Fairweather has become well known for devising a model community program in which psychiatric patients live together in community lodges and work together in tcams as independent businesses providing various needed services to the community. These programs will be discussed in more detail later in the chapter. At this point it is sufficient to note that a follow-up study of patients in the lodge program showed that they realized substantial benefits when compared with a matched control group of patients who entered typical psychiatric aftercare programs. Patients in the lodge program had assured employment while those in routine aftercare, almost to the last person, were unable to find full-time work. Residents of the lodge spent five or six times as much time out of hospital as patients in the control group. Lodge patients were more satisfied with their lives in the community, but very little difference was found between the level of symptoms manifested by the two groups of patients.[12] We cannot conclude from this study that employment alone led to the patients' success, for the lodge program offered, in addition, assured accommodation and a relatively sheltered environment coupled with opportunities for autonomy, an important role within the lodge society and enhanced self-esteem.

One study might be cited as *failing* to support the notion that employment improves outcome in psychosis. Psychologist Robert Walker and his co-workers developed a program of assured employment in industry for Veterans Administration clients – both inpatient and outpatient. They compared the progress over six months of a group of 14 of these patients with 14 similar patients who were placed in the hospital workshop and who were left to find regular employment on leaving hospital. Half of the patients in each group were schizophrenic. The researchers found no difference between the two groups in the amount of inpatient care required during the six-month period. The failure to find a difference in outcome, however, may have been a consequence of the fact that the control-group patients received the benefit of in-hospital work therapy and had surprisingly high rates of success in finding employment after discharge. The employment records of the two groups, in fact, were comparable.[13]

As much research appears to have been done on the effects of work therapy as on the benefits of work itself. Some writers, foremost among them rehabilitation psychologist William Anthony, have painted a dismal picture of the efficacy of inpatient work therapy programs.[14] Such pessimism, however, is not justified by a thorough examination of the available research. True, one study conducted at Fort Logan Mental Health Center in Denver found that patients placed in the hospital sheltered workshop stayed in hospital longer than a similar group who were not given work therapy; rehospitalization rates for the two groups were similar.[15] Other pieces of research on the effects of work therapy, nevertheless, are more positive.

Numerous early postwar studies revealed that institutionalized patients who were given routine work around the hospital improved dramatically.[16] We know, however, that more or less any activating experience improves the condition of neglected, regressed, long-stay hospital patients. A more recent study of a state hospital rehabilitation program, published in 1965, compared patients in work therapy with a matched group in routine ward care. The patients who received work therapy stayed out of hospital for longer periods after discharge, or if they remained in hospital they showed greater clinical improvement. The condition of the patients in the control group actually worsened.[17]

A study of patients treated in a Veterans Administration hospital showed that people with schizophrenia placed in the work therapy Member Employee Program were half as likely to be rehospitalized as a control group. Neurotic patients placed in the same program, however, showed no benefit.[18]

Finally, a British study aiming to compare the outcome for schizophrenic patients in work therapy and in occupational therapy (arts and crafts activities) placed 50 patients randomly in the two types of treatment. After six months the patients in work therapy showed greater willingness and ability to work and greater skills in forming relationships.[19]

Overall, these studies show that people with mental illness who are working are more likely to stay out of hospital than unemployed patients and they *suggest* that employment may contribute to the patients' success. Work therapy also appears to offer some benefit to people with mental illness. The studies do not show, however, that working patients have fewer symptoms. The provision of work may improve the social functioning of the mentally ill, but it is not clear that it leads to symptomatic improvement. The definitive research on the latter point remains to be done. There is a good deal of evidence of an impressionistic or anecdotal nature, however, suggesting that patients' symptoms improve if they are working regularly. The following report provides an interesting example.

HELP WANTED: Ten factory workers wanted for private employment. Must have a history of mental illness to qualify.

The production work force of a toy company was recruited by this advertisement when it was run in a California newspaper in 1960. Eleven mentally ill applicants were hired; over half of them were schizophrenic, and all had been unemployed for a year or more. The work force proved to be efficient and, as the company expanded, more mentally ill people were hired. The company's personnel director, physician Ray Poindexter, reported

> that the type, severity, and duration of the mental illness was not related to job performance. Disappearance of symptoms accompanied the opportunity to perform for an employer who had confidence in his employees and whose success in business depended on their work.[20]

This illustration allows us to see that there is no contradiction between the repeated finding, on the one hand, that successfully employed patients may be highly disturbed[21] and the possibility, on the other hand, that the patient's condition may improve substantially with employment.

We may conclude that the limited volume of clinical research provides moderate support for the central thesis of this book, which is based on macrostatistical data, that the availability of employment influences outcome in schizophrenia. If this thesis is correct, we must accept that improvement in the course of schizophrenia requires a change in the relationship between the mentally ill person and the labor force – a point which has been little recognized in psychiatry. Given that a return to full employment seems scarcely feasible in any of the modern economies of the Western world,[22] how can such a change be achieved?

To address this question, we must first examine the current status of vocational rehabilitation for the mentally ill.

VOCATIONAL REHABILITATION PROGRAMS

Fewer than 15 per cent of the seriously mentally ill in the United States are in full-time or part-time competitive employment.[23] At least a quarter of a million schizophrenic people in the United States, we can estimate, are unemployed but potentially productive members of society. Sheltered work and other vocational placements are available for fewer than a tenth of these individuals.[24] In Britain the situation is little better.[25] The depressed economy and the labor glut on both sides of the Atlantic stand in the way of improvement in these services.

Sheltered workshops

It has become clear that industrial therapy programs cannot exist without financial subsidies from government or other sources. Such programs use marginally productive workers and cannot successfully compete for work on the open market against more efficient enterprises. This observation is well accepted in Europe, but in the United States, where rehabilitation services are poorly funded, the hope prevails that vocational services can break even.[26] Sheltered workshops ordinarily obtain work from industry by bidding for contracts. The work obtained is often a series of repetitive tasks which would lead to high staff turnover under usual economic conditions if performed in-house by the private company's own employees. When business is in decline, however, such sources of work begin to dry up. Companies may cut back production, perform more work in-house or go out of business. Competition for available contracts can become severe. Under these conditions sheltered workshops may go out of business, lower their bidding rates so far that they lose money or cut back operations and lay off disabled employees. In the sheltered workshop of the Mental Health Center of Boulder County, Colorado, for example, the number of clients employed fluctuates, with economic conditions, between 35 and 50; in hard times the waiting list for placement may be several months long.

Mental health agencies, often ambivalent about offering sheltered work in the first instance, are unlikely to pay extra to keep it going. In consequence, one of two things is likely to happen. Lower-functioning clients, who require a greater subsidy, may be screened out or they may be hired at a piece-work rate which pays so little that it is not worth their while to work. Either way, the end result is that only the more productive patients remain on the rolls.

Where subsidies are freely available, there is a limit to their use, for subsidized workshops end up competing with one another. "In Wales, for instance," report British rehabilitation specialists Nancy Wansbrough and Philip Cooper,

> Remploy [a subsidized company employing the disabled] and Blind Workshops were at one time fighting each other quite hard for contracts. Hospital Industrial Therapy Units were also thought to be accepting work at unrealistic prices and undercutting sheltered workshops of every sort.[27]

Under cut-throat conditions such as these it is not surprising that many sheltered workshops in Britain and the United States become financially insolvent and close down.

CONSUMER-OPERATED BUSINESSES

Given the limitations of sheltered work, we might well expect that independent businesses operated by consumers of mental health services themselves would be a more satisfactory rehabilitation model. Such employment would hopefully be of higher status and more rewarding than a workshop, offer a greater variety of jobs and be more adaptable to the clients' needs than competitive employment. A number of effective models, in fact, have been established along these lines.

Remploy is a company, established in Britain in 1945, which employs severely disabled people to produce a variety of goods. Among the company products are furniture, knitwear, leather goods and textiles. In 1977, at 87 factories distributed across the country, nearly 8,000 disabled people were employed. Of these, a fifth suffered from some kind of a mental disability, but most of these employees had a developmental disability or a non-psychotic mental disorder. Fewer than 5 per cent of all employees suffered from a psychosis. Twenty-two of the factories at that time employed no mentally disabled people at all.[28]

Some independent businesses have been established which employ only the mentally ill. George Fairweather and his colleagues, for example, created an innovative program of this type in the San Francisco Bay area of northern California. The positive results of their program were described earlier in this chapter. In 1963 a group of 15 chronic mental patients moved from hospital into a set of former motel buildings – the lodge. Initially under the direction of a psychologist, they organized themselves into work teams and contracted with area residents and businesses to provide janitorial and gardening services. Residents of the lodge assumed such tasks as business manager and cook and, as professional supervision and financial support were progressively withdrawn, the lodge developed within a few years into an autonomous and self-sufficient business enterprise.[29] Several similar programs have since been established, from Anchorage, Alaska, to Concord, New Hampshire, usually affiliated with state mental hospitals. They have achieved varying degrees of success. Few have developed to the same level of autonomy as Fairweather's original model, and many have closed down.[30]

Worker cooperatives

Nowhere have consumer-run enterprises proven as successful as in the worker cooperatives and "social enterprises" of northern Italy, Switzerland, Germany and other west European countries. In Trieste and Pordenone, Italy, and Geneva, Switzerland, cooperative businesses employ a mixed work force of mentally disabled and healthy workers in manufacturing and service enterprises. In Trieste, the consortium of cooperatives includes a beauty shop, a bicycle rental service, a café, a restaurant, a hotel, a leather goods factory, a furniture workshop and even a sea-going yacht. In nearby Pordenone, the successful enterprises include an office-cleaning business, an elegant crafts boutique, a horticultural nursery, collecting money from public telephones, mail delivery, landscaping, park upkeep, making park furniture, repairing and maintaining public buildings and providing nursing aides for hospitals and nursing homes and home help for the disabled. In Geneva, the cooperative ventures include a publishing house, cooperative housing and a café.[31]

Some small and some large, the cooperatives compete successfully with local businesses by bidding for and winning contracts. They employ substantial numbers of severely mentally ill clients. In 1990, the production of the Trieste consortium totalled nearly $4.5 million (£3 million) and, in Pordenone, $7.5 million (£5 million). In each of these Italian consortia about half of the regular workers are mentally ill or otherwise handicapped, earning a full standard wage for the job and, generally, working full-time. In addition, some mentally ill people work part-time for the cooperatives as trainees and receive a modest rehabilitation income. Unlike most British or American programs for the seriously mentally ill, the cooperatives advertise widely and have high community visibility. Thus, the scale and impact of the cooperatives exceed anything that vocational programs generally achieve elsewhere.

Social enterprises in Germany are generally not run as worker cooperatives, but efforts have been made to create partnerships between workers and management. The main objective of these enterprises is to provide permanent full-wage work for people with psychiatric disabilities. They also employ non-disabled workers at competitive salaries. There are more than 100 social enterprises in Germany, employing over 1,000 people. These non-profit companies are usually specialized firms producing foods (often health foods) or technical products, or providing domestic services, such as moving, painting and repairs and offering office services and printing. Often about 30 per cent of the company's net income is derived from government subsidies in the form of wage supplements which are awarded for each disabled worker at a diminishing rate over three years. Unless new disabled workers are hired, subsidies dwindle until the company has to survive on earnings alone. With careful planning this is feasible, and only a small number of the 105 social enterprises established in Germany in the past ten years have been forced to shut down.[32]

Mental health agencies in other countries have recently been trying to establish non-profit cooperative enterprises similar to the European models. Monadnock Family Services in Keene, New Hampshire, has successfully set up a consumer-owned and managed cooperative with projects that include buying, renovating and selling two houses.[33] The Mental Health Center of Boulder County, Colorado, is attempting to develop new consumer-employing enterprises (described below) including a property repair business. A plan to develop a consumer-cooperative pharmacy for the mentally ill in Boulder has been abandoned owing to changes in Medicaid reimbursement mechanisms in Colorado, but would be viable elsewhere (see below). Following the Italian design, a consortium can be managed by a council of workers, professionals and business people. Successful enterprises employ an integrated work force of mentally disabled and healthy workers, the proportion varying with the size and profitability of the enterprise. The necessity to be productive, cost-effective and self-sustaining are weighed against the desire to provide rehabilitative opportunities for the mentally ill.

Overcoming difficulties with consumer-run businesses

Ultimately, consumer-operated businesses confront the same problems as sheltered workshops. The available work may be quite menial. True self-sufficiency, moreover, is difficult to achieve. The European cooperatives, for example, use varying amounts of public subsidy. In Trieste, in 1991, the subsidy, in the form of direct grants, donated space, rehabilitation stipends for trainee workers and staff time contributed by the mental health service, amounted to nearly half of the total budget; in Geneva, the equivalent subsidy is close to a third and in Pordenone, about a tenth. Similarly, Fairweather's California lodge program almost collapsed when research funds were pulled out, and the project only survived because residents' earnings were supplemented by Veterans Administration pensions. Replication projects of the lodge model have required substantial subsidies to survive.[34] Each year Remploy has to subsidize substantial business losses: in 1977 the difference between expenditure and income amounted to $38 million (around £16 million at that time). It would be cheaper, in fact, to put Remploy's disabled employees on social security than to keep them at work.[35]

We should not be misled into thinking that such businesses for the disabled are not cost-effective merely because they require financial subsidies. We must also take into account the likelihood of increased treatment expenses (including hospital care) and increased social cost (such as involvement of the criminal justice system) if psychotic patients are left drifting idle and unsupported.

As economic conditions worsen, consumer-run businesses, like many small operations, are increasingly likely to fail. Fairweather recognized that his demonstration model lodge, begun in 1963, operated during a period of continuous expansion in the American economy and within range of a prosperous trading area. As such, it had unusual opportunities to flourish.[36] Later replication projects of his model have encountered trouble in finding contracts as times have become harder. In Britain, organizations which would like to follow the lead of the Peter Bedford Trust and John Bellars Ltd protest that suitable work cannot be found.[37]

A mental health agency can give a consumer-employing enterprise a competitive advantage by contracting with the business for needed services. Janitorial and cleaning services are often thought of in this context, but these jobs, in fact, are not popular with many mentally ill people: the work is menial and does not pay well. More clients, especially men, are interested in construction and property repair jobs such as plumbing, wiring, painting, roofing and so on. In a survey conducted at the Mental Health Center in Boulder, Colorado, less than a quarter of the male clients expressed an interest in janitorial work; more than a third, however, were interested in property repair.[38] Consequently, the agency has started a small property repair business employing a non-disabled lead contractor at $13 an hour (at current exchange rates, about £8.50 an hour), and a number of part-time consumer assistants for upwards of $5 (£3.30) an hour. The business has taken over the property maintenance which previously cost the agency $30,000 (£20,000) a year, and could expand to serve other businesses and local government departments. Other agency contracts, such as courier services, might similarly be switched to consumer-employing enterprises.

Many successful projects, in fact, have relied heavily on government sources of work. In Pordenone, about 90 per cent of the cooperative's work contracts are made with public agencies such as hospitals, schools, the post office or the fire station, and in Trieste, about 60 per cent of contractual work is for public agencies, including the mental health service. The core of the British John Bellars program is office-cleaning contracts won from the Department of Health and Social Security and the London borough of Islington.[39] In Britain, government departments, such as the Post Office and the Ministry of Defence, are required to give priority in the placement of contracts to institutions like Remploy which are supported by government funds.[40] In the United States, government work is less commonly awarded to rehabilitation programs. A scheme designed to award federal government contracts to sheltered workshops does exist in the United States, but it is burdened with red tape and initial investment requirements and is widely considered to be unworkable for the majority of small programs. Local government contracts are more feasible.

AN ECONOMIC DEVELOPMENT APPROACH

Another way to improve the market advantage of a consumer-employing business is to develop enterprises which exploit the purchasing power of the consumer group – an approach which has the additional merit of recirculating money through the community to produce an economic multiplier effect. This is equivalent to establishing local ownership of the ghetto grocery store so that outside owners do not drain capital from the neighborhood. Following this approach, the author, with Paul Polak, a Canadian psychiatrist and Third World economic development expert, interviewed 50 mentally ill people living in Boulder, Colorado, to learn about their personal finances and to spot potential money-making opportunities. The consumers control a number of sizable markets, it emerges: the average mentally ill person in Boulder consumes $2,000 (£1,300) a month in psychiatric treatment, accommodation, food, medication and other goods and services. Consumer-owned enterprises which could serve the mentally ill and benefit from their spending capacity include: (1) a consumer-cooperative pharmacy, (2) treatment-related services for other clients, (3) housing cooperatives, (4) cafeterias and (5) courier/transportation services.[41]

A consumer-oriented pharmacy for the mentally ill

There are several reasons to believe that a consumer-cooperative pharmacy for the mentally ill can be a viable and profitable consumer enterprise in many parts of the United States. In the first place, medication is one of the largest consumer markets which clients control: the total expenditure on medication in Boulder averages $90 (£60) a month for each seriously mentally ill person. A pharmacy which shares the profits from these medications with the consumer group will capture much of this business. Secondly, public mental health agencies, in most states of the union, may purchase medications at substantially lower prices than retail pharmacies through the state purchasing consortium. In California and Maryland, for example, the public purchasing price allows a 30 to 33 per cent profit on the maximum allowable Medicaid retail price. In Colorado, however, recent changes in Medicaid reimbursement of public pharmacy sales have reduced this profit margin to a much lower level.

The idea of a consumer-cooperative pharmacy, in which mentally ill people share in ownership, jobs and profits, was originally proposed by James Mandiberg, Director of the Mental Health Bureau for Santa Clara County, California. Under this model, a consumer/professional/business-person board administers all or part of the profits for the consumer group, investing them in consumer-oriented projects and services such as a drop-in center/cafeteria, an advocacy and support network, or other consumer-employing businesses. Paul Polak, Loren Mosher and the author conducted a feasibility study in Maryland and Colorado to see if this model is viable. We concluded that, in many states, a cooperative pharmacy would be profitable in a mental health system with a catchment area of 250,000 and a caseload of more than 3,000 clients: it would capture 60 prescriptions a day and make a net profit of $40,000 (£27,000) a year. Smaller mental health agencies could cooperate with other groups of users to enlarge their market to a profitable size.[42]

There are additional benefits to the development of a specialty pharmacy affiliated with a mental health agency. Customers receive more education on the effects of medication than is usual in a retail pharmacy: education is a primary part of the pharmacist's job and consumers can be employed to deliver medication and teach customers about their use and effects. Computerized prescription-tracking can spot potential drug interactions and provide information on current medication to mental health staff when clients come in at night with an emergency. Successful economic development projects produce benefits in several areas – in this case, consumer management skills, group cohesion, consumer employment, availability of affordable medication, professional and consumer education, and emergency services.[43]

More consumer-cooperative enterprises

Medication is a large market, averaging over $1,000 (£670) a year per client in Boulder. The consumption of psychiatric treatment is more than ten times this amount. If consumers could participate in providing these services, the potential for improving their financial and work situation would be considerable. An innovative program which trains mental health consumers with long-term mental illness to work as service providers within the mental health system will be described in the next chapter.

Another large area of consumption by the mentally ill is accommodation. If consumers were cooperative property owners instead of tenants, this could be an important form of economic advancement. The possibility of developing housing cooperatives for the mentally ill will also be addressed in the next chapter.

SUPPORTED EMPLOYMENT IN INDUSTRY

Higher-functioning, productive patients often do well in a job in a private business with supervision from a job coach. In the supported employment program of the Mental Health Center in Boulder, Colorado, nearly twenty clients occupy such slots. Several of these jobs are clerical positions in government offices and banks, others are in shops and department stores and food services at the university.[44] The client receives supervision from a mental health center job coach during the early stages of working. For seriously mentally ill clients, such attention may be essential for success. Under the stress of learning a new job and meeting new people symptoms of psychosis may appear. The person may feel co-workers are talking about him or her, for example, or plotting some harm; consequently the client may want to quit. Help in adjusting to the job can avert such problems, and the professional supervision can also be reassuring to the employer and to other employees. Supervision becomes less necessary as the patient and others involved become more comfortable.

The placement may be permanent, when it is termed continuous supported employment, or it may be limited to a few months, when it is referred to as transitional employment. At the end of the transitional period the employee may be hired permanently by the company or he or she may move on to other competitive employment. A major problem with transitional employment for the mentally ill is that skills developed in one job do not automatically transfer to another. When the training period ends, clients may not be much better placed to land a permanent job.

Supported employment programs have been developed by many rehabilitation agencies. Fountain House in New York has around 150 transitional jobs in a variety of small businesses and large firms and banks. Most of these jobs are unskilled positions such as messenger, mail clerk and kitchen helper.[45] Thresholds, in Chicago, has a large continuous supported employment program.[46] Sometimes groups of clients are placed in the same employment setting; when they work together as a permanent team, such sheltered working groups may be termed enclaves. Group placements may be found in a number of businesses including a car-accessory company in Croydon, England,[47] a cafeteria in Chicago and a department store in New York City.[48]

Supervised job openings are not hard to develop, even during hard times. Supported employment has several attractions for employers. Job-hiring costs and turnover are reduced. Job training is done by the professional job coach. If the client-employee is unable to work one day, the agency ensures that someone else does the work, even if the job coach has to do it himself or herself. The jobs are often low-paid but essential to the production process, and the promise of reliability is of considerable benefit to the employer. The difficulty, indeed, is not so much in creating such job openings, but in finding clients to fill them. One of the primary reasons for this is the problem of economic disincentives to work.

ECONOMIC DISINCENTIVES TO WORK

When Paul Polak and the author interviewed 50 mentally ill people in Boulder, Colorado, and surveyed many others, it became apparent that there are serious financial disincentives to work. For example, the income and benefits of mentally ill people in Boulder who work part-time add up to little more than for those who are unemployed. Part-time workers receive an average of $245 more a month in earned income than the unemployed, but $156 less from Social Security, food stamps and benefits. This amounts to, what economists term, an "implicit tax" of 64 per cent on earned income. Thus, someone working part-time for a minimum wage ($4.25 an hour) would actually keep, in real terms, $1.57 an hour.[49] This client's case illustrates the situation:

Jennifer, a 28-year-old single woman with schizoaffective disorder, was receiving a Supplemental Security Income (SSI) pension of $409 (£255) a month. She took a 25-hour-a-week job as a teacher's aide for developmentally disabled children, earning $6.63 an hour. In so doing, her SSI dropped by $315 a month, she lost $17 a month in food stamps, and her rent subsidy went down by $143. Now that she was working, she could no longer stop at her parents' house and eat lunch every day, and she was often too tired to go there to eat at night: as a result, the cost of her food and meals went up by $110 a month. Overall, she found herself ahead by no more than $73 a month. The decision to continue in the job became based, therefore, not on economic gains, which were insignificant, but on the opposing factors of stress and self-esteem. Initially, because the disabled pupil to whom she was assigned was so difficult, she decided she would quit: when she was given an easier child to work with, however, she resolved to continue in the job. Without an analysis of her economic situation, her ambivalence about working would not have appeared as rational as, in fact, it was, and might have been blamed on schizophrenic apathy, deficits in functioning or just plain laziness.[50]

The situation seems to be better for full-time workers. In our sample, these subjects meet an implicit tax of only 23 per cent and, after deducting the implicit tax, are keeping an average of $5 an hour of their earnings.[51] Many mentally ill people, however, are incapable of moving straight into full-time work.

In response to these disincentives, most mentally disabled people identify a minimum earnings level which makes work an economically sensible choice – what economists term their "reservation wage."[52] More than three-quarters of the clients we surveyed in Boulder rule out the option of taking a job at the official minimum wage ($4.25 an hour), but over 60 per cent would be willing to work for $5 an hour and 80 per cent would work for $6 an hour.[53] At the present time, if we are to employ significant numbers of the mentally ill in Boulder, we need to find or create jobs which pay $5 an hour or more.

WELFARE REFORM

There is nothing novel about the observation that support payments create obstacles to employment. The mentally ill merely illustrate the larger problem of chronic welfare dependency. A single mother receiving Aid to Families with Dependent Children (AFDC) in the United States, for example, may find that it does not pay her to return to work because of loss of dollar benefits, food stamps and Medicaid, and the additional cost of child care and payroll taxes.[54]

In recent years, political attention in the United States has been focused on finding solutions to work disincentives and welfare dependency. Congress revised the Work Incentive Program in 1981, and passed the Family Support Act in 1988 – offering education and job placement, and extending certain benefits for up to a year after recipients leave the rolls – but these attempts at reform have had relatively little impact.[55]

Consequently, more far-reaching recommendations to restructure welfare are gaining support. In the run-up to the 1992 presidential election, candidate Clinton endorsed many of the proposals of Harvard economist David Ellwood. Ellwood emphasizes that the primary problem underlying welfare dependency is not a lack of training programs or tough work requirements but the fact that welfare recipients cannot earn enough to make work a viable economic choice. He proposes that welfare be time-limited and that government ensure that welfare recipients be provided with work which pays enough to prevent poverty. The minimum wage should be increased, he suggests, and public jobs provided for those who cannot find work in the private sector.[56] Writer Mickey Kaus, in a similar vein, argues for eliminating cash assistance altogether and replacing it with a program of guaranteed jobs, like the Depression-era Works Progress Administration (WPA), that would pay a little less than the minimum wage.[57]

SOCIAL POLICY INNOVATIONS FOR THE MENTALLY ILL

Such welfare reform proposals are not generally thought of as including the mentally and physically disabled because, it is assumed, the disabled cannot be required to work and, in addition, there is a concern that it will be hard enough to create sufficient jobs for the non-disabled. Social policy innovations could produce dramatic savings, however, if they were to reduce the number of mentally ill on disability pension rolls. In the two largest disability pension programs in the United States, Social Security Disability Insurance (SSDI) and Supplemental Security Income (SSI), the number of mentally disordered adults has been increasing dramatically in recent years and, in 1991, amounted to more than 1.3 million people.[58] There are a number of ways, in fact, in which we might create economic incentives and a steeper income gradient for mentally ill people entering the labor force – mechanisms which could improve their economic and psychological condition, quality of life and productivity while reducing the cost to government of their treatment and support. We could:

- Raise the minimum wage but not raise disability pensions;
- Reduce disability benefits more gradually when disabled people begin to work;
- Substitute guaranteed jobs at a non-poverty wage instead of a disability pension for all but the most disabled; or
- Pay underproductive disabled workers a wage subsidy to make work worth while.

Adjust the minimum wage

We could keep disability pensions at a lower level than the minimum wage by raising the minimum wage but not pensions. In Boulder, a wage of $5

(£3.30) an hour (plus health insurance) would encourage many more people on disability benefits to choose work, but there are problems with this approach. Raising the minimum wage, currently $4.25 (£2.80), for all Americans would be expensive, although it is bound to happen eventually. More importantly, both minimum wage work and disability pensions are below the poverty level; it would be hard to justify leaving the disabled in poverty if other Americans were advancing financially.

Graduated benefit reduction

We could establish a graduated reduction scheme for disability benefits for beginning workers which would hold the implicit tax rate (the loss of prior income versus the increase in new income) to no more than 35 per cent, even when loss of other benefits, such as food stamps and rent subsidy, are taken into account. In the United States, the more liberal trial work regulations under SSDI, compared to the rapid cut-off of SSI benefits, help maintain the income of beginning workers and are associated with improved employment rates.[59] A suitable plan – an even more liberal version of current SSDI regulations – would be to allow the beginning worker to earn up to, say, $500 (£330) a month with no loss of pension and, when that earning level is reached, to reduce benefits by 35 cents for every dollar earned. Disability support payments should be reinstated immediately if employment is terminated for whatever reason. This plan looks expensive but if it put enough of the disabled to work it would, in fact, save money.

Guaranteed jobs

In the context of a national scheme of the type that Ellwood proposes – including raising the minimum wage, changing AFDC to a temporary system of support and providing guaranteed jobs for all – we could establish something similar for the disabled.

One reason for the success of the worker cooperatives in northern Italy is the greater work incentive resulting from limited access to disability pensions. In Trieste, only the most severely disabled mentally ill (those with 80 per cent disability) receive a disability pension (about $830 or £550 a month). The remainder of the mentally ill must work for pay. Less productive patients work half-time as trainees in the cooperative and receive a rehabilitation stipend of about $290 (£190) a month with the possibility of an incentive award of $125. Trainee pay, therefore, is $3.60 to $5.20 an hour. Fully productive workers are employed full-time for $920 (£610) a month ($5.75 an hour). In Pordenone, the income gradient is essentially similar except that all full-time workers are paid at a higher rate – $6.65 an hour.

The contrast is clear from these monthly cash income figures:

	Trieste	Boulder
Unemployed	0	$522
Part-time employment	$290 to $415	$698
Full-time employment	$920	$1,503

The income gradient is much more gradual for Boulder patients entering part-time employment, and is even more gradual when non-cash benefits are included. Clearly, the mentally ill in Boulder do not have as great an economic incentive to begin part-time work. The Italian model works well with the availability of guaranteed jobs through the cooperative for the mentally ill; without this, the unemployed would have no means of support.

To achieve the same effect, we could (a) limit disability pensions to the most disabled; (b) guarantee jobs for the remainder of the disabled in private industry, in sheltered workshops or in consumer cooperatives; and (c) pay a wage subsidy which covers the difference between the worker's productive capacity and the minimum wage. Regulations governing benefits, such as SSI and SSDI, could be waived to allow payments to be diverted into a wage subsidy scheme. The employer or cooperative would be reimbursed the difference between the worker's rate of production and his or her rate of pay. There is already a time-study process, established by the U.S. Department of Labor, which can be used to measure this difference.[60]

Wage subsidy

To be realistic, waiting for guaranteed jobs could be like waiting for the return of full employment. Nevertheless, in the absence of Ellwood-style reforms, we could still use the wage subsidy approach for underproductive workers in consumer cooperatives or supported employment. In fact, if we are to make work rewarding for those with a diminished level of functioning, it is essential to provide a subsidy which raises wages from the actual productive earning capacity to the client's reservation wage – around $5 an hour.

Wage subsidies would make it possible to modify the features of the traditional sheltered workshop. If workers were paid at or above the minimum wage rate, workshops would become more like mainstream employment and might join a consortium of cooperatives. The workshop labor force could be expanded to include a greater proportion of fully productive, non-handicapped people; new types of contracts could be sought to broaden the range of tasks. Such changes would improve work satisfaction, reduce the stigma which many clients associate with workshop employment and encourage the enrollment of currently unemployed people.

Can wage subsidies be generated locally, without radical changes in national disability pension fund regulations? In worker cooperatives, some enterprises, such as the consumer-oriented pharmacy described above, will be profitable and will cover part of the wage subsidy expense for less productive workers. Some of the cooperative businesses in Trieste and Pordenone (office cleaning, landscaping, nursing aides, restaurant) are self-sustaining and balance the costs of the less profitable enterprises in the consortia. The number of subsidized workers is dependent upon the overall profitability of the consortium.

In addition, if we could anticipate treatment cost savings for patients who become employed we might reasonably look to the mental health treatment budget for a wage subsidy. The cost of outpatient treatment of the unemployed patient is so high in Boulder (around $2,000 a month) that the expense of providing a wage supplement for half-time work for unemployed clients could be met by a mere 10 per cent reduction in the amount of treatment required. Psychiatric treatment costs are only half as high for part-time employed clients in Boulder, but it is not clear if the treatment costs are lower, in part, because the patients are working.[61] It seems logical that work will reduce treatment costs, purely because the client who is in a work setting for a large part of the week is not available to be in treatment. Being in a productive role, moreover, may enhance a client's self-esteem and reduce alienation so much that his or her level of functioning will improve.

Can treatment costs be reduced by employing patients? There is almost no research which addresses this question. As we saw earlier in this chapter, a number of studies have shown that patients who are working are much less likely to be rehospitalized than those who are unemployed, regardless of the patient's level of pathology. Research which addresses the question of cost directly, however, is extremely limited. An uncontrolled study conducted at the Mental Health Center of Boulder County found that psychiatric treatment costs were a third less for patients who were enrolled in the sheltered workshop than for those who were on the workshop waiting list. Clients waiting for workshop placement used substantially more inpatient and residential care and day care. The groups were non-randomly selected, however, and it is possible that the patients on the waiting list were less stable than those who were already enrolled.[62]

Research on this topic would help in the design of new treatment and rehabilitation strategies. However, mental health agencies in a capitated funding system (under which agencies may spend funds in any way considered cost-effective) can conduct real-life experiments with cost-shifting. For example, agencies in Utah and elsewhere, which are beginning to operate under a capitated Medicaid plan, might reasonably offer a wage subsidy to patients with the highest outpatient treatment costs, and track the subsequent cost of their care.

Full employment is not on the horizon, but innovations in social policy – in the design of disability pensions, job programs and health care funding – could well create dramatic improvements in the quality of life and integration of the mentally ill in our society.

SUMMARY

- Clinical research indicates that mentally ill people who are working stay out of hospital longer than unemployed patients.
- The research suggests, but does not prove, that employment may be the cause of the person's better functioning.
- There is no evidence in the clinical research that working leads to an improvement in the symptoms of psychosis.
- Work therapy appears to benefit psychotic patients.
- Long-term sheltered work is necessary for many of the mentally ill.
- Worker cooperatives successfully employ large numbers of mentally ill people in parts of Italy and other European countries.
- Both sheltered work and consumer-run businesses become less viable as the economy declines.
- Consumer-run enterprises can gain a market advantage by contracting to provide services to public agencies or to the consumer group.
- A consumer-cooperative specialty pharmacy for the mentally ill is a viable enterprise for many U.S. communities.
- The mentally ill encounter economic disincentives to work which may be alleviated by a more gradual reduction of disability benefits for beginning workers.
- Wage subsidies encourage the employment of lower-functioning patients and might pay for themselves by a reduction in treatment costs.

Chapter 12

Desegregating schizophrenia

It is easy to tell horror stories, and there are plenty in this book. It is harder to come up with ways to alleviate the plight of the mentally ill in the Western world. How can we help schizophrenic people re-enter society as it is presently structured and achieve a genuine degree of social integration? In this chapter we will look at practical answers to this question.

COMMUNITY SUPPORT SYSTEMS

The treatment programs of the Mental Health Center of Boulder County, Colorado, will frequently be used as examples. They illustrate what is possible given the usual level of community mental health funding[1] and a commitment to provide decent care for the most seriously ill patients. This center, like a number of others across the United States, was designated a model community support system for severely disturbed patients by the U.S. National Institute of Mental Health in the 1970s and has continued to add new programs since that time.

The services and programs that may be offered by a community support system range from individual counseling through psychosocial rehabilitation and vocational services to family support and public education. Services may be offered to patients in hospital, group homes, independent living or wherever the client can be found, whether it be in jail or a shelter for the homeless. The functions of such a system may be succinctly expressed by the following commandments. The treatment agency shall:

- adopt total responsibility for the severely disabled client's welfare, including helping the patient acquire such material resources as food, shelter, clothing and medical care;
- aggressively pursue the client's interests – ensuring that other social agencies fulfill their obligations, for example, or actively searching for patients who drop out of treatment;
- provide a range of supportive services which can be tailored to fit each patient's needs and which will continue as long as they are needed;

- educate the patient to live and work in the community; and
- offer support to family, friends and community members.[2]

Community support, then, comprises everything the old, long-stay institutions used to furnish and a host of additional services besides, which are essential for community tenure. By these means, if they are all supplied, we may virtually eliminate the revolving-door phenomenon.

Keeping the patient in the community, however, does not necessarily mean that he or she, in any real sense, is recovered (though it may well help in that recovery). Required in addition, as the earlier chapters have argued, are efforts to raise the degraded social status of the schizophrenic person, to offer him or her a meaningful role in life leading to a sense of worth and a reduction of alienation. Given these criteria, treatment becomes more than just a matter of providing services to patients and their relatives – it becomes social action, political lobbying and community education directed towards the desegregation of a minority group.

ESCAPING THE GHETTO

The ghettoes of the long-term mentally ill are the nursing homes, inner-city boarding homes, Skid Row missions and jails. How do we help these people break out? In Boulder County the mental health center has never placed physically healthy schizophrenic people in nursing homes. The administrators of the center have actively discouraged local nursing home operators from opening wards for chronically ill psychiatric patients, arguing that nursing homes cannot provide an adequate quality of care and environment for such patients. Recent federal legislation now prevents the expenditure of Medicaid funds on treating physically healthy mentally ill in nursing homes; this statute has reduced one of the worst abuses of psychiatric patients in the United States.

An outreach team from the mental health center goes to the Boulder shelter for the homeless every week, and when mentally ill people are located there or living on the streets, efforts are made to provide treatment and accommodate them in one of the residential facilities described below. Another outreach team goes to the local jail with a similar mission.[3]

Harmful and degrading though it is, increasing numbers of people suffering from psychosis are ending up in U.S. local jails (as described in Chapter 8). To cope with this problem it is important that mental health agencies accept that the local jail is part of their community and supply outreach services to the inmates. The object of such programs should be to arrange the transfer of all psychotic inmates to an appropriate treatment setting. This goal requires the development of working relationships with criminal court judges. Only in those rare instances when a judge will not release a mentally ill person because the crime is too serious, or when a psychotic inmate refuses to be transferred to a treatment setting and is too mildly disturbed for involuntary measures, should we resort to treating people with psychosis behind bars.[4]

It has, in fact, become routine in most areas of the United States for people suffering from psychosis to be treated in jail with antipsychotic drugs and to be detained for extended periods – largely because the public mental hospitals are filled to capacity and offer only brief care. Often the people with psychosis who spend most time in jail are those who have proved particularly difficult to treat in community programs. The task of mental health administrators and action groups, therefore, is to put pressure on their legislators to maintain the adequacy and capacity of the public psychiatric hospitals and to sustain the funding for an array of community treatment programs such as those described below.

INTENSIVE RESIDENTIAL TREATMENT

Cedar House is a large house for fifteen psychiatric patients in a residential and business district of the city of Boulder. It functions both as an alternative to acute care in a psychiatric hospital and as a half-way house. Like a psychiatric hospital it offers all the usual diagnostic and treatment services but, costing less than a third of private hospital treatment, it is feasible for patients to remain in residence for quite long periods of time if necessary. Usually admitted with some kind of an acute psychiatric problem (most often an acute psychotic relapse), a client may stay anywhere from a day to a year; the average period is around two weeks.

Unlike a psychiatric hospital, Cedar House is non-coercive. No patients can be strapped down, locked in or medicated unwillingly. Staff must encourage patients to comply voluntarily with treatment requirements and house rules. The people who cannot be managed are those who repeatedly walk away or run away and those who are violent. Since the alternative for patients who are unable to stay at Cedar House is hospital treatment, which none prefers, the large majority of residents accept the necessary restrictions. Very few patients, as we shall see, need to be transferred to hospital. In practice, virtually all clients with psychotic depression, most of those with schizophrenia and many with acute mania can be treated at Cedar House through all phases of their illness. There is no doubt that a large number of the people treated in this residential facility would be subjected to coercive measures, such as restraints or seclusion, if they were admitted to a hospital where such approaches are available and routinely used. The avoidance of coercion is the first step in maintaining the psychotic patient's status and self-esteem. As the moral-treatment advocates recognized, to cultivate the patient's self-control is to elicit his or her collaboration in treatment.

Like the York Retreat, also, the environment is similar to that of a middle-class home, not a hospital. Residents and staff may bring their pets with them to the house. A bird may be heard singing in one of the bedrooms and a dog shares the comfortable furniture with the residents. The floors are carpeted, a fire burns in the hearth, shelves of books are available, residents and visitors come and go fairly freely, staff and patients interact casually, eat together and are encouraged to treat one another with mutual respect. As in Tuke's establishment, the goal is to allow therapists and clients alike to retain their dignity and humanity and to foster cooperation.

In line with this emphasis, each resident is intimately involved in running the household. He or she is responsible for specific tasks which are assigned and supervised by one of the residents. These cooperative living arrangements reduce treatment costs, increase the resident's sense of belonging and can be useful training for people with problems in day-to-day functioning. A full-scale, therapeutic community style of patient government has not been established. In view of the relatively brief length of patient stay and the necessity for staff and administration to exercise close control over patients' admission and discharge (in order to make room for new acute admissions at all times) patient government is not considered workable. The ethos of the community, however, calls for residents routinely to assist in the care of others.

Residential treatment of this intensity requires a staffing pattern similar to that of a hospital. A mental health worker and a nurse are on duty at all times. At night, one of the two is awake and the other sleeps. On weekdays, two experienced therapists work with the patients. A psychiatrist is present for three hours a day, a team leader directs the program and a secretarial assistant manages the office work and the purchasing of household supplies. The treatment setting calls for staff who are tolerant and empathic and it brings out their capacity independently to find inventive solutions to difficult problems.

There is no commonly used form of psychiatric treatment (except for electro-convulsive therapy) and no diagnostic measure which cannot be provided for residents of this treatment facility. Patients with acute or chronic organic brain disorders, for example, can be evaluated using the laboratories and diagnostic equipment of local hospitals. Consulting physicians provide treatment for medical problems.

An essential step in the treatment of people entering Cedar House is the evaluation of the patient's social system. What has happened to bring the patient in for treatment at this particular time? What are his or her financial circumstances, living arrangements and work situation? Have there been recent changes? Are there family tensions? From the answers to such questions as these, a plan may be made which will hopefully diminish the chances of relapse after the patient leaves residential treatment.

In some cases the solution may be straightforward. The patient has been living on the street, sleeping in doorways on cold nights and eating out of garbage cans. Floridly psychotic at the time of admission, he (or, more rarely, she) may show few positive features of illness after a day or two of warmth and good food. This person needs help in applying for welfare entitlements and finding a place to live and, probably, a lot of supervision while settling into a new pattern of living. Another patient may relapse into acute psychosis after starting a job or losing one. He or she needs on-the-job counseling.

Other situations can be more difficult to ameliorate. A patient and his or her family members may be at loggerheads, periodically inflaming the patient to psychotic outbursts or the family members to angry rejection; yet none of the parties wishes to separate. Although the patient is calm and well while in residential treatment, meticulous family negotiations may be necessary before the patient can be discharged.

Most such seriously disturbed psychotic patients will benefit from taking some kind of psychoactive medication. The period of residential treatment allows the opportunity to spend time observing the patient's illness and selecting the most suitable drug (an antipsychotic may not be the best choice), monitoring and adjusting the dosage to minimize side effects and evaluating the benefits. An added advantage of the more leisurely pace of residential treatment (compared with brief hospitalization), as outlined in Chapter 10, is that it allows an opportunity to see if low doses of medication will be effective and for selected psychotic patients to be treated without antipsychotic drugs.[5]

What has been described so far is just one approach to the community treatment of the acutely ill psychotic patients – an intensive residential treatment program. Other good methods for treating such clients during the acute phase of their illness have been developed. Two of these will be described next.

FOSTER CARE FOR THE ACUTELY ILL

As part of Southwest Denver Community Mental Health Services in Colorado, in the 1970s and 1980s, Canadian community psychiatrist Paul Polak and his team developed an innovative method of caring for the acutely psychotic patient. They found several families in the neighborhood who were willing to take one or two acutely disturbed patients into their homes. Nurses, a psychiatrist and other staff from the mental health agency worked with the foster family to provide care and treatment for the disturbed person. The patient's own family also participated. Medications were used freely and were closely monitored by the medical staff. The average length of stay for such patients was ten days.

Foster families were chosen for their warmth and acceptance. Each client was given his or her own room and was treated as a guest. When able, the patient helped with shopping, cooking and household tasks. Often he or she would become friendly with the foster family and remain in touch through telephone calls, letters or visits.

This program, which did everything possible to maintain the client's status and connection with the community, proved workable and effective. In operation for two decades, it was a viable alternative to hospital care for all but a handful of patients. A two-year study using random assignment of patients showed that the community homes were more effective in some respects than a psychiatric hospital in providing intensive treatment, one important advantage being that clients treated in the family homes felt better about themselves and their treatment.[6]

Southwest Denver Mental Health Center no longer exists as an independent agency and the system of family sponsor homes is not in operation. A system of family crisis homes based on the Southwest Denver model, however, is currently in operation at Dane County Mental Health Center in Madison, Wisconsin. Six family homes provide care to a wide variety of people in crisis, most of whom would otherwise have spent time in hospital; many of these clients suffer from acute psychotic illness and some are acutely suicidal. Violence and safety are almost never a problem, in part because of careful selection of appropriate clients and in part because clients feel honored to be invited into another person's home; they try to behave with the courtesy of house guests. These crisis homes induce the patient to exercise self-control – a key strength of human-scale domestic alternatives to hospital care.[7]

INTENSIVE COMMUNITY SUPPORT

Another approach to the problem of caring for the most severely disturbed psychotic patients is to follow them so closely in the community – providing support at every step – that psychotic relapse is more or less eliminated. Leonard Stein, an American community psychiatrist, Mary Ann Test, a social worker, and their colleagues in Madison, Wisconsin, put such a program into effect in the 1970s. A similar program is provided now by the mental health center in Madison, with leadership from psychiatrist Ron Diamond. Available twenty-four hours a day, seven days a week, mental health staff visit patients in their own homes. They help their chronically mentally ill clients learn to do laundry, shopping, cooking, grooming and budgeting. They assist them in finding work and in settling disputes with landlords. If a patient does not show up for work or treatment one day, the staff member goes to his or her home to discover the reason. Staff help patients to expand their social lives and they provide support to the patients' families. Early signs of the return of psychosis are immediately detected and lead to active treatment measures. In essence, the patient is watched and helped as closely as he or she would be on many hospital wards, but the treatment is provided instead in the patient's own neighborhood. This type of daily practical help and advocacy has come to be termed "case management."

When these measures fail, the patient may be admitted briefly to hospital; such a move is rarely necessary, however. In a study of the course of illness in patients referred for admission to hospital with a severe psychiatric problem, it was found that nearly all of those randomly assigned to the Stein and Test intensive community treatment program in Madison could be treated without hospital care; of the patients assigned to standard outpatient care, on the other hand, nearly all were initially treated in hospital. At the end of a year the rate of readmission to hospital was 6 per cent for clients of the intensive community treatment team, in contrast to 58 per cent for patients in routine outpatient care. Mobile and intensive community treatment had put a stop to the revolving door.

The clients in this program reaped other benefits. Compared with the patients in standard community care, they had fewer symptoms, greater self-esteem and were more satisfied with their lives after one year of treatment. They were more likely to be living independently and had spent less time in jail.[8] This was accomplished, furthermore, with no increase in social cost to the patient's family or the community; there was no increased burden of social disruption or suicidal gestures.[9]

A program at the Mental Health Center of Boulder County, based on the Madison model, provides similar services and achieves equivalent results. In Boulder, the 20 per cent of the agency's psychotic patients with the greatest likelihood of relapse are assigned to an intensive community treatment team. Caseloads are small: each therapist is responsible for only 12 to 15 clients. The services they receive, when necessary, include:

- daily, flexible, unscheduled contact;
- twice daily medication monitoring;
- daily administration of funds (the therapist may be payee for the client's disability pension);
- supervised and subsidized housing;
- assistance with acquiring entitlements, housing and health care; and
- advocating for clients with social agencies and the criminal justice system.

Because medication can be administered daily, few clients assigned to this team receive long-acting intramuscular (depot) antipsychotic drugs. Patients appreciate this fact: almost none chooses intramuscular medication, even though coming in daily for oral medication is a chore – a telling comment on the dislike that clients have for the increased side effects associated with depot medications. Patients with bipolar disorder show the greatest improvement after assignment to the team, presumably because their lithium carbonate or other mood-stabilizing medication is carefully monitored. Clients whose mental illness is complicated by drug and alcohol abuse also do better on this team: in part this is because their money is often disbursed in modest daily amounts – too little to get too drunk or high. Their illness, consequently, is less severe, their rent is paid regularly and they are less likely to be admitted to hospital psychotic, hungry and homeless half-way through the month.

Before they were assigned to this intensive treatment team in 1984, 28 per cent of a sample of these severely disturbed clients were revolving-door patients with several hospital admissions a year; six years later, fewer than 5 per cent were in this frequent-admission category. With treatment, most of the group developed a stable course of illness. Only 4 per cent of the cohort had originally been free of hospital admissions over a two-year period; six years after assignment to intensive treatment nearly 60 per cent were this stable.

In Britain, where more psychiatric hospital beds are available (there are ten times as many beds *per capita* in Manchester, England, as in Boulder, Colorado[10]), most of these very disturbed patients would be in hospital. Are they better off in the community? In a comparison of Boulder clients in intensive outpatient treatment with patients in long-term care in the psychiatric ward of a general hospital in Manchester it was found that psychopathology was greater in the Boulder outpatient sample but their quality of life scores were better.[11] Patients maintained outside hospital with intensive services continue to be quite disturbed, it appears, but they enjoy life more. The reason is fairly clear: few people, well or ill, like to live in an institution – if they can get the same services outside hospital they are more contented.

WHICH PROGRAM?

We have now examined three programs aimed at boosting both the social functioning and quality of life of the most severely disabled psychotic patients. All three rely upon the cost savings from reduced use of expensive psychiatric hospital beds to make the program affordable; a small mental health center could scarcely afford to establish all of these programs, though an agency serving a large catchment area might be able to. Each program has its merits and drawbacks. If you had to choose, which one should be used in which circumstances?

Cedar House is a relatively expensive program. The required level of staffing imposes high fixed costs which cannot be reduced without seriously altering the nature of the program. Such costs would not be justifiable for an agency with a small catchment area (much below 200,000 persons). For small agencies and scattered populations, the family care program and the mobile treatment team would be more suitable. By comparison with these programs, furthermore, Cedar House is more institutional. By treating patients a stage further removed from their usual surroundings it may be somewhat more like a hospital in stigmatizing its clientele.

On the other hand, the two programs that are more deeply immersed in the community rely more heavily upon drug treatment for their success. Periods of hospitalization have to be brief; psychotic behavior must be efficiently brought under control if the patient is to remain in the community. As mentioned previously, the intensive residential program allows treatment decisions, including decisions on the use of medications, to be taken at a more measured pace and it offers the possibility of instituting low-dose or non-neuroleptic treatment in selected cases. This feature, in and of itself, some would consider to be a humanizing force.

DO WE NEED PSYCHIATRIC HOSPITALS?

In the 1960s, politicians and mental health professionals alike were heralding the death of the psychiatric hospital – but it is still with us. Does it serve a useful purpose? Even using one of the intensive community treatment programs described above, there remains a handful of patients who cannot be adequately cared for outside a hospital. A few patients, for example, consistently refuse any type of treatment and will always walk away from an open-door establishment; a few become violent at times and, if they fail to improve with treatment, represent a danger to mental health staff and members of the public. Some people with psychosis routinely make their illnesses worse by the constant abuse of hallucinogenic drugs, by heavy drinking or by sniffing glue and volatile solvents.

Attempts to treat such patients in the community are more likely to fail. These mentally ill people will be found in jail, held for minor offenses; they will be committed by the criminal courts to forensic psychiatric hospitals for more serious offenses; or they will end up living on the streets, leading degrading lives and becoming physically debilitated. The effort to help such patients, nevertheless, will have put an immense strain on the community support system. Many hours of work will have been put into makeshift treatment plans which have little hope of success.

The number of patients that cannot be treated in the community is extremely small, however. During 1993, around four psychotic patients from Boulder County were in long-term public hospital care, placed there by the mental health center. Another fifteen psychotic mental health center patients, at any time, are likely to be receiving medium- or short-term hospital treatment (lasting from a few days to three months) before returning to community care.[12] These patients are drawn from a county population of 225,000 people and a caseload of over 2,000 mental health center clients. The number of patients in long-term non-forensic hospital care emerges as fewer than 1 per cent of all the functionally psychotic patients in treatment at the mental health center.

It is important to identify these few clients and arrange for them to receive hospital care as the humane course of treatment. This may be more easily said than done. Long-term hospital care in the United States is virtually a thing of the past. State budget cuts have so reduced hospital capacity that the ward staff feel obliged to discharge any patient who loses his or her psychotic symptoms regardless of what the patient's trajectory is likely to be after release. Community mental health administrators must first fight to see a bare sufficiency of hospital beds funded; and then they must stand firm against the pressure to discharge from the hospital patients who cannot be properly treated once they leave.

If community support services were provided on a truly comprehensive basis, we would need only small hospitals but they would serve a highly specialized function. Based on the experience in Boulder and elsewhere, only one or two hospital beds for adults (aged 18–60) would be needed for each 10,000 of the general population. (Mental health staff working with the population of large cities might arrive at a higher estimate for the number of required hospital beds. States with a mental illness statute which does not permit involuntary outpatient treatment would also need more hospital beds.) A substantial proportion of the patients, however, would be long-term and highly resistant or unresponsive to treatment. Locked doors would be necessary for many of these clients, but their hopes of improvement would depend upon their being provided with work therapy; a range of varied but low-stress recreational activities; skilled, humane care in small attractive units; and access to a pleasant, open-air environment. In other words, they would be as unlike nursing homes as it is possible for such places to be.

AN ALTERNATIVE TO LONG-TERM HOSPITAL CARE

One reason that the number of patients in Boulder County in long-term hospital care is so low is because an open-door domestic alternative to hospital has been established for some of these very difficult-to-treat clients. Friendship House is a long-term intensive-treatment household for five very disturbed young and middle-aged adults. Each of these people has been ill for over a decade with a brittle psychosis which has shown relatively little benefit from psychiatric medication. Many have significant problems with substance abuse in addition to their mental illness. Most are somewhat uncooperative with treatment and so volatile and lacking in social skills that they have been unable to live outside an inpatient setting for more than a few weeks or months since the illness began, even when surrounded by an elaborate array of community supports. These residents represent a new generation of the severely ill who have become chronically institutionalized in an era when few indigent people in the United States get to stay in a hospital for any time at all.

The household is a cooperative venture between the Mental Health Center of Boulder County and the Naropa Institute, a Buddhist university with an East–West psychology training program. It is a cost-effective application of the principles embodied in contemplative therapy – an approach which emphasizes patience and compassion[13] – to the rehabilitation of the very ill. Within the household, each resident is provided with his or her own team comprised of a part-time therapist (paid) and some part-time psychology interns (all unpaid). The remaining staff include two resident house-parents and a program director. All of these staff work with the residents to create a therapeutic community and learning environment in which compassion, respect and openness are core values. The program has been successful in bringing equilibrium to the lives of people who had not known stability since they became ill, and in encouraging people who had been in involuntary treatment for years to accept voluntary treatment. What makes this program work are the same things that make Cedar House work. It is small and domestic. It is so much more pleasant than being in hospital that people will draw upon all their resources of self-control in order to stay there – the essence of moral treatment.

SUPERVISED APARTMENTS

Like one's job, a powerful indicator of status is one's living environment. The unemployed schizophrenic person, unless living with his or her family, is likely to occupy seedy, low-rent rooms, a boarding house or a nursing home. Many, having fallen ill early in life, have little experience of independent living. Some have poor judgment and lack the capacity to manage a household. For such people, supervised and subsidized housing is a necessity.

Several mental health agencies have demonstrated that cooperative apartments (or group homes, as they are often called) work well for chronically ill patients who are leaving mental hospital after several years of residence.[14] The same approach has been shown to be viable also for young adult psychotic patients who have not spent years in mental hospitals. Apartment programs for such clients exist in Fareham, England,[15] for example, in Madison, Wisconsin, and in Boulder, Colorado. For these patients, however, often more volatile, disruptive and subject to relapse, a more intensive level of supervision is required. In the Boulder supervised living program, staff members hold house meetings for the residents at least once weekly in their apartments and provide individual outpatient counseling in addition. Help with household management often includes sorting out problems with "crashers" – initially welcome guests who end up exploiting the residents or stealing from them. The advantage of such group living is that it offers a substitute family to clients who may have difficulties in setting up a stable family of their own or in living with their parents. Achieving amiable domestic relations, however, may require the therapist to arbitrate a considerable number of disputes.

For many schizophrenic people, living alone is the best arrangement – the stresses of cooperative living may provoke relapse; others find loneliness to be a major problem. Supervised apartments in Boulder range in size from one- to eight-person households. At some of the larger houses a university student is hired to live in (rent free) and to provide a little supervision in the evenings. These larger houses can accommodate clients who have more limited capacity for independent living. By supplying increasing amounts of staff support on the premises it is possible to develop a range of community living arrangements up to the level of the traditional, staffed half-way house, for clients with progressively lower levels of functioning.

In high-rent Boulder, some form of rent subsidy is necessary for clients who must often exist on limited Social Security income. Such financial assistance is available through the federal Department of Housing and Urban Development, either as direct rent subsidies or as grants to mental health agencies to build or buy new accommodation. In most instances, the center operates as a tenant, subleasing the house or apartment to the patients.

RESIDENTIAL SETTINGS BASED ON MUTUAL SUPPORT

Some residential settings provide security and support for the residents by developing a strong sense of community and employing the tenants in staff positions. An interesting cooperative housing project of this type, Columbia University Community Services, operates five apartment buildings on the Upper West Side of Manhattan for mentally ill and mentally healthy poor people. In this project, a private non-profit housing corporation owns the buildings (obtained cheaply from the city of New York), the mental health agency at Columbia University provides treatment and practical assistance (case management) to all tenants, and a board composed of residents, mental health staff and representatives of the landlord screens potential tenants and manages the day-to-day operations of the building. Some tenants are given paid jobs on the 24-hour-a-day "tenant patrol" which provides security and assistance to the residents.[16]

Another residential program in California – the clustered apartment project of Santa Clara County Mental Health Center – was designed to build community strength among clients living independently in apartments in the same neighborhood. These were to be communities of mentally ill people based on mutual support and interdependence – assertively non-clinical in style. Staff were encouraged to abandon traditional roles and to become, instead, community organizers. It was hoped that these strengthened communities would develop ways to support their members so that hospital admission for acute psychiatric distress became less necessary. As the project took shape, each of the communities developed different strengths. In one program, all of the staff were drawn from among the consumer group. In another, the program developed a strong sense of community around its Latino identity. In a third, community members provided respite care in a crisis apartment to members who were acutely disturbed. The programs varied in the extent to which they met the needs of new or established members but they were all successful in building a sense of empowerment among the residents.[17]

LONG-TERM FOSTER CARE

Many patients who have not yet developed the ability to live independently may do well in long-term foster care. Dr. Polak's short-term foster care program was established to treat acutely ill patients. In other mental health programs, however, a client moves in to live with a foster family when his or her condition is stable and may stay as long as he or she wishes. Fort Logan Mental Health Center in Denver, Colorado, has successfully operated such a system of family care for many years. Their clients often graduate to independent living. The boarding-out schemes in operation in Salisbury and in Hampshire, England, are similar.[18]

SMALL IS BEAUTIFUL

There is an important common quality to each of the model treatment programs discussed so far – the setting is small. This factor can have a powerful influence upon the patient's social role and sense of worth. Where there are relatively few members of a group the contribution of each is seen as correspondingly more important. Students in small high schools, for example, have been found to have a better developed sense of responsibility and usefulness than students in large schools. In the small schools each student is more likely to be relied upon to contribute to sporting events, the band, dramatic productions and similar activities. Studies have shown that people in small settings such as these are more active and that they tackle more varied, difficult and useful tasks. In consequence, they feel challenged, valued and better satisfied with themselves.[19]

A patient living in a small community setting, therefore, where he or she is called upon to contribute to the operation of the household, will be more valued for any special abilities and will develop greater self-esteem and practical skills. More than this, he or she will be better accepted and socially integrated. As in the Third World village, where there is no labor surplus, it is necessary to accept those who are available to do the job. Where there are more people than are strictly required, the research of psychologist Roger Barker reveals, deviance and individual differences are not tolerated nearly as well.[20] This is one reason why boarding homes and nursing homes containing scores or hundreds of patients have such a pernicious influence on the course of schizophrenia.

COOPERATIVELY-OWNED HOUSING

If mentally ill people were to become property owners instead of tenants, this would be a form of social and economic advancement. Housing cooperatives provide a mechanism for poor people to own their accommodation and offer a number of advantages besides. They not only provide long-term affordable housing, they also create a better quality of life for residents, particularly those with special needs, by developing a strong feeling of community. They build leadership skills among members of the cooperative through the financial, maintenance and managerial tasks required for the operation of the housing. Housing cooperatives can be hard to establish, however, as both mortgage lenders and potential residents may be put off by the cooperative governance structure.[21]

There are a number of reasons why cooperative housing is more affordable. Each member owns a share of the cooperative corporation and then leases his or her own housing unit from the corporation. Since members are "leasers," therefore, they qualify for rent subsidies, including federal Section 8 certificates. Nevertheless, they retain ownership rights, including the ability to profit from resale of the share. Since departing members could sell their shares at an escalated current market value, a mechanism is required to ensure permanent affordability; this is achieved through a "limited equity" formula. Under this arrangement, the cooperative buys back shares, when the owner departs, at a predetermined rate of appreciation. Another financial advantage is that the ongoing cost of operating a cooperative tends to be lower than that of rental apartments because of resident involvement in management and the absence of a profit line in the budget.[22]

The basic financing method for establishing a cooperative is a blanket mortgage, based on the value of the building, for which the cooperative corporation is liable. Members pay an initial membership price and a monthly assessment. Members can obtain cooperative share loans, backed by the individual's cooperative share, to allow them to meet the membership price. For example, poor families joining the Hillrise Mutual Housing Association in Lancaster, Pennsylvania, are required to pay a membership price of $1,500, but most pay $300 in cash and finance the rest through a share loan. Low-income housing cooperatives in the United States may obtain subsidies through local government low-interest loans and grants, home-ownership assistance programs and property tax forgiveness.[23]

In fact, there are relatively few successful examples of cooperative home ownership for the mentally ill because of a variety of problems. The mentally ill tend to be a fairly mobile group with little capital or monthly income. If hospitalized for a prolonged period, the person may lose benefits and be unable to pay the monthly assessment. Recipients of supplemental security income (SSI), furthermore, cannot accumulate capital to purchase housing without adversely affecting their eligibility for benefits.

One novel attempt to develop a housing cooperative for the mentally ill achieved only limited success. The Mental Health Law Project in New York filed a class-action suit on behalf of a large number of mentally ill clients whose social security benefits had been suspended during the Reagan Administration.[24] The suit was successful and the clients were due to receive large, retroactive payments. Ironically, this could have led to their funds being discontinued again, as their assets would have exceeded the maximum allowable under social security regulations. To avoid this outcome, the Mental Health Law Project established a housing trust to receive the clients' retroactive payments. The project was only partially successful, however, because, by the time the necessary waiver of regulations had been obtained from the Social Security Administration allowing the clients to invest their assets in future housing, most of the clients had spent their awards. The number of remaining participants was too small to leverage private development funds to create low-cost housing. The trust, however, continues to be a suitable vehicle for those who need to shelter retroactive SSI payments and want to invest them in housing.[25]

A small-scale attempt to create a housing association in which mentally ill people participate in a limited equity housing agreement, the Newell Street Cooperative in Pittsfield, Massachusetts, also ended in failure. The project obtained a waiver which allowed state rent subsidies (like HUD Section 8 subsidies) to be applied to the purchase of a four-apartment building; when the rent subsidy program was trimmed, however, the cooperative collapsed. During the one-year period that the cooperative was in operation significant improvements were noted in the participants' management skills, self-esteem and sense of mastery.[26]

Despite difficulties and failures, however, housing cooperatives for the mentally ill are a viable concept. Some chapters of the National Alliance for the Mentally Ill (a U.S. organization of relatives and friends of mentally ill people), including the Greater Chicago branch, have established non-profit housing trusts. The residents of these housing projects are usually mentally ill relatives of the investors; if one of the residents moves, the investor may dispose of his/her share to another family or claim a tax deduction. A trust of this type can establish small homes or large apartment complexes and can contract with a local mental health agency to provide appropriate services on the premises. The settings may include disabled and non-disabled residents. The National Alliance for the Mentally Ill has proposed a low-cost revolving loan fund which, by building a large reservoir of capital, could access favorable loan rates. Although plans of this type do not necessarily place ownership of the property in the hands of the mentally ill themselves, they are a valuable source of stable and affordable housing.[27]

PSYCHOTHERAPY

Serious questions have been raised as to the efficacy of psychotherapy in general and its value in schizophrenia in particular. The research suggests that insight-oriented, uncovering psychotherapy has little or no application in psychosis and that environmental considerations, psychosocial interventions and various types of drug treatment are usually of more immediate relevance.[28] None of the treatment approaches discussed so far would be possible, however, without some of the basic ingredients of psychotherapy. The schizophrenic patient and the therapist must be able to form a relationship of mutual trust and to work through disagreements which arise between them in the course of treatment. The therapist should also be able to help the patients resolve conflicts with other people which may surface. The patient should feel free to discuss concerns about his or her life, illness and treatment. Where denial is preventing the patient from recognizing problems, the therapist must be able to approach the issues sensitively; and where resistance holds the patient back from a useful course of action, the therapist must attempt to uncover the reasons. In other words, while social considerations and drug therapy are important, they must be humanized if the schizophrenic patient is to re-enter society.

The frustration of failure inherent in working in an inadequate system of care can lead staff to feel a degree of contempt for their clients. Such an attitude can be expressed in jokes which attribute negative characteristics to their psychotic patients or in more subtle forms of denigration. Sociologist David Rosenhan, for example, revealed that hospital staff often fail to respond to a patient's question, passing by as if the inquirer were not present.[29] Therapy which hopes to increase the schizophrenic person's sense of worth must begin with respect; and professionals with the greatest authority within a treatment agency are under the heaviest obligation to demonstrate respect for the clientele on all occasions. In a similar vein, therapy should aspire to identify and emphasize the patient's special strengths and individuality and not aim merely to control pathology.

An important element in avoiding frustration in therapy for the patient, relatives and therapist alike is to set suitable expectations. Like the moral-treatment pioneers, we should look for a certain level of self-control and performance from the psychotic patient, but goals must be achievable. The client should not be encouraged to apply for work which is beyond his or her current capacity; the family should be warned that the ambitions for their relative may need to be restricted in every sphere; and the therapist should not see the patient's occasional relapse as a failure.

While the patient may be given the hope that medication will one day be unnecessary, such an option should not be seen as an end in itself. The patient's goals should be to do well and to feel good – the medication is a tool toward that end. The patient, however, may identify the medicine with the illness and see it as a stigmatizing and controlling force (which it often is, of course). To get around this problem one may do a number of things: help the patient identify certain goals and the extent to which medication can assist in reaching them; discuss the patient's reaction to the illness, to the medication, to control and to stigma as separate but related issues; and delegate to the patient authority over his or her own medications at the earliest workable opportunity so that he or she can set the dosage to achieve the desired benefit.

The schizophrenic patient does not respond well to ambiguity in therapy or to a neutral and distant therapist. Communication should be straightforward, expectations clear-cut and the therapist should not hesitate to act as a role-model for the patient. Psychotic experiences may be discussed frankly, not to uncover dynamic origins, but to alleviate the client's fears and perplexity about them and to identify stresses which provoke their appearance. The emphasis in therapy, though, needs to be on problems in daily living – work, personal and family relationships, finances and accommodation – and a major goal of treatment should be the reduction of stress in these areas.

Paradoxically, the therapist for psychotic clients will find that he or she is encouraging many patients that they can overcome their disability and accomplish more, while he or she must persuade the others that they suffer from an illness and should accept restrictions and limit their horizons. As argued in Chapter 8, this phenomenon is exacerbated by the stigma of mental illness. To consider oneself both mentally ill and capable creates cognitive dissonance: patients tend either to accept the label of mental illness and adopt the associated stereotype of incompetence or they reject the notion that they are ill or disabled. The solution is to proceed slowly, to avoid confronting the receptive patient too harshly with success and to avoid vigorously attacking the denial of the patient who rejects the illness label.

Herein lies one of the potential advantages of group therapy for psychotic patients. Cognitive-dissonance research demonstrates that people are more likely to change their attitudes if they can be encouraged to express in public an opinion different from their usual belief. By bringing together in a therapy group psychotic patients who variously accept or reject the illness label and who have a variety of levels of functioning, one may hope that the less competent patients will accept the possibility of becoming more capable and that those who deny their illness will change their opinion. A group focus on practical accomplishments and the development of social skills is indicated. A review of the research on the effectiveness of group psychotherapy for outpatients with psychosis suggests, in fact, that such treatment is particularly valuable in boosting both the clients' levels of social functioning and their morale.[30]

FAMILY THERAPY

While individual and group psychotherapy are universally applied in the treatment of schizophrenia – useful integrating forces which are sometimes overrated and sometimes undervalued – family therapy is an often neglected approach. This neglect is the more indefensible in light of the evidence that family therapy can be as effective in the treatment of schizophrenia as the antipsychotic drugs. From the outset, however, it should be clear that family therapy, here, does not mean efforts to uncover the root cause of the psychosis in family dynamics. As indicated in Chapter 1, there is little evidence to suggest that family pathology contributes to the *development* of schizophrenia. The successful family therapy programs, rather, have concentrated upon the influence of the family environment on the *course* of the condition, and have relied heavily upon practical support and education as the essential ingredients.

In Chapter 10, the research conducted by Julian Leff and his associates in London on the family environment of schizophrenic people was reviewed in some detail. These researchers have shown that schizophrenic patients who return to a home in which their relatives are critical and overinvolved have a higher relapse rate than those who return to a low-stress home. The greater the proportion of time the patient spends with high-stress relatives, the greater the risk of relapse. Since this early British research was conducted, more than a score of similar studies have been carried out in several countries around the world, nearly all of them confirming the original findings. If the results of these studies are pooled so that hundreds of cases are included we see that the overall rate of relapse in the critical and overinvolved families is more than twice the rate in the families without these features – 50 per cent *versus* 23 per cent at the end of a year.[31]

Four studies of family therapy for people with high-relapse schizophrenia (who are taking medication) have now been conducted using random assignment of cases to therapy or to a control group. Each shows a marked degree of benefit for family treatment. In the control groups relapse rates are as high as might be expected for high-risk cases who are taking medication – usually around 50 per cent over the course of nine months; patients receiving family therapy, however, experience relapse rates of under 10 per cent.[32] If we look back to Figure 10.2, we may see that antipsychotic drugs reduce the rate of relapse in schizophrenic patients spending large amounts of time in high-stress households from a virtual certainty to a 50–50 chance. Now we see that family intervention can change the stress pattern of such a household and almost eliminate the remaining risk (at least over a nine-month period).

What are the elements of effective family therapy? In each of the four studies the family intervention is rather similar. In a study conducted by Julian Leff, for example, the family treatment comprised (a) a series of sessions of education about mental illness, (b) participation in a relatives' group, and (c) individual family therapy conducted in the patient's home. The relatives' group, which was the central component of the program, offered support for the relatives, who often felt isolated and lonely, practical strategizing for those who were having trouble coping with difficult behavior and role-playing to assist in the development of new attitudes.[33]

A broad review of the research on family therapy in psychosis in fact suggests that it has repeatedly been found to be of value.[34] We should conclude that to withhold family assistance where we can identify high levels of stress is equivalent to withholding drug treatment from patients whom we know will do poorly without it.

FAMILY EDUCATION AND SUPPORT

Many families of mentally ill people feel that "therapy" implies pathology and, hence, blame. Other approaches can be less stigmatizing and less expensive. Education for the mentally ill and their relatives, for example, can be provided as an evening class. Such courses have been run annually at the Mental Health Center of Boulder County for over a decade, sponsored by local organizations of the mentally ill and their relatives. An outline of the topics for one series of classes is set out in Table 12.1. Such a course can be run at low cost, for the speakers may be drawn from among the agency consumers and staff and community professionals. For the teacher, the class is an agreeable experience; rarely does one encounter students so hungry for knowledge and so interested in the subject matter. For the students, the class is more than an educational program. On each occasion the course has been run, the participants have gained support from the informal sharing of experiences – the recognition that they are not alone, that other people have found strategies for the problems with which they have been struggling in isolation. With no specific direction from the mental health professionals, the relatives form themselves into a self-help group.

CONSUMER GROUPS

Many observers would argue that one of the most important developments in psychiatry in the past twenty years has been the growth of organizations of relatives of people with serious mental illness. In the United States the

Table 12.1 *Facts about Mental Illness*: A course for people with mental illness and their family members

Class*	Topic
1	*What is Mental Illness?* The main features of schizophrenia and manic-depressive illness
2	*The Experience of Psychosis* People who have suffered episodes of serious mental illness describe the experience
3	*Schizophrenia: Its Causes and Outcome* Why do people develop schizophrenia? Who recovers and why? The latest research
4	*Manic-Depressive (Bipolar) Illness: Its Causes and Outcome* How does the illness progress, with and without treatment?
5	*Medications* How do medications help? What are their side effects and what can be done about them?
6	*Community Support and Treatment* Housing, financial support and treatment. Dealing with substance abuse and mental illness when they occur together
7	*Coping with Mental Illness* People who suffer from mental illness or have a mentally ill family member talk about mastering the symptoms, handling crises and gaining independence

* Each class runs for 90 minutes

National Alliance for the Mentally Ill has lobbied for improvements in services for people with mental illness, influencing decisions to direct public mental health funding to the most seriously disturbed and to focus research efforts on schizophrenia. Media reports on the mentally ill have changed in tone in response to a drive by the Alliance to reduce stigma and to establish a new openness about psychiatric illness.

In Britain the National Schizophrenia Fellowship, established a few years earlier than its American counterpart, has been similarly active in providing emotional support for its members, lobbying for needed services, fostering public education and sponsoring research. Its publications have covered such topics as inadequate services, mental health law and the importance of work for the mentally disabled.[35]

Many are hopeful that the next decade will see an equivalent growth in the organization of *direct* or *primary* consumers of mental health services. This would help to balance the paternalism and control, which are unavoidable elements of relapse prevention programs, with the empowerment offered by consumer-run services. Across the United States, the consumer movement is gathering momentum. Two organizations, the National Mental Health Consumer Association and the National Alliance of Mental Patients, vie for membership, sponsor national conferences, send speakers to professional meetings, combat stigma through media presentations and lobby for political objectives. Consumers are appointed to the governing boards of many mental health centers, and state regulations in California require that the boards of residential facilities include consumer members. The statewide consumer organization in Utah, U-Can-Du, employs a staff of three consumers, holds an annual state consumer conference and is involved in system advocacy, providing input into the state mental health planning process.

CONSUMER-RUN SERVICES

In recent years, in the U.S.A. and elsewhere, consumers of mental health services have become increasingly involved in running their own programs. Consumer organizations have set up drop-in centers, support groups, speakers' bureaux, telephone hot-lines and a variety of other services. Utah's statewide consumer network is composed of 17 local organizations, one of which operates a café, and another, a drop-in center and a housing cooperative with a half-a-million dollar annual budget.

A consumer action group in Denver has opened its own psychiatric clinic. The Capitol Hill Action and Recreation Group (CHARG) is a coalition of consumers and professionals which has established a consumer-run drop-in center and a full-scale psychiatric clinic for the treatment of severely ill people. The clinic is directly accountable to an elected consumer board and to a second board comprising professionals and other interested people. All matters of clinic policy require the consent of the consumer board. CHARG also provides consumer advocates for patients at the local state hospital, in boarding homes and in other locations. The advocates visit the hospital wards, attend treatment planning meetings and accompany clients to court hearings; among other services, they help clients find apartments, apply for public assistance, appeal adverse Social Security rulings and contest involuntary treatment certifications.[36]

Patients who are admitted to the locked psychiatric ward of San Francisco General Hospital are provided with a peer counselor – someone who also suffers from mental illness and has had inpatient treatment. The peer counselor's job is to humanize the hospital environment by offering advice and support which are completely distinct from the professional hospital treatment. (Only in unusual circumstances does the peer counselor talk to the staff about information gathered from the patient.) The volunteer peer counselors are trained and supervised by Carol Patterson, a social worker who is herself a consumer.[37]

An innovative program in Denver, Colorado, at the Regional Assessment and Training Center (RATC), has trained mental health consumers with long-term mental illness to work as aides to case managers within the state mental health system, as residential counselors and as vocational rehabilitation staff.[38] Trainees with well-controlled major mental illness receive 21 credit hours of college education during six weeks of class-room training and a 14-week field placement. Classroom courses include mathematics, writing, interviewing techniques, case management skills, crisis intervention and professional ethics. Following the supervised intern-ship in a community mental health program, trainees earn a certificate from the local Community College and are guaranteed employment with a community mental health program. As case manager aides, the program graduates help mentally ill clients with budgeting, applying for welfare entitlements and finding housing, and they counsel their clients on treat-ment, work and other issues. As vocational aides, the graduates act as job coaches and train clients in successful work habits. By 1992, the sixth year of the program's operation, over 70 consumers had been trained and placed in employment with the Colorado mental health system and, at last count, 62 per cent of the program graduates had completed a year or more of successful employment.[39]

This program has continued successfully after initial demonstration grant funds, which paid the salaries of the consumer staff, have been terminated, and has been replicated in other states of the union. In Houston, Texas, a similar program has trained and placed 50 consumer case managers, and other replication projects have been established in Washington state, Utah and Oregon – all without demonstration grants.[40] The consumer aides are paid a standard wage but are still relatively cheap ($5.50 or £3.70 an hour); they perform tasks (for example, apartment hunting) which profes-sionals are happy to see others take on and they achieve some things which professionals cannot. In particular, they serve as role models for clients who are struggling to manage their lives better and they effectively reduce the antagonism that many clients show toward treatment. The consumer staff also raise the staff and patient level of optimism about outcome from illness.

THE DEATH OF DAY CARE

Developments in community treatment and consumer-run programs have made traditional day care more or less obsolete. Day care programs are in essence a transfer of the institutional setting to the community. Writing of British practice, psychiatrist Mounir Ekdawi concludes:

> Severely disabled people attending a day unit have often led dependent, institutional lives for many years; nevertheless, it often seems that their past hospital experience was, if anything, richer and more socially stimulating.[41]

For many patients, day care offers close observation, daily medica-tion monitoring and a welcome release from an otherwise aimless exis-tence. These advantages, however, can be achieved, with much greater empowerment and rehabilitative potential, through a combination of intensive outpatient treatment (described above) and a Fountain House style of clubhouse with consumer involvement.

Organizations such as Fountain House, in New York City, and Thresholds, in Chicago, have gained international prominence for establishing a model in which people with mental illness are involved in running a program which meets many of their recreational, social and vocational needs. In these programs, clients are called "members" and work with staff in running the operations of the clubhouse – putting out the daily newsletter, working in the food service, staffing the reception desk or serving in the clubhouse thrift shop (second-hand clothes store). The clubhouse is open in the evenings, on weekends and on holidays, providing a refuge for people who cannot fit in well elsewhere. Psychiatric treatment is definitively not part of the program. Instead the emphasis is on developing work skills and job opportunities for the members.[42]

For example, at the Chinook Clubhouse in Boulder, which is modeled on Fountain House, staff locate jobs for the members in local businesses and train and support them as they settle into the new work. In preparation for this, the members join clubhouse work groups like those at Fountain House. The program is not for everyone, however; lower-functioning clients are scared off by the emphasis on work and higher-functioning clients are not keen to mingle with other mentally ill people. A substantial proportion, nevertheless, take part in the program and report a distinct improvement in their quality of life.

Recently clubhouses with even more consumer involvement have sprung into being. Spiritmenders Community Center in San Francisco's inner city was established by the San Francisco Network of Mental Health Clients. The program is democratically run and is funded and maintained solely by mental health service consumers. It offers a number of activities, a safe place to drop in and socialize (important in the inner city), and education for its members and the general public. It aims to empower its members through peer counseling, advocacy and by fostering self-advocacy. Members clearly do not see the center as being part of the traditional mental health system. As one of the organizers frames their goal,

> efforts are made to prevent those situations that force individuals to receive involuntary services and/or other mental health services.[43]

As discussed in Chapter 8, the existential neurosis is a problem which stands in the way of recovery from schizophrenia for people living in the community. To combat this obstacle we can use ingredients of the therapeutic community approach which helped us tackle the institutional syndrome in the postwar decades – the normalizing effect of small, domestic treatment settings coupled with patient participation in their own treatment and control over their environment. How these ingredients may be added to community care has been discussed in this chapter. We are left, however, with the problem of confronting the stigma of mental illness.

COMMUNITY EDUCATION

Although the mentally ill have been in the community for four decades, we have scarcely begun to educate the public about the nature of major mental illness. Community mental health professionals in Italy have taken this challenge far more seriously and have succeeded to a greater extent. Leading up to 1978, when Italy enacted its mental health reform law, daily newspaper articles, radio broadcasts, television interviews, discussions and books all involved the general public, politicians and union officials in a debate which was theirs, not just for psychiatrists.[44] In Trieste, the emptying of the mental hospital in the 1970s was celebrated with a city-wide parade and other festive occasions; the old mental hospital was thrown open to the public for film festivals, repertory theater and art exhibitions;[45] businesses employing the mentally ill became very prominent in the public eye, advertised by brilliantly designed brochures filled with graphic art. These initiatives, writes sociologist Michael Donelly,

> mobilised a wide sympathy and interest among the people of Trieste, and probably displaced at least some of the fears which the breaking down of the asylum walls would otherwise have occasioned.[46]

Newspaper coverage of mental illness in Britain and the United States is generally limited to reports of crimes committed by "former mental patients" or, more rarely, shocking disclosures of the degraded conditions of the deinstitutionalized mentally ill. Organizations such as the National Alliance for the Mentally Ill and the National Schizophrenia Fellowship have appreciated that a more sensitive portrayal of mental illness is required if the associated stigma is to be lifted.

To this end, a series of radio programs were produced in Boulder, with the support of the local Alliance for the Mentally Ill, which attempted to reveal the human side of psychosis. Parents of a schizophrenic man talk about their son's illness, in one program, describing both his disturbed behavior and his talents – revealing their love for him and their sense of tragic loss. In other programs, patients describe the inner world of psychosis and the frustrations of trying to be understood, of trying to get help and of mere survival.[47] Such first-hand accounts are moving – for those who hear them. Most radio stations, unfortunately, are not interested; the material does not fit with the usual programming.

We have far to go before the schizophrenic person is welcome in Western society and before he or she can view himself or herself as an equal and useful member of society. Until that time schizophrenia is likely to continue to be a malignant condition.

We have the knowledge, nevertheless, to render the illness benign. We would need to:

- treat the acute phase of the illness in small, domestic, non-coercive settings which reflect the humane principles of moral treatment;
- ensure adequate psychological and clinical support in the community, including a full range of independent and supervised, non-institutional accommodation;
- give recognition and support for the care offered by the schizophrenic person's family, and provide family education and counseling;
- provide guaranteed jobs and training for the mentally disabled – work which is neither too demeaning nor too stressful;
- establish economic incentives to work – a more gradual reduction of disability benefits for disabled workers and wage subsidies for the severely handicapped;
- encourage economic and social advancement through consumer-cooperative businesses, housing and services;
- fight for the rights of people with schizophrenia and their families to participate as fully integrated members of society, taking the issue before the public through the media; and
- use the antipsychotic drugs as a supplement to these measures, not as a substitute for them.

Parts of this plan would be expensive but overall it may cost little more than our current vast expenditure on the treatment and support of schizophrenic people and on the associated disruption, crime and imprisonment which result from inadequate care. Our society is inherently unequal, however, and to provide such a quality of life for the person with schizophrenia is scarcely feasible since such a large proportion of the population – including an army of unemployed – would be left in worse circumstances. To render schizophrenia benign we may, in essence, have to restructure our provisions for all of the poor.

Notes

INTRODUCTION

1 Harris, M., *Cultural Materialism: The Struggle for a Science of Culture*, New York: Random House, 1979. See also the preface to Marx, K., *A Contribution to the Critique of Political Economy*, New York: International Publishers, 1970; first published 1859.

1 WHAT IS SCHIZOPHRENIA?

1 Lee, R. B., "!Kung bushman subsistence: An input–output analysis," in A. P. Vayda (ed.), *Environment and Cultural Behavior: Ecological Studies in Cultural Anthropology*, Garden City, New York: Natural History Press, 1969, pp. 47–9.
2 This is a broad definition of political economy as is commonly used in anthropology. It is drawn from Harris, M., *Culture, Man, and Nature*, New York: Thomas Y. Crowell, 1971, p. 145. Similarly broad definitions may be found in Lange, O., *Political Economy*, vol. 1, New York: Macmillan, 1959 ("Political economy is concerned with the social laws of production and distribution"); and in Marshall, A., *Principles of Economics*, 8th edn., London: Macmillan, 1920, p.1 ("Economics is a study of mankind in the ordinary business of life: it examines that part of individual and social action which is most closely connected with the attainment and with the use of material requisites of well being").
3 Szasz, T. S., *The Myth of Mental Illness: Foundations of a Theory of Personal Conduct*, revised edn., New York: Harper & Row, 1974.
4 American Psychiatric Association, *Diagnostic and Statistical Manual of Mental Disorders*, 3rd edn.-Revised (DSM-III-R), Washington, D.C., 1987.
5 Kraepelin, E., *Dementia Praecox and Paraphrenia*, Edinburgh: Livingstone, 1919, pp. 38–43.
6 Leff, J., *Psychiatry Around the Globe: A Transcultural View*, New York: Marcel Dekker, 1981, ch. 5.
7 Bleuler, E., *Dementia Praecox, or the Group of Schizophrenias*, translated by J. Zinkin, New York: International Universities Press, 1950. The German language edition first appeared in 1911.
8 Ibid., pp. 246–7.
9 Ibid., p. 248.
10 Ibid., pp. 258–9.
11 Ibid., p. 471.
12 Ibid., p. 475.

13 Ibid., p. 476.
14 Ibid., p. 471.
15 Ibid., p. 472.
16 Ibid., p. 480.
17 Ibid., p. 478.
18 Ibid., p. 479.
19 Langfeldt, G., "The prognosis in schizophrenia and the factors influencing the course of the disease," *Acta Psychiatrica et Neurologica Scandinavica*, supplement 13, 1937.
20 Leff, *Psychiatry Around the Globe*, pp. 37–40; Wing, J. K., *Reasoning About Madness*, New York: Oxford University Press, 1978.
21 Cooper, J. E., Kendell, J. E., Gurland, B. J. *et al.*, *Psychiatric Diagnosis in New York and London*, Maudsley Monograph Number 20, London: Oxford University Press, 1972.
22 World Health Organization, *The International Pilot Study of Schizophrenia*, vol. 1, Geneva, 1973.
23 Cade, J. F. J., "Lithium salts in the treatment of psychotic excitement," *Medical Journal of Australia*, 36: 349 *et seq.*, 1949.
24 Schou, M., Juel-Nielsen, N., Stromgren, E. and Voldby, H., "The treatment of manic psychoses by the administration of lithium salts," *Journal of Neurology, Neurosurgery and Psychiatry*, 17: 250 *et seq.*, 1954.
25 Fieve, R. R., "Lithium therapy," in H. I. Kaplan, A. M. Freedman and B. J. Sadock (eds.), *Comprehensive Textbook of Psychiatry-III*, vol. 31, Baltimore: Williams & Wilkins, 1980, pp. 2348–52. The reference is to p. 2348.
26 American Psychiatric Association, *Diagnostic and Statistical Manual of Mental Disorders*, 3rd edn. (DSM-III), Washington, D.C., 1980, pp. 181–203.
27 Taylor, M. A. and Abrams, R., "The prevalence of schizophrenia: A reassessment using modern diagnostic criteria," *American Journal of Psychiatry*, 135: 945–8, 1978; Helzer, J., "Prevalence studies in schizophrenia," presented at the World Psychiatric Association Regional Meeting, New York, October 30–November 3, 1981; Endicott, J., Nee, J., Fleiss, J. *et al.*, "Diagnostic criteria for schizophrenia: Reliabilities and agreement between systems," *Archives of General Psychiatry*, 39: 884–9, 1982; Jablensky, A., Sartorius, N., Ernberg, G. *et al.*, "Schizophrenia: Manifestions, incidence and course in different cultures: A World Health Organization ten-country study," *Psychological Medicine*, supplement 20, 1992, p. 97; Warner, R. and de Girolamo, G., *Epidemiology of Mental Disorders and Psychosocial Problems: Schizophrenia*, Geneva: World Health Organization, 1994.
28 Ciompi, L, "Catamnestic long-term study on the course of life and aging of schizophrenics," *Schizophrenia Bulletin*, 6: 606–18, 1980.
29 Jablensky *et al.*, "Schizophrenia: Manifestations, incidence and course."
30 Kiev, A., *Transcultural Psychiatry*, New York: Free Press, 1972, p. 45.
31 Strauss, J. S. and Carpenter, W. T., *Schizophrenia*, New York: Plenum, 1981, ch. 2.
32 Gottesman, I. I., *Schizophrenia Genesis: The Origins of Madness*, New York: W. H. Freeman, 1991, pp. 94–7.
33 Heston, L. L., "Psychiatric disorders in foster-home-reared children of schizophrenic mothers," *British Journal of Psychiatry*, 112: 819–25, 1966; Kety, S. S., Rosenthal, D., Wender, P. H. and Shulsinger, F., "The types and prevalence of mental illness in the biological and adoptive families of adopted schizophrenics," in D. Rosenthal and S. S. Kety (eds.), *The Transmission of Schizophrenia*, Oxford: Pergamon, 1968, pp. 345 *et seq.* ; Kety, S. S., Rosenthal, D., Wender,

P. H. *et al.*, "Mental illness in the biological and adoptive families of adopted individuals who have become schizophrenic," in R. R. Fieve, D. Rosenthal and H. Brill (eds.), *Genetic Research in Psychiatry*, Baltimore: Johns Hopkins University Press, 1975, pp. 147 *et seq.*

34 Gottesman, *Schizophrenia Genesis*, p. 103.

35 Twin studies of the inheritance of schizophrenia are summarized in Gottesman, *Schizophrenia Genesis*, pp. 105–32.

36 Kallman, F. J., "The genetic theory of schizophrenia: An analysis of 691 schizophrenic twin index families," *American Journal of Psychiatry*, 103: 309–22, 1946.

37 Kringlen, E., "An epidemiological-clinical twin study of schizophrenia," in Rosenthal and Kety (eds.), *The Transmission of Schizophrenia*, pp. 49 *et seq.*

38 Meltzer, H. Y. and Stahl, S. M., "The dopamine hypothesis of schizophrenia: A review," *Schizophrenia Bulletin*, 2: 19–76, 1976; Haracz, J. L., "The dopamine hypothesis: An overview of studies with schizophrenic patients," *Schizophrenia Bulletin*, 8: 438–69, 1982.

39 Reynolds, G. P., "Beyond the dopamine hypothesis: The neurochemical pathology of schizophrenia," *British Journal of Psychiatry*, 155: 305–16, 1989; Wyatt, R. J., Alexander, R. C., Egan, M. F. and Kirch, D. G., "Schizophrenia: Just the facts. What do we know, how well do we know it?," *Schizophrenia Research*, 1: 3–18, 1988.

40 Weinberger, D. R. and Kleinman, J. E., "Observations on the brain in schizophrenia," in A. J. Frances and R. E. Hales (eds.), *Psychiatry Update: American Psychiatric Association Annual Review: Volume 5*, Washington, D.C.: American Psychiatric Press, 1986, pp. 42–67.

41 Averback, P. "Lesions of the nucleus ansa peduncularis in neuropsychiatric disease," *Archives of Neurology*, 38: 230–5, 1981; Stevens, J. R., "Neuropathology of schizophrenia," *Archives of General Psychiatry*, 39: 1131–9, 1982; Weinberger and Kleinman, "Observations on the brain in schizophrenia," pp. 52–5.

42 Weinburger, D. R., DeLisi, L. E., Perman, G. P. *et al.*, "Computer tomography in schizophreniform disorder and other acute psychiatric disorders," *Archives of General Psychiatry*, 39: 778–83, 1982; Van Horn, J. D. and McManus, I. C., "Ventricular enlargement in schizophrenia: A meta-analysis of studies of the ventricle:brain ratio (VBR)," *British Journal of Psychiatry*, 160: 687–97, 1992; Weinberger and Kleinman, "Observations on the brain in schizophrenia," pp. 43–8; Wyatt *et al.*, "Schizophrenia: Just the facts," p. 12.

43 Weinberger and Kleinman, "Observations on the brain in schizophrenia," p. 47.

44 Weinburger *et al.*, "Computer tomography in schizophreniform disorder," p. 782.

45 Weinberger and Kleinman, "Observations on the brain in schizophrenia," p. 46–7.

46 Weinburger *et al.*, "Computed tomography in schizophreniform disorder," p. 782.

47 McNeil, T. F., "Perinatal influences in the development of schizophrenia," in H. Helmchen and F. A. Henn (eds.), *Biological Perspectives of Schizophrenia*, New York: John Wiley, 1987, pp. 125–38.

48 Reveley, A. M., Reveley, M. A., Clifford, C. A. *et al.*, "Cerebral ventricular size in twins discordant for schizophrenia," *Lancet*, 1: 540–1, 1982; Suddath, R. L., Christison, G., Torrey, E. F. *et al.*, "Quantitative magnetic resonance imaging in twin pairs discordant for schizophrenia," *Schizophrenia Research*, 2: 129, 1989.

49 Weinberger and Kleinman, "Observations on the brain in schizophrenia," p. 47.

50 Bradbury, T. N. and Miller, G. A., "Season of birth in schizophrenia: a review of evidence, methodology and etiology," *Psychology Bulletin*, 98: 569–94, 1985.

51 Eaton, W. W., Day, R. and Kramer, M., "The use of epidemiology for risk factor research in schizophrenia, An overview and methodologic critique," in M. T. Tsuang and J. L. Simpson (eds.), *Handbook of Schizophrenia, Volume 3: Nosology, Epidemiology and Genetics*, Amsterdam: Elsevier Science Publishers, 1988.

52 Warner and de Girolamo, *Epidemiology of Mental Disorders*.

53 Beiser, M. and Iacono, W. G., "An update on the epidemiology of schizophrenia," *Canadian Journal of Psychiatry*, 35: 657–68, 1990.

54 Watson, C. G., Kucala, T., Tilleskjor, C. and Jacobs, L., "Schizophrenic birth seasonality in relation to the incidence of infectious diseases and temperature extremes," *Archives of General Psychiatry*, 41: 85–90, 1984; Torrey, E. F., Rawlings, R. and Waldman, I. N., "Schizophrenic births and viral disease in two states," *Schizophrenia Research*, 1: 73–7, 1988; Mednick, S. A., Parnas, J. and Schulsinger, F., "The Copenhagen high-risk project, 1962–1986," *Schizophrenia Bulletin*, 13: 485–95, 1987; O'Callaghan, E., Sham, P., Takei, N. *et al.*, "Schizophrenia after prenatal exposure to 1957 A2 influenza epidemic," *Lancet*, 337: 1248–50; Barr, C. E., Mednick, S. A. and Munk-Jørgensen, P., "Exposure to influenza epidemics during gestation and adult schizophrenia: A 40–year study," *Archives of General Psychiatry*, 47: 869–74, 1990.

55 Kendell, R. E. and Kemp, I. W., "Maternal influenza in the etiology of schizophrenia," *Archives of General Psychiatry*, 46: 878–82, 1989; Bowler, A. E. and Torrey, E. F., "Influenza and schizophrenia: Helsinki and Edinburgh," *Archives of General Psychiatry*, 47: 876–7, 1990.

56 Sham, P. C., O'Callaghan, E., Takei, N. *et al.*, "Schizophrenia following prenatal exposure to influenza epidemics between 1939 and 1960," *British Journal of Psychiatry*, 160: 461–6, 1992.

57 Sacchetti, E., Calzeroni, A., Vita, A. *et al.*, "The brain damage hypothesis of the seasonality of births in schizophrenia and major affective disorders: Evidence from computerized tomography," *British Journal of Psychiatry*, 160: 390–7, 1992.

58 Joseph, M. H., Frith, C. D. and Waddington, J. L., "Dopaminergic mechanisms and cognitive deficit in schizophrenia: A neurobiological model," *Psychopharmacology*, 63: 273–80, 1979; Strauss and Carpenter, *Schizophrenia*, ch. 7; Freedman, R., Waldo, M., Bickford-Wimer, P. and Nagamoto, H., "Elementary neuronal dysfunctions in schizophrenia," *Schizophrenia Research*, 4: 233–43, 1991.

59 Freedman *et al.*, "Elementary neuronal dysfunctions in schizophrenia," pp. 233–6.

60 Ibid., pp. 238–9.

61 Adler, L. E., Hoffer, L. J., Griffiths, J. *et al.*, "Normalization by nicotine of deficient auditory sensory gating in the relatives of schizophrenics," *Biological Psychiatry*, 32: 607–16, 1992.

62 Franzen, G. and Ingvar, D. H., "Abnormal distribution of cerebral activity in chronic schizophrenia," *Journal of Psychiatric Research*, 12: 199–214, 1983; Weinberger and Kleinman, "Observations on the brain in schizophrenia," pp. 48–52.

63 Weinberger and Kleinman, "Observations on the brain in schizophrenia," p. 52.

64 Lawrence, D. H., *Apocalypse and the Writings on Revelation*, Cambridge: Cambridge University Press, 1980, p. 149. *Apocalypse* was first published in 1931.

65 Cooper, D., *The Death of the Family*, New York: Vintage Books, 1971.
66 Fromm-Reichmann, F., "Notes on the development of treatment of schizophrenia by psychoanalytic psychotherapy," *Psychiatry*, 11: 263–73, 1948.
67 Lidz, T., Fleck, S. and Cornelison, A., *Schizophrenia and the Family*, New York: International Universities Press, 1965.
68 Bateson, G., Jackson, D. and Haley, J., "Towards a theory of schizophrenia," *Behavioral Science*, 1: 251–64, 1956.
69 Laing, R. D. and Esterton, A., *Sanity, Madness and the Family: Families of Schizophrenics*, Baltimore: Penguin Books, 1970.
70 Wynne, L. C. and Singer, M., "Thought disorder and family relations," *Archives of General Psychiatry*, 9: 199–206, 1963.
71 Hirsch, S. and Leff, J., *Abnormality in Parents of Schizophrenics*, London: Oxford University Press, 1975.
72 Woodward, J. and Goldstein, M., "Communication deviance in the families of schizophrenics: A comment on the misuse of analysis of covariance," *Science*, 197: 1096–7, 1977.
73 Tienari, P., Lahti, I., Sorri, A. *et al.*, "The Finnish adoptive family study of schizophrenia: Possible joint effects of genetic vulnerability and family environment," *British Journal of Psychiatry*, 155: supplement 5, 29–32, 1989.
74 Brown, G. W., Birley, J. L. T. and Wing, J. K., "Influence of family life on the course of schizophrenic disorders: A replication," *British Journal of Psychiatry*, 121: 241–58, 1972; Vaughn, C. E. and Leff, J. P., "The influence of family and social factors on the course of psychiatric illness: A comparison of schizophrenic and depressed neurotic patients," *British Journal of Psychiatry*, 129: 125–37, 1976; Parker, G. and Hadzi-Pavlovic, D., "Expressed emotion as a predictor of schizophrenic relapse: An analysis of aggregated data," *Psychological Medicine*, 20: 961–5, 1990; Kavanagh, D. J., "Recent developments in expressed emotion and schizophrenia," *British Journal of Psychiatry*, 160: 601–20, 1992.
75 Tarrier, N., Vaughn, C. E., Lader, M. H. and Leff, J. P., "Bodily reaction to people and events in schizophrenics," *Archives of General Psychiatry*, 36: 311–15, 1979; Sturgeon, D., Kuipers, L., Berkowitz, R. *et al.*, "Psychophysiological responses of schizophrenic patients to high and low expressed emotion relatives," *British Journal of Psychiatry*, 138: 40–5, 1981.
76 Warner, R. and Atkinson, M. "The relationship between schizophrenic patients' perceptions of their parents and the course of their illness," *British Journal of Psychiatry*, 153: 344–53, 1988.
77 Brown *et al.*, "Influence of family life on the course of schizophrenic disorders;" Vaughn and Leff, "The influence of family and social factors on the course of psychiatric illness;" Leff, J. and Vaughn, C., "The role of maintenance therapy and relatives' expressed emotion in relapse in schizophrenia," *British Journal of Psychiatry*, 139: 102–4, 1981.
78 Warner, R., Miklowitz, D. and Sachs-Ericsson, N., "Expressed emotion, patient attributes and outcome in psychosis," presented at Royal College of Psychiatrists Spring Quarterly Meeting, Leicester, April 16–17, 1991.
79 Cheek, F. E., "Family interaction patterns and convalescent adjustment of the schizophrenic," *Archives of General Psychiatry*, 13: 138–47, 1965; Angermeyer, M. C., "'Normal deviance': Changing norms under abnormal circumstances," presented at the Seventh World Congress of Psychiatry, Vienna, July 11–16, 1983.
80 Wig, N. N., Menon, D. K. and Bedi, H., "Coping with schizophrenic patients in developing countries," presented at the Seventh World Congress of Psychiatry, Vienna, July 11–16, 1983.

81 Brown, G. W. and Birley, J. L. T., "Crises and life changes and the onset of schizophrenia," *Journal of Health and Social Behavior*, 9: 203–14, 1968.
82 Jacobs, S. and Myers, J., "Recent life events and acute schizophrenic psychosis: A controlled study," *Journal of Nervous and Mental Disease*, 162: 75–87, 1976; Ventura, J., Nuechterlein, K. H., Lukoff, D. *et al.*, "A prospective study of stressful life events and schizophrenic relapse," *Journal of Abnormal Psychology*, 98: 407–11, 1989.
83 Day, R., Nielsen, J. A., Korten, G. *et al.*, "Stressful life events preceding the acute onset of schizophrenia: A cross-national study from the World Health Organization," *Culture, Medicine and Psychiatry*, 11: 123–205, 1987.
84 Norman, M. G. and Malla, A. K., "Stressful life events and schizophrenia. I: A review of the research," *British Journal of Psychiatry*, 162: 161–6, 1989.
85 Ventura, J., Nuechterlein, K. H., Hardesty, J. P. and Gitlin, M., "Life events and schizophrenic relapse after withdrawal of medication," *British Journal of Psychiatry*, 161: 615–20, 1992.
86 Dohrenwend, B. and Egri, G., "Recent stressful life events and episodes of schizophrenia," *Schizophrenia Bulletin*, 7: 12–23, 1981; Andrews, G. and Tennant, C., "Life event stress and psychiatric illness," *Psychological Medicine*, 8: 545–9, 1978.

2 HEALTH, ILLNESS AND THE ECONOMY

1 Thompson, E. P., *The Making of the English Working Class*, New York: Vintage, 1966, pp. 330–1.
2 Ibid., p. 325.
3 Doyal, L., *The Political Economy of Health*, Boston: South End Press, 1981.
4 Antonovsky, A., "Social class, life expectancy and overall mortality," in E. G. Jaco, *Patients, Physicians and Illness: A Sourcebook in Behavioral Science and Health*, 2nd edn., New York: Free Press, 1972, pp. 5–30; Lerner, M., "Social differences in physical health," in J. Kosa, A. Antonovsky and I. K. Zola, *Poverty and Health: A Sociological Analysis*, Cambridge, Massachusetts: Harvard University Press, 1969, pp. 69–167.
5 Comstock, G. W., "Fatal arteriosclerotic heart disease, water hardness at home and socioeconomic characteristics," *American Journal of Epidemiology*, 94: 1–8, 1971; Kitagawa, F. M. and Hauser, P. M., *Differential Mortality in the United States: A Study in Socioeconomic Epidemiology*, Cambridge, Massachusetts: Harvard University Press, 1973, pp. 11–33, 78–9; Weinblatt, E., Ruberman, W., Goldberg, J. D. *et al.*, "Relation of education to sudden death after myocardial infarction," *New England Journal of Medicine*, 299: 60–5, 1978; Lown, B., Desilva, R. A, Reich, P. and Murawski, B. J., "Psychophysiological factors in sudden cardiac death," *American Journal of Psychiatry*, 137: 1325–35, 1980.
6 Doyal, *Political Economy of Health*, p. 65.
7 Lerner, "Social differences in physical health," p. 107.
8 McDonough, J. R., Garrison, G. E. and Hames, C. G., "Blood pressure and hypertensive disease among negroes and whites in Evans County, Georgia," in J. Stamler, R. Stamler and T. N. Pullman (eds.), *The Epidemiology of Hypertension*, New York: Grune & Stratton, 1967; Dawber, T. R., Kannel, S. B., Kagan, A. *et al.*, "Environmental factors in hypertension," in Stamler, Stamler and Pullman, *Epidemiology of Hypertension*; Borhani, N. O. and Borkman, T. S., *Alameda County Blood Pressure Study*, Berkeley: California State Department of Public Health, 1968; Shekelle, R. B., Ostfeld, A. M. and Paul, O., "Social status and incidence of coronary heart disease," *Journal of*

Chronic Disability, 22: 381–94, 1969; Syme, S. L., Oakes, T. W., Friedman, G. D. *et al.*, "Social class and differences in blood pressure," *American Journal of Public Health*, 64: 619–20, 1974; Hypertension Detection and Follow-up Program Cooperative Group, "Race, education and prevalence of hypertension," *American Journal of Epidemiology*, 106: 352–61, 1977.

9 Schwab, J. J. and Traven, N. D., "Factors related to the incidence of psychosomatic illness," *Psychosomatics*, 20: 307–15, 1979.

10 Eyer, J. and Sterling, P., "Stress-related mortality and social organization," *Review of Radical Political Economics*, 9: 1–44, 1977.

11 Coates, D., Moyer, S. and Wellman, B., "The Yorklea Study of urban mental health: Symptoms, problems and life events," *Canadian Journal of Public Health*, 60: 471–81, 1969.

12 Myers, J. K., Lindenthal, J. J. and Pepper, M. P., "Social class, life events and psychiatric symptoms: A longitudinal study," in B. S. Dohrenwend and B. P. Dohrenwend (eds.), *Stressful Life Events: Their Nature and Effects*, New York: Wiley, 1974; Dohrenwend, B. S., "Social status and stressful life events," *Journal of Personal and Social Psychology*, 28: 225–35, 1973.

13 Pearlin, L. I. and Radabaugh, D. W., "Economic strains and coping functions of alcohol," *American Journal of Sociology*, 82: 652–63, 1976.

14 Faris, R. E. L. and Dunham, H. W., *Mental Disorders in Urban Areas: An Ecological Study of Schizophrenia and Other Psychoses*, Chicago: University of Chicago Press, 1939.

15 Schroeder, C. W., "Mental disorders in cities," *American Journal of Sociology*, 48: 40–8, 1942.

16 Gerard, D. L. and Houston, L. G., "Family setting and the social ecology of schizophrenia," *Psychiatric Quarterly*, 27: 90–101, 1953.

17 Gardner, E. A. and Babigian, H. M., "A longitudinal comparison of psychiatric service to selected socioeconomic areas of Monroe County, New York," *American Journal of Orthopsychiatry*, 36: 818–28, 1966.

18 Klee, G. D., Spiro, E., Bahn, A. K. and Gorwitz, K., "An ecological analysis of diagnosed mental illness in Baltimore," in R. R. Monroe, G. D. Klee and E. B. Brody (eds.), *Psychiatric Epidemiology and Mental Health Planning*, Washington, D.C.: American Psychiatric Association, 1967, pp. 107–48.

19 Sundby, P. and Nyjus, P., "Major and minor psychiatric disorders in males in Oslo: An epidemiological study," *Acta Psychiatrica Scandinavica*, 39: 519–47, 1963.

20 Hare, E. H., "Mental illness and social conditions in Bristol," *Journal of Mental Science*, 102: 349–57, 1956.

21 Clark, R. E., "Psychoses, income and occupational prestige," *American Journal of Sociology*, 54: 433–40, 1949.

22 Hollingshead, A. B. and Redlich, F. C., *Social Class and Mental Illness*, New York: Wiley, 1958.

23 Srole, L., Langner, R. S., Michael, S. T. *et al.*, *Mental Health in the Metropolis: The Midtown Manhattan Study* (2 vols.), New York: McGraw-Hill, 1962.

24 Leighton, D. C., Harding, J. S., Macklin, D. B. *et al.*, *The Character of Danger: Psychiatric Symptoms in Selected Communities*, New York: Basic Books, 1963, pp. 279–94.

25 Ödegard, Ö., "The incidence of psychoses in various occupations," *International Journal of Social Psychiatry*, 2: 85–104, 1956.

26 Stein, L., "'Social class' gradient in schizophrenia," *British Journal of Preventive and Social Medicine*, 11: 181–95, 1957.

27 Eaton, W. W., "Epidemiology of schizophrenia," *Epidemiologic Reviews*, 7: 105–26, 1985.

28 Goldberg, E. M. and Morrison, S. L., "Schizophrenia and social class," *British Journal of Psychiatry*, 109: 785–802, 1963.
29 Turner, R. J. and Wagenfeld, M. O., "Occupational mobility and schizophrenia: An assessment of the social causation and social selection hypotheses," *American Sociological Review*, 32: 104–13, 1967.
30 Kohn, M. L., "Social class and schizophrenia: A critical review and a reformulation," *Schizophrenia Bulletin*, issue 7: 60–79, 1973, p. 64.
31 Cancro, R., "Overview of schizophrenia," in H. I. Kaplan, A. M. Freedman and B. J. Sadock (eds.), *Comprehensive Textbook of Psychiatry-III*, Baltimore: Williams & Wilkins, 1980, pp. 1093–104. The reference is to p. 1097.
32 Weiner, H., "Schizophrenia: etiology," in Kaplan, Freedman and Sadock, *Comprehensive Textbook of Psychiatry-III*, pp. 1121–52. The quotation is on p. 1139.
33 Strauss, J. S. and Carpenter, W. T., *Schizophrenia*, New York: Plenum, 1981, p. 131.
34 Turner and Wagenfeld, "Occupational mobility and schizophrenia."
35 Kohn, "Social class and schizophrenia," p. 62.
36 Leighton, D. C., Hagnell, O., Leighton, A. H. *et al.*, "Psychiatric disorder in a Swedish and a Canadian community: An exploratory study," *Social Science and Medicine*, 5: 189–209, 1971.
37 Brown, G. W., Davidson, S., Harris, T. *et al.*, "Psychiatric disorder in London and North Uist," *Social Science and Medicine*, 11: 367–77, 1977; Rutter, M., Yule, B., Quinton, D. *et al.*, "Attainment and adjustment in two geographical areas: III. Some factors accounting for area differences," *British Journal of Psychiatry*, 126: 520–9, 1975.
38 Nielsen, J. and Nielsen, J. A., "A census study of mental illness in Samsö," *Psychological Medicine*, 7: 491–503, 1977.
39 Mandel, E., *Long Waves of Capitalist Development: The Marxist Interpretation*, Cambridge: Cambridge University Press, 1980; Saul, S. B., *The Myth of the Great Depression, 1873–1896*, London: Macmillan, 1969; Church, R. A., *The Great Victorian Boom, 1850–1873*, London: Macmillan, 1975.
40 Willcox, W. G., "A study in vital statistics," *Political Science Quarterly*, 8 (1), 1893.
41 Hooker, R. H., "On the correlation of the marriage rate with foreign trade," *Journal of the Royal Statistical Society*, 64: 485, 1901.
42 Ogburn, W. F. and Thomas, D. S., "The influence of the business cycle on certain social conditions," *Journal of the American Statistical Association*, 18: 324–40, 1922.
43 Thomas, D. S., *Social Aspects of the Business Cycle*, New York: Gordon & Breach, 1968. First published by Knopf in 1927.
44 Catalano, R. and Dooley, C. D., "Economic predictors of depressed mood and stressful life events in a metropolitan community," *Journal of Health and Social Behavior*, 18: 292–307, 1977; Dooley, D. and Catalano, R., "Economic, life, and disorder changes: Time-series analyzes," *American Journal of Community Psychology*, 7: 381–96, 1979.
45 Dooley and Catalano, op. cit., p. 393.
46 Dooley, D., Catalano, R., Jackson, R. and Brownell, A., "Economic, life, and symptom changes in a nonmetropolitan community," *Journal of Health and Social Behavior*, 22: 144–54, 1981.
47 Ibid.
48 Gore, S., "The effect of social support in moderating the health consequences of unemployment," *Journal of Health and Social Behavior*, 19: 157–65, 1978.

49 Brenner, M. H., *Estimating the Social Costs of National Economic Policy: Implications for Mental and Physical Health, and Criminal Aggression*, prepared for the Joint Economic Committee of the Congress of the United States, Washington, D.C.: U.S. Government Printing Office, 1976.

50 Ibid., p. 41.

51 Ibid., p. 39.

52 Kasl, S. V., "Mortality and the business cycle: Some questions about research strategies when utilizing macro-social and ecological data," *American Journal of Public Health*, 69: 784–8, 1979, p. 786.

53 Mandel, E., *Marxist Economic Theory*, vol. 1, translated by B. Pearcel, New York: *Monthly Review Press*, 1968, ch. 11.

54 Samuelson, P. A., *Economics*, 11th edn., New York: McGraw-Hill, 1980, ch. 14.

55 Eyer and Sterling, "Stress-related mortality;" Eyer, J., "Prosperity as a cause of death," *International Journal of Health Services*, 7: 125–50, 1977; Eyer, J., "Does unemployment cause the death rate peak in each business cycle? A multifactor model of death rate change," *International Journal of Health Services*, 7: 625–62, 1977.

56 Eyer and Sterling, "Stress-related mortality."

57 Bunn, A. R., "Ischaemic heart disease mortality and the business cycle in Australia," *American Journal of Public Health*, 69: 772–81, 1979.

58 Brenner, M. H., "Fetal, infant, and maternal mortality during periods of economic instability," *International Journal of Health Services*, 3: 145–59, 1973.

59 Hewitt, M., *Wives and Mothers in Victorian Industry*, Westport, Connecticut: Greenwood Press, 1958, pp. 115–16.

60 Ibid., chs. 2, 3, 8, 9, 10.

61 Thomas, *Social Aspects of the Business Cycle*, footnote on p. 111.

62 Kinnersly, P., *The Hazards of Work: How to Fight Them*, London: Pluto Press, 1973, cited in Doyal, *Political Economy of Health*, p. 67.

63 Doyal, *Political Economy of Health*, p. 74.

64 Lown *et al.*, "Sudden cardiac death;" Rahe, R. H., Bennett, L., Rorio, M. *et al.*, "Subjects' recent life changes and coronary heart disease in Finland," *American Journal of Psychiatry*, 130: 1222–6, 1973.

65 Rabkin, S. W., Mathewson, F. A. L. and Tate, R. B., "Chronobiology of cardiac sudden death in men," *Journal of the American Medical Association*, 244: 1357–8, 1980, p. 1358.

66 Rogot, E., Fabsitz, R. and Feinleib, M., "Daily variation in U.S.A. mortality," *American Journal of Epidemiology*, 103: 198–211, 1976.

67 Russek, H. I. and Zohman, B. L., "Relative significance of heredity, diet and occupational stress in coronary heart disease of young adults," *American Journal of Medical Science*, 235: 266–77, 1958.

68 Liljefors, I. and Rahe, R. H., "An identical twin study of psychosocial factors in coronary heart disease in Sweden," *Psychosomatic Medicine*, 32: 523 *et seq.*, 1970; Theorell, T. and Rahe, R. H., "Behavior and life satisfaction characteristics of Swedish subjects with myocardial infarction," *Journal of Chronic Disability*, 25: 139 *et seq.*, 1972; Flodérus, B., "Psycho-social factors in relation to coronary heart disease and associated risk factors," *Nordisk Hygienisk Tidskrift*, supplement 6, 1974.

69 Friedman, M., Rosenman, R. H. and Carroll, V., "Changes in the serum cholesterol and blood clotting time in men subjected to cyclic variation of occupational stress," *Circulation*, 17: 852–61, 1958.

70 Theorell, T., "Life events before and after the onset of a premature myocardial infarction," in Dohrenwend and Dohrenwend, *Stressful Life Events*, pp. 101–17.

71 Theorell, T., Lind, E. and Flodérus, B., "The relationship of disturbing life-changes and emotions to the early development of myocardial infarction and other serious illnesses," *International Journal of Epidemiology*, 4: 281–93, 1975.
72 Haynes, S. G., Feinleib, M., Levine, S. *et al.*, "The relationship of psychosocial factors to coronary heart disease in the Framingham Study: II. Prevalence of coronary heart disease," *American Journal of Epidemiology*, 107: 384–402, 1978.
73 Senate Bill 3916 (1972) sought

> to provide for research for solutions to the problems of alienation among American workers in all occupations and industries and technical assistance to those companies, unions, State and local governments seeking to find ways to deal with the problem.

Quoted in Rubin, L. B., *Worlds of Pain: Life in the Working Class Family*, New York: Basic Books, 1976, footnote on p. 233.
74 Marx, K., *The Economic and Philosophic Manuscripts of 1844*, New York: International Publishers, 1964; Novack G., "The problem of alienation," in E. Mandel and G. Novack, *The Marxist Theory of Alienation*, New York: Pathfinder Press, 1973, pp. 53–94; Ollman, B., *Alienation: Marx's Conception of Man in Capitalist Society*, Cambridge: Cambridge University Press, 1971.
75 Garson, B., *All the Livelong Day: The Meaning and Demeaning of Routine Work*, New York: Penguin, 1977, p. 95.
76 Ibid., p. 88.
77 Ibid., p. 204.
78 Terkel, S., *Working*, New York: Avon, 1975, p. 2.
79 Ibid., p. 3.
80 Rubin, *Worlds of Pain*, p. 169.
81 Ibid., p. 183.
82 Jahoda, M. and Rush, H., *Work, Employment and Unemployment*, University of Sussex Science Policy Research Unit Occasional Paper, no. 12, Brighton: University of Sussex, 1980, pp. 15–16.
83 Kornhauser, A., *Mental Health of the Industrial Worker: A Detroit Study*, New York: Wilcy, 1965, p. 270.
84 Jahoda and Rush, *Work, Employment and Unemployment*, pp. 16–17.
85 Kornhauser, *Mental Health of the Industrial Worker*, pp. 260–2.
86 Kohn, M. L. and Schooler, C., "Occupational experience and psychological functioning: An assessment of reciprocal effects," *American Sociological Review*, 38: 97–118, 1973.
87 Dalgard, O. S., "Occupational experience and mental health, with special reference to closeness of supervision," *Psychiatry and Social Science*, 1: 29–42, 1981.
88 Kasl, S. V., "Changes in mental health status associated with job loss and retirement," in Barrett, Rose and Klerman, *Stress and Mental Disorder*, pp. 179–200. The reference is to pp. 182–3.
89 Ibid.; Kasl, S. V. and Cobb, S., "Blood pressure changes in men undergoing job loss: A preliminary report," *Psychosomatic Medicine*, 22: 19–38, 1970.
90 Liem, R. and Rayman, P., "Health and social costs of unemployment: Research and policy considerations," *American Psychologist*, 37: 1116–23, 1982.
91 Little, C., "Technical-professional unemployment: Middle-class adaptability to personal crisis," *Sociological Quarterly*, 17: 262–74, 1976.
92 Eisenberg, P. and Lazarsfeld, P. F., "The psychological effects of unemployment," *Psychological Bulletin*, 35: 358–90, 1938.

93 Liem and Rayman, "Health and social costs of unemployment," p. 1120.
94 Strangle, W. G., "Job loss: A psychological study of worker reactions to a plant closing in a company town in Southern Appalachia," Doctoral dissertation, School of Industrial and Labor Relations, Cornell University, Ithaca, New York, 1977.
95 Warr, P., "Studies of psychological well-being," presented at the British Psychological Society Symposium on Unemployment, London, 1980.
96 Parnes, H. S. and King, R., "Middle-aged job loser," *Industrial Gerontology*, 4: 77–95, 1977.
97 Lahelma, E., "Unemployment and mental well-being: Elaboration of the relationship," *International Journal of Health Services*, 22: 261–74, 1992.
98 Studnicka, M., Studnicka-Benke, A., Wögerbauer, G. *et al.*, "Psychological health, self-reported physical health and health service use: Risk differential observed after one year of unemployment," *Social Psychiatry and Psychiatric Epidemiology*, 26: 86–91, 1991.
99 Hendry, L. B., Shucksmith, J. and Love, J. G., *Lifechances: Developing Adolescent Lifestyles*, London: Routledge, 1991.
100 Warr, P., Jackson, P. and Banks, M., "Unemployment and mental health: Some British studies," *Journal of Social Issues*, 44: 47–68, 1988.
101 Kessler, R. C., Turner, J. B. and House, J. S., "Effects of unemployment on health in a community survey: Main, modifying, and mediating effects," *Journal of Social Issues*, 44: 69–85, 1988.
102 Brenner, S-E. and Starrin, B., "Unemployment and health in Sweden: Public issues and private troubles," *Journal of Social Issues*, 44: 125–40, 1988.
103 Theorell, Lind and Flodérus, "Disturbing life changes."
104 Coates, Moyer and Wellman, "The Yorklea Study."
105 Eyer, J. and Sterling, P., "Stress-related mortality;" Brenner, *Social Costs of National Economic Policy*; Henry, A. F. and Short, J. F., *Suicide and Homicide*, Glencoe, Illinois: Free Press, 1954; Vigderhous, G. and Fishman, G., "The impact of unemployment and familial integration on changing suicide rates in the U.S.A., 1920–1969," *Social Psychiatry*, 13: 239–48, 1978; Hamermesh, D. S. and Soss, N. M., "An economic theory of suicide," *Journal of Political Economy*, 82: 83–98, 1974; Ahlburg, D. A. and Shapiro, M. O., "The darker side of unemployment," *Hospital and Community Psychiatry*, 34: 389, 1983.
106 Vigderhous and Fishman, "Impact of unemployment;" Ahlburg and Shapiro, "The darker side of unemployment."
107 Dooley, D., Catalano, R., Rook, K. and Serxner, S., "Economic stress and suicide: Multilevel analyzes. Part I: Aggregate time-series analyzes of economic stress and suicide," *Suicide and Life-Threatening Behavior*, 19: 321–36, 1989.
108 Pierce, A., "The economic cycle and the social suicide rate," *American Sociological Review*, 32: 457–62, 1967.
109 Personal communication from J. P. Marshall to D. Dooley and R. Catalano, cited in Dooley, D. and Catalano, R., "Economic change as a cause of behavioral disorder," *Psychological Bulletin*, 87: 450–68, 1980, p. 455; Yang, B., "The economy and suicide: A time-series study of the U.S.A.," *American Journal of Economics and Sociology*, 51: 87–99, 1992.
110 Durkheim, E., *Suicide*, Glencoe, Illinois: Free Press, 1951, p. 243.
111 Hamermesh and Soss, "An economic theory of suicide.'
112 Powell, E., "Occupation, status and suicide: Towards a redefinition of anomie," *American Social Review*, 22: 131–9, 1958.
113 Resnik, N. L. P. and Dizmang, L. H., "Observations on suicidal behavior among American Indians," *American Journal of Psychiatry*, 127: 58–63, 1971.

114 Dublin, L. I., *Suicide: A Sociological and Statistical Study*, New York: Ronald Press, 1963, ch. 8; Hamermesh and Soss, "An economic theory of suicide."
115 Yap, R. M., "Aging and mental health in Hong Kong," in R. H. Williams (ed.), *Processes of Aging: Social and Psychological Perspectives*, vol. 2, New York: Atherton, 1963, pp. 176–91.
116 Lendrum, F. C., "A thousand cases of attempted suicide," *American Journal of Psychiatry*, 13: 479–500, 1933; Sainsbury, P., *Suicide in London: An Ecological Study*, London: Chapman & Hall, 1955; Morris, J. B., Kovacs, M., Beck, A. and Wolffe, S., "Notes towards an epidemiology of urban suicide," *Comprehensive Psychiatry*, 15: 537–47, 1974; Sanborn, D. E., Sanborn, C. J. and Cimbolic, P., "Occupation and suicide," *Diseases of the Nervous System*, 35: 7–12, 1974; Shepherd, D. M. and Barraclough, B. M., "Work and suicide: An empirical investigation," *British Journal of Psychiatry*, 136: 469–78, 1980.
117 Olsen, J. and Lajer, M., "Violent death and unemployment in two trade unions in Denmark," *Social Psychiatry*, 14: 139–45, 1979.
118 Breed, W., "Occupational mobility and suicide among white males," *American Sociological Review*, 28: 179–88, 1963; Portersfield, A. L. and Gibbs, J. P., "Occupational prestige and social mobility of suicides in New Zealand," *American Journal of Sociology*, 66: 147–52, 1960; Sanborn, Sanborn and Cimbolic, "Occupation and suicide;" Shepherd and Barraclough, "Work and suicide."
119 Platt, S., "Unemployment and suicidal behaviour: A review of the literature," *Social Science and Medicine*, 19: 93–115, 1984.
120 Tuckman, J. and Labell, M., "Study of suicide in Philadelphia," *Public Health Reports*, 73: 547–53, 1958; Shepherd and Barraclough, "Work and suicide;" Fruensgaard, K., Bejaminsen, S., Joensen, S. and Helstrup, K., "Psychosocial characteristics of a group of unemployed patients consecutively admitted to a psychiatric emergency department," *Social Psychiatry*, 18: 137–44, 1983.
121 Rogot, Fabsitz and Feinleib, "Daily variation in U.S.A. mortality;" Baldamus, W., *The Structure of Sociological Inference*, New York: Barnes & Noble, 1976, p. 94. Curiously, Baldamus presents the data on the daily frequency of suicide declining from Monday to Sunday as an example of a phenomenon which defies explanation. This, he argues, is because of "the difficulty of visualizing a characteristic quality inherent in each day of the week." His experience of the work week is clearly different from that of the average working person.
122 Brenner, M. H., *Mental Illness and the Economy*, Cambridge, Massachusetts: Harvard University Press, 1973.
123 Pollock, H. M., "The Depression and mental disease in New York State," *American Journal of Psychiatry*, 91: 736–71, 1935; Mowrer, E. R., "A study of personal disorganization," *American Sociological Review*, 4: 475–87, 1939; Dayton, N. A., *New Facts on Mental Disorders: Study of 89,190 Cases*, Springfield, Illinois: Charles C. Thomas, 1940; Dunham, H. W., *Sociological Theory and Mental Disorder*, Detroit, Michigan: Wayne State University Press, 1959; Pugh, T. F. and MacMahon, B., *Epidemiologic Findings in the United States Mental Hospital Data*, Boston: Little, Brown, 1962.
124 Brenner, *Mental Illness and the Economy*, p. 45.
125 Marshall, J. R. and Funch, D. P., "Mental illness and the economy: A critique and partial replication," *Journal of Health and Social Behavior*, 20: 282–9, 1979.
126 Dear, M., Clark, G. and Clark, S., "Economic cycles and mental health care policy: An examination of the macro-context for social service planning," *Social Science and Medicine*, 136: 43–53, 1979.

127 Ahr, P. R., Gorodezky, M. J. and Cho, D. W., "Measuring the relationship of public psychiatric admissions to rising unemployment," *Hospital and Community Psychiatry*, 32: 398–401, 1981.
128 Parker, J. J., "Community mental health center admissions and the business cycle: A longitudinal study," Doctoral dissertation, Department of Sociology, University of Colorado, Boulder, 1979.
129 Brenner, *Mental Illness and the Economy*, ch. 9.
130 Ahr, Gorodezky and Cho, "Public psychiatric admissions;" Draughon, M., "Relationship between economic decline and mental hospital admissions continues to be significant," *Psychological Reports*, 36: 882, 1975.

3 RECOVERY FROM SCHIZOPHRENIA

1 Strecker, H. P., "Insulin treatment of schizophrenia," *Journal of Mental Science*, 84: 146–55, 1938; Freyhan, F. A., "Course and outcome of schizophrenia," *American Journal of Psychiatry*, 112: 161–7, 1955; Leiberman, D. M., Hoenig, J. and Auerback, I., "The effect of insulin coma and E.C.T. on the three year prognosis of schizophrenia," *Journal of Neurology, Neurosurgery and Psychiatry*, 20: 108–13, 1957; and Ödegard, Ö., "Changes in the prognosis of functional psychoses since the days of Kraepelin," *British Journal of Psychiatry*, 113: 813–22, 1967.
2 Kelly, D. H. W. and Sargant, W., "Present treatment of schizophrenia: A controlled follow-up study," *British Medical Journal*, 2: 147–50, 1965; Holmboe, R., Noreik, K. and Astrup, C., "Follow-up of functional psychoses at two Norwegian mental hospitals," *Acta Psychiatrica Scandinavica*, 44: 298–310, 1968; Gross, G. and Huber, G., "Zur Prognose der Schizophrenien," *Psychiatrica Clinica* (Basel), 6: 1–16, 1973; Cottman, S. B. and Mezey, A. G., "Community care and the prognosis of schizophrenia," *Acta Psychiatrica Scandinavica*, 53: 95–104, 1976; and Bland, R. C., Parker, J. H. and Orn, H., "Prognosis in schizophrenia: Prognostic predictors and outcome," *Archives of General Psychiatry*, 35: 72–7, 1978.
3 Lehmann, H. E., "Schizophrenia: Clinical features," in H. I. Kaplan, A. M. Freedman and B. J. Sadock (eds.), *Comprehensive Textbook of Psychiatry-III*, Baltimore: Williams & Wilkins, 1981, p. 1187.
4 Horwitz, W. A. and Kleinman, C., "Survey of cases discharged from the Psychiatric Institute and Hospital," *Psychiatric Quarterly*, 10: 72–85, 1936; Henisz, J. "A follow-up study of schizophrenic patients," *Comprehensive Psychiatry*, 7: 524–8, 1966; Bockoven, J. S. and Solomon, H. C., "Comparison of two five-year follow-up studies: 1947 to 1952 and 1967 to 1972," *American Journal of Psychiatry*, 132: 796–801, 1975; and Harrow, M., Grinker, R. R., Silverstein, M. L. and Holzman, P., "Is modern-day schizophrenic outcome still negative?" *American Journal of Psychiatry*, 135: 1156–62, 1978.
5 Stephen, J. H., "Long-term prognosis and follow-up in schizophrenia," *Schizophrenia Bulletin*, 4: 25–47, 1978.
6 Bleuler, M., "A 23-year longitudinal study of 208 schizophrenics and impressions in regard to the nature of schizophrenia," in D. Rosenthal and S. S. Kety, *The Transmission of Schizophrenia*, Oxford: Pergamon, 1968, p. 3.
7 Ibid., p. 5.
8 Ibid., p. 6.
9 The studies included in Table 3.1 are listed in the general bibliography.
10 Kirchhof, T., *Geschichte der Psychiatrie*, Leipzig: Franz Deuticke, 1912.
11 Source of unemployment statistics: U.S., 1881–9, Eyer, J. and Sterling, P.,

"Stress-related mortality and social organization," *Review of Radical Political Economics*, 9: 1–44, 1977; 1890–1970, U.S. Bureau of the Census, *Historical Statistics of the United States: Colonial Times to 1970: Part I*, Washington, D.C.: 1975; 1970–1985, U.S. Bureau of the Census, *Statistical Abstract of the United States: 1990*, Washington, D.C.: 1990; U.K., 1881–7, Mitchell, B. R. and Deane, P., *Abstract of British Historical Statistics*, Cambridge: Cambridge University Press, 1962; 1888–1970, Mitchell, B. R., *European Historical Statistics, 1750–1970*, New York: Columbia University Press, 1978; 1970–1985, Organisation for Economic Cooperation and Development, *Labour Force Statistics*, Paris: 1992.

12 Lehmann, "Schizophrenia: Clinical features," p. 1178.

13 American Psychiatric Association, *Diagnostic and Statistical Manual of Mental Disorder*, 3rd edn. (DSM-III), Washington, D.C., 1980.

4 DEINSTITUTIONALIZATION

1 Davis, J. M., "Organic therapies," in H. I. Kaplan, A. M. Freedman and B. J. Sadock (eds.), *Comprehensive Textbook of Psychiatry-III*, Baltimore: Williams & Wilkins, 1981, pp. 2257–89. The quotation is on p. 2257.

2 Ödegard, Ö., "Pattern of discharge from Norwegian psychiatric hospitals before and after the introduction of the psychotropic drugs," *American Journal of Psychiatry*, 120: 772–8, 1964.

3 Norton, A., "Mental hospital ins and outs: A survey of patients admitted to a mental hospital in the past 30 years," *British Medical Journal*, i: 528–36, 1961.

4 Shepherd, M., Goodman, N. and Watt, D. C., "The application of hospital statistics in the evaluation of pharmacotherapy in a psychiatric population," *Comprehensive Psychiatry*, 2: 11–19, 1961.

5 Lewis, A., untitled paper, in R. B. Bradley, P. Deniker and C. Radouco-Thomas (eds.), *Neuropsychopharmacology*, vol. 1, Amsterdam: Elsevier, 1959, pp. 207–12, cited in Scull, A., *Decarceration: Community Treatment and the Deviant – A Radical View*, Englewood Cliffs, New Jersey: Prentice-Hall, 1977, p. 82.

6 Pugh, T. F. and MacMahon, B., *Epidemiologic Findings in United States Mental Hospital Data*, Boston: Little, Brown, 1962.

7 Chittick, R. A., Brooks, G. W. and Deane, W. N., *Vermont Project for the Rehabilitation of Chronic Schizophrenic Patients: Progress Report*, Vermont State Hospital, 1959, cited in Scull, *Decarceration*, p. 82.

8 Epstein, L. J., Morgan, R. D. and Reynolds, L., "An approach to the effect of ataraxic drugs on hospital release rates," *American Journal of Psychiatry*, 119: 36–45, 1962.

9 Linn, E. L., "Drug therapy, milieu change, and release from a mental hospital," *Archives of Neurology and Psychiatry*, 81: 785–94, 1959.

10 Brill, H. and Patton, R. E., "Analysis of population reduction in New York State mental hospitals during the first four years of large-scale therapy with psychotropic drugs," *American Journal of Psychiatry*, 116: 495–509, 1959, p. 495.

11 Scull, *Decarceration*, p. 83.

12 Davis, "Organic therapies," p. 2257.

13 Freudenberg, R. K., Bennet, D. H. and May, A. R., "The relative importance of physical and community methods in the treatment of schizophrenia," in *International Congress of Psychiatry, Zurich, 1957*, Fussli, 1959, pp. 157–78. Quotation is from p. 159.

14 All of the information in this paragraph is from Clark, D. H., *Social Therapy in Psychiatry*, Baltimore: Penguin, 1974, pp. 22–5; and Langsley, D. G., "Community psychiatry," in Kaplan, Freedman and Sadock, *Comprehensive Textbook of Psychiatry*, pp. 2836–53. The reference is to pp. 2839–40.
15 Jones, M., *Social Psychiatry in Practice*, Baltimore: Penguin, 1968, p. 17; Clark, *Social Therapy in Psychiatry*, p. 29.
16 Clark, *Social Therapy in Psychiatry*, pp. 25–6.
17 Ödegard, "Pattern of discharge," p. 776.
18 Rathod, N. H., "Tranquillisers and patients' environment," *Lancet*, i: 611–13, 1958.
19 The statistics in this paragraph are from Scull, *Decarceration*, p. 149.
20 Bassuk, E. L. and Gerson, S., "Deinstitutionalization and mental health services," *Scientific American*, 238(2): 46–53, February 1978, p. 50.
21 These examples are from Langsley, "Community psychiatry," p. 2847; and Lamb, H. R. and Goertzel, V., "The demise of the state hospital: A premature obituary?" *Archives of General Psychiatry*, 26: 489–95, 1972.
22 Lehman, A. F., Ward, N. C. and Linn, L. S., "Chronic mental patients: The quality of life issue," *American Journal of Psychiatry*, 139: 1271–6, 1982.
23 Lamb, H. R., "The new asylums in the community," *Archives of General Psychiatry*, 36: 129–34, 1979.
24 Van Putten, T. and Spar, J. E., "The board and care home: Does it deserve a bad press?" *Hospital and Community Psychiatry*, 30: 461–4, 1979. This reference is to pp. 461–2.
25 Bassuk and Gerson, "Deinstitutionalization," p. 49.
26 Morgan, C. H., "Service delivery models." Prepared for the Special National Workshop on Mental Health Services in Local Jails, Baltimore, Maryland, September 27–9, 1978; Gibbs, J. J., "Psychological and behavioral pathology in jails: A review of the literature," presented at the Special National Workshop on Mental Health Services in Local Jails, 1978; Olds, E., *A Study of the Homeless, Sick and Alcoholic Persons in the Baltimore City Jail*, Baltimore: Baltimore Council of Social Agencies, 1956; Arthur Bolton Associates, Report to the California State Legislature, October 1976; Swank, G. E. and Winer, D., "Occurrence of psychiatric disorder in a county jail population," *American Journal of Psychiatry*, 133: 1331–6, 1976; unidentified author, "Mental ill inmates untreated, says GAO," *Psychiatric News*, February 6, 1981, p. 1; Torrey, E. F., Stieber, J., Ezekiel, J. *et al.*, *Criminalizing the Seriously Mentally Ill: The Abuse of Jails as Mental Hospitals*, Washington, D.C.: Public Citizens Health Research Group, 1992, pp. iv and 15.
27 Roth, L. H. and Ervin, F. R., "Psychiatric care of federal prisoners," *American Journal of Psychiatry*, 128: 424–30, 1971.
28 Rollin, H., "From patients into vagrants," *New Society*, January 15, 1970, pp. 90–3.
29 Tidmarsh, D. and Wood, S., "Psychiatric aspects of destitution: A study of the Camberwell Reception Centre," in J. K. Wing and A. M. Haily (eds.), *Evaluating a Community Psychiatric Service: The Camberwell Register 1964–1971*, London: Oxford University Press, 1972, pp. 327–40.
30 Rollin, "From patients into vagrants," p. 92; National Schizophrenia Fellowship, *Home Sweet Nothing: The Plight of Sufferers from Chronic Schizophrenia*, Surbiton: 1971; Coid, J., "How many psychiatric patients in prison?" *British Journal of Psychiatry*, 145: 78–86, 1984; Gunn, J., Maden, A. and Swinton, M., "Treatment needs of prisoners with psychiatric disorders," *British Medical Journal*, 303: 338–41, 1991.

31 Morris, B., "Recent developments in the care, treatment, and rehabilitation of the chronic mentally ill in Britain," *Hospital and Community Psychiatry*, 34: 159–63, 1983.
32 Korer, J., *Not the Same as You: The Social Situation of 190 Schizophrenics Living in the Community*, Dalston, London: Psychiatric Rehabilitation Association, 1978; Ebringer, L. and Christie-Brown, J. R. W., "Social deprivation amongst short stay psychiatric patients," *British Journal of Psychiatry*, 136: 46–52, 1980.
33 Hencke, D., "Squalor in mental homes kept secret," *Guardian*, July 20, 1983, p. 1; Hencke, D., "Hospital report reveals faults," *Guardian*, July 22, 1983, p. 3.
34 Scull, *Decarceration*, p. 152.
35 Fraser, D., *The Evolution of the British Welfare State: A History of Social Policy Since the Industrial Revolution*, New York: Harper & Row, 1973, pp. 212–16; Leiby, J., *A History of Social Welfare and Social Work in the United States*, New York: Columbia University Press, 1978, p. 289.
36 Ödegard, Ö., "Changes in the prognosis of functional psychoses since the days of Kraepelin," *British Journal of Psychiatry*, 113: 813–22, 1967, p. 819.
37 Foucault, M., *Madness and Civilization: A History of Insanity in the Age of Reason*, New York: Vintage Books, 1965, p. 49.
38 Parry-Jones, W. L., *The Trade in Lunacy: A Study of Private Madhouses in England in the Eighteenth and Nineteenth Centuries*, London: Routledge & Kegan Paul, 1972, p. 72.
39 All the material in this paragraph is taken from Sinfield, A., *What Unemployment Means*, Oxford: Martin Robertson, 1981, pp. 130–1.
40 Clark, *Social Therapy in Psychiatry*, p. 23.
41 Ödegard, "Prognosis of functional psychoses," p. 819.
42 Pugh and MacMahon, *Epidemiologic Findings*.
43 Camberwell Group prevalence study, 1965, cited in Torrey, E. F., *Schizophrenia and Civilization*, New York: Jason Aronson, 1980, p. 89.
44 McGowan, J. F. and Porter, T. L., *An Introduction to the Vocational Rehabilitation Process*, Washington, D.C.: U.S. Department of Health, Education and Welfare, Vocational Rehabilitation Administration, 1967.
45 Tizard, J. and O'Connor, N., "The employment of high-grade mental defectives. I," *American Journal of Mental Deficiency*, 54: 563–76, 1950.
46 Field, M. G. and Aronson, J., "The institutional framework of Soviet psychiatry," *Journal of Nervous and Mental Disease*, 138: 305–22, 1964; Field, M. G. and Aronson, J., "Soviet community mental health services and work therapy: A report of two visits," *Community Mental Health Journal*, 1: 81–90, 1965; Hein, G., "Social psychiatric treatment of schizophrenia in the Soviet Union," *International Journal of Psychiatry*, 6: 346–62, 1968; Gorman, M., 'Soviet psychiatry and the Russian citizen," *International Journal of Psychiatry*, 8: 841–57, 1969.
47 Maxwell Jones, personal communication.
48 Maddison, A., *Economic Growth in the West*, New York: Twentieth Century Fund, 1964, p. 220.
49 de Plato, G. and Minguzzi, G. F., "A short history of psychiatric renewal in Italy," *Psychiatry and Social Science*, 1: 71–7, 1981.
50 Donnelly, M., *The Politics of Mental Health in Italy*, London: Routledge, 1992.
51 For a fuller discussion of this analysis see Warner, R., "Mental hospital and prison use: An international comparison," *Mental Health Administration*, 10: 239–58, 1983.
52 World Health Organization, *World Health Statistics Annual 1977*, vol. III, Geneva: 1977; Maxwell Jones and Loren Mosher, personal communications.

53 Field and Aronson, "Institutional framework of Soviet psychiatry;" Field and
   Aronson, "Soviet community mental health;" Hein, "Soviet psychiatric treat-
   ment;" Gorman, "Soviet psychiatry;" Wing, J. R., *Reasoning About Madness*,
   New York: Oxford University Press, 1978.

5 MADNESS AND THE INDUSTRIAL REVOLUTION

1 Charles-Gaspard de la Rive, a Swiss doctor. Quoted in Foucault, M., *Madness
  and Civilization: A History of Insanity in the Age of Reason*, New York: Vintage
  Books, 1973, p. 242. Also quoted in Jones, K., *A History of the Mental Health
  Services*, London: Routledge & Kegan Paul, 1972, p. 47. According to Foucault
  the passage appeared in a letter to the editors of the *Bibliothèque Britannique*;
  according to Jones it was written in the visitors' book of the Retreat. One
  assumes both are correct, and that Dr. de la Rive used the same material twice.
2 Daniel Hack Tuke stated that the name Retreat was suggested by his grand-
  mother, William Tuke's daughter-in-law, to convey the idea of a haven. Quoted
  by Jones, *History of Mental Health Services*, p. 47.
3 These details of moral treatment at the York Retreat are drawn from the
  following sources: Mora, G., "Historical and theoretical trends in psychiatry,"
  in H. I. Kaplan, A. M. Freedman and B. J. Sadock (eds.), *Comprehensive
  Textbook of Psychiatry-III*, Baltimore: Williams & Wilkins, 1980, pp. 4–98. The
  reference is to pp. 55–7; Jones, *History of Mental Health Services*, pp. 45–54;
  Foucault, *Madness and Civilization*, pp. 241–55.
4 Thurnam, J., *Observations and Essays on the Statistics of Insanity*, London:
  Simpkin, Marshall, 1845, reprint edition New York: Arno Press, 1976. Quoted
  in Jones, *History of Mental Health Services*, p. 66.
5 Both passages are from Godfrey Higgins' letter to the *York Herald*, 10 January
  1814. Quoted in Jones, *History of Mental Health Services*, p. 70.
6 Both quotations are from Dickens, C. and Wills, W. H., "A curious dance
  around a curious tree," in H. Stone (ed.), *Charles Dickens' Uncollected
  Writings from Household Words 1850–1859*, Bloomington: Indiana University
  Press, 1968, pp. 381–91. The passages quoted are on pp. 382–3.
7 Parry-Jones, W. L., *The Trade in Lunacy: A Study of Private Madhouses in
  England in the Eighteenth and Nineteenth Centuries*, London: Routledge &
  Kegan Paul, 1972, p. 289.
8 Scull, A., "Moral treatment reconsidered: Some sociological comments on an
  episode in the history of British psychiatry," in A. Scull (ed.), *Madhouses,
  Mad-doctors, and Madmen: The Social History of Psychiatry in the Victorian
  Era*, Philadelphia: University of Pennsylvania Press, 1981, pp. 105–18. This
  reference is on p. 107.
9 Foucault, *Madness and Civilization*, p. 68.
10 Ibid., pp. 74–5.
11 Ibid., pp. 68–78; Scull, "Moral treatment reconsidered," pp. 106–10.
12 Dr. de la Rive's remarks are translated from the original French which was
   quoted in Jones, *History of Mental Health Services*, p. 49.
13 *Regolamento dei Regi Spedali di Santa Maria Nuova de Bonifazio*. Hospital
   regulations prepared under the supervision of Vincenzo Chiarugi in 1793.
   Quoted in Mora, "Historical and theoretical trends," p. 55.
14 Daquin, J., *La Philosophie de la folie*, Chambéry, 1791, cited in Mora,
   "Historical and theoretical trends," p. 57.
15 Mora, "Historical and theoretical trends," p. 54.
16 Jones, *History of Mental Health Services*, p. 44.

17 Ferriar, J., *Medical Histories and Reflections* (3 vols.), London: Cadell & Davies, vol. 2, pp. 111–12. Quoted in Scull, "Moral treatment reconsidered," p. 106.
18 Mora, "Historical and theoretical trends," pp. 58–9.
19 Ibid., p. 54.
20 Hobsbaum, E. J., *The Age of Revolution 1789–1848*, New York: New American Library, p. 37.
21 Ibid., p. xv.
22 Ibid., p. 46.
23 Ibid., p. 38.
24 Ibid., pp. 40, 103.
25 Ibid., pp. 72, 77.
26 Tuma, E. H., *European Economic History: Tenth Century to the Present*, Palo Alto, California: Pacific Books, 1979, p. 202.
27 Hobsbaum, *Age of Revolution*, p. 79.
28 Inglis, B., *Poverty and the Industrial Revolution*, London: Panther Books, 1972, p. 78; Piven, F. F. and Cloward, R. A., *Regulating the Poor: The Functions of Public Welfare*, New York: Vintage Books, 1972, p. 21.
29 Ashton, T. S., *The Industrial Revolution 1760–1830*, Oxford: Oxford University Press, 1968, p. 46.
30 Ibid., p. 46.
31 Hobsbawm, *Age of Revolution*, pp. 93, 212.
32 Maidstone Poor Law authorities. Quoted in Jones, *History of Mental Health Services*, p. 18.
33 Jones, *History of Mental Health Services*, p. 18.
34 Ibid., pp. 10–12.
35 Parry-Jones, *Trade in Lunacy*, p. 30.
36 Scull, A., *Museums of Madness: The Social Organization of Insanity in Nineteenth-Century England*, London: Allen Lane (New York: St. Martin's Press), 1979, p. 39.
37 Ibid., pp. 27–34, 247; Jones, *History of Mental Health Services*, pp. 88–9.
38 Foucault, *Madness and Civilization*, p. 232.
39 Ibid., pp. 234–40.
40 Parry-Jones, *Trade in Lunacy*, p. 204.
41 Scull, *Museums of Madness*, pp. 71–3; Scull, "Moral treatment reconsidered,' pp. 112–15.
42 It had been difficult enough to maintain mentally disabled relatives at home before the Industrial Revolution, as revealed by a cottager's petition of 1681 in the Lancashire Quarter Sessions Records, quoted in Allderidge, P., "Hospitals, madhouses and asylums: Cycles in the care of the insane," *British Journal of Psychiatry*, 134: 321–34, 1979, p. 327.
43 Best, G., *Mid-Victorian Britain 1851–70*, Bungay, Suffolk: Fontana, 1979, p. 161.
44 Scull, *Museums of Madness*, pp. 224, 244.
45 Jones, *History of Mental Health Services*, pp. 48, 123.
46 Ibid., pp. 93–6.
47 Thurnam, *Statistics of Insanity*, pp. 138–9.
48 Walton, J., "The treatment of pauper lunatics in Victorian England: The case of Lancaster Asylum, 1816–1870," in Scull, *Madhouses, Mad-doctors, and Madmen*, pp. 166–97. This reference is on p. 168. Jones, *History of Mental Health Services*, pp. 114–21.
49 Walton, "Pauper lunatics in Victorian England," p. 180.

50 Ibid., pp. 186–91; Scull, *Museums of Madness*, pp. 214–18.
51 Parry-Jones, *Trade in Lunacy*, p. 290.
52 Ibid., p. 288.
53 Ibid., p. 177.
54 Ibid., p. 175.
55 Ibid., pp. 175, 185.
56 Ibid., pp. 154, 185–6.
57 Thurnam, *Statistics of Insanity*, p. 36.
58 Ibid., calculated from Table 12.
59 Tuke, D. H., *Chapters in the History of the Insane in the British Isles*, London: Kegan Paul, Trench, 1882, p. 491.
60 Walton, "Pauper lunatics in Victorian England," p. 182.
61 For a discussion of the standard of living debate see: Taylor, A. J. (ed.), *The Standard of Living in Britain in the Industrial Revolution*, London: Methuen, 1975.
62 Harrison, J. F. C., *Early Victorian Britain 1832–51*, Bungay, Suffolk: Fontana, 1979, p. 34; Hobsbawm, E. J., *Labouring Men: Studies in the History of Labour*, London: Weidenfeld & Nicolson, 1968, pp. 72–82.
63 Mayhew, H., *London Labour and the London Poor II*, p. 338. Quoted in E. P. Thompson, *The Making of the English Working Class*, New York: Vintage Books, 1966, p. 250.
64 Hobsbawm, E. J., *Industry and Empire*, Harmondsworth, Middlesex: Penguin, 1969, p. 161.
65 Church, R. A., *The Great Victorian Boom 1850–1873*, London: Macmillan, 1975, pp. 72–3.
66 Piven and Cloward, *Regulating the Poor*, pp. 32–8.
67 Flinn, M. W., *British Population Growth 1700–1850*, London: Macmillan, 1970, p. 57; Kemmerer, D. L. and Hunter, M. H., *Economic History of the United States*, Totowa, New Jersey: Littlefield, Adams, 1967, pp. 61, 65; Boorstin, D. J., *The Americans: Volume II: The National Experience*, Harmondsworth, Middlesex: Penguin, p. 46.
68 Boorstin, *The National Experience*, p. 51.
69 Hunt, E. H., *British Labour History 1815–1914*, London: Weidenfeld & Nicolson, 1981, p. 108; Tucker, R. S., "Real wages of artisans in London, 1729–1935," in Taylor, *Standard of Living in the Industrial Revolution*, p. 33.
70 Rothman, D. J., *The Discovery of the Asylum: Social Order and Disorder in the New Republic*, Boston: Little, Brown, 1971, p. 158.
71 Ibid., p. 160.
72 Ibid., pp. 160, 205.
73 Garraty, J. A., *Unemployment in History: Economic Thought and Public Policy*, New York: Harper, 1979, p. 109.
74 This material on the corporate asylums is drawn from Scull, A., "The discovery of the asylum revisited: Lunacy reform in the new American republic," in Scull, *Madhouses, Mad-doctors, and Madmen*, pp. 144–65; and Rothman, *Discovery of the Asylum*, pp. 130–54.
75 For example, see Caplan, R. B., *Psychiatry and the Community in Nineteenth-Century America*, New York: Basic Books, 1969, p. 4.
76 Mora, "Historical and theoretical trends," p. 62.
77 Rothman, *Discovery of the Asylum*, p. 277.
78 Ibid., p. 151.
79 Dain, N., *Disordered Minds: The First Century of Eastern State Hospital in Williamsburg, Virginia 1766–1866*, Williamsburg, Virginia: Colonial Williamsburg Foundation, 1971, pp. 66, 107.

80 The Boston Prison Discipline Society report. Quoted in Dain, *Disordered Minds*, p. 62.
81 Dain, *Disordered Minds*, pp. 43, 127.
82 Grob, G. N., *Mental Institutions in America: Social Policy to 1875*, New York: Free Press, 1973, p. 392.
83 Rothman, *Discovery of the Asylum*, pp. 144–51; Dain, N., *Concepts of Insanity in the United States, 1789–1865*, New Brunswick, New Jersey: Rutgers University Press, p. 128.
84 Bockoven, J. S., "Moral treatment in American psychiatry," *Journal of Nervous and Mental Disease*, 124: 167–94, 292–321, 1956. This reference is to p. 181.
85 Thurnam, *Statistics of Insanity*, Table 16.
86 Rothman, *Discovery of the Asylum*, p. 149.
87 Dickens, C., *American Notes for General Circulation*, Harmondsworth, Middlesex: Penguin, 1972, p. 97.
88 Ibid., p. 122.
89 Ibid., p. 140.
90 Dickens and Wills, "A curious dance," p. 386–91.
91 Dickens, *American Notes*, p. 141.
92 Rothman, *Discovery of the Asylum*, p. 283.
93 Ibid., pp. 144–6.
94 Caplan, *Psychiatry and the Community*, p. 43.
95 Ibid., pp. 37–8; Grob, *Mental Institutions in America*, p. 179.
96 Hall, B., *Travels in North America in the Years 1827 and 1828*, Edinburgh: Cadell, 1829. Quoted in Bromberg, W., *From Shaman to Psychotherapist: A History of the Treatment of Mental Illness*, Chicago: Henry Regnery, 1975, p. 124; and cited in Caplan, *Psychiatry and the Community*, p. 90; and in Tourney, G., "A history of therapeutic fashions in psychiatry, 1800–1966," *American Journal of Psychiatry*, 124: 784–96, 1967. According to Scull in "Discovery of the asylum revisited," p. 164. E. S. Abdy made similar remarks in his *Journal of a Residence and Tour in the United States of North America*, London: Murray, 1835.
97 Bromberg, *Shaman to Psychotherapist*, p. 125.
98 Quoted in Bromberg, *Shaman to Psychotherapist*, p. 125.
99 Deutsch, A., *The Mentally Ill in America*, New York: Columbia University Press, 1949, ch. 11.
100 See Caplan, *Psychiatry and the Community*, pp. 90–1 for a detailed list of the flaws in the recovery statistics.
101 Bromberg, *Shaman to Psychotherapist*, p. 124; Parry-Jones, *Trade in Lunacy*, pp. 202–5.
102 Thurnam, *Statistics of Insanity*, p. 57.
103 Ibid., Table 6.
104 Pliny Earle published his views on the curability of insanity as an article in 1876, and later in book form: *The Curability of Insanity: A Series of Studies*, Philadelphia: Lippincott, 1887. See Rothman, *Discovery of the Asylum*, p. 268; Caplan, *Psychiatry and the Community*, p. 93; Bromberg, *Shaman to Psychotherapist*, p. 126.
105 Bockoven, J. S., *Moral Treatment in Community Mental Health*, New York: Springer, 1972, ch. 5.
106 Rothman, *Discovery of the Asylum*, p. 357.
107 Bockoven, *Moral Treatment*, p. 67.
108 An exception would be Grob, *Mental Institutions in America*, pp. 184–5. After

reviewing Dr. Park's follow-up study of Dr. Woodward's patients, Grob concludes that it indicates "a record that compares quite favorably with mid-twentieth century discharge rates from mental hospitals."

109 Ray, I., *American Journal of Insanity*, 16: 1–2, 1861–2. Quoted in Caplan, *Psychiatry and the Community*, pp. 73–4.
110 Rothman, *Discovery of the Asylum*, p. 266.
111 Ibid., p. 281; Scull, "Discovery of the asylum revisited," pp. 157–9.
112 Scull, "Discovery of the asylum revisited," p. 159.
113 Mora, "Historical and theoretical trends," p. 73.
114 "The German asylum tradition issued more from the prison than the monastery, and this is, according to Kirchhof, the reason for their tremendous use of coercive measures." Ellenburger, H. F., "Psychiatry from ancient to modern times," in S. Arieti (ed.), *American Handbook of Psychiatry*, vol. I, New York: Basic Books, 1974, pp. 3–27. This reference is on p. 22.

6 LABOR, POVERTY AND SCHIZOPHRENIA

1 Brenner, M. H., *Mental Illness and the Economy*, Cambridge, Massachusetts: Harvard University Press, 1973, p. 207.
2 Scull, A. T., *Decarceration: Community Treatment and the Deviant – A Radical View*, Englewood Cliffs, New Jersey: Prentice-Hall, 1977, p. 157; Sharfstein, S. S. and Nafziger, J. C., "Community care: Costs and benefits for a chronic patient," *Hospital and Community Psychiatry*, 27: 170–3, 1976; Murphy, J. G. and Datel, W. E., "A cost-benefit analysis of community versus institutional living," *Hospital and Community Psychiatry*, 27: 165–70, 1976.
3 All quotations in this paragraph are drawn from Marsden, D. and Duff, E., *Workless: Some Unemployed Men and Their Families*, Baltimore: Penguin, 1975, pp. 191–202.
4 Eisenberg, P. and Lazarsfeld, P. F., "The psychological effects of unemployment," *Psychological Bulletin*, 35: 358–90, 1938; The Pilgrim Trust, *Men Without Work*, New York: Greenwood Press, 1968, p. 143 *et seq*.
5 Bemporad, J. R. and Pinsker, H., "Schizophrenia: The manifest symptomatology," in S. Arieti and E. B. Brody (eds.), *American Handbook of Psychiatry*, vol. III, New York: Basic Books, 1974, pp. 525–50. The quotation is on p. 540.
6 Marsden and Duff, *Workless*, p. 211.
7 Israeli, N., "Distress in the outlook of Lancashire and Scottish unemployed," *Journal of Applied Psychology*, 19: 67–9, 1935.
8 Ibid., p. 67.
9 Brenner, *Mental Illness and the Economy*, pp. 38, 56, 169.
10 Brown, G. W., Birley, J. L. T. and Wing, J. K., "Influence of family life on the course of schizophrenic disorders: A replication," *British Journal of Psychiatry*, 121: 241–58, 1972; Vaughn, C. E. and Leff, J. P., "The influence of family and social factors on the course of psychiatric illness," *British Journal of Psychiatry*, 129: 125–37, 1976.
11 Leff, J., "Preventing relapse in schizophrenia," presented at the World Psychiatric Association Regional Meeting, New York City, October 30–November 3, 1981.
12 Brown, G. W., Bone, M., Dalison, B. *et al.*, *Schizophrenia and Social Care*, London: Oxford University Press, 1966.
13 Wing, J. K. and Brown, G. W., *Institutionalism and Schizophrenia*, London: Cambridge University Press, 1970.

14 Huessy, H. R., "Discussion," *Schizophrenia Bulletin*, 7: 178–80, 1981.
15 Brown, G. W. and Birley, J. L. T., "Crises and life changes and the onset of schizophrenia," *Journal of Health and Social Behavior*, 9: 203–14, 1968.
16 Engels, F., *The Condition of the Working Class in England*, London: Granada, 1969, p. 117. First published in Leipzig in 1845.
17 Marx, K., *Capital*, vol. I, New York: International Publishers, 1967; reproduction of the English edition of 1887, p. 632.
18 Ibid., p. 643.
19 Ibid., pp. 743–4.
20 Ibid., p. 644.
21 Braverman, H., *Labor and Monopoly Capital: The Degradation of Work in the Twentieth Century*, New York: Monthly Review Press, 1974, pp. 386–401.
22 Anderson, C. H., *The Political Economy of Class*, Englewood Cliffs, New Jersey: Prentice-Hall, 1974, p. 149.
23 Silk, L., "Stocks jump as jobs slump: So what's next?," *New York Times*, October 10, 1982, p. E1; Pear, R., "Ranks of U.S. poor reach 35.7 million, the most since '64," *New York Times*, September 4, 1992, pp. A1 and A10; Bovee, T., "More American workers holding low-paying jobs," Associated Press report in *Boulder Daily Camera*, May 12, 1992, p. 5A.
24 Mora, G., "Historical and theoretical trends in psychiatry," in H. I. Kaplan, A. M. Freedman and B. J. Sadock (eds.), *Comprehensive Textbook of Psychiatry-III*, Baltimore: Williams & Wilkins, 1980, pp. 4–98. The material in this paragraph is from pp. 73–91.
25 Scull, A. T., *Museums of Madness: The Social Organization of Insanity in Nineteenth Century England*, London: Allen Lane (New York: St. Martin's Press), 1979, pp. 196–9.
26 Clark, D. H., *Social Therapy in Psychiatry*, Baltimore: Penguin, 1974, p. 23.
27 Mora, "Historical and theoretical trends," pp. 80, 90.
28 Among those making an ideological switch in tune with the economy was psychiatrist Werner Mendel, nationally recognized in the 1970s for his advocacy of community treatment of schizophrenia. Appearing for the City and County of Denver, the defendants in the case, Dr. Mendel modified his earlier views and testified that community care and vocational rehabilitation for schizophrenic people just do not work. In his deposition of May 7, 1983, for the Probate Court (case number 81–MH-270) and the District Court (civil action number 81–CV-6961) of the City and County of Denver, he claimed that it would be just as well for schizophrenic people if the whole mental health profession disappeared overnight. His pessimistic appraisal grew largely out of his own research and experience with a program treating psychotic patients in Los Angeles through a period of increasing unemployment and declining mental health funds.
29 For positive evaluations of the efficacy of psychosocial treatment and community support systems see Mosher, L. R. and Keith, S. J., "Psychosocial treatment: Individual, group, family, and community support approaches,' *Schizophrenia Bulletin*, 6: 11–41, 1980; Stein, L. I. and Test, M. A., "Alternative to mental hospital treatment: I. Conceptual model, treatment program, and clinical evaluation," *Archives of General Psychiatry*, 37: 392–7, 1980; Weisbrod, B. A., Test, M. A. and Stein, L. I., "Alternative to mental hospital treatment: II. Economic benefit-cost analysis," *Archives of General Psychiatry*, 37: 400–51, 1980; Test, M. A. and Stein, L. I., "Alternative to mental hospital treatment: III. Social cost," *Archives of General Psychiatry*, 37: 409–12, 1980; Pasamanick, G., Scarpitti, F. and Dinitz, S., *Schizophrenics in the Community: An Experimental Study in the Prevention of Hospitalization*, New York: Appleton-Century-Crofts,

1967; Mosher, L. R., Menn, A. Z. and Mathews, S., "Soteria: Evaluation of a home-based treatment for schizophrenia," *American Journal of Orthopsychiatry*, 45: 455–69, 1975; Polak, P. R. and Kirby, M. W., "A model to replace psychiatric hospitals," *Journal of Nervous and Mental Disease*, 162: 13–22, 1976.

30 Aronson, E., *The Social Animal*, 2nd edn., San Francisco: W. H. Freeman, 1976, pp. 186–9.

31 Clark, *Social Therapy in Psychiatry*, ch. 2.

32 Carstairs, G. M., "Advances in psychological medicine," *Practitioner*, Symposium on Advances in Treatment, 187: 495–504, 1961. Quoted in Jones, K., *A History of the Mental Health Services*, London: Routledge & Kegan Paul, 1972, p. 292.

33 Star, S., "The public's idea of mental illness," presented at National Association for Mental Health meeting, Chicago, Illinois, November 1955; Cumming, E. and Cumming, J., *Closed Ranks: An Experiment in Mental Health Education*, Cambridge, Massachusetts: Harvard University Press, 1957; Nunally, J. C., *Popular Conceptions of Mental Health*, New York: Holt, Rinehart & Winston, 1961.

34 Lemkau, P. V. and Crocetti, G. M., "An urban population's opinion and knowledge about mental illness," *American Journal of Psychiatry*, 118: 692–700, 1962; Meyer, J. K., "Attitudes toward mental illness in a Maryland community," *Public Health Reports*, 79: 769–72, 1964.

35 D'Arcy, C. and Brockman, J., "Changing public recognition of psychiatric symptoms? Blackfoot revisited," *Journal of Health and Social Behavior*, 17: 302–10, 1976; Olmsted, D. W. and Durham, K., "Stability of mental health attitudes: A semantic differential study," *Journal of Health and Social Behavior*, 17: 35–44, 1976.

36 Jones, *History of Mental Health Services*, p. 291.

37 Ibid., pp. 283, 289–91, 304.

38 Dickens, C., *American Notes for General Circulation*, Harmondsworth, Middlesex: Penguin, 1972; first published 1842, p. 100.

39 Clark, *Social Therapy in Psychiatry*, p. 21.

40 Brenner, *Mental Illness and the Economy*, pp. 170–2.

41 Thurnam, J., *Observations and Essays on the Statistics of Insanity*, London: Simpkin, Marshall, 1845; reprint edn., New York, Arno Press, 1976, p. 27.

42 Ödegard, Ö., "Statistical study of factors influencing discharge from psychiatric hospitals," *Journal of Mental Science*, 106: 1124–33, 1960.

43 Salokangas, R. K. R., "Prognostic implications of the sex of schizophrenic patients," *British Journal of Psychiatry*, 142: 145–51, 1983.

44 Beck, J. C., "Social influences on the prognosis of schizophrenia," *Schizophrenia Bulletin*, 4: 86–101, 1978.

45 World Health Organization, *Schizophrenia: An International Follow-up Study*, Chichester: Wiley, 1979, pp. 162, 273, 278, 286; Jablensky, A., Sartorius, N., Ernberg, M. *et al.*, "Schizophrenia: Manifestations, incidence and course in different cultures: A World Health Organization ten-country study," *Psychological Medicine*, supplement 20, 1992, tables 4.16 and 4.17.

46 Brenner, *Mental Illness and the Economy*, p. 170.

47 Henry, A. F. and Short, J. F., *Suicide and Homicide*, Glencoe, Illinois: Free Press, 1954.

48 Brenner, *Mental Illness and the Economy*, p. 53.

49 Cooper, B., "Social class and prognosis in schizophrenia: Parts I and II," *Journal of Preventive and Social Medicine*, 15: 17–30, 31–41, 1961.

50 Ibid., p. 36.

51 Brooke, E. M., "Report on the Second International Congress for Psychiatry,

Zurich," vol. III, 1957, p. 52. Cited in Cooper, "Social class and prognosis in schizophrenia," p. 19.
52 Hollingshead, A. B. and Redlich, F. C., *Social Class and Mental Illness*, New York: Wiley, 1958.
53 Myers, J. K. and Bean, L. L., *A Decade Later: A Follow-up of Social Class and Mental Illness*, New York: Wiley, 1968.
54 Astrachan, B. M., Brauer, L., Harrow, M. *et al.*, "Symptomatic outcome in schizophrenia," *Archives of General Psychiatry*, 31: 155–60, 1974.
55 World Health Organization, *Schizophrenia*, p. 288.
56 Wing, J. K., Denham, J. and Munro, A. B., "Duration of stay of patients suffering from schizophrenia," *British Journal of Preventive and Social Medicine*, 13: 145–8, 1959; Carstairs, G. M., Tonge, W. L., O'Connor, N. *et al.*, *British Journal of Preventive and Social Medicine*, 9: 187 *et seq.*, 1955, cited in Cooper, "Social class and prognosis in schizophrenia," p. 19.
57 Ödegard, "Discharge from psychiatric hospital," pp. 1127–9.
58 Astrachan *et al.*, "Symptomatic outcome from schizophrenia," pp. 159–60.
59 Ciompi, L., "Catamnestic long-term study on the course of life and aging of schizophrenics," *Schizophrenia Bulletin*, 6: 606–18, 1980.
60 Mitchell, B. R., *European Historical Statistics 1750–1970*, abridged edn., New York: Columbia University Press, 1978.
61 Ciompi, "Life and aging of schizophrenics," p. 615.
62 Ellman, M., *Socialist Planning*, Cambridge: Cambridge University Press, 1979, p. 257.
63 Ibid., p. 161.
64 Barker, D., "Moscow mayor has his say on jobless," *Guardian*, July 11, 1983.
65 Wing, J. K., *Reasoning About Madness*, Oxford: Oxford University Press, 1978; Field, M. G. and Aronson, J., "Soviet community mental health services and work therapy: A report of two visits," *Community Mental Health Journal*, 1: 81–90, 1965; Hein, G., "Social psychiatric treatment of schizophrenia in the Soviet Union," *International Journal of Psychiatry*, 6: 346–62, 1968.
66 World Health Organization, *Schizophrenia*, p. 160.

7 SCHIZOPHRENIA IN THE THIRD WORLD

1 Gunderson, J. G. and Mosher, L. R., "The cost of schizophrenia," *American Journal of Psychiatry*, 132: 901–6, 1975.
2 Collomb, H., "Bouffées délirantes en psychiatrie Africaine," *Transcultural Psychiatric Research*, 3: 29–34, 1966. This reference is to p. 29.
3 Schwartz, R., "Beschreibung einer ambulanten psychiatrischen Patientenpopulation in der Grossen-Kabylie (Nordalgerien): Epidemiologische und Klinische Aspekte," *Social Psychiatry* (West Germany), 12: 207–18, 1977.
4 Smartt, C. G. F., "Mental maladjustment in the East African," *Journal of Mental Science*, 102: 441–66, 1956.
5 Opler, M. K., "The social and cultural nature of mental illness and its treatment," in S. Lesse (ed.), *An Evaluation of the Results of the Psychotherapies*, Springfield, Illinois: C. C. Thomas, 1968, pp. 280–91.
6 Tewfik, G. I., "Psychoses in Africa," in *Mental Disorders and Mental Health in Africa South of the Sahara*, CCTA/CSA-WFMH-WHO meeting of specialists on mental health, Bukavu, London: 1958.
7 Field, M. J., *Search for Security: An Ethno-psychiatric Study of Rural Ghana*, Chicago: Northwestern University Press, 1962.
8 Fortes, M. and Mayer, D. Y., "Psychosis and social change among the Tallensi

of northern Ghana," in S. H. Foulkes and G. S. Prince (eds.), *Psychiatry in a Changing Society*, London: Tavistock, 1969, pp. 33–73.

9 Berne, E., "Some oriental mental hospitals," *American Journal of Psychiatry*, 106: 376–83, 1949; Seligman, C. G., "Temperament, conflict and psychosis in a stone-age population," *British Journal of Medical Psychology*, 9: 187–202, 1029; Jilek, W.G. and Jilek-Aall, L., "Transient psychoses in Africans," *Psychiatrica Clinica* (Basel), 3: 337–64, 1970.

10 Murphy, H. B. M., "Cultural factors in the genesis of schizophrenia," in D. Rosenthal and S. S. Kety (eds.), *The Transmission of Schizophrenia*, Oxford: Pergamon, 1968, p. 138.

11 American Psychiatric Association, *Diagnostic and Statistical Manual of Mental Disorders (DSM-III-R)*, Washington, D.C.: 1987.

12 Wintrob, R. M., "Malaria and the acute psychotic episode," *Journal of Nervous and Mental Disease*, 156: 306–17, 1973.

13 Rin, H. and Lin, T., "Mental illness among Formosan aborigines as compared with the Chinese in Taiwan," *Journal of Mental Science*, 108: 134–46, 1962.

14 De Wet, J. S. Du T., "Evaluation of a common method of convulsion therapy in Bantu schizophrenics," *Journal of Mental Science*, 103: 739–57, 1957. This reference is to p. 745.

15 Laubscher, B. J. F., *Sex, Custom and Psychopathology: A Study of South African Pagan Natives*, London: Routledge & Kegan Paul, 1937; Simons, H. J., "Mental disease in Africans: Racial determinism," *Journal of Mental Science*, 104: 371–88, 1958.

16 Westermeyer, J., "Psychosis in a peasant society: Social outcomes," *American Journal of Psychiatry*, 137: 390–4, 1980. This reference is to p. 393.

17 Ibid.

18 Westermeyer, J. and Wintrob, R., "'Folk' criteria for diagnosis of mental illness in rural Laos: On being insane in sane places," *American Journal of Psychiatry*, 136: 755–61, 1979, p. 755.

19 Westermeyer, J., "Dr. Westermeyer replies," *American Journal of Psychiatry*, 138: 699, 1981.

20 Brown, G. W., Bone, M., Dalison, B. and Wing, J. K., *Schizophrenia and Social Care*, London: Oxford University Press, 1966.

21 Kulhara, P. and Wig, N. N., "The chronicity of schizophrenia in North West India: Results of a follow-up study," *British Journal of Psychiatry*, 132: 186–90, 1978.

22 Murphy, H. B. M. and Raman, A. C., "The chronicity of schizophrenia in indigenous tropical peoples," *British Journal of Psychiatry*, 118: 489–97, 1971.

23 Waxler, N. E., "Is outcome for schizophrenia better in nonindustrial societies? The case of Sri Lanka," *Journal of Nervous and Mental Disease*, 167: 144–58, 1979.

24 Lo, W. H. and Lo, T., "A ten-year follow-up study of Chinese schizophrenics in Hong Kong," *British Journal of Psychiatry*, 131: 63–6, 1977.

25 Tsoi, W. F., Kok, L. P. and Chew, S. K., "A five-year follow-up study of schizophrenia in Singapore," *Singapore Medical Journal*, 26: 171–7, 1985.

26 Verghese, A., John, J. K., Rajkumar, S. *et al.*, "Factors associated with the course and outcome of schizophrenia in India: Results of a two-year multicentre follow-up study," *British Journal of Psychiatry*, 154: 499–503, 1989.

27 World Health Organization, *Schizophrenia: An International Follow-up Study*, Chichester, England: Wiley, 1979.

28 Jablensky, A., Sartorius, N., Ernberg, G. *et al.*, "Schizophrenia: Manifestations, incidence and course in different cultures: A World Health Organization ten-country study," *Psychological Medicine*, supplement 20, 1992, p. 97.

29 Harris, M., *Culture, Man and Nature: An Introduction to General Anthropology*, New York: Thomas Y. Crowell, 1971, p. 480.
30 Lambo, T., "The importance of cultural factors in psychiatric treatment," in I. Al-Issa and W. Dennis (eds.), *Cross-Cultural Studies of Behavior*, New York: Holt, Rinehart & Winston, 1970, pp. 548–52.
31 World Health Organization, *Schizophrenia*, p. 104.
32 Wing, J. K., "The social context of schizophrenia," *American Journal of Psychiatry*, 135: 1333–9, 1978.
33 World Health Organization, *Schizophrenia*, p. 104.
34 Sahlins, M., *Stone Age Economics*, Chicago: Aldine-Atherton, 1972, pp. 63–4; Neff, W. S., *World and Human Behavior*, Chicago: Aldine, 1968; Sharp, L., "People without politics," in V. F. Ray (ed.), *Systems of Political Control and Bureaucracy in Human Societies*, Seattle: University of Washington Press, 1958, p. 6.
35 Lee, R. E., *The !Kung San: Men, Women and Work in a Foraging Society*, New York: Cambridge University Press, 1979.
36 Richards, A. I., *Land, Labour and Diet in Northern Rhodesia*, London: Oxford University Press, 1961, appendix E; Guillard, J., "Essai de mesure de l'activité d'un paysan Africain: Le Toupouri," *L'Agronomie Tropicale*, 13: 415–28, 1958. Both works are cited in Sahlins, *Stone Age Economics*, pp. 62–4.
37 Eyer, J. and Sterling, P., "Stress-related mortality and social organization," *The Review of Radical Political Economics*, 9: 1–44, 1977. This reference is to p. 15.
38 Fei, H. and Chang, C., *Earthbound China: A Study of Rural Economy in Yunnan*, Chicago: University of Chicago Press, 1945, pp. 30–4, 145; Eyer and Sterling, "Stress-related mortality," p. 15.
39 Sahlins, *Stone Age Economics*, ch. 2.
40 Chayanov, A. V., *The Theory of Peasant Economy*, Homewood, Illinois: Richard D. Irwin, 1966, p. 77, cited in Sahlins, *Stone Age Economics*, p. 89.
41 Richards, *Land, Labour and Diet*, p. 402; Douglas, M., "Lele economy as compared with the Bushong," in G. Dalton and P. Bohannen, *Markets in Africa*, Evanston, Illinois: Northwestern University Press, 1962, p. 231, cited in Sahlins, *Stone Age Economics*, pp. 52–4.
42 Linn, J. F., *Cities in the Developing World: Policies for Their Equitable and Efficient Growth*, New York: World Bank/Oxford University Press, 1983, pp. 36–42; Squire, L., *Employment Policy in Developing Countries*, New York: World Bank/Oxford University Press, 1981, pp. 66–75, 83–90.
43 World Health Organization, *Schizophrenia*, ch. 10.
44 Doyal, L, *The Political Economy of Health*, Boston: South End Press, 1981, pp. 112–13; Fortes and Mayer, "Psychosis among the Tallensi."
45 World Health Organization, *Schizophrenia*, pp. 271, 283.
46 Squire, *Employment Policy in Developing Countries*, p. 71.
47 World Health Organization, *Schizophrenia*, p. 283.
48 Ibid., pp. 287–8.
49 McGoodwin, J. R., "No matter how we asked them, they convinced us that they suffer," *Human Organization*, 37: 378–83, 1978.
50 Paul, B. D., "Mental disorder and self-regulating processes in culture: A Guatemalan illustration," in R. Hunt (ed.), *Personalities and Cultures: Readings in Psychological Anthropology*, Garden City, New York: Natural History Press, 1967.
51 Gelfand, M., "Psychiatric disorders as recognized by the Shona," in A. Kiev (ed.), *Magic, Faith and Healing*, New York: Free Press, 1964, pp. 156–73.
52 Collomb, "Bouffées délirantes en psychiatrie Africaine," p. 30.

53 Rogler, L. H. and Hollingshead, A. B., *Trapped: Families and Schizophrenia*, New York: Wiley, 1965, p. 254.
54 Erinosho, O. A. and Ayonrinde, A., "Educational background and attitude to mental illness among the Yoruba in Nigeria," *Human Relations*, 34: 1–12, 1981.
55 D'Arcy, C. and Brockman, J., "Changing public recognition of psychiatric symptoms? Blackfoot revisited," *Journal of Health and Social Behavior*, 17: 302–10, 1976.
56 Ibid.
57 Binitie, A. O., "Attitude of educated Nigerians to psychiatric illness," *Acta Psychiatrica Scandinavica*, 46: 391–8, 1970.
58 Colson, A. C., "The perception of abnormality in a Malay village," in N. N. Wagner and E. Tan (eds.), *Psychological Problems and Treatment in Malaysia*, Kuala Lumpar: University of Malaya Press, 1971.
59 Leff, J., *Psychiatry Around the Globe: A Transcultural View*, New York: Marcel Dekker, 1981, p. 19.
60 Westermeyer and Wintrob, "'Folk' diagnosis in rural Laos;" Westermeyer, J. and Kroll, J., "Violence and mental illness in a peasant society: Characteristics of violent behaviors and 'folk' use of restraints," *British Journal of Psychiatry*, 133: 529–41, 1978.
61 Edgerton, R. B., "Conceptions of psychosis in four East African societies," *American Anthropologist*, 68: 408–25, 1966.
62 Edgerton, R. B., *The Individual in Cultural Adaption*, Berkeley: University of California Press, 1971, p. 188.
63 Edgerton, "Psychosis in four East African societies."
64 Ibid., p. 417.
65 Rin and Lin, "Mental illness among Formosan aborigines."
66 Waxler, N. E., "Is mental illness cured in traditional societies? A theoretical analysis," *Culture, Medicine and Psychiatry*, 1: 233–53, 1977. This reference is to p. 242.
67 World Health Organization, *Schizophrenia*, p. 105.
68 Levy, J. E., Neutra, R. and Parker, D., "Life careers of Navajo epileptics and convulsive hysterics," *Social Science and Medicine*, 13: 53–66, 1979.
69 Sontag, S., *Illness as Metaphor*, New York: Vintage Books, 1979.
70 Eliade, M., *Shamanism: Archaic Techniques of Ecstasy*, Princeton: Princeton University Press/Bollingen Paperback, 1972; Black Elk, *The Sacred Pipe*, Baltimore: Penguin, 1971.
71 Rogler and Hollingshead, *Trapped: Families and Schizophrenia*, p. 254.
72 Ozturk, O. M., "Folk treatment of mental illness in Turkey," in Kieva, *Magic, Faith and Healing*, p. 349.
73 Benedict, R., *Patterns of Culture*, Boston: Houghton-Mifflin, 1934, pp. 267–8.
74 Ackernecht, E. H., "Psychopathology, primitive medicine and primitive culture," *Bulletin of the History of Medicine*, 14: 30–67, 1943; and Silverman, J., "Shamans and acute schizophrenia," *American Anthropologist*, 69: 21–31, 1967.
75 Torrey, E. F., *The Mind Game: Witchdoctors and Psychiatrists*, New York: Emerson Hall, 1972; Torrey, E. F., *Schizophrenia and Civilization*, New York: Jason Aronson, 1980.
76 Silverman, "Shamans and acute schizophrenia," p. 29.
77 Linton, R., *Culture and Mental Disorders*, Springfield, Illinois: Charles C. Thomas, 1956.
78 Mischel, W. and Mischel, F., "Psychological aspects of spirit possession," *American Anthropologist*, 60: 249–60, 1958.

79 Prince, R., "Indigenous Yoruba psychiatry," in Kiev, *Magic, Faith and Healing*, pp. 84–120.
80 Messing, S. D., "Group therapy and social status in the Zar cult of Ethiopia," in J. Middleton (ed.), *Magic, Witchcraft and Curing*, Garden City, New York: Natural History Press, 1967, pp. 285–93.
81 Fox, J. R., "Witchcraft and clanship in Cochiti therapy," in Middleton, *Magic, Witchcraft and Curing*, pp. 255–84.
82 Dawson, J., "Urbanization and mental health in a West African community," in Kiev, *Magic, Faith and Healing*, pp. 305–42.
83 Benedict, *Patterns of Culture*, p. 72.
84 Kaplan, B. and Johnson, D., "The social meaning of Navajo psychopathology and psychotherapy," in Kiev, *Magic, Faith and Healing*, pp. 203–29; Leighton, A. H. and Leighton, D. C., "Elements of psychotherapy in Navaho religion," *Psychiatry*, 4: 515–23, 1941.
85 Waxler, "Is mental illness cured in traditional societies?," p. 241.
86 World Health Organization, *Schizophrenia*, p. 288; Jablensky *et al.*, "Schizophrenia: Manifestations, incidence and course in different cultures," Table 4.17.
87 Hare, E. H., "Mental illness and social conditions in Bristol," *Journal of Mental Science*, 103: 349–57, 1956; Stein, L., "'Social class' gradient in schizophrenia," *British Journal of Preventive and Social Medicine*, 11: 181–95, 1957; Cooper, B., "Social class and prognosis in schizophrenia: Part I," *British Journal of Preventive and Social Medicine*, 15: 17–30, 1961; Jaco, E. G., "The social isolation hypothesis and schizophrenia," *American Sociological Review*, 19: 567–77, 1954.
88 Lévi-Strauss, C., *Structural Anthropology*, Harmondsworth, Middlesex: Penguin, 1972, p. 180.
89 Warner, W. L., *A Black Civilization*, New York: Harper, 1937, pp. 241–2.
90 Beiser, M. and Collomb, H., "Mastering change: Epidemiological and case studies in Senegal, West Africa," *American Journal of Psychiatry*, 138: 455–9, 1981.
91 El-Islam, M. F., "A better outlook for schizophrenics living in extended families," *British Journal of Psychiatry*, 135: 343–7, 1979.
92 Wig, N. N., Menon, D. K. and Bedi, H., "Coping with schizophrenic patients in developing countries: A study of expressed emotions in the relatives," presented at the Seventh World Congress of Psychiatry, Vienna, July 11–16, 1983; Leff, *Psychiatry Around the Globe*, p. 157.

8 THE SCHIZOPHRENIC PERSON IN WESTERN SOCIETY

1 Kraft, S. and Shulins, N., "Cardboard is home for box people," Associated Press release in the *Boulder Daily Camera*, January 17, 1982, p. 5.
2 Hopper, K., Baxter, E. and Cox, S., "Not making it crazy: The young homeless patients in New York City," *New Directions for Mental Health Services*, no. 14: 33–42, 1982.
3 U.S. Department of Health and Human Services, *Toward a National Plan for the Chronically Mentally Ill*, Report to the Secretary by the Steering Committee on the Chronically Mentally Ill, Washington, D.C.: Department of Health and Human Services Publication Number (ADM) 81–1077, 1981, part 2, p. 11.
4 Reich, R. and Siegel, L., "The emergence of the Bowery as a psychiatric dumping ground," *Psychiatric Quarterly*, 50: 191–201, 1978; Reich, R. and Siegel, L., "The chronically mentally ill shuffle to oblivion," *Psychiatric Annals*, 3: 35–55, 1973.

5 Spitzer, R. L., Cohen, G., Miller, D. J. and Endicott, J., "The psychiatric status of 100 men on Skid Row," *International Journal of Social Psychiatry*, 15: 230–4, 1969.
6 Baxter, E., and Hopper, K., "The new mendicancy: Homeless in New York City," *American Journal of Orthopsychiatry*, 52: 393–408, 1982. This reference is to p. 398.
7 Ibid., pp. 398–400.
8 Hopper, Baxter and Cox, "Not making it crazy," p. 34.
9 Priest, R. G., "A U.S.A.–U.K. comparison," *Proceedings of the Royal Society of Medicine*, 63: 441–5, 1970.
10 Bogue, D. J., *Skid Row in American Cities*, Chicago: Community and Family Study Center, University of Chicago, 1963, p. 208.
11 Farr, R., unpublished mimeograph, 1983.
12 Torrey, E. F., "The real twilight zone," *Washington Post*, August 26, 1983.
13 Morse, G. and Calsyn, R., "Mentally disturbed homeless people in St. Louis: Needy, willing, but underserved," *Journal of Mental Health*, 14: 74–94, 1986.
14 Colorado Bar Association, Report concerning the implementation of the Colorado Act for the Care and Treatment of the Mentally Ill, submitted to the Board of Governors of the Colorado Bar Association by the Disability Law Committee on July 31, 1981, p. 22.
15 Interagency Council on the Homeless, *Outcasts on Main Street*, Washington, D.C., 1992, p. x.
16 Freeman, S. J. J., Formo, A., Alumpur, A. G. and Sommers, A. F., "Psychiatric disorder in a Skid-Row mission population," *Comprehensive Psychiatry*, 20: 454–62, 1979.
17 Edwards, G., Williamson, V., Hawker, A. *et al.*, "Census of a Reception Centre," *British Journal of Psychiatry*, 114: 1031–9, 1968.
18 Tidmarsh, D. and Wood, S., "Psychiatric aspects of destitution: A study of the Camberwell Reception Centre," in J. K. Wing and A. M. Hailey (eds.), *Evaluating a Community Psychiatric Service: The Camberwell Register 1964–1971*, London: Oxford University Press, 1972.
19 Patch, I. C. L., "Homeless men," *Proceedings of the Royal Society of Medicine*, 63: 437–41, 1970.
20 Priest, R. G., "The Edinburgh homeless: A psychiatric survey," *American Journal of Psychotherapy*, 25: 191–213, 1971.
21 Stark, C., Scott, J., Hill, M. *et al.*, *A Survey of the "Long-Stay" Users of DSS Resettlement Units: A Research Report*, London: Department of Social Security.
22 Her Majesty's Stationery Office, *Homeless Single Persons*, London: 1966.
23 Rollin, J., "From patients to vagrants," *New Society*, January 15, 1970, pp. 90–3.
24 Lim, M. H., "A psychiatric emergency clinic: A study of attendances over six months," *British Journal of Psychiatry*, 143: 460–1, 1983.
25 Torrey, E. F., Stieber, J., Ezekiel, J. *et al.*, *Criminalizing the Seriously Mentally Ill: The Abuse of Jails as Mental Hospitals*, Public Citizens' Health Research Group and the National Alliance for the Mentally Ill, Washington D.C., 1992, p. 15; Swank, G. E. and Winer, D., "Occurrence of psychiatric disorder in a county jail population," *American Journal of Psychiatry*, 133: 1331–3, 1976; Petrich, J., "Rate of psychiatric morbidity in a metropolitan county jail population," *American Journal of Psychiatry*, 133: 1439–44, 1976; Lamb, H. R. and Grant, R. W., "The mentally ill in an urban county jail," *Archives of General Psychiatry*, 39: 17–22, 1982.
26 Warner, R., "Psychotics in jail," presented at the Mental Health Center of

Boulder County Symposium on Controversial Issues in Community Care, Boulder, Colorado, March 27, 1981.

27 Torrey *et al.*, *Criminalizing the Seriously Mentally Ill*, pp. 1–3.

28 Ibid., p. 4.

29 Cherry, A. L., "On jailing the mentally ill," *Health and Social Work*, 3: 189–92, 1978.

30 Roth, L. H. and Ervin, F. R., "Psychiatric care of federal prisoners," *American Journal of Psychiatry*, 128: 424–30, 1971; Kaufman, E., "The violation of psychiatric standards of care in prisons," *American Journal of Psychiatry*, 137: 566–70, 1980.

31 James, J. F., Gregory, D., Jones, R. K. and Rundell, O. H., "Psychiatric morbidity in prisons," *Hospital and Community Psychiatry*, 31: 674–7, 1980.

32 Unpublished data from the Division of Community Psychiatry, University of Washington, 1988, cited in Jemelka, R., Trupin, E. and Chiles, J. A., "The mentally ill in prisons: A review," *Hospital and Community Psychiatry*, 40: 481–5, 1989.

33 Neighbors, H. W., "The prevalence of mental disorder in Michigan prisons," *DIS Newsletter*, Department of Psychiatry, University of Washington, St. Louis, 7: 8–11, 1987.

34 Jemelka, R. *et al.*, "The mentally ill in prisons."

35 Stelovich, S., "From the hospital to the prison: A step forward in deinstitutionalization?" *Hospital and Community Psychiatry*, 31: 674–7, 1980.

36 Torrey, *et al.*, *Criminalizing the Seriously Mentally Ill*, p. i.

37 Goldfarb, R., *Jails: The Ultimate Ghetto*, Garden City, New York: Anchor Press, 1975, p. 89.

38 Ibid.

39 Ibid.

40 Kaufman, "Violation of psychiatric standards," p. 567.

41 Ibid., p. 568.

42 Velde, R. W., associate administrator of the Law Enforcement Assistance Administration of the U.S. Department of Justice, writing in *The Correctional Trainer*, Newsletter for Illinois Correctional Staff Training, Fall 1979, p. 109.

43 Goldfarb, *Jails*; Kaufman, "Violation of psychiatric standards."

44 Waldron, R. J. and Pospichal, T. J., "The relationship between unemployment rates and prison incarceration rates," NCJRS microfiche, 1980; Jankovic, I., "Labor market and imprisonment," *Crime and Social Justice*, 8: 17–31, 1977; Carlson, K., Evans, P. and Flanagan, J., *American Prisons and Jails: Volume II: Population Trends and Projections*, Washington, D.C.: U.S. Department of Justice, National Institute of Justice, 1980; Greenberg, D. G., "The dynamics of oscillatory punishment processes," *Journal of Criminal Law and Criminology*, 68: 643–51, 1977; Brenner, M. H., *Estimating the Social Costs of National Economic Policy: Implications for Mental and Physical Health and Criminal Aggression*, Washington, D.C.: U.S. Government Printing Office, 1976; Nagel, J. H., "Crime and incarceration: A reanalysis," NCJRS microfiche, 1977; Nagel, W. G., "A statement on behalf of a moratorium on prison construction," proceedings of the 106th Annual Congress of the American Correctional Association, Denver, August 1976, pp. 79–87.

45 Warner, R., "The effect of the labor market on mental hospital and prison use: An international comparison," *Administration in Mental Health*, 10: 239–58, 1983.

46 U.S. DHHS, *Toward a National Plan*, part 2, p. 20.

47 A study of the chronically mentally ill in Los Angeles board and care homes

found two-thirds to be schizophrenic: see Lehman, A. F., Ward, A. C. and Linn, L. S., "Chronic mental patients: The quality of life issue," *American Journal of Psychiatry*, 139: 1271–6, 1982.

48 U.S. DHHS, *Toward a National Plan*, Part 2, p. 19. Minkoff, K., "A map of the chronic mental patient," in J. A. Talbott (ed.), *The Chronic Mental Patient*, Washington, D.C.: American Psychiatric Association, 1978, pp. 18–19.

49 Gunderson, J. G. and Mosher, L. R., "The cost of schizophrenia," *American Journal of Psychiatry*, 132: 901–5, 1975; Minkoff, "Map of the chronic mental patient," p. 13.

50 Minkoff ("Map of the chronic mental patient," p. 13) calculates that there were about 1.1 million schizophrenic patients in treatment in 1977–8. The figure is derived from the prevalence statistic in the Monroe County case register of 4.78 per 1,000 of the general population. The commonly cited figure of 2 million Americans with schizophrenia is a crude *lifetime* prevalence estimate. Here we are concerned with *active* cases of schizophrenia and the lower point-prevalence rate is the appropriate figure.
    The estimate of 1.1 million schizophrenic patients refers to patients *in treatment* in the course of a year. As we have seen, however, close to 200,000 schizophrenic people may be on Skid Row or in jail. To account for these persons we should adjust the number of American schizophrenic people upwards to 1.25 million.

51 Binder, R. L., "The use of seclusion on an inpatient crisis intervention unit," *Hospital and Community Psychiatry*, 30: 266–9, 1979.

52 Wadeson, J. and Carpenter, W. T., "The impact of the seclusion room experience," *Journal of Nervous and Mental Disease*, 163: 318–28, 1976.

53 Telintelo, S., Kuhlman, T. L. and Winget, C., "A study of the use of restraint in a psychiatric emergency room," *Hospital and Community Psychiatry*, 34: 164–5, 1983.

54 Sologg, P. H., "Behavioral precipitants of restraint in the modern milieu," *Comprehensive Psychiatry*, 19: 179–84, 1978. This reference is to p. 182.

55 Mattson, M. R. and Sacks, M. H., "Seclusion: Uses and complications," *American Journal of Psychiatry*, 135: 1210–13, 1978. This reference is to p. 1211.

56 Colorado Bar Association Report, pp. 9–10. Subsequently, conditions at the two Colorado State Hospitals have substantially improved.

57 "In Your Community," radio program in the series "Breakdown," produced at Seven Oaks Productions, Boulder, Colorado, by R. Warner and K. Kindle.

58 Anonymous, "On being diagnosed schizophrenic," *Schizophrenia Bulletin*, 3: 4, 1977.

59 Star, S., "The public's idea about mental illness," presented at the National Association for Mental Health meeting, Chicago, Illinois, November 1955.

60 Cumming, E. and Cumming, J., *Closed Ranks: An Experiment in Mental Health Education*, Cambridge, Massachusetts: Harvard University Press, 1957.

61 Nunally, J. C., *Popular Conceptions of Mental Health: Their Development and Change*, New York: Holt, Rinehart & Winston, 1961, p. 46.

62 Ibid., p. 51.

63 Ibid., p. 233.

64 Lemkau, P. V. and Crocetti, G. M., "An urban population's opinions and knowledge about mental illness," *American Journal of Psychiatry*, 118: 692–700, 1962; Meyer, J. K., "Attitudes toward mental illness in a Maryland community," *Public Health Reports*, 79: 769–72, 1964; Bentz, W. K., Edgerton, J. W. and Kherlopian, M., "Perceptions of mental illness among people in a rural area," *Mental Hygiene*, 53: 459–65, 1969; Crocetti, G., Spiro, J. R. and Siassi, I., "Are

the ranks closed? Attitudinal social distance and mental illness," *American Journal of Psychiatry*, 127: 1121–7, 1971.
65 Cockerham, W. C., *Sociology of Mental Disorder*, Englewood Cliffs, New Jersey: Prentice-Hall, 1981, pp. 295–9.
66 Olmsted, D. W. and Durham, K., "Stability of mental health attitudes: A semantic differential study," *Journal of Health and Social Behavior*, 17: 35–44, 1976.
67 D'Arcy, C. and Brockman, J., "Changing public recognition of psychiatric symptoms? Blackfoot revisited," *Journal of Health and Social Behavior*, 17: 302–10, 1976.
68 Miller, D. and Dawson, W. H., "Effects of stigma on re-employment of ex-mental patients," *Mental Hygiene*, 49: 281–7, 1965.
69 Aviram, U. and Segal, S. P., "Exclusion of the mentally ill: Reflection of an old problem in a new context," *Archives of General Psychiatry*, 29: 126–31, 1973.
70 Tringo, J. L., "The hierarchy of preference toward disability groups," *Journal of Special Education*, 4: 295–306, 1970.
71 Lamy, R. E., "Social consequences of mental illness," *Journal of Consulting Psychology*, 30: 450–5, 1966.
72 Lamb, H. R., "Roots of neglect of the long-term mentally ill," *Psychiatry*, 42: 201–7, 1979.
73 Munoz, R. A. and Morrison, J. R., "650 private psychiatric patients," *Journal of Clinical Psychiatry*, 40: 114–16, 1979.
74 Page, S., "Social responsiveness toward mental patients: The general public and others," *Canadian Journal of Psychiatry*, 25: 242–6, 1980.
75 Scheper-Hughes, N., *Saints, Scholars and Schizophrenics: Mental Illness in Rural Ireland*, Berkeley: University of California Press, 1979, p. 89.
76 Giovannoni, J. M. and Ullman, L. P., "Conceptions of mental health held by psychiatric patients," *Journal of Clinical Psychology*, 19: 398–400, 1963; Manis, M., Houts, P. S. and Blake, J. B., "Beliefs about mental illness as a function of psychiatric status and psychiatric hospitalization," *Journal of Abnormal and Social Psychology*, 67: 226–33, 1963; Crumpton, E., Weinstein, A. D., Acker, C. W. and Annis, A. P., "How patients and normals see the mental patient," *Journal of Clinical Psychology*, 23: 46–9, 1967.
77 Bentinck, C., "Opinions about mental illness held by patients and relatives," *Family Process*, 6: 193–207, 1967; Swanson, R. M. and Spitzer, S. P., "Stigma and the psychiatric patient career," *Journal of Health and Social Behavior*, 11: 44–51, 1970.
78 Scheff, T. J., *Being Mentally Ill: A Sociological Theory*, Chicago: Aldine, 1966.
79 Phillips, D. L., "Public identification and acceptance of the mentally ill," *American Journal of Public Health*, 56: 755–63, 1966.
80 Rosenhan, D. L., "On being sane in insane places," *Science*, 179: 250–8, 1973.
81 Gove, W. R., "Labeling and mental illness," in W. R. Gove (ed.), *The Labeling of Deviance: Evaluating a Perspective*, New York: Halsted, 1975.
82 Strauss, J. S. and Carpenter, W. T., *Schizophrenia*, New York: Plenum, 1981, p. 128.
83 Festinger, L., *A Theory of Cognitive Dissonance*, Stanford, California: Stanford University Press, 1957; Festinger, L. and Carlsmith, J. M., "Cognitive consequences of forced compliance," *Journal of Abnormal and Social Psychology*, 58: 203–10, 1959.
84 Van Putten, J., Crumpton, E. and Yale, C., "Drug refusal in schizophrenia and the wish to be crazy," *Archives of General Psychiatry*, 33: 1443–6, 1976.

85 Lamb, H. R. and Goertzel, V., "Discharged mental patients – Are they really in the community?" *Archives of General Psychiatry*, 24: 29–34, 1971; Wing, J. K., "The social context of schizophrenia," *American Journal of Psychiatry*, 135: 1333–9, 1978.
86 Doherty, E. G., "Labeling effects in psychiatric hospitalization: A study of diverging patterns of inpatient self-labeling processes," *Archives of General Psychiatry*, 32: 562–8, 1975.
87 Warner, R., Taylor, D., Powers, M. and Hyman, J., "Acceptance of the mental illness label by psychotic patients: Effects on functioning," *American Journal of Orthopsychiatry*, 59: 398–409, 1989.
88 Pattison, E. M., DeFrancisco, D., Wood, P. *et al.*, "A psychosocial kinship model for family therapy," *American Journal of Psychiatry*, 132: 1246–51, 1975; Cohen, C. I. and Sokolovsky, J., "Schizophrenia and social networks: Ex-patients in the inner city," *Schizophrenia Bulletin*, 4: 546–60, 1978; Pattison, E. M. and Pattison, M. L., "Analysis of a schizophrenic psychosocial network," *Schizophrenia Bulletin*, 7: 135–43, 1981; Lipton, F. R., Cohen, C. I., Fischer, E. and Katz, S. E., "Schizophrenia: A network crisis," *Schizophrenia Bulletin*, 7: 144–51, 1981; Minkoff, "Map of the chronic mental patient," p. 25.
89 Lipton *et al.*, "A network crisis."
90 Westermeyer, J. and Pattison, E. M., "Social networks and mental illness in a peasant society," *Schizophrenia Bulletin*, 7: 125–34, 1981.
91 Cohen and Sokolovsky, "Schizophrenia and social networks."
92 Yarrow, M., Clausen, J. and Robbins, P., "The social meaning of mental illness," *Journal of Social Issues*, 11: 33–48, 1955.
93 Kreisman, D. E. and Joy, V. D., "Family response to the mental illness of a relative: A review of the literature," *Schizophrenia Bulletin*, issue 10: 34–57, 1974.
94 Hatfield, A., "Psychosocial costs of schizophrenia to the family," *Social Work*, 23: 355–9, 1978. This reference is to p. 358.
95 Creer, C., "Living with schizophrenia," *Social Work Today*, 6: 2–7, 1975.
96 Grinspoon, L., Courtney, P. H. and Bergen, H. M., "The usefulness of a structured parents' group in rehabilitation," in M. Greenblatt, D. J. Levinson and G. L. Klerman, *Mental Patients in Transition: Steps in Hospital–Community Rehabilitation*, Springfield, Illinois: Charles C. Thomas, 1961, p. 245.
97 Maddox, S., "Profiles: Tom Hansen," *Boulder Monthly*, January 1979, p. 19.
98 Brown, G. W., Birley, J. L. T. and Wing, J. K., "Influence of family life on the course of schizophrenic disorders: A replication," *British Journal of Psychiatry*, 121: 241–58, 1972; Vaughn, C. E. and Leff, J. P., "The influence of family and social factors on the course of psychiatric illness," *British Journal of Psychiatry*, 129: 125–37, 1976.
99 Marx, K., *The Economic and Philosophic Manuscripts of 1844*, New York: International Publishers, 1964; Novack, G., "The problem of alienation," in E. Mandel and G. Novack, *The Marxist Theory of Alienation*, New York: Pathfinder Press, 1973, pp. 53–94; Ollman, B., *Alienation: Marx's Conception of Man in Capitalist Society*, Cambridge: Cambridge University Press, 1971.
100 Robinson, J. P. and Shaver, P. R., *Measures of Social Psychological Attitudes*, Ann Arbor, Michigan: Institute for Social Research, 1969, p. 249.
101 Fromkin, K. R., "Gender differences among chronic schizophrenics in the perceived helpfulness of community-based treatment programs," unpublished doctoral dissertation, Department of Psychology, University of Colorado, 1985.

102 Robinson and Shaver, *Measures of Social Psychological Attitudes*, p. 271.
103 Safer, D. J., "Substance abuse by young adult chronic patients," *Hospital and Community Psychiatry*, 38: 853–858, 1985; Atkinson, R. M., "Importance of alcohol and drug abuse in psychiatric emergencies," *California Medicine*, 118: 1–4, 1973.
104 Warner, R., Taylor, D., Wright, J. *et al.*, "Substance use among the mentally ill: Prevalence, reasons for use and effects on illness," *American Journal of Orthopsychiatry*, in press.
105 Henry, J., *Culture Against Man*, New York: Random House, 1964.
106 Berreman, G. D., "Structure and function of caste systems," in G. DeVos and H. Wagatsuma, *Japan's Invisible Race: Caste in Culture and Personality*, Berkeley, California: University of California Press, 1972, pp. 277–307. The reference is to p. 288.
107 Harris, M., *Culture, Man, and Nature*, New York: Thomas Y. Crowell, 1971, ch. 18.

9 THE INCIDENCE OF SCHIZOPHRENIA

 1 Barker, D. J. P., "Rise and fall of Western diseases," *Nature*, 338: 371–2, 1989.
 2 Barker, D. J. P. and Phillips, D. I. W., *Lancet*, ii: 567–70, 1984, cited in Barker, "Rise and fall of Western diseases."
 3 Kraepelin, E., *Dementia Praecox and Paraphrenia*, Edinburgh: Livingstone, 1927, p. 1145.
 4 Babigian, H. M., "Schizophrenia: Epidemiology," in H. I. Kaplan, A. M. Freedman and B. J. Sadock (eds.), *Comprehensive Textbook of Psychiatry – III*, Baltimore: Williams & Wilkins, 1980, pp. 1113–21. The reference is to p. 1115; Wing, J. K., "Epidemiology of schizophrenia," *British Journal of Psychiatry*, 9: 25–31, 1975.
 5 Warner, R. and de Girolamo, G., *Epidemiology of Mental Health and Psychosocial Problems: Epidemiology of Schizophrenia*, Geneva: World Health Organization, in press, Table 3.
 6 Torrey, E. F., *Schizophrenia and Civilization*, New York: Jason Aronson, 1980.
 7 Jeste, D. V., Carman, R., Lohr, J. B. and Wyatt, R. J., "Did schizophrenia exist before the eighteenth century?," *Comprehensive Psychiatry*, 26: 493–503, 1985; Ellard, J., "Did schizophrenia exist before the eighteenth century?," *Australia and New Zealand Journal of Psychiatry*, 21: 306–14, 1987.
 8 Jeste *et al.*, "Schizophrenia before the eighteenth century."
 9 Ellard, "Schizophrenia before the eighteenth century."
10 Hare, E., "Was insanity on the increase?," *British Journal of Psychiatry*, 142: 439–5, 1983.
11 Scull, A., *Museums of Madness: The Social Organization of Insanity in Nineteenth-Century England*, London: Allen Lane, 1979, p. 225.
12 Tuke, D. H., "Increase in insanity in Ireland," *Journal of Mental Science*, 40: 549–58, 1894.
13 Hare, "Was insanity on the increase?'
14 Hare, E., "Schizophrenia as a recent disease," *British Journal of Psychiatry*, 153: 521–31, 1988.
15 Jablensky, A., "Epidemiology of schizophrenia: A European perspective," *Schizophrenia Bulletin*, 12: 52–73, 1986.
16 Bamrah, J. S., Freeman, H. L. and Goldberg, D. P., "Epidemiology in Salford, 1974–84: Changes in an urban community over ten years," *British*

Journal of Psychiatry, 159: 802–10, 1991; Castle, D., Wessely, S., Der, G. and Murray, R. M., "The incidence of operationally defined schizophrenia in Camberwell, 1965–84," *British Journal of Psychiatry*, 159: 790–4, 1991; de Alarcon, J., Seagroatt, V. and Goldacre, M., "Trends in schizophrenia (letter)," *Lancet*, 335: 852–3, 1990; Der, G., Gupta, S. and Murray, R. M., "Is schizophrenia disappearing?" *Lancet*, 335: 513–16, 1990; Dickson, W. E. and Kendell, R. E., "Does maintenance lithium therapy prevent recurrences of mania under ordinary clinical conditions?," *Psychological Medicine*, 16: 521–30, 1986; Eagles, J. M., Hunter, D. and McCance, C., "Decline in the diagnosis of schizophrenia among first contacts with psychiatric services in north-east Scotland, 1969–1984," *British Journal of Psychiatry*, 152: 793–8, 1988; Eagles, J. M. and Whalley, L. J., "Decline in the diagnosis of schizophrenia among first admissions to Scottish mental hospitals from 1969–78," *British Journal of Psychiatry*, 146: 151–4, 1985; Folnegović, Z., Folnegović-Šmalc, V. and Kulčar, Ž., "The incidence of schizophrenia in Croatia," *British Journal of Psychiatry*, 156: 363–5, 1990; Häfner, H. and an der Heiden, W., "The Mannheim case register: The long-stay population," in G. H. M. M. ten Horn, R. Giel, W. H. Gulbinat and J. H. Henderson (eds.), *Psychiatric Case Registers in Public Health*, Amsterdam: Elsevier, 1986, pp. 28–38; Harrison, G., Cooper, J. E. and Gancarczyk, R., "Changes in the administrative incidence of schizophrenia," *British Journal of Psychiatry*, 159: 811–16, 1991; Joyce, P. R., "Changing trends in first admissions and readmissions for mania and schizophrenia in New Zealand," *Australian and New Zealand Journal of Psychiatry*, 21: 82–6, 1987; Munk-Jørgensen, P., "Decreasing first-admission rates of schizophrenia among males in Denmark from 1970 to 1984," *Acta Psychiatrica Scandinavica*, 73: 645–50, 1986; Munk-Jørgensen, P. and Jørgensen, P., "Decreasing rates of first-admission diagnoses of schizophrenia among females in Denmark from 1970 to 1984," *Acta Psychiatrica Scandinavia*, 74: 379–83, 1986; Munk-Jørgensen, P. and Mortensen, P. B., "Incidence and other aspects of the epidemiology of schizophrenia in Denmark, 1971–1987," *Journal of Psychiatry*, 1992 (in press); Parker, G., O'Donnell, M. and Walter, S., "Changes in the diagnoses of the functional psychoses associated with the introduction of lithium," *British Journal of Psychiatry*, 146: 377–82, 1985.
17 Strömgren, E., "Changes in the incidence of schizophrenia," *British Journal of Psychiatry*, 150: 1–7, 1967; Crow, T. J., "Trends in schizophrenia" (letter), *Lancet*, 335: 851, 1990.
18 Parker *et al.*, "Changes in the diagnoses of the functional psychoses."
19 Dickson and Kendell, "Does maintenance lithium therapy prevent recurrences of mania?"; Eagles *et al.*, "Decline in the diagnosis of schizophrenia."
20 Kendell, R. E., Malcolm, D. E. and Adams, W., "The problem of detecting changes in the incidence of schizophrenia," *British Journal of Psychiatry*, 162: 212–18, 1993.
21 Crow, "Trends in schizophrenia;" Munk-Jørgensen and Mortensen, "Incidence and other aspects of the epidemiology of schizophrenia in Denmark."
22 Graham, P. M., "Trends in schizophrenia" (letter), *Lancet*, 335: 1214, 1990; de Alarcon, J. *et al.*, "Trends in schizophrenia."
23 Cooper, J. E., Goodhead, D., Craig, T. *et al.*, "The incidence of schizophrenia in Nottingham," *British Journal of Psychiatry*, 151: 619–26, 1987.
24 Gottesman, I. I., *Schizophrenia Genesis: The Origins of Madness*, New York: W. W. Freeman, 1991, p. 102.
25 Barker, "Rise and fall of Western diseases."
26 Gupta, S. and Murray, R. M., "The changing incidence of schizophrenia: Fact or artefact?" *Directions in Psychiatry*, 11:1–8, 1991.

27 Rose, A. M., "The prevalence of mental disorders in Italy," *International Journal of Social Psychiatry*, 10: 87–100, 1964.
28 Rao, S., "Caste and mental disorders in Bihar," *American Journal of Psychiatry*, 122: 1045–55, 1966.
29 Nandi, D. N., Mukherjee, S. P., Boral, G. C. *et al.*, "Socio-economic status and mental morbidity in certain tribes and castes in India: A cross-cultural study," *British Journal of Psychiatry*, 136: 73–85, 1980.
30 Dube, K. C. and Kumar, N., "Epidemiological study of schizophrenia," *Journal of Biosocial Science*, 4: 187–95, 1972.
31 Elnagar, M. N., Maitra, P. and Rao, M. N., "Mental health in an Indian rural community," *British Journal of Psychiatry*, 118: 499–503, 1971.
32 Lin, T., "A study of the incidence of mental disorder in Chinese and other cultures," *Psychiatry*, 16: 313–36, 1953, pp. 326–7; Lin, T., Rin, H., Yeh, E. *et al.*, "Mental disorders in Taiwan, fifteen years later: A preliminary report," in W. Candill and T. Lin (eds.), *Mental Health Research in Asia and the Pacific*, Honolulu: East–West Center Press, 1969, pp. 66–91.
33 McNeil, T. F., "Perinatal influences in the development of schizophrenia," in H. Helmchen and F. A. Henn, *Biological Perspectives of Schizophrenia*, New York: John Wiley, 1987, pp. 125–38.
34 Goodman, R., "Are complications of pregnancy and birth causes of schizophrenia?," *Developmental Medicine and Child Neurology*, 30: 391–5, 1988.
35 Wilcox, J. A. and Nasrallah, H. A., "Perinatal insult as a risk factor in paranoid and non-paranoid schizophrenia," *Psychopathology*, 20: 285–7, 1987; Schwarzkopf, S. B., Nasrallah, H. A., Olson, S'C. *et al.*, "Perinatal complications and genetic loading in schizophrenia; Preliminary findings," *Psychiatry Research*, 27: 233–9, 1989.
36 Cannon, T. D., Mednick, S. A. and Parnas, J., "Genetic and perinatal determinants of structural brain deficits in schizophrenia," *Archives of General Psychiatry*, 46: 883–9, 1989; Fish, B., Marcus, J., Hans, J. L. *et al.*, "Infants at risk of schizophrenia: Sequelae of a genetic neurointegrative defect," *Archives of General Psychiatry*, 49: 221–35, 1992.
37 North, A. F. and MacDonald, H. M., "Why are neonatal mortality rates lower in small black infants of similar birth weights?," *Journal of Pediatrics*, 90: 809–10, 1977.
38 Cannon *et al.*, "Genetic and perinatal determinants."
39 Lane, E. and Albee, G. W., "Comparative birthweights of schizophrenics and their siblings," *Journal of Psychiatry*, 64: 227–31, 1966; Stabenau, J. R. and Pollin, W., "Early characteristics of MZ twins discordant for schizophrenia," *Archives of General Psychiatry*, 17: 723–34, 1967.
40 Gupta and Murray, "The changing incidence of schizophrenia."
41 Eagles, J. M., "Is schizophrenia disappearing?," *British Journal of Psychiatry*, 158: 834–5, 1991.
42 Arieti, S., *The Interpretation of Schizophrenia*, New York: Basic Books, 1974, p. 494; Leff, J., *Psychiatry Around the Globe: A Transcultural View*, Second edition, London: Gaskell, 1988, p. 163.
43 U.S. Department of Health, Education and Welfare, *Vital Statistics of the United States*, Washington, D.C.: U.S. Government Printing Office, 1923; Malzberg, B., "A statistical study of mental diseases among natives of foreign white parentage in New York State," *Psychiatric Quarterly*, 10: 127–42, 1936; Malzberg, B., *Social and Biological Aspects of Mental Disease*, Utica, New York: State Hospital Press, 1940; Malzberg, B., "Are immigrants psychologically

326 Notes to pages 205–206

disturbed?," in S. C. Plog and R. B. Edgerton (eds.), *Changing Perspectives in Mental Illness*, New York: Holt, Rinehart & Winston, 1969, pp. 395–421.
44 Eitinger, L., "The incidence of mental disease among refugees in Norway," *Journal of Mental Science*, 105: 326–38, 1959.
45 Hemsi, L. K., "Psychiatric morbidity of West Indian immigrants," *Social Psychiatry*, 2: 95–100, 1967.
46 Bagley, C., "The social aetiology of schizophrenia in immigrant groups," *International Journal of Social Psychiatry*, 17: 292–304, 1971; Giggs, J., "High rates of schizophrenia among immigrants in Nottingham," *Nursing Times*, 69: 1210–12, 1973; Rwegellera, G. G. C., "Psychiatric morbidity among West Africans and West Indians living in London," *Psychological Medicine*, 7: 317–29, 1977; Carpenter, L. and Brockington, I. F., "A study of mental illness in Asians, West Indians, and Africans living in Manchester," *British Journal of Psychiatry*, 137: 201–5, 1980; Bebbington, P. E., Hurry, J. and Tennant, C., "Psychiatric disorders in selected immigrant groups in Camberwell," *Social Psychiatry*, 16: 43–51, 1981; Dean, G., Walsh, D., Downing, H. and Shelley, E., "First admissions of native born and immigrants to psychiatric hospitals in South East England, 1976," *British Journal of Psychiatry*, 139: 506–12, 1981; Harrison, G., Owens, D., Holton, T. *et al.*, "A prospective study of severe mental disorder in Afro-Caribbean patients," *Psychological Medicine*, 18: 643–57, 1988.
47 Cochrane, R., "Mental illness in immigrants to England and Wales: An analysis of mental hospital admissions, 1971," *Social Psychiatry*, 12: 25–35, 1977; Cochrane, R. and Bal, S. S., "Migration and schizophrenia: An examination of five hypotheses," *Social Psychiatry*, 22: 181–91, 1987; Glover, G. R., "The pattern of psychiatric admissions of Caribbean-born immigrants in London," *Social Psychiatry and Psychiatric Epidemiology*, 24: 49–56, 1989.
48 Cade, J. F. J. and Krupinski, J., "Incidence of psychiatric disorders in Victoria in relation to country of birth," *Medical Journal of Australia*, 49: 400–4, 1962.
49 Halevi, H. S., "Frequency of mental illness among Jews in Israel," *International Journal of Social Psychiatry*, 9: 268–82, 1963.
50 Cochrane, "Mental illness in immigrants to England and Wales."
51 Malzberg, "Are immigrants psychologically disturbed?," pp. 416–17.
52 Bland, R. C. and Orn, H., "Schizophrenia: Sociocultural factors," *Canadian Journal of Psychiatry*, 26: 186–8, 1981.
53 Bagley, C. and Binitie, A., "Alcoholism and schizophrenia in Irishmen in London," *British Journal of Addiction*, 65: 3–7, 1970; Clare, A. W., "Alcoholism and schizophrenia in Irishmen in London: A reassessment," *British Journal of Addiction*, 69: 207–12, 1974.
54 Arieti, *The Interpretation of Schizophrenia*, pp. 499–501.
55 Ödegard, Ö., "Emigration and insanity," *Acta Psychiatrica et Neurologica Scandinavica*, supplement 4, 1932.
56 Royes, K., "The incidence and features of psychoses in a Caribbean community," *Proceedings of the 3rd World Congress of Psychiatry*, 2: 1121–5, 1962; Burke, A. W., "First admissions and planning in Jamaica," *Social Psychiatry*, 9: 39–45, 1974.
57 Clare, "Alcoholism and schizophrenia in Irishmen;" Walsh, D., O'Hare, A., Blake, B. *et al.*, "The treated prevalence of mental illness in the Republic of Ireland – The three county register study," *Psychological Medicine*, 10: 465–70, 1980.
58 Adelstein, A. M. and Marmot, M. G., "The health of migrants in England and Wales: Causes of death," in J. K. Cruickshank and D. G. Beevers (eds.), *Ethnic Factors in Health and Disease*, Kent, England: Wright, 1989.

59 Lumb, K. M., Congdon, P. G. and Lealman, G. T., "A comparative review of Asian and British born maternity patients in Bradford, 1974–8," *Journal of Epidemiology and Community Health*, 35: 106–9, 1981.

60 Terry, P. B., Condie, R. G., Bissenden, J. G. and Keridge, D. F., "Ethnic differences in incidence of very low birthweight and neonatal deaths among normally formed infants," *Archives of Disease of Childhood*, 62: 709–11, 1987; Griffiths, R., White, M. and Stonehouse, M., "Ethnic differences in birth statistics from central Birmingham," *British Medical Journal*, 298: 94–5, 1989.

61 Tuck, S. M., Cardozo, L. D., Studd, J. W. W. *et al.*, "Obstetric characteristics in different social groups," *British Journal of Obstetrics and Gynaecology*, 90: 892–7, 1983.

62 World Health Organization, "Deliveries and complications of pregnancy, childbirth and the puerperium," *World Health Statistics Report*, 21: 468–71, 1968.

63 Terry, P. B., Condic, R. G., Settatree, R. S., "Analysis of ethnic differences in perinatal statistics," *British Medical Journal*, 281: 1307–8, 1980.

64 Terry *et al.*, "Incidence of very low birthweight and neonatal deaths;" Griffiths *et al.*, "Ethnic differences in birth statistics."

65 Harrison *et al.*, "Severe mental disorder in Afro-Caribbean patients."

66 McGovern, D. and Cope, R. V., "First psychiatric admission rate of first and second generation Afro-Caribbeans," *Social Psychiatry*, 22: 139–49, 1987.

67 Wessely, S., Castle, D., Der, G. and Murray, R., "Schizophrenia and Afro-Caribbeans: A case-control study," *British Journal of Psychiatry*, 159: 795–801, 1991.

68 Thomas, C. S., Stone, K., Osborne, M. *et al.*, "Psychiatric morbidity and compulsory admission among U.K.-born Europeans, Afro-Caribbeans and Asians in Central Manchester," *British Journal of Psychiatry*, 163: 91–9, 1993.

69 Harrison, G., "Searching for the causes of schizophrenia: The role of migrant studies," *Schizophrenia Bulletin*, 16: 663–671, 1990; Eagles, J. M., "The relationship between schizophrenia and immigration: Are there alternatives to psychosocial hypotheses?," *British Journal of Psychiatry*, 159: 783–9, 1991.

70 Wing, J. K., "Schizophrenic psychoses: Causal factors and risks," in P. Williams, G. Wilkinson and K. Rawnsley (eds.), *The Scope of Epidemiological Psychiatry*, London: Routledge & Kegan Paul, 1989, pp. 225–39.

71 Harrison, "Searching for the causes of schizophrenia."

72 Warner and de Girolamo, *Epidemiology of Schizophrenia*, section 3.2.2.

73 Jablensky, A., Sartorius, N., Ernberg, G. *et al.*, "Schizophrenia: Manifestations, incidence and course in different cultures: A World Health Organization ten-country study," *Psychological Medicine*, supplement 20, 1992.

74 ni Nuallain, M., O'Hare, A. and Walsh, W., "Incidence of schizophrenia in Ireland," *Psychological Medicine*, 17: 943–8, 1987.

75 Häfner, H. and Gattaz, W. F., "Is schizophrenia disappearing?," *European Archives of Psychiatry and Clinical Neuroscience*, 240: 374–6, 1991.

76 "Relationships between aging and schizophrenia now being studied," *Clinical Psychiatry News*, September, 1982, pp. 1, 24; Strauss, J. S. and Carpenter, W. T., *Schizophrenia*, New York: Plenum, 1981, p. 73.

77 U.S. Bureau of the Census, *Historical Statistics of the United States: Colonial Times to 1970*, Washington, D.C.: 1975, Series D 29–41, p. 131 and Series D 87–101, p. 135.

78 U.S. Bureau of the Census, *Social Indicators 1976*, Washington, D.C.: 1977, Table 8/5, pp. 372–3.

10 ANTIPSYCHOTIC DRUGS: USE, ABUSE AND NON-USE

1 Davis, J. M., "Antipsychotic drugs," in H. I. Kaplan, A. M. Freedman and B. J. Sadock (eds.), *Comprehensive Textbook of Psychiatry – III*, Baltimore: Williams & Wilkins, 1981, p. 2257.
2 Gardos, G. and Cole, J. O., "Maintenance antipsychotic therapy: Is the cure worse than the disease?" *American Journal of Psychiatry*, 133: 32–6, 1976.
3 Rogers *v.* Okin, Federal District Court, Boston, Civil Action 75–1610–T (D. Mass. 1979); Rennie *v.* Klein, 462 F. Supp. 1131 (D. N.J. 1978); Goedecke *v.* State of Colorado, Supreme Court of Colorado, Civil Action 28179, 1979.
4 Past president of the American Psychiatric Association, Alan Stone, speaking at the 1978 Annual Meeting of the Southern Psychiatric Association. Quoted in Ford, M. D., "The psychiatrist's double bind: The right to refuse medication," *American Journal of Psychiatry*, 137, 332–9, 1980. This reference is to p. 332.
5 Gutheil, T. G., "In search of true freedom: Drug refusal, involuntary medication, and 'rotting with your rights on,'" *American Journal of Psychiatry*, 137: 327–8, 1980.
6 Chouinard, G., Annable, L., Ross-Chouinard, A. and Nestoros, J. N., "Factors related to tardive dyskinesia," *American Journal of Psychiatry*, 136: 79–83, 1979; Fann, W. E., Davis, J. M. and Janowsky, D. S., "The prevalence of tardive dyskinesia in mental hospital patients," *Diseases of the Nervous System*, 33: 182–6, 1972; Smith, J. M., Kucharski, L. T., Oswald, W. T. and Waterman, L. J., "A systematic investigation of tardive dyskinesia in inpatients," *American Journal of Psychiatry*, 136: 918–22, 1979.
7 Chouinard *et al.*, "Factors related to tardive dyskinesia," p. 79.
8 Singh, M. M. and Kay, S. R., "Dysphoric response to neuroleptic treatment in schizophrenia: Its relationship to autonomic arousal and prognosis," *Biological Psychiatry*, 14: 277–94, 1979; Van Putten, T., May, P. R. A. and Marder, S. R., "The hospital and optimal chemotherapy in schizophrenia," *Hospital and Community Psychiatry*, 30: 114–17, 1979.
9 Leff, J. P. and Wing, J. K., "Trial of maintenance therapy in schizophrenia," *British Medical Journal*, 3: 559–604, 1971.
10 Cole, J. O., Goldberg, S. C. and Klerman, G. L., "Phenothiazine treatment in acute schizophrenia," *Archives of General Psychiatry*, 10: 246–61, 1964.
11 Pasamanick, B., Scarpetti, F. and Cinitz, S., *Schizophrenics in the Community: An Experimental Study in the Prevention of Rehospitalization*, New York: Appleton-Century-Crofts, 1967; Goldberg, S. C., Schooler, N. R., Hogarty, G. E. and Roper, M., "Prediction of relapse in schizophrenic outpatients treated by drug and sociotherapy," *Archives of General Psychiatry*, 34: 171–84, 1977; Hogarty, G. E. and Ulrich, R. F., "Temporal effects of drug and placebo in delaying relapse in schizophrenic outpatients," *Archives of General Psychiatry*, 34: 297–307, 1977.
12 For thorough reviews of research on the dopamine hypothesis of schizophrenia see Meltzer, H. Y. and Stahl, S. M., "The dopamine hypothesis of schizophrenia: A review," *Schizophrenia Bulletin*, 2: 19–76, 1976; and Haracz, J. L., "The dopamine hypothesis: An overview of studies with schizophrenic patients," *Schizophrenia Bulletin*, 8: 438–69, 1982.
13 Smythies, J. R. and Adey, W. T., *The Neurological Foundation of Psychiatry*, New York: Academic Press, 1966, pp. 150–7.
14 Melamud, N., "Psychiatric disorder with intracranial disorders of the limbic system," *Archives of Neurology* (Chicago), 17: 113–24, 1967; Horowitz, M. J. and Adams, J. E., "Hallucinations on brain stimulation: Evidence for revision of the Penfield hypothesis," in W. Keup (ed.), *Origins and Mechanisms of*

Hallucinations, New York: Plenum Publishing, 1970, pp. 13–22; Torrey, E. F. and Peterson, M. R., "Schizophrenia and the limbic system," *Lancet*, 2: 942–6, 1974.

15 Meltzer and Stahl list nine studies on this topic, the large majority of which show that HVA (homovanillic acid) and 5HIAA (5–hydroxyindolacetic acid) are not elevated in the cerebrospinal fluid of schizophrenic people.

16 Bowers, M. B., "Central dopamine turnover in schizophrenic syndromes," *Archives of General Psychiatry*, 31: 50–4, 1974.

17 Three groups of researchers have found elevated dopamine binding capacity in the limbic system of both drug-treated and drug-free schizophrenic people; the elevation is greater in the drug-treated patients. These studies are: Owen, F., Cross, A. J., Crow, T. J. *et al.*, "Increased dopamine receptor sensitivity in schizophrenia," *Lancet*, 2: 223–6, 1978; Lee, T. and Seeman, P., "Elevation of brain neuroleptic/dopamine receptors in schizophrenia," *American Journal of Psychiatry*, 137: 191–7, 1980; and Reisine, T. D., Rossor, M., Spokes, E. *et al.*, "Opiate and neuroleptic receptor alterations in human schizophrenic brain tissue," *Advances in Biochemical Psychopharmacology*, 21: 443–50, 1980. Studies from two other laboratories show elevation of dopamine binding capacity in drug-treated schizophrenic patients only. These studies include: Reynolds, G. P., Riederer, P., Jellinger, K. and Gabriel, E., "Dopamine receptors and schizophrenia: The neuroleptic drug problem," *Neuropharmacology*, 20: 1319–20, 1981; and Mackay, A. V. P., Iverson, L. L., Rossor, M. *et al.*, "Increased brain dopamine and dopamine receptors in schizophrenia," *Archives of General Psychiatry*, 39: 991–7, 1982.

18 Goldberg, M. E. and Salama, A. I., "Tolerance to drum stress and its relationship to dopamine turnover," *European Journal of Pharmacology*, 17: 202–7, 1972.

19 Bowers, "Central dopamine turnover."

20 Burt, D. R., Creese, I. and Snyder, S. H., "Antischizophrenic drugs: Chronic treatment elevates dopamine receptor binding in brain," *Science*, 196: 326–8, 1977; Muller, P. and Seeman, P., "Brain neurotransmitter receptors after long-term haloperidol: Dopamine, acetylcholine, serotonin, α-noradrenergic and naloxone receptors," *Life Sciences*, 21: 1751–8, 1977.

21 See footnote 17 in this chapter.

22 Rosen, B., Engelhardt, D. M., Freedman, N. *et al.*, "The hospitalization proneness scale as a predictor of response to phenothiazine treatment. I: Prevention of psychiatric hospitalization," *Journal of Nervous and Mental Disease*, 146: 476–80, 1968.

23 Rosen, B., Engelhardt, D. M., Freedman, N *et al.*, "The hospital proneness scale as a predictor of response to phenothiazine treatment. II: Delay of psychiatric hospitalization," *Journal of Nervous and Mental Disease*, 152: 405–11, 1971.

24 Goldstein, M. J., "Premorbid adjustment, paranoid status, and patterns of response to phenothiazine in acute schizophrenia," *Schizophrenia Bulletin*, 3: 24–37, 1970; Evans, J. R., Rodnick, E. H., Goldstein, M. J. and Judd, L. L., "Premorbid adjustment, phenothiazine treatment, and remission in acute schizophrenics," *Archives of General Psychiatry*, 27: 486–90, 1972.

25 Judd, L. L., Goldstein, M. J., Rodnick, E. H. and Jackson, N. L. P., "Phenothiazine effects in good premorbid schizophrenics divided into paranoid non-paranoid status," *Archives of General Psychiatry*, 29: 207–11, 1973.

26 Goldstein, M. J., Rodnick, E. H., Evans, J. R. *et al.*, "Drug and family therapy in the aftercare of acute schizophrenics," *Archives of General Psychiatry*, 35: 1169–77, 1978.

27 Rappaport, L. M., Hopkins, H. K., Hall, K. *et al.* "Are there schizo-phrenics for whom drugs may be unnecessary or contra-indicated?," *International Pharmacopsychiatry*, 13: 100–11, 1978, p. 107.
28 Carpenter, W. T., McGlashan, T. H. and Strauss, J. S., "The treatment of acute schizophrenia without drugs: An investigation of some current assumptions," *American Journal of Psychiatry*, 134: 14–20, 1977, p. 19.
29 Klein, D. G. and Rosen, B., "Premorbid asocial adjustment and response to phenothiazine treatment among schizophrenic inpatients," *Archives of General Psychiatry*, 29: 480–5, 1973.
30 Goldberg *et al.*, "Prediction of relapse," p. 171.
31 May, P. R. A., Tuma, A. H. and Dixon, W. J., "Schizophrenia – A follow-up study of results of treatment. I: Design and other problems," *Archives of General Psychiatry*, 33: 474–8, 1976; May, P. R. A., Tuma, A. H. and Dixon, W. J., "Schizophrenia: A follow-up study of the results of five forms of treatment," *Archives of General Psychiatry*, 38: 776–84, 1981.
32 Schooler, N. R., Goldberg, S. C., Boothe, H. and Cole, J. O., "One year after discharge: Community adjustment of schizophrenic patients," *American Journal of Psychiatry*, 123: 986–95, 1967.
33 Pasamanick *et al.*, *Schizophrenics in the Community*.
34 National Institute of Mental Health Psychopharmacology Service Center Collaborative Study Group, "Phenothiazine treatment in acute schizophrenia," *Archives of General Psychiatry*, 10: 246–61, 1964.
35 Mosher, L. R. and Menn, A. Z., "Community residential treatment for schizophrenia: Two-year follow-up," *Hospital and Community Psychiatry*, 29: 715–23, 1978. This reference is to p. 722.
36 Matthews, S. M., Roper, M. T., Mosher, L. R. and Menn, A. Z., "A non-neuroleptic treatment for schizophrenia: Analysis of the two-year postdischarge risk of relapse," *Schizophrenia Bulletin*, 5: 322–33, 1979.
37 Ciompi, L., Dauwalder, H-P., Maier, C. *et al.*, "The pilot project 'Soteria Berne:'" Clinical experiences and results," *British Journal of Psychiatry*, 161, supplement 18: 145–53, 1992; Ciompi, L., Dauwalder, H-P., Aebi, E. *et al.*, "A new approach to acute schizophrenia: Further results of the pilot project 'Soteria Berne,'" lecture given at the tenth International Symposium on the Psychotherapy of Schizophrenia, Stockholm, Sweden, August 11–15, 1991.
38 Davis, J., "Overview: Maintenance therapy in psychiatry. 1: Schizophrenia," *American Journal of Psychiatry*, 132: 1237–45, 1975.
39 Brown, G. W. and Birley, J. L. T., "Crises and life changes and the onset of schizophrenia," *Journal of Health and Social Behavior*, 9: 203–14, 1968; Birley, J. L. T. and Brown, G. W., "Crises and life changes preceding the onset or relapse of acute schizophrenia: Clinical aspects," *British Journal of Psychiatry*, 116: 327–33, 1970; Strahilevitz, M., "Possible interaction of environmental and biological factors in the etiology of schizophrenia," *Canadian Psychiatric Association Journal*, 19: 207–17, 1974; Jacobs, S. C. and Myers, J., "Recent life events and acute schizophrenic psychosis: A controlled study," *Journal of Nervous and Mental Disease*, 162: 75–87, 1976; Leff, J. P. and Vaughn, C. E., "The interaction of life events and relatives' expressed emotion in schizophrenia and depressive neurosis," *British Journal of Psychiatry*, 136: 146–53, 1980; Dohrenwend, B. P. and Egri, G., "Recent stressful life events and episodes of schizophrenia," *Schizophrenia Bulletin*, 7: 12–23, 1981; Spring, B., "Stress and schizophrenia: Some definitional issues," *Schizophrenia Bulletin*, 7: 24–33, 1981.
40 Wing, J. K., "The social context of schizophrenia," *American Journal of Psychiatry*, 135: 1333–9, 1978. This reference is to p. 1335.

41 Brown, G. W., Birley, J. L. T. and Wing, J. K., "Influence of family life on the course of schizophrenic disorders: A replication," *British Journal of Psychiatry*, 121: 241–58, 1972; Vaughn, C. E. and Leff, J. P., "The influence of family and social factors on the course of psychiatric illness: A comparison of schizophrenic and depressed neurotic patients," *British Journal of Psychiatry*, 129: 125–37, 1976.

42 Leff, J. P. and Vaughn, C. E., "The role of maintenance therapy and relatives' expressed emotion in relapse of schizophrenia: A two-year follow-up," *British Journal of Psychiatry*, 139: 40–5, 1981.

43 Leff and Vaughn, "Interaction of life events and expressed emotion."

44 Sturgeon, D., Kuipers, L., Berkowitz, R. *et al.*, "Psychophysiological responses of schizophrenic patients to high and low expressed emotion relatives," *British Journal of Psychiatry*, 138: 40–5, 1981.

45 Tarrier, N., Vaughn, C. E., Lader, M. H. and Leff, J. P., "Bodily reaction to people and events in schizophrenics," *Archives of General Psychiatry*, 36: 311–15, 1979.

46 Paul, G. L., Tobias, L. L. and Holly, B. L., "Maintenance psychotropic drugs in the presence of active treatment programs: A 'triple-blind' withdrawal study with long-term mental patients," *Archives of General Psychiatry*, 27: 106–15, 1972.

47 Ibid.

48 Paul, G. L. and Lentz, R. J., *Psychosocial Treatment of Chronic Mental Patients: Milieu versus Social Learning Programs*, Cambridge, Massachusetts: Harvard University Press, 1977.

49 Goldberg *et al.*, "Prediction of relapse."

50 Hogarty, G. E., Goldberg, S. C., Schooler, N. R. and the Collaborative Study Group, "Drug and sociotherapy in the aftercare of schizophrenic patients. III: Adjustment of nonrelapsed patients," *Archives of General Psychiatry*, 31: 609–18, 1974.

51 Hogarty, G. E., Goldberg, S. C., Schooler, N. R. *et al.*, "Drug and sociotherapy in the aftercare of schizophrenic patients. II: Two-year relapse rates," *Archives of General Psychiatry*, 31: 603–8, 1974.

52 Goldberg *et al.*, "Prediction of relapse," p. 171.

53 Leff, J. P., "Preventing relapse in schizophrenia," presented at the World Psychiatric Association Regional Meeting, New York, October 30–November 3, 1981; Berkowitz, R., Kuipers, L., Eberlein-Fries, R. and Leff, J. P., "Lowering expressed emotion in relatives of schizophrenics," *New Direction in Mental Health Services*, 12: 27–48, 1981.

54 Falloon, I. R. H., Boyd, J. L., McGill, C. W. *et al.*, "Family management in the prevention of exacerbations of schizophrenia: A controlled study," *New England Journal of Medicine*, 306: 1437–40, 1982.

55 Schmidt, L. J., Reinhardt, A. M., Kane, R. L. and Olsen, D. M., "The mentally ill in nursing homes: New back wards in the community," *Archives of General Psychiatry*, 34: 687–91, 1977.

56 Sheehan, S., "A reporter at large," *New Yorker*, May 25, June 1, June 8, June 15, 1981.

57 *In the interest of Edmiston*, Civil Action 80 MH 378 (Denver Probate Court, December 17, 1980).

58 Jick, H., "Reserpine and breast cancer: A perspective," *Journal of the American Medical Association*, 233: 896, 1975; Schyve, P. M., Smithline, F. and Meltzer, H. Y., "Neuroleptic-induced prolactin level elevation and breast cancer: An emerging clinical issue," *Archives of General Psychiatry*, 35: 1291–1301, 1978;

Gulbinat, W., Dupoint, A., Jablensky, A. *et al.*, "Cancer incidence of schizo-phrenic patients," *British Journal of Psychiatry*, 161, supplement 18: 75–85, 1992.

59 Quitkin, F., Rifkin, A. and Klein, D. F., "Very high dosage versus standard dosage fluphenazine in schizophrenia," *Archives of General Psychiatry*, 32: 1276–81, 1975; McGlashan, T. H. and Carpenter, W. T., "Postpsychotic depression in schizophrenia," *Archives of General Psychiatry*, 33: 231–9, 1976; Van Putten, T. and May, P. R. A., "'Akinetic depression' in schizophrenia," *Archives of General Psychiatry*, 35: 1101–7, 1978; Hogarty, G. E., Schooler, N. R., Ulrich, R. *et al.*, "Fluphenazine and social therapy in the aftercare of schizophrenic patients: Relapse analyzes of a two-year controlled study of fluphenazine decanoate and fluphenazine hydrochloride," *Archives of General Psychiatry*, 36: 1283–94, 1979; Goldstein *et al.*, "Drug and family therapy."

60 Hirsh, S., "Do neuroleptics cause depression in the schizophrenias?" presented at the World Psychiatric Association Regional Meeting, New York, October 30–November 3, 1981; Moller, H. and von Zerssen, G., "Depressive states occurring during clinical treatment of 280 schizophrenic inpatients," presented at the World Psychiatric Association Regional Meeting, New York, October 30–November 3, 1981.

61 Hartlage, L. C., "Effects of chlorpromazine on learning," *Psychological Bulletin*, 64: 235–45, 1965; Bruening, S. E., Davis, V. J., Matson, J. L. and Ferguson, D. G., "Effects of thioridazine and withdrawal dyskinesias on workshop per-formance of mentally retarded young adults," *American Journal of Psychiatry*, 139: 1447–54, 1982.

62 *Physicians' Desk Reference*, 47th Edition, Montvale, New Jersey: Medical Economics Data, 1993, pp. 2093–7.

63 Taylor, D. P., Riblet, L. A., Stanton, H. C. *et al.*, "Dopamine and anti-anxiety activity," *Pharmacology, Biochemistry and Behavior*, vol. 17, supplement 1, pp. 25–35, 1982; Haefely, W. E., "Behavioral and neuropharmacological aspects of drugs used in anxiety and related states," in M. A. Lipton, A. DiMascio and K. F. Killam (eds.), *Psychopharmacology: A Generation of Progress*, New York: Raven Press, 1978; Nestoros, J. N., "Benzodiazepines in schizophrenia: A need for a reassessment," *International Pharmacopsychiatry*, 15: 171–9, 1980; Bunney, G. S. and Aghajanian, G. K., "The effect of antipsychotic drugs on the firing of dopaminergic neurons: A reappraisal," in G. Sedvall, G. Uvnäs and Y. Zotterman, *Antipsychotic Drugs: Pharmaco-dynamics and Pharmacokinetics*, New York: Pergamon, 1976.

64 Feldman, P. E., "An analysis of the efficacy of diazepam," *Journal of Neuropsychiatry*, 3, supplement 1: S62–S67, 1962; Pignatoro, F. P., "Experience with chemotherapy in refractory psychiatric disorders," *Current Therapeutic Research*, 4: 389–98, 1962; Maculans, G. A., "Comparison of diazepam, chlor-prothixene and chlorpromazine in chronic schizophrenic patients," *Diseases of the Nervous System*, 25: 164–8, 1964; Kramer, J. C., "Treatment of chronic hallucinations with diazepam and phenothiazines," *Diseases of the Nervous System*, 28: 593–4, 1967; Irvine, B. M. and Schaecter, F., "'Valium' in the treatment of schizophrenia," *Medical Journal of Australia*, i: 1387, 1969; Trabucchi, M. and Ba, G., "Are benzodiazepines an antipsychotic agent?," *Southern Medical Journal*, 72: 636, 1979; Ansari, J. M. A., "Lorazepam in the control of acute psychotic symptoms and its comparison with flupenthixol," in E. Usdin, H. Eckert and I. S. Forrest (eds.), *Phenothiazines and Structurally Related Drugs*, New York: Elsevier/North-Holland, 1980; Beckman, H. and Haas, S., "High-dose diazepam in schizophrenia," *Psychopharmacology*, 71:

70–82, 1980; Lingjaerde, O., "Effect of the benzodiazepine derivative estazolam in patients with auditory hallucinations: A multicentre double-blind cross-over study," *Acta Psychiatrica Scandinavica*, 65: 339–54, 1982; "Diazepam shown to reduce many schizophrenic symptoms," *Psychiatric News*, August 20, 1982; Haas, S., Emrich, H. M. and Beckmann, H., "Analgesic and euphoric effects of high-dose diazepam in schizophrenia," *Neuropsychobiology*, 8: 123–8, 1982. Several similar studies are listed in the review article – Nestoros, "Benzodiazepines in schizophrenia," – which draws the conclusion that benzodiazepines have generally positive effects in schizophrenia.

65 The following studies yield equivocal results: Hollister, L. E., Bennett, J. L., Kimbell, I. *et al.*, "Diazepam in newly admitted schizophrenics," *Diseases of the Nervous System*, 24: 746–50, 1963; Kellner, R., Wilson, R. M., Muldawer, M. D. and Pathak, D., "Anxiety in schizophrenia: The responses to chlordiazepoxide in an intensive design study," *Archives of General Psychiatry*, 32: 1246–54, 1975; Jimerson, D. C., Van Kammen, D. P., Post, R. M. *et al.*, "Diazepam in schizophrenia: A preliminary double-blind trial," *American Journal of Psychiatry*, 139: 489–91, 1982. Clearly negative results are reported in: Lehmann, H. E. and Ban, T. A., "Notes from the log-book of a psychopharmacological research unit II," *Canadian Psychiatric Association Journal*, 9: 111–13, 1964; Weizman, A., Weizman, S., Tyano, S. *et al.*, "The biphasic effect of gradually increased doses of diazepam on prolactin secretion in acute schizophrenic patients," *Israeli Annals of Psychiatry*, 17: 233–40, 1979; Ruskin, P., Averbukh, I., Belmaker, R. H. and Dasberg, H., "Benzodiazepines in chronic schizophrenia," *Biological Psychiatry*, 14: 557–8, 1979; Karson, C. N., Weinberger, D. R., Bidelow, L. and Wyatt, R. J., "Clonazepam treatment of chronic schizophrenia: Negative results in a double-blind, placebo-controlled trial," *American Journal of Psychiatry*, 139: 1627–8, 1982. For a generally negative review of the value of the benzodiazepines in schizophrenia, see Greenblatt, D. J. and Shader, R. I., *Benzodiazepines in Clinical Practice*, New York: Raven Press, 1974, ch. 4.

66 Beckman and Haas, "High-dose diazepam in schizophrenia;" Feldman, "The efficacy of diazepam;" Maculan, "Diazepam in chronic schizophrenic patients;" and "Diazepam shown to reduce many schizophrenic symptoms," *Psychiatric News*, August 20, 1982.

67 Gardos and Cole, "Maintenance antipsychotic therapy."

68 Phillips, L., "Case history data and prognosis in schizophrenia," *Journal of Nervous and Mental Disease*, 117: 515–25, 1953; Stephens, J. H., Astrup, C. and Mangrum, J. C., "Prognostic factors in recovered and deteriorated schizophrenics," *American Journal of Psychiatry*, 122: 1116–21, 1966; Marder, S. R., van Kammen, D. P., Docherty, J. P. *et al.*, "Predicting drug-free improvement in schizophrenic psychosis," *Archives of General Psychiatry*, 36: 1080–5, 1979.

69 Bromet, E., Harrow, M. and Kasl, S., "Premorbid functioning and outcome in schizophrenics and nonschizophrenics," *Archives of General Psychiatry*, 30: 203–7, 1974; Strauss, J. S. and Carpenter, W. T., "The prognosis of schizophrenia: Rationale for a multidimensional concept," *Schizophrenia Bulletin*, 4: 56–77, 1978; Bland, R. C., Parker, J. H. and Orn, H., "Prognosis in schizophrenia: Prognostic predictors and outcome," *Archives of General Psychiatry*, 35: 72–7, 1978.

70 Harrow, M., Bromet, E. and Quinlan, D., "Predictors of post-hospital adjustment in schizophrenia: Thought disorders and schizophrenic diagnosis," *Journal of Nervous and Mental Disease*, 158: 25–32, 1974; Strauss, J. S. and Carpenter, W. T., "Characteristic symptoms and outcome in schizophrenia," *Archives of*

General Psychiatry, 30: 429–34, 1974; Carpenter, W. T., Barko, J. J., Strauss, J. S. and Hawk, A. B., "Signs and symptoms as predictors of outcome: A report from the International Pilot Study of Schizophrenia," *American Journal of Psychiatry*, 135: 940–5, 1978.

71 Strauss, J. S. and Carpenter, W. T., "The prediction of outcome in schizophrenia. I: Characteristics of outcome," *Archives of General Psychiatry*, 27: 739–46, 1972; Hawk, A. B., Carpenter, W. T. and Strauss, J. S., "Diagnostic criteria and five-year outcome in schizophrenia: A report from the International Pilot Study of Schizophrenia," *Archives of General Psychiatry*, 32: 343–7, 1975.

72 Strauss, J. S. and Carpenter, W. T., "The prediction of outcome in schizophrenia. II: Relationships between predictor and outcome variables: A report from the WHO International Pilot Study of Schizophrenia," *Archives of General Psychiatry*, 31: 37–42, 1974; Strauss, J. S. and Carpenter, W. T., "Prediction of outcome in schizophrenia. III: Five-year outcome and its predictors," *Archives of General Psychiatry*, 34: 159–63, 1977; Mintz, J., O'Brien, C. P. and Luborsky, L., "Predicting the outcome of psychotherapy for schizophrenics: Relative contributions of patient, therapist, and treatment characteristics," *Archives of General Psychiatry*, 33: 1183–6, 1976.

73 Kant, O., "The incidence of psychoses and other mental abnormalities in the families of recovered and deteriorated schizophrenic patients," *Psychiatric Quarterly*, 16: 176–86, 1942; Vaillant, G. E., "Prospective prediction of schizophrenic remission," Archives of General Psychiatry, 11: 509–18, 1964; Welner, J. and Strömgen, E., "Clinical and genetic studies on benign schizophreniform psychoses based on a follow-up," *Acta Psychiatrica Scandinavica*, 33: 377–99, 1958; McCabe, M. S., Fowler, R. C., Cadoret, R. J. and Winokur, G., "Familial differences in schizophrenia with good and poor prognosis", *Psychological Medicine*, 1: 326–32, 1971; Fowler, R. D., McCabe, M. S., Cadoret, R. J. and Winokur, G., "The validity of good prognosis schizophrenia," *Archives of General Psychiatry*, 26: 182–5, 1972; Taylor, M. A. and Abrams, R., "Manic-depressive illness and good prognosis schizophrenia," *American Journal of Psychiatry*, 132: 741–2, 1975.

74 Fowler *et al.*, "The validity of good prognosis schizophrenia," p. 182.

75 Ibid., p. 183; McCabe, "Familial differences in schizophrenia," pp. 327, 331.

76 Taylor and Abrams, "Manic-depressive illness and good prognosis schizophrenia," p. 742.

77 Hirschowitz, J., Casper, R., Garver, D. L. and Chang, S., "Lithium response in good prognosis schizophrenia," *American Journal of Psychiatry*, 137: 916–20, 1980.

78 Mosher, L. R., Menn, A. and Matthews, S. M., "Soteria: Evaluation of a home-based treatment for schizophrenia," *American Journal of Orthopsychiatry*, 45: 455–67, 1975. This reference is to p. 458.

79 Ibid., pp. 460–1.

80 Ibid., p. 458.

11 WORK

1 Tuke, S., *Description of the Retreat*, London: Dawson, 1964, facsimile of 1813 edn. Quoted in Scull, A. T., *Museums of Madness: The Social Organization of Insanity in Nineteenth-Century England*, London: Allen Lane (New York: St. Martin's Press), 1979, p. 69.

2 Ellis, W. C., *A Treatise on the Nature, Symptoms, Causes, and Treatment of Insanity*, London: Samuel Holdsworth, 1838, p. 197.

3 Todd, E., unpublished letter in the Institute of Living archives, Hartford, Connecticut, 1830. Quoted in Braceland, F. J., "Rehabilitation," in S. Arieti (ed.), *American Handbook of Psychiatry*, 2nd edn., vol. 5, New York: Basic Books, 1975, pp. 683–700. The quotation is on p. 684.

4 Browne, W. A. F., *What Asylums Were, Are, and Ought to Be: Being the Substance of Five Lectures Delivered before the Managers of the Montrose Royal Lunatic Asylum*, Edinburgh: Black, 1837, pp. 229–31. Quoted in Scull, *Museums of Madness*, pp. 105–6.

5 Carlyle, T., "Inaugural address at Edinburgh University, 1866," in M. Strauss (ed.), *Familiar Medical Quotations*, Boston: Little, Brown, 1968.

6 Freud, S., "Civilization and Its Discontents," in J. Strachey (ed.), *Standard Edition of the Complete Psychological Works of Sigmund Freud*, vol. 21, London: Hogarth Press, 1953–1966. First published in 1930.

7 Wansbrough, N. and Cooper, O., *Open Employment after Mental Illness*, London: Tavistock, 1980, pp. 2–4; Fairweather, G. W., Sanders, D. H., Maynard, H. *et al.*, *Community Life for the Mentally Ill*, Chicago: Aldine, 1969, pp. 13–14; Patterson, C. H., "Evaluation of the rehabilitation potential of the mentally ill patient," in L. P. Blum and R. K. Kujoth (eds.), *Job Placement of the Emotionally Disturbed*, Metuchen, New Jersey: Scarecrow Press, 1972, pp. 188–215. The reference is to pp. 189–91.

8 Stringham, J. A., "Rehabilitating chronic neuropsychiatric patients," *American Journal of Psychiatry*, 108: 924–8, 1952.

9 Cohen, L., "Vocational planning and mental illness," *Personnel and Guidance Journal*, 34: 28–32, 1955.

10 Brown, G. W., Carstairs, G. M. and Topping, G., "Post-hospital adjustment of chronic mental patients," *Lancet*, ii: 685–9, 1958.

11 Freeman, H. E. and Simmons, O. G., *The Mental Patient Comes Home*, New York: Wiley, 1963, ch. 4.

12 Fairweather *et al.*, *Community Life for the Mentally Ill*, ch. 12.

13 Walker, R., Winick, W., Frost, E. S. and Lieberman, J. M., "Social restoration of hospitalized psychiatric patients through a program of special employment in industry," *Rehabilitation Literature*, 30: 297–303, 1969.

14 Anthony, W. A., Buell, G. W., Sharatt, S. and Althoff, M. D., "The efficacy of psychiatric rehabilitation," *Psychological Bulletin*, 78: 447–56, 1972.

15 Barbee, M. S., Berry, K. L. and Micek, L. A., "Relationship of work therapy to psychiatric length of stay and readmission," *Journal of Consulting and Clinical Psychology*, 33: 735–8, 1969.

16 Wing, J. K. and Brown, G. W., *Institutionalism and Schizophrenia: A Comparative Study of Three Mental Hospitals 1960–68*, Cambridge: Cambridge University Press, 1970; Peffer, P. A., "Money: A rehabilitation incentive for mental patients," *American Journal of Psychiatry*, 110: 84–92, 1953. Two similar examples are given in Linn, L., "Occupational therapy and other activities," in H. I. Kaplan, A. M. Freedman and B. J. Sadock (eds.), *Comprehensive Textbook of Psychiatry – III*, Baltimore: Williams & Wilkins, 1980, pp. 2382–90. The reference is to pp. 2385–6.

17 Johnson, R. F. and Lee, H., "Rehabilitation of chronic schizophrenics: Major results of a three-year program," *Archives of General Psychiatry*, 12: 237–40, 1965.

18 Kunce, J. T., "Is work therapy really therapeutic?," *Rehabilitation Literature*, 31: 297–9, 320, 1970.

19 Miles, A., "Long-stay schizophrenic patients in hospital workshops: A comparative study of an industrial unit and an occupational therapy department,"

British Journal of Psychiatry, 119: 611–20, 1971; Miles, A., "The development of interpersonal relationships among long-stay patients in two hospital workshops," *British Journal of Medical Psychology*, 45: 105–14, 1972.

20 Poindexter, W. R., "Screening ex-patients for employability," in Blum and Kujoth, *Job Placement of the Emotionally Disturbed*, pp. 152–7. The quotation is on pp. 155–6.

21 Lowe, C. M., "Prediction of posthospital work adjustment by the use of psychological tests," in Blum and Kujoth, *Job Placement of the Emotionally Disturbed*, pp. 239–48; Patterson, "Evaluation of rehabilitation potential," p. 196; Freeman and Simmons, *The Mental Patient Comes Home*, p. 61; Brown, Carstairs and Topping, "Post-hospital adjustment of chronic mental patients."

22 For a full discussion of this issue see Chapter 11 of the first edition of Warner, R., *Recovery from Schizophrenia: Psychiatry and Political Economy*, London: Routledge & Kegan Paul, 1985. Also see Hawkins, K., *Unemployment: Facts, Figures and Possible Solutions for Britain*, Harmondsworth, Middlesex: Penguin, 1979; Scott, M. and Laslett, R. A., *Can We Get Back to Full Employment?*, New York: Holmes & Meier, 1979; Samuelson, P. A., *Economics*, 11th edn., New York: McGraw-Hill, 1980; Thurow, L. C., *The Zero-Sum Society: Distribution and the Possibilities for Economic Change*, Harmondsworth, Middlesex: Penguin, 1980, ch. 7; Friedman, M., "The role of monetary policy," *American Economic Review*, 58: 1–17, 1968; Phelps, E. S., "Phillips curve, expectations of inflation, and optimal unemployment over time," *Economica*, 34: 254–81, 1967; Jay, P., *A General Hypothesis of Employment, Inflation and Politics*, London: Institute of Economic Affairs, Occasional Paper 46, 1976; Bluestone, B. and Harrison, B., *The Deindustrialization of America*, New York: Basic Books, 1982, ch. 8.

23 Anthony, W. A. and Blanch, A., "Supported employment for persons who are psychiatrically disabled: An historical and conceptual perspective," *Psychosocial Rehabilitation Journal*, 11: 5–23, 1987. This reference is to p. 6; Farkas, M., Rogers, S. and Thurer, S., "Rehabilitation outcome for the recently deinstitutionalized psychiatric patient," *Hospital and Community Psychiatry*, 38: 864–70, 1987.

24 Glasscote, R. M., Cumming, E., Rutman, I. *et al.*, *Rehabilitating the Mentally Ill in the Community*, Washington, D.C.: Joint Information Service of the American Psychiatric Association and the National Association for Mental Health, 1971, p. 200; U.S. Department of Labor, *Sheltered Workshop Study, Volume II: Study of Handicapped Clients in Sheltered Workshops and Recommendations of the Secretary*, Washington, D.C.: 1979, p. 31.

25 Wansbrough and Cooper, *Open Employment after Mental Illness*, p. 38.

26 Black, B., *Industrial Therapy for the Mentally Ill in Western Europe*, New York: Altro Service Bureau, 1966.

27 Wansbrough and Cooper, *Open Employment after Mental Illness*, p. 38.

28 Ibid., pp. 36–8.

29 Fairweather *et al.*, *Community Life for the Mentally Ill*.

30 Backer, T. E. and Glaser, E. M. (eds.), *Case Studies of Fairweather Hospital–Community Treatment Program*, Los Angeles: Human Interaction Research Institute, 1979.

31 Information about Italian and Swiss cooperatives reported throughout this chapter was gathered by the author during a series of visits in 1991. Further information is available on the Pordenone cooperatives in Conte, S. and Comis, S., "Social enterprise in Italy," presented at the Third Congress of the World Association for Psychosocial Rehabilitation, October 13–16, 1991; and

on the Trieste cooperatives in Dell'Acqua, P. and Dezza, M. G. C., "The end of the mental hospital: A review of the psychiatric experience in Trieste," *Acta Psychiatrica Scandinavica*, supplement 316: 45–69, 1985; De Leonardis, O., Mauri, D., Rotelli, F., "Deinstitutionalization, another way: The Italian mental health reform," *Health Promotion*, 1: 151–64, 1986.

32 Stastny, P., Gelman, R. and Mayo, H., "The European experience with social firms in the rehabilitation of persons with psychiatric disabilities," unpublished report of a study visit to Germany and Austria, May, 1992.

33 Boyles, P., "Mentally ill gain a foothold in working world," *Boston Sunday Globe*, June 5, 1988.

34 Backer and Glaser, *Case Studies of Fairweather Programs*, pp. 58, 90.

35 Wansbrough and Cooper, *Open Employment after Mental Illness*, p. 37.

36 Fairweather *et al.*, *Community Life for the Mentally Ill*, pp. 140–1.

37 Wansbrough and Cooper, *Open Employment after Mental Illness*, pp. 53–4.

38 Warner, R. and Polak, P., "An economic development approach to the mentally ill in the community," Concept paper written under contract to the National Institute of Mental Health, Rockville, Maryland, January 16, 1993, p. 24.

39 Wansbrough and Cooper, *Open Employment after Mental Illness*, pp. 53–4.

40 Ibid., p. 37.

41 Warner and Polak, "An economic development approach."

42 Polak, P., Warner, R. and Mosher, L. R., "Final report: Feasibility study on the development of a consumer-oriented system of pharmacies for the seriously mentally ill." Prepared for the Robert Wood Johnson Foundation, Princeton, New Jersey, January 15, 1992.

43 Warner and Polak, "An economic development approach," pp. 18–19.

44 Details of the Boulder supported employment program, and other material in this chapter, were provided by Ruth Arnold, Coordinator of Vocational Services at the Mental Health Center of Boulder County, Colorado. An overview of supported employment in the United States is available in Anthony and Blanch, "Supported employment for persons who are psychiatrically disabled."

45 Glasscote *et al.*, *Rehabilitating the Mentally Ill*, p. 55.

46 Personal communication, Jerry Dincin, 1988.

47 Wansbrough and Cooper, *Open Employment after Mental Illness*, p. 47.

48 Glasscote *et al.*, *Rehabilitating the Mentally Ill*, pp. 55, 134.

49 Warner and Polak, "An economic development approach," p. 12.

50 Ibid., p. 12.

51 Ibid., p. 13.

52 Berndt, E. R., *The Practice of Econometrics: Classic and Contemporary*, Reading, Massachusetts: Addison-Wesley, 1990, ch. 11, pp. 593–651.

53 Warner and Polak, "An economic development approach," p. 13.

54 Sancton, T., "How to get America off the dole," *Time*, May 25: p. 44–7, 1992. The reference is to p. 47.

55 Haskins, R., "Congress writes a law: Research and welfare reform," *Journal of Policy Analysis and Management*, 10: 616–32, 1991. This reference is to p. 620; Sancton, "How to get America off the dole," p. 46.

56 Ellwood, D., *Poor Support*, New York: Basic Books, 1988.

57 Kaus, M., "The work ethic state," *New Republic*, July 7: 22–33, 1986.

58 Scheffler, R., "Financing mental health services," presented at NIMH workshop on Organizing and Financing Services for People with Severe Mental Disorders, Park City, Utah, December 9–11, 1992.

59 Jacobs, H. E., Wissusik, M. A., Collier, R. *et al.*, "Correlations between

psychiatric disabilities and vocational outcome," *Hospital and Community Psychiatry*, 43: 365–9, 1992. This reference is to p. 368.
60 Roberts, J. D. and Ward, I. M., *Commensurate Wage Determination for Service Contracts*, Columbus, Ohio: Ohio Industries for the Handicapped, 1987.
61 Warner and Polak, "An economic development approach," p. 8.
62 Ellis, R. H. and Young, C., "Cost savings associated with sheltered workshop employment," Brief Report no. 2, Colorado Division of Mental Health Evaluation Services, February 25, 1983.

12 DESEGREGATING SCHIZOPHRENIA

1 The Mental Health Center of Boulder, County, Inc., is a comprehensive community mental health center which offers a full range of psychiatric services to the 225,000 residents of the mixed urban and rural region of Boulder County, Colorado. Clients' fees are on a sliding scale and services for the indigent are free. The Center sees more than 6,300 clients a year; over 2,100 cases are active at any one time and about 650 of these suffer from functional psychoses.

The Center employs 340 part-time and full-time staff (280 full-time equivalent employees). Around two-thirds of the full-time equivalent employees provide clinical services and one-third have administrative and clerical duties.

The Center's budget for 1991–2 was $11.1 million (£7.4 million). The sources of revenue were as follows:

Federal government	$481,000
State government	$304,000
Local government (cities and county)	$2,234,000
Fees and health insurance (including Medicaid)	$5,500,000
Other sources	$2,589,000

2 Turner, J. C. and Tenhoor, W. J., "The NIMH community support program: Pilot approach to a needed social reform," *Schizophrenia Bulletin*, 4: 319–48, 1978.
3 Warner, R., "Jail services and community care for the mentally ill in Boulder County, Colorado," in H. J. Steadman, D. W. McCarty and J. P. Morrisey, *The Mentally Ill in Jail: Planning for Essential Services*, New York: Guilford Press, 1989, pp. 198–213.
4 Ibid.
5 Warner, R., Wollesen, C. *et al.*, "Cedar House: A non-coercive hospital alternative in Boulder, Colorado," in R. Warner (ed.), *Alternatives to Hospital for Acute Psychiatric Treatment*, Washington, D.C.: American Psychiatric Press, in press, ch. 1.
6 Polak, P. R., Kirby, M. W. and Deitchman, W. S., "Treating acutely ill psychotic patients in private homes," in R. Warner, *Alternatives to Hospital for Acute Psychiatric Treatment*, ch. 12; Brook, B. D., Cortes, M., March, R. and Sundberg-Stirling, M., "Community families: An alternative to psychiatric hospital intensive care," *Hospital and Community Psychiatry*, 27: 195–7, 1976.
7 Bennett, R., "The crisis home program of Dane County," in Warner, *Alternatives to Hospital for Acute Psychiatric Treatment*, ch. 13.
8 Stein, L. I. and Test, M. A., "Alternative to mental hospital treatment: I. Conceptual model, treatment program, and clinical evaluation," *Archives of General Psychiatry*, 37: 392–7, 1980.
9 Stein, L. I. and Test, M. A., "Alternative to mental hospital treatment: III. Social cost," *Archives of General Psychiatry*, 37: 409–12, 1980.
10 Warner, R. and Huxley, P., "Psychopathology and quality of life among mentally ill patients in the community: British and U.S. samples compared," *British Journal of Psychiatry*, in press.

11 Ibid.
12 To this number we should add about 20 psychotic patients who have been placed in the forensic unit of the state hospital by the Boulder County criminal courts. Other psychotic patients from Boulder County receive inpatient and outpatient care in the private sector. It is not possible to say how many of these patients would be in hospital treatment if they were under the care of the mental health center. One may safely assume, however, that virtually none of the people in treatment with the private sector for psychosis is a candidate for long-term hospital care – such patients rapidly pass the point of being able to pay for private hospital treatment, the limited provisions of their health insurance having been exhausted.
13 Podvoll, E. M., *The Seduction of Madness: Revolutionary Insights into the World of Psychosis and a Compassionate Approach to Recovery at Home*, New York: HarperCollins Publishers, 1990.
14 Sandall, H., Hawley, T. T. and Gordon, G. C., "The St. Louis community homes program: Graduated support for long-term care," *American Journal of Psychiatry*, 132: 617–22, 1975.
15 Morris, B., "Residential units," in J. K. Wing and B. Morris (eds.), *Handbook of Psychiatric Rehabilitation Practice*, Oxford: Oxford University Press, 1981, pp. 99–121. The reference is to p. 109.
16 Personal communication, Ellen Baxter and Ezra Susser; Warner, R., "Creative Programming," in S. Ramon (ed.), *Beyond Community Care*, Basingstoke, Hampshire: Macmillan, 1991, pp. 114–35.
17 Mandiberg, J., "Can interdependent mutual support function as an alternative to hospitalization?," in Warner, *Alternatives to Hospital for Acute Psychiatric Treatment*, ch. 11.
18 Morris, "Residential units," p. 106.
19 Barker, R. G., *Ecological Psychology: Concepts and Methods for Studying the Environment of Human Behavior*, Stanford: Stanford University Press, 1968, ch. 7.
20 Ibid.
21 Davis, M. and Thompson, B., *Cooperative Housing: A Development Primer*, Washington, D.C.: National Cooperative Business Association, 1992.
22 Ibid.
23 Ibid.
24 City of New York *v.* Bowen.
25 Leonard Rubenstein, personal communication.
26 Kathy Burns, personal communication.
27 Laurie Flynn, personal communication.
28 Sartorius, N., de Girolamo, G., Andrews, G. *et al.* (eds.), *Treatment of Mental Disorders: A Review of Effectiveness*, Washington, D.C.: American Psychiatric Press, 1993.
29 Rosenhan, D. L., "On being sane in insane places," *Science*, 179: 250–8, 1973.
30 Mosher, L. R. and Keith, S. J., "Research on the psychosocial treatment of schizophrenia: A summary report," *American Journal of Psychiatry*, 136: 623–31, 1979.
31 Kavanagh, D. J., "Recent developments in expressed emotion and schizophrenia," *British Journal of Psychiatry*, 160: 601–20, 1992.
32 Goldstein, M. J., Rodnick, E. H., Evans, J. R. *et al.*, "Drug and family therapy in the aftercare treatment of acute schizophrenia," *Archives of General Psychiatry*, 35: 169–77, 1978; Leff, J. P., Kuipers, L., Berkowitz, R. *et al.*, "A controlled trial of intervention in the families of schizophrenic patients," *British Journal*

of Psychiatry, 141: 121–34, 1982; Falloon, I. R. H., Boyd, J. L., McGill, C. W. *et al.*, "Family management in the prevention of exacerbations of schizophrenia," 306: 1437–40, 1982; Hogarty, G. E., Anderson, C. M., Reiss, D. J. *et al.*, "Family psychoeducation, social skills training, and maintenance chemotherapy in the aftercare treatment of schizophrenia: I. One-year effects of a controlled study of relapse and expressed emotion," *Archives of General Psychiatry*, 43: 633–42, 1986.

33 Leff *et al.*, "A controlled trial of intervention in the families of schizophrenic patients."

34 Mosher and Keith, "Research on the psychosocial treatment of schizophrenia."

35 Pyke-Lees, P., "The National Schizophrenia Fellowship," in Wing and Morris, *Handbook of Psychiatric Rehabilitation*, pp. 126–9.

36 Jones, L., *A Matter of Community II*, Denver, Colorado: Capitol Hill Action and Recreation Group.

37 Warner, "Creative Programming."

38 Sherman, P. S. and Porter, R., "Mental health consumers as case management aides," *Hospital and Community Psychiatry*, 42: 494–8, 1991.

39 Warner, R. and Polak, P., "An economic development approach to the mentally ill in the community," Washington, D.C.: NIMH Community Support Program document, 1993.

40 Ibid.

41 Ekdawi, M. K., "The role of day units in rehabilitation," in Wing and Morris, *Handbook of Psychiatric Rehabilitation*, pp. 95–8. The quotation is from p. 98.

42 Beard, J. H., Propst, R. and Malamud, T. J., "The Fountain House Model of Psychiatric Rehabilitation," *Psychosocial Rehabilitation Journal*, 5: 47–53, 1982.

43 Hasher, R., "Spiritmenders: A client-operated community center," presented at American Psychiatric Association annual meeting, San Francisco, May 6–11, 1989.

44 Scheper-Hughes, N. and Lovell, A. M., *Psychiatry Inside Out: Selected Writings of Franco Basaglia*, New York: Columbia University Press, 1987, p. xvii.

45 Donelly, M., *The Politics of Mental Health in Italy*, London: Routledge, 1992.

46 Ibid., p.67.

47 *Breakdown*, a series of eight, 15–minute programs produced at Seven Oak Productions, Boulder, by Richard Warner and Konnie Kindle.

Bibliography

STUDIES OF THE OUTCOME OF SCHIZOPHRENIA IN TABLE 3.1

Ackner, B. and Oldham, A. J., "Insulin treatment of schizophrenia: A three-year follow-up of a controlled study," *Lancet*, i: 504–6, 1962.

Astrup, C., Fossum, A. and Holmboe, R., *Prognosis in Functional Psychoses*, Springfield, Illinois: Charles C. Thomas, 1963.

Astrup, C. and Noreik, K., *Functional Psychoses: Diagnostic and Prognostic Models*, Springfield, Illinois: Charles C. Thomas, 1966.

Beck, M. N., "Twenty-five and thirty-five year follow up of first admissions to mental hospitals," *Canadian Psychiatric Association Journal*, 13: 219–29, 1968.

Biehl, H., Maurer, K., Schubart, B. *et al.*, "Prediction of outcome and utilization of medical services in a prospective study of first onset schizophrenics: Results of a prospective 5-year follow-up study," *European Archives of Psychiatry and Neurological Sciences*, 236: 139–47, 1986.

Bland, R. C. and Orn, H., "Fourteen-year outcome in early schizophrenia," *Acta Psychiatrica Scandinavica*, 58: 327–38, 1978.

Bland, R. C., Parker, J. H. and Orn, H., "Prognosis in schizophrenia," *Archives of General Psychiatry*, 35: 72–7, 1978.

Bleuler, E., *Dementia Praecox, or the Group of Schizophrenias*, New York: International Universities Press, 1950.

Bleuler, M., *The Schizophrenic Disorders: Long-term Patient and Family Studies*, New Haven: Yale University Press, 1978.

Bond, E. D., "Results in 251 cases five years after admission to a hospital for mental diseases," *Archives of Neurology and Psychiatry*, 6: 429–39, 1921.

Bond, E. D. and Braceland, F. J., "Prognosis in mental disease," *American Journal of Psychiatry*, 94: 263–74, 1937.

Braatöy, T., "The prognosis in schizophrenia, with some remarks regarding diagnosis and therapy," *Acta Psychiatrica et Neurologica Scandinavica*, 11: 63–102, 1936.

Breier, A., Schreiber, J., Dyer, J. and Pickar, D., "National Institute of Mental Health longitudinal study of chronic schizophrenia: Prognosis and predictors of outcome," *Archives of General Psychiatry*, 48: 239–46, 1991.

Briner, O., *Zentralblatt für die gesamte Neurologie und Psychiatrie*, 162: 582, cited in E. Guttman, W. Mayer-Gross and E. Slater, "Short-distance prognosis of schizophrenia," *Journal of Neurological Psychiatry*, 2: 25–34, 1939.

Brown, G. W., Bone, M., Dalison, B. and Wing, J. K., *Schizophrenia and Social Care*, London: Oxford University Press, 1966.

Carter, A. B., 'The prognostic factors of adolescent psychosis," *Journal of Mental Science*, 88: 31–81, 1942.

Cheney, C. O. and Drewry, P. H., "Results of non-specific treatment in dementia praecox," *American Journal of Psychiatry*, 95: 203–17, 1938.

Cole, N. J., Brewer, D. L. and Branch, C. H. H., "Socioeconomic adjustment of a sample of schizophrenic patients," *American Journal of Psychiatry*, 95: 203–17, 1938.

Coryell, W. and Tsuang, M. T., "Outcome after 40 years in DSM III schizophreniform disorder," *Archives of General Psychiatry*, 43: 324–28, 1986.

Cottman, S. B. and Mezey, S. B., "Community care and the prognosis of schizophrenia," *Acta Psychiatrica Scandinavica*, 53: 95–104, 1976.

Eitinger, L., Laane, C. L. and Langfeldt, G., "The prognostic value of the clinical picture and the therapeutic value of physical treatment in schizophrenia and the schizophreniform states," *Acta Psychiatrica et Neurologica Scandinavica*, 33: 33–53, 1958.

Engelhardt, D. M., Rosen, B., Feldman, J. *et al.*, "A 15-year follow-up of 646 schizophrenic outpatients," *Schizophrenia Bulletin*, 8: 493–503, 1982.

Errera, P. A., "Sixteen-year follow-up of schizophrenic patients seen in an outpatient clinic," *Archives of Neurology and Psychiatry*, 78: 84–8, 1957.

Evensen, H., *Dementia Praecox*, Oslo: Kristiania, 1904.

Freyhan, F. A., "Course and outcome of schizophrenia," *American Journal of Psychiatry*, 112: 161–7, 1955.

Fröshaug, H. and Ytrehus, A., "The problems of prognosis in schizophrenia," *Acta Psychiatrica Scandinavica*, supplement 169: 176–87, 1963.

Fromenty, L., "Les remissions dans la schizophrénie statistique sur leur fréquence et leur durée avant l'insulinthérapie," *Encephale*, 1: 275–86, 1937.

Gerloff, W., "Über Verlauf und Prognose der Schizophrenie," *Archiv für Psychiatrie und Nervenkrankheiten*, 106: 585–98, 1936.

Guttman, E., Mayer-Gross, W. and Slater, E., "Short-distance prognosis of schizophrenia," *Journal of Neurological Psychiatry*, 2: 25–34, 1939.

Hall, J. C., Smith, K. and Shimkunas, A., "Employment problems of schizophrenic patients," *American Journal of Psychiatry*, 123: 536–40, 1966.

Harris, A., Linker, I., Norris, V. and Shepherd, M., "Schizophrenia: A prognostic and social study," *British Journal of Social and Preventive Medicine*, 10: 107–14, 1956.

Harrow, M., Grinker, R. R., Silverstein, M. L. and Holzman, P., "Is modern-day schizophrenia outcome still negative?," *American Journal of Psychiatry*, 135: 1156–62, 1978.

Hastings, D. W., "Follow-up results in psychiatric illness," *American Journal of Psychiatry*, 114: 1057–65, 1958.

Helgason, L., "Twenty years' follow-up of first psychiatric presentation for schizophrenia: What could have been prevented?," *Acta Psychiatrica Scandinavica*, 81: 231–5, 1990.

Henisz, J., "A follow-up study of schizophrenic patients," *Comprehensive Psychiatry*, 7: 524–8, 1966.

Hoenig, J. and Hamilton, M. W., "Schizophrenia in an extramural service," *Comprehensive Psychiatry*, 7: 81–9, 1966.

Holmboe, R. and Astrup, C., "A follow-up study of 255 patients with acute schizophrenia and schizophreniform psychoses," *Acta Psychiatrica et Neurologica Scandinavica*, supplement 125, 1957.

Holmboe, R., Noreik, K. and Astrup, C., "Follow-up of functional psychoses at two Norwegian mental hospitals," *Acta Psychiatrica Scandinavica*, 44: 298–310, 1968.

Horwitz, W. A. and Kleiman, C., "Survey of cases of dementia praecox discharged from the Psychiatric Institute and Hospital," *Psychiatric Quarterly*, 10: 72–85, 1936.

Huber, G., Gross, G. and Schuttler, R., "A long-term follow-up study of schizophrenia: Psychiatric course of illness and prognosis," *Acta Psychiatrica Scandinavica*, 52: 49–57, 1975.

Hunt, R. C., Feldman, H. and Fiero, R. P., "Spontaneous remission in dementia praecox," *Psychiatric Quarterly*, 12: 414–25, 1938.

Jablensky, A., Sartorius, N., Ernberg, G. *et al.*, "Schizophrenia: manifestations, incidence and course in different cultures. A World Health Organization ten-country study," *Psychological Medicine*, monograph supplement 20, 1991, p. 97.

Johanson, E., "A study of schizophrenia in the male: A psychiatric and social study based on 138 cases with follow-up," *Acta Psychiatrica et Neurologica Scandinavica*, supplement 125, 1958.

Johnstone, E. C., Frith, D. C., Gold, A. and Stevens, M., "The outcome of severe acute schizophrenia illness after one year," *British Journal of Psychiatry*, 134: 28–33, 1979.

Jönnson, S. A. T. and Jönnson, H., "Outcome in untreated schizophrenia: A search for symptoms and traits with prognostic meaning in patients admitted to a mental hospital in the pre-neuroleptic era," *Acta Psychiatrica Scandinavica*, 85: 313–20, 1992.

Kelly, D. H. W. and Sargant, W., "Present treatment of schizophrenia," *British Medical Journal*, 1: 147–50, 1965.

Kraepelin, E., *Dementia Praecox and Paraphrenia*, Edinburgh: Livingstone, 1919.

Langfeldt, G., "The prognosis in schizophrenia and factors influencing the course of the disease," *Acta Psychiatrica et Neurologica Scandinavica*, supplement 13, 1939.

Leiberman, D. M., Hoenig, J. and Auerbach, I., "The effect of insulin coma and E.C.T. on the 3 year prognosis of schizophrenia," *Journal of Neurology, Neurosurgery and Psychiatry*, 20: 108–13, 1957.

Lemke, R., "Untersuchungen über die soziale Prognose der Schizophrenie unter besonders Beruchsicktigung des encephalographischen Befundes," *Archive für Psychiatrie und Nervenkrankheiten*, 104: 89–136, 1935.

Levenstien, S., Klein, D. F. and Pollack, M., "Follow-up study of formerly hospitalized voluntary psychiatric patients: The first two years," *American Journal of Psychiatry*, 122: 1102–9, 1966.

Leyberg, J. T., "A follow-up study on some schizophrenic patients," *British Journal of Psychiatry*, 111: 617–24, 1965.

Malamud, W. and Render, I. N., "Course and prognosis in schizophrenia," *American Journal of Psychiatry*, 95: 1039–57, 1939.

Mandelbrote, B. M. and Folkard, S., "Some factors related to outcome and social adjustment in schizophrenia," *Acta Psychiatrica Scandinavica*, 37: 223–35, 1961.

Marengo, J., Harrow, M., Sands, J. and Galloway, C., "European versus U.S. data on the course of schizophrenia," *American Journal of Psychiatry*, 148: 606–11, 1991.

Marneros, A., Deister, A. and Rohde, A., "Comparison of long-term outcome of schizophrenic, affective and schizoaffective disorders," *British Journal of Psychiatry*, 161, supplement 18: 44–51, 1992.

Masterson, J. F., "Prognosis in adolescent disorders: Schizophrenia," *Journal of Nervous and Mental Disease*, 124: 219–32, 1956.

Mayer-Gross, W., "Die schizophrenie," in O. Bumke (ed.), *Handbuch der Geisteskrankheiten*, vol. 9, Berlin: Springer, 1932, p. 534.

Möller, H-J., von Zerssen, D., Werner-Eilert, K. and Wüschner-Stockheim, M., "Outcome in schizophrenic and similar paranoid psychoses," *Schizophrenia Bulletin*, 8: 99–108, 1982.

Müller, V., "Katamnestische Erhebungen über den Spontanverlauf der Schizophrenie," *Monatsschrift für Psychiatrie und Neurologie*, 122: 257–76, 1951.

Munk-Jørgensen, P. and Mortensen, P. B., "Social outcome in schizophrenia: A 13-year follow-up," *Social Psychiatry and Psychiatric Epidemiology*, 27: 129–34, 1992.

Murdoch, J. H., "Crime in schizophrenic reaction types," *Journal of Mental Science*, 79: 286–97, 1933.

Niskanen, P. and Achté, K. A., "Prognosis in schizophrenia: A comparative follow-up study of first admissions for schizophrenic and paranoid psychoses in Helsinki in 1950, 1960 and 1965," *Psychiatria Fennica Year Book 1971*, 1971, pp. 117–26.

Norton, A., "Mental hospital ins and outs: A survey of patients admitted to a mental hospital in the past 30 years," *British Medical Journal*, 1: 528–36, 1961.

Otto-Martiensen, J., *Zeitschrift für Psychiatrie*, 77: 295 *et seq.*, 1921, cited in R. Lemke, "Untersuchungen über die soziale Prognose der Schizophrenie unter besonders Beruchsichtigung des encephalographischen Befundes," *Archives für Psychiatrie und Nervenkrankheiten*, 104: 89–136, 1935.

Prudo, R. and Blum, H. M., "Five-year outcome and prognosis in schizophrenia: A report from the London field research centre of the International Pilot Study of Schizophrenia," *British Journal of Psychiatry*, 150: 345–54, 1987.

Rennie, T. A. C., "Follow-up study of 500 patients with schizophrenia admitted to the hospital from 1913–1923," *Archives of Neurology and Psychiatry*, 42: 877–91, 1939.

Romano, J. and Ebaugh, F. G., "Prognosis in schizophrenia," *American Journal of Psychiatry*, 95: 583–96, 1938.

Rosanoff, A. J., "A statistical study of prognosis in insanity," *Journal of the American Medical Association*, 62: 3–6, 1914.

Rupp, C. and Fletcher, E. K., "A five to ten year follow-up study of 641 schizophrenic cases," *American Journal of Psychiatry*, 96: 877–88, 1940.

Salokangas, R. K. R., "Prognostic implications of the sex of schizophrenic patients," *British Journal of Psychiatry*, 142: 145– 51, 1983.

Scottish Schizophrenia Research Group, "The Scottish first episode schizophrenia study: VIII. Five-year follow-up: Clinical and psychosocial findings," *British Journal of Psychiatry*, 161: 496–500, 1992.

Shepherd, M., Watt, D., Falloon, I. and Smeeton, N., "The natural history of schizophrenia: A five-year follow-up study of outcome and prediction in a representative sample of schizophrenics," *Psychological Medicine*, monograph supplement 15: 1–46, 1989.

Stalker, H., "The prognosis in schizophrenia," *Journal of Mental Science*, 85: 1224–40, 1939.

Stearns, A. W., "The prognosis in dementia praecox," *Boston Medical and Surgical Journal*, 167: 158–60, 1912.

Stephens, J. H., "Long-term course and prognosis in schizophrenia," *Seminars in Psychiatry*, 2: 464–85, 1970.

Stone, M. H., "Exploratory psychotherapy in schizophrenia-spectrum patients: A reevaluation in the light of long-term follow-up of schizophrenic and borderline patients," *Bulletin of the Menninger Clinic*, 50: 287–306, 1986.

Strecker, E. A. and Willey, G. F., "Prognosis in schizophrenia," *Journal of Mental Science*, 73: 9–39, 1927.

Tsuang, M. T., Woolson, R. F. and Fleming, J. A., "Long-term outcome of major psychoses: I. Schizophrenia and affective disorders compared with psychiatrically symptom-free surgical conditions," *Archives of General Psychiatry*, 36: 1295–301, 1979.

Vaillant, G. E. and Funkenstein, D. H., "Long-term follow-up (10–15 years) of schizophrenic patients with Funkenstein (adrenalin-mecholyl) tests," in P. H. Hoch and J. Zubin (eds.), *Psychopathology of Schizophrenia*, New York: Grune & Stratton, 1966.

Vaillant, G. E., Semrad, E. V. and Ewalt, J. R., "Current therapeutic results in schizophrenia," *New England Journal of Medicine*, 271: 280–3, 1964.

Wirt, R. D. and Simon, W., *Differential Treatment and Prognosis in Schizophrenia*, Springfield, Illinois: Charles C. Thomas, 1959.

Wootton, L. H., Armstrong, R. W. and Lilly, D., "An investigation into the after-histories of discharged mental patients," *Journal of Mental Science*, 81: 168–72, 1935.

World Health Organization, *Schizophrenia: An International Follow-Up Study*, Chichester, England: Wiley, 1979.

Name index

Abrams, Richard 239
Achtè, K. A. 64, 66
Ackner, B. 64
Adler, Alfred 139
Alarcon, J. de 198
d'Alembert, Jean Le Roud 105
Anderson, Charles 137
Anthony, William 248
Arieti, Silvano 206
Ashton, T. S. 107
Astrup, C. 64
Awl, William 122

Bamrah, J. S. 198
Barbigian, H. M. 210n
Barker, D. J. P. 194n
Barker, Roger 277
Basaglia, Franco 97
Bassuk, Ellen 89
Bateson, Gregory 26
Bean, L. L. 145
Beck, James 144
Beck, M. N. 62
Bell, George 86
Benedict, Ruth 166
Biehl, H. 68
Bland, R. C. 66
Bleuler, Eugen 9–11, 15, 16, 60, 78, 139
Bleuler, Manfred 57–8, 64
Bluestone, Barry 48
Blum, H. M. 68
Bockoven, Sanbourne 124, 125
Bogue, Donald 173
Bond, E. D. 60
Boorstin, Daniel 114
Bowers, Malcolm 219
Braatöy, T. 60
Braceland, F. J. 60

Breier, A. 70
Brenner, Harvey 38–9, 40, 41, 42n, 52, 129, 131, 143, 144
Brigham, Amariah 122
Brill, Henry 85
Briner, O. 62
Brown, G. W. 64, 247
Browne, W. A. F. 245, 246
Buckley, K. A. H. 132n
Bunn, Alfred 40
Burrows, George 122
Byrd, Mary 172

Cabanis, Georges 105
Cancro, Robert 34
Carlyle, Thomas 245–6
Carpenter, William 18, 34, 182, 225, 231, 232
Carstairs, Morris 140
Carter, A. B. 62
Castle, D. 198
Catalano, Ralph 36–7, 38
Caudill, W. 202n
Cheney, C. P. 62
Chew, S. K. 153
Chiarugi, Vicenzo 105, 106, 108
Ciompi, Luc 15, 146, 228
Clark, David 94, 142
Clark, Robert 32
Clinton, William 260
Cobb, Sidney 47, 48
Cockerham, William 180
Cohen, Leon 247
Cole, N. J. 66
Conolly, John 111, 120
Cooper, B. 145–6
Cooper, David 25
Cooper, Philip 251

Subject index

352 Subject index

Britain 24, 75, 106–7, 122, 235, 254; Afro-Caribbeans 206, 207; asylum standards 118; centers of trade and manufacturing 30–1; County Asylum Act (1808) 108; day care 286; dwindling cure rates for insanity during growth of industrialism 157; efforts to introduce into psychiatric hospitals methods of work therapy 142; government departments 255; incidence rate for treated schizophrenia 195; industrial illness 44; Industrial Revolution 106; industrializing 203; jails 93; labor (19th-c.) 113–14; moral treatment 112; newspaper coverage of mental illness 288; patients unresponsive to antipsychotic drugs 217; postwar labor shortage 94; psychiatry 15, 113, 114; recent apparent decrease in incidence of schizophrenia greatest in most prosperous regions 204; social-insurance schemes for the totally and permanently disabled 92; stagnation in psychiatric rehabilitation 95; unemployment 72, 73–4, 133, 137; Victorian, admission rates higher for pauper lunatics 145; vocational rehabilitation 250; see also England; Great Depressions; Scotland; social psychiatry revolution; Wales
British Columbia 168
Buckinghamshire, St John's Hospital, Stone 84
business cycles 35–7, 38–40, 41, 44, 132, 144; see also economic booms; economic conditions; economic downturns; economic recession

Caesarean sections 203, 206
Cali 154, 155, 156, 160, 165
California 232, 249, 252, 256, 285; Agnews State Hospital, San Jose 89–90, 224; Camarillo State Hospital 223; Fairweather's lodge program 254; patients in seclusion 178; San Mateo County 90; Santa Clara County Mental Health Center 276; state hospitals 84; University of 223–4; see also Los Angeles; San Francisco
Cameroon 158

Canada 44, 62, 66, 97, 205; mental hospitals 131; see also under individual provinces and cities
cardiovascular-renal disease 38
Caribbean see Afro-Caribbeans
case management 271
castes 33, 190, 200, 211; high 201, 202; low 201; merchant 201
catatonia 8, 237
catecholamines 218
CATEGO system 154
central nervous system 218–19; organic changes of 125; see also brain
cerebral atrophy 23
cerebral strokes 38
cerebral syphilis 8
cerebrospinal fluid 219
Chambéry 105
Chandigarh 27, 156, 170, 208; Postgraduate Institute of Medical Education and Research 152
CHARG (Capitol Hill Action and Recreation Group) 285
Chicago 31–2, 173, 279; Thresholds 258, 287
childbirth 202–4
childhood 23, 26, 40, 43, 203, 206
China, Yunnan Province 159; see also Formosa; Hong Kong; Taiwan
chlorpromazine 82, 84, 86, 222–3, 224, 225
cigarette-smoking 39
classes see castes; social class
close supervision 45, 47
clozapine 235
coercion 72, 104, 105, 127; avoidance of 267
cognitive dissonance theory 182–6, 281
Colombia 13; see also Cali
Colorado 24, 25, 129–30, 140, 177, 188; Foundation for Medical Care 179; State Hospital 179; see also Boulder; Denver
Columbia University Community Services 276
communication 4, 18, 26
communism 95, 147
communities 276–7; education 288; lodges 248; rehabilitation 10, 100; schizophrenics living in 91; services/support systems 140, 265–6, 274; 'therapeutic' 87, 275, 287; treatment 57, 189, 267–9, 273

242; poor 17, 161, 222, 223, 225, 227, 228; worst outlook 14
progressive and humane measures 118
prolactin 234
promazine 222–3
pseudo-patients 181
psychiatric hospitals *see* asylums; hospitals
psychiatric philosophy 139
psychiatry/psychiatrists: American 12–13, 75, 78, 86, 115, 121–2; British 13, 15, 113, 114; community 179; European 75; ideology may be influenced by changes in the economy 139; middle-class clientele 126; pessimism in 72; reforms 97; stagnation 91–2; treatment 72, 99, 201; *see also* DSM-III-R; social psychiatry revolution
psychoanalytic theories 9, 12, 240
psychopathology 139, 228, 272
psychopharmacology 233
psychoses 75, 87, 91, 100, 134, 168, 252; acute, foster care for 269–70; affective 14, 199; alcohol-related 123; atypical 14, 156, 157; brief 14, 149–50, 163; chronic 120, 123, 126, 140; common features of 4; conception of the cause of 164; control of florid features of 89; culture-bound 163; developed late in life 238; diagnosis of 13, 162; disorders 137; drug-induced 4, 150; drug-withdrawal supersensitivity 231; early signs of return immediately detected 270; economic hardship and 143; episodes of 18, 22, 58, 144, 150, 161–2; experiences discussed frankly 281; fear and guilt 149; full-blown 15; group psychotherapy for outpatients 282; high status in 165–7; homeless suffering from 174; human side of 288; jailed sufferers 175, 266, 267; late-onset involutional, female patients 51; malarial 150; marginal 127; mental condition of many people with 133; mild 21, 238; natural healing processes of 10; neglected 139; notion that employment improves outcome in 248; organic 99, 150, 151; parasitic, nutritional and infectious disorders, which may develop into 150; patient living in

inadequate setting 88; perpetuation of 136; potential for improvement in the course of 142; precipitants of 19; prevalence of 35, 109; process 58; prognosis 12, 15, 127; prolonged withdrawal 237; psychogenic 8; psychotherapy in 280; recovery from 126, 141, 145, 158, 169, 232; refugees likely to suffer from 205; schizophrenic 144; schizophreniform 12, 14, 78; senile 99; severe 164, 270; short duration 15; significant underreporting in peasant communities 200; stable disorder 133; supernatural explanation for features 162; supersensitivity hypothesis 226; Third World 149–50, 187; treatment of 11, 72, 164, 165, 175, 189, 216; triggering 28; true increase in occurrence of 135; understanding of 139; unemployment and 148; women suffering from 172; worsening, with drink/drug abuse 273; *see also* acute psychosis; delusions; depression; functional psychosis; hallucinations; manic-depressive psychosis; psychotic relapse; psychotic symptoms
psychosocial treatment 231, 232, 233, 234; family-oriented 224
psychosomatic illness 31
psychosurgery 57, 72, 139
psychotherapy 86, 226, 280–2; dynamic uncovering 242; intensive dynamic 240; overenthusiastic 233
psychotic relapse 27, 90, 133, 269; greatest likelihood of 271; more or less eliminated 270; preventing 228; subject to 275; valuable defense against 166
psychotic symptoms 5, 15, 145, 153, 156, 160, 166, 242, 248, 274; amphetamine and exacerbation of 218; controlling 237; denied 181; dramatic relief from 215; fewer 232, 271; folk treatment of 162; rebounding, after withdrawal of antipsychotic drug treatment 221; remission of 159; tendency to persist 183; under the stress of learning a new job and meeting new people 257
public health insurance 130
Pueblo Indians 167